History of the Jews of Jasło
Yizkor (Memorial) Book of the Jewish Community of Jaslo, Poland

Translation of
Toldot Yehudei Yaslo

**Originally in Hebrew
Edited by Moshe Nathan Even Chaim (Rapaport)
Published by Jaslo Society, Tel Aviv 1953**

Translated and Edited by William Leibner
Edited by Phyllis Kramer

Published by JewishGen

**An Affiliate of the Museum of Jewish Heritage - A Living Memorial to the Holocaust
New York**

History of the Jews of Jaslo
Yizkor (Memorial) Book of the Jewish Community of Jaslo, Poland

Translation of *Toldot Yehudei Jaslo*

Translated and Edited by William Leibner
Copyright © 2013 by JewishGen, Inc.
All rights reserved.
First Printing: July 2013, Av 5773
Second Printing, September 2019, Elul 5779

Translator and Project Coordinator: William Leibner
Edited by Phyllis Kramer
Layout by Joel Alpert
Images Scanned by Ken Bruss
Cover Design by Jan R. Fine
Publicity by Sandra Hirschhorn
Indexing by Diane Salman

Published by JewishGen, Inc.
An Affiliate of the Museum of Jewish Heritage
A Living Memorial to the Holocaust
36 Battery Place, New York, NY 10280

Printed in the United States of America by Lightning Source, Inc.

Library of Congress Control Number (LCCN): 2013939696
ISBN: 978-1-939561-08-4 (hard cover: 324 pages, alk. paper)

JewishGen and the Yizkor Books in Print Project

This book has been published by the **Yizkor Books in Print Project,** as part of the **Yizkor Book Project** of **JewishGen, Inc.**

JewishGen, Inc. is a non-profit organization founded in 1987 as a resource for Jewish genealogy. Its website [www.jewishgen.org] serves as an international clearinghouse and resource center to assist individuals who are researching the history of their Jewish families and the places where they lived. JewishGen provides databases, facilitates discussion groups, and coordinates projects relating to Jewish genealogy and the history of the Jewish people. In 2003, JewishGen became an affiliate of the **Museum of Jewish Heritage - A Living Memorial to the Holocaust** in New York.

The **JewishGen Yizkor Book Project** was organized to make more widely known the existence of Yizkor (Memorial) Books written by survivors and former residents of various Jewish communities throughout the world. Later, volunteers connected to the different destroyed communities began cooperating to have these books translated from the original language—usually Hebrew or Yiddish—into English, thus enabling a wider audience to have access to the valuable information contained within them. As each chapter of these books was translated, it was posted on the JewishGen website and made available to the general public.

The **Yizkor Books in Print Project** began in 2011 as an initiative to print and publish Yizkor Books that had been fully translated, so that hard copies would be available for purchase by the descendants of these communities and also by scholars, universities, synagogues, libraries, and museums.

These Yizkor books have been produced almost entirely through the volunteer effort of researchers from around the world, assisted by donations from private individuals. The books are printed and sold at near cost, so as to make them as affordable as possible. Our goal is to make this important genre of Jewish literature and history available in English in book form, so that people can have the personal histories of their ancestral towns on their bookshelves for themselves and for their children and grandchildren.

A list of all published translated Yizkor Books can be found at:
http://www.jewishgen.org/Yizkor/ybip.html

Lance Ackerfeld, Yizkor Book Project Manager

Joel Alpert, Yizkor Book in Print Project Coordinator

JewishGen
Yizkor Book Project

This book is presented by the
Yizkor Books in Print Project
Project Coordinator: Joel Alpert

Part of the
Yizkor Books Project of JewishGen, Inc.
Project Manager: Lance Ackerfeld

These books have been produced solely through volunteer effort
of individuals from around the world. The books are printed and
sold at near cost, so as to make them as affordable as possible.

Our goal is to make this history and important genre of Jewish
literature available in English in book form so that people can have
the near-personal histories of their ancestral towns on their bookshelves for themselves and for their children and grandchildren.

Any donations to the Yizkor Books Project are appreciated.

Please send donations to:
Yizkor Book Project
JewishGen
36 Battery Place
New York, NY 10280

JewishGen, Inc. is an affiliate of the
Museum of Jewish Heritage
A Living Memorial to the Holocaust

Hebrew Title Page of Original Book

משה נתן אבן-חיים
בן חיים ראפופורט

תולדות יהודי יאסלו

מראשית התישבותם בתוך העיר
עד ימי החורבן על ידי
הנאצים וגרודיהם,
פושעי האנושיות
בתקופת המאה
ה-20

בהוצאת ארגון "יוצאי יאסלו" בארץ ישראל

תשי"ג   תל-אביב   1953

Translation of the Hebrew Title Page of Original Book

Moshe Nathan Even Chaim
Ben Chaim (Rapaport)

Toldot Yehudei Jaslo

The Jewish History of Jaslo

From its inception to its destruction
by the Nazis and their helpers,
criminals of humanity in
the 20th century

Published by the association of former residents of Jaslo in Israel.
Tel Aviv   1953

משה נתן אבן־חיים (ראפופורט) / תולדות יהודי יאסלו.

זכור ד׳ לבני אדום.

אשרי שישלם לך את גמולך שגמלת לנו,

אשרי שיאחז ונפץ את עולליך אל הסלע.

(תהלים קל״ז.)

נר ד׳ נשמת אדם.

מונוגרפיה מקיפה על חיי קהלת יאסלו, מראשית
ההתהוותה והתפתחותה, משנת תרכ״ה (1865) בערך,
עד ימי השואה והחורבן במלחמת העולם השניה
משנות תרצ״ט (1939). בה חרבה הקהלה עד היסוד.

Translation of previous page

Moshe Nathan Even Chaim (Rapaport) / Toldot Yehudei Jasło

Psalm 137 (By the rivers of Babylon)

Remember, Lord what the Edomites did...
Happy is the one who repays you according to what you have to us.
Happy is the one who seizes your infants and dashes them against the rocks.

G-d's candle represents the soul of man

An extensive description of Jewish life in Jasło since about 1865 to the beginning of its destruction in 1939 and the obliteration of the Jewish community during the Shoah days of World War II.

חסר ויתיר, משגה, טעות ושכחה
נ ח ל ת כ ל א ד ם ה ם,
ואין בן אדם שולט עליהם.
(Errare humanum est).

נדפס בישראל
Printed in Israel

דפוס ספר, תל-אביב, רח' הרצל 50

Translation of previous page

Please excuse omissions, inaccuracies,
errors and spellings for they were not intentional.

Latin expression: To err is human.

Printed in Israel

Pepper printing, 61 Herzl St. Tel Aviv.

The author - Moshe Nathan Even Chaim

Acknowledgements

The publication of this book would not have happened without the dedication of William Leibner, who translated and edited the book and coordinated the efforts to place the contents on the web site of Yizkor Books Project of JewishGen, Inc. Special thanks also to Phyllis Kramer who also edited the book. Thanks to Ken Bruss who scanned images from the original book so that they could be included. Thanks also to Jan R. Fine for the cover design and to Sandra Hirschhorn for handling publicity of the distribution of this book. Special thanks to Joel Alpert for his full devotion to the task of publishing the book that will enable many people to read the fascinating story of Jewish community of Jaslo in Poland.

אֵל מָלֵא רַחֲמִים שׁוֹכֵן בַּמְּרוֹמִים, הַמְצֵא מְנוּחָה נְכוֹנָה

עַל כַּנְפֵי הַשְּׁכִינָה בְּמַעֲלוֹת קְדוֹשִׁים טְהוֹרִים וְגִבּוֹרִים,

כְּזֹהַר הָרָקִיעַ מַזְהִירִים, לְנִשְׁמוֹת הַקְּדוֹשִׁים שֶׁנִּלְחֲמוּ בְּכָל

מַעַרְכוֹת יִשְׂרָאֵל, בַּמַּחְתֶּרֶת וּבַצָּבָא הַהֲגָנָה לְיִשְׂרָאֵל וְשֶׁנָּפְלוּ

בְּמִלְחַמְתָּם וּמָסְרוּ נַפְשָׁם עַל קְדֻשַׁת הַשֵּׁם, הָעָם וְהָאָרֶץ,

בַּעֲבוּר שֶׁאָנוּ מִתְפַּלְלִים לְעִלּוּי נִשְׁמוֹתֵיהֶם. לָכֵן בַּעַל

הָרַחֲמִים יַסְתִּירֵם בְּסֵתֶר כְּנָפָיו לְעוֹלָמִים וְיִצְרֹר בִּצְרוֹר

הַחַיִּים אֶת נִשְׁמוֹתֵיהֶם, יהוה הוּא נַחֲלָתָם, בְּגַן עֵדֶן מְנוּחָתָם,

וְיָנוּחוּ בְשָׁלוֹם עַל מִשְׁכָּבוֹתָם וְתַעֲמֹד לְכָל יִשְׂרָאֵל זְכוּתָם

וְיַעַמְדוּ לְגוֹרָלָם לְקֵץ הַיָּמִין, וְנֹאמַר אָמֵן.

May the Father of mercies who dwelleth on high, in His mighty compassion, remember those living, upright and blameless ones, the holy congregations, who laid down their lives for the sanctification of the divine name. Beloved and faithful were they in life, and in death were not separated; swifter than eagles and stronger than lion to do the will of their Master and the desire of their Rock. May our God remember them for good with the other righteous of the world and avenge the blood of the people which has been shed; as it is written in the Torah: "Sing aloud, O ye nations, for God doth bring to judgment those who shed the blood of His servants.' Wherefore should the nations say: "Where is their God?' Let the retribution of Thy servants' blood be made known among the nations in our sight. God will judge among the nations and He will emerge triumphant.

El Molay Rachamim
The Hebrew prayer for the departed for Yizkor and the English translation.

Foreword for the Translation

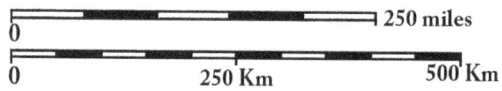

BALTIC SEA

LITHUANIA

RUSSIA

Vilnius ●

POLAND

BELARUS

GERMANY

● Poznan   Warsaw ●

● Lodz

● Prague

● Krakow

CZECH REPUBLIC

Jaslo ●

UKRAINE

SLOVAKIA

250 miles

0

0   250 Km   500 Km

POLAND - Current Borders

Map of Poland with Jaslo

Map of Poland with Jaslo indicated (in Hebrew)

Jasło, Galicia, Poland

A Short History

Not in the Original Yizkor Book

By William Leibner

The city of Jasło is located in southeastern Poland, east of Krakow. It is a small county town with a population of about 37,347 inhabitants as of the Polish census of June 2, 2009. The city is considered one of the oldest communities in Poland. In the 12th century, the village of Jasło belonged to the Cisterian Monastery of Pszebnica. Jasło became royal property in 1366 and received municipal status in 1589. The municipality excluded Jews from residing in Jasło. The ban would last several hundred years. Jews did enter Jasło from nearby communities on fair or market days. In the 15th and 16th century, Jasło became a very important commercial center, especially in the trade with Hungary. The city became a center for the production of wool and flax. Jasło was destroyed several times by Tartars, Hungarians and Swedes. In the second half of the 17th century following the Swedish invasion, there were large fires and severe floods caused by the Wasiolka and Wisloka rivers that encircle the city. Epidemics ensued that slowed the development of the city until the middle of the 19th century when growth resumed. In 1860 Jaslo became a district city and was connected to the railway system in 1884. Oil was discovered in the area in 1863 and exploitation began immediately. An oil refinery was built in Niglowic about two kilometers from the city in 1890 and a public high school was opened the same year. While Jasło was not seriously damaged during World War I, the economic dislocations played havoc with the local economy and pauperized the Jewish population, which depended extensively on commerce.

Jews were mentioned in Jasło by the 14th century and in 1565 mention was made of a document pertaining to a Jewish community in Jasło. But in 1589 the King of Poland granted the city the right to exclude Jews from the city except on market and fair days. It seems that the law was not strictly implemented because in 1765 eight Jews or two Jewish families lived in the city. A document dated 1783 states that Jasło had no Jews and therefore the local situation was much better than other places where Jews resided. With the partition of Poland, Jaslo was attached to the Austrian Empire. The latter converted the city to a district city and all provincial government offices were opened in Jasło. The Austrians also repealed the anti-Jewish residence laws, enabling Jews to move to Jaslo proper. Some Jews did settle in the suburb of Jasło called Olszewica where they opened businesses, workshops and built the first wooden study center. With the cancellation in 1860 of the ban on Jews living in Jasło, a few Jewish families moved to the city proper and settled in the area known as the Targowica square. At a later date, the Jews moved to other areas in the city. The Polish residents did not approve of their new neighbors and tried to stop the Jewish expansion but in vain.

Chaim Steinhaus and Leibish Winfeld, both natives of Zmigrod, were the first Jews to settle in Jaslo, in about 1870. Soon Jews began to flock to the city in great numbers from the nearby small towns: Zmigrod, Osiek, Dukla, Brzostek, Kolaczyce and Fristig.

By 1910, Jasło had a Jewish population of 2,262. The number kept growing until the war. The revolving fund of the Jewish community for the year 1913 lists 535 merchants, mainly small traders, 62 artisans, seven farmers, 15 professionals (lawyers, doctors and teachers) ,and 25 others. Many Jewish engineers, supervisors and clerks worked at the oil refinery.

(District of Jasło, region of Krakow)

Year	Total Population	Jews
1765	(?)	909
1880	3,302	433
1890	4,527	934
1900	6,571	1,524
1910	10,116	2,262
1921	10,391	2,445
1931	10,013	1,512

Statistical chart of population composition of Jaslo.

Notice the sharp drop in the Jewish column between 1921 and 1931. It is true that some Jews left Jaslo but not in such great numbers. The change was due to the change of questions. In 1921 the main question was: "what language do you use at home, please check off." In 1931, there were several questions that had to be answered in writing and many people could not write the answer in Polish. The government was interested in reducing the numbers of the Jewish minority.

As we look at the numbers we see the great growth of Jewish Jasło through the years 1880-1910. A Jewish kehilla - community organisation was established, a cemetery opened, many social, religious, help fund cultural groups and associations were established. The beautiful synagogue was finished in 1906. Rabbi Yona Tzanger was the spiritual leader of the community followed by Rabbi Avraham Heshel Rubin and later his son Rabbi Tzwi Yossef Rubin. His son, Rabbi Elimelech Rubin, was the last rabbi in Jaslo and perished in the Shoa. Dr. Avraham Kornhauser helped to establish a Zionist club in 1905. Jasło also had a large Jewish professional intelligentsia that influenced Jewish life. The small merchants were the backbone of the Jewish economic life of the city in those days, and they greatly suffered during World War I. Following the war, the American Joint had to financially support the community. Slowly, normal life resumed but the business community began to suffer from the various anti-Jewish campaigns and boycotts that continued until the outbreak of World War II. Jewish life continued to grow in Jaslo but at a slower pace. The Zionist movement gained new adherents daily and soon there were various Zionist groups and youth groups in the city. The Zionists challenged the religious leadership of the Jewish community. The Jewish population was still overwhelmingly religious. The Jews elected six Jewish councilmen in the municipal elections of 1933 and five in the elections of 1939 out of a total of 24 seats. The anti-Semitic campaigns against the Jews continued unabated throughout 1938. Jews were often attacked and beaten. Jewish stores and institutions were intimidated. The Germans entered Jaslo on September 8, 1939. Many Jewish families and single men fled east. Their trip was soon halted by the rapid advance of the Germans.

Many of the Jews began to trek back home to Jasło and some never made it. The Germans began a campaign of terror aimed at the Jews. Jewish stores and homes were broken into and robbed. Several transports of Jews arrived from Western Polish areas annexed to the Reich and from Krakow. These shipments were rather large and one of them exceeded 3,000 people. Jasło also received Jews from the villages in the vicinity. The Germans appointed a Judenrat in Jasło headed by the wood merchant Yaakow Goldstein. The main task of the Judenrat was of course to provide slave labor to the Germans. Conditions in Jasło deteriorated rapidly, resulting in epidemics and starvation. The local J.S.S. (Jewish Self Assistance Help) office assisted 500 people in Jaslo in February 1942. A ghetto was established in the Targowica area. The ghetto was sealed with barbed wire and one guarded gate was left open. A census taken in January of the ghetto indicated that there were 2,300 Jews in the Jasło ghetto. Large and small actions against Jews took their toll and the Jewish population steadily declined. On August 18, 1942, the ghetto of Jaslo was liquidated.

Posters had appeared the previous days, the 17th or 16th of August 1942 calling on all Jews of the ghetto of Jasło to assemble at the Targowica square on August 18, 1942, at 6 AM. That evening, Polish, Ukrainian and German police formations surrounded the ghetto. The Jews began to assemble at the designated place and later in the day, police forces began to comb the city for hidden Jews.

Any Jew found hiding was shot on the spot. The assembled Jews were ordered to surrender all their valuable possessions and were then frisked. The selection followed. About 200 young and strong men and women were removed from the area to clear the ghetto afterward. The old and sick were transported by trucks to the forest near the village of Wiazica where they were shot and buried in prepared pits. The remainder of the Jews were kept in the square without food or water until the afternoon. But no train arrived, so they were marched on foot throughout the city to the elevated monastery of Wizitka on top of the hill, a distance of 500 meters from the railway station. There the Jasło Jews awaited the train that arrived the 19th or 20th of August 1942 and took them to the death camp of Belzec. The surviving group of the selection was led to a specially created small ghetto.

They would clean the ghetto area and later would be dispersed to various camps. Jasło thus became "Judenrein" except for the few Jews who were hidden by Poles. On January 11, 1945, the Russian Army liberated the city of Jasło and found 20 Jews who had survived in the vicinity of the city.

Jaslo was almost totally destroyed by the Germans in their fight with the Russians.

There is a memorial monument erected by the residents of Jaslo near the village of Wiazica where the mass killings took place. Some Jewish mass graves were also located there. It is estimated that about 2,000 Jews from Jaslo, Frysztak, Tarnow and Zmigrod were killed near the village. The memorial is the only reminder of the once flourishing Jewish community of Jaslo.

Thus ended Jewish life in Jaslo.

William Leibner
March 3, 2013
Jerusalem, Israel

Notes to the Reader:

Within the text the reader will note "{34}" standing ahead of a paragraph. This indicates that the material translated below was on page 34 of the original book. However, when a paragraph was split between two pages in the original book, the marker is placed in this book after the end of the paragraph for ease of reading.

Note that the letter *"w"* is used in this translation where most likely it would be sounded like *"vee."* Examples are " Awraham," "Tzwi," " Yaakow," " Zeew "and "Dawid."

Alternate names: Jasło [Polish], Yasla [Yiddish], Jaslau [German], Yaslo.

Jaslo is located 174 mi South of Warsaw, at 49°45' North Latitude and 21°28' East Longitude.

Table of Contents

Addendums:
  P1 - Contributors to the publication
  P2 - The Author

Supplementary material

  Prepared by William Leibner - Updated list, not in original book

History of the Jews of Jaslo

by Moshe Nathan Even Chaim (Rapaport)

Missing, extra, mistakes, omissions
Is part of man's creation?
No man is perfect
(To err is human)

Printed in Israel

Pepper Printing House

Herzl St. 61, Tel Aviv

[Page 2]

All the revenues from the book
"The History of the Jews in Jaslo"
are dedicated to a charitable fund, the author

[Page 3]

"The History of the Jews in Jaslo"

Moshe Nathan Even Chaim (Rapaport)

Oh! G-d Remember your promise to the people.
Blessed are the ones that will be paid for their deeds
Blessed be He that destroyed the bonds of servitude
The light of G-d is the soul of men.

An encompassing monogram of Jewish life in Jaslo from its
inception about 1865, development to the days of the shoah and
destruction of World War II, that started in 1939, and finished with
the total destruction of the Jewish community.

[Page 4]

In Memory of my father Chaim and my
mother Yuta, my sister Rivka and her
husband Eliyahu and their two daughters;

Hannah and Sarah. In memory of my two
brothers, Yehuda and Issachar Dov.

In Memory of all the inhabitants of the
Jewish community of Jaslo that were killed
outside their home.

May G-d avenge the misdeeds.

Memorial Prayer for All Departed

O merciful G-d who dwellst on high and are full of compassion, grant perfect rest beneath the shelter of Thy divine presence among the holy and pure who shine as the brightness of the firmament to our departed residents of the Jewish community of Jaslo and vicinity. Amongst them, torah scholars, scholars, yeshiva students, children, aged people, old and youngsters, babies, children and mothers, fathers, mothers, sons and daughters that were killed, burned, butchered, choked, drowned, shot, murdered, and buried alive by the enemy, descendants of Amalek. The Jews were innocents except for the fact that they were children of Jacob that sanctified the name of G-d.

May their souls be bound up in the bonds of eternal life. Grant that their memories ever inspire us to noble and consecrated living.

Amen

[Page 6]

Memorial Statement

When a person dies, the burial society comes and tends to all the necessities that are required to prepare the body for burial and finally bury the body in accordance with Jewish custom. People of the community leave their homes and come to pay respect to the deceased. Following the period of mourning, the relatives place the tombstone with the standard inscription. We take solace in our belief and we pray that the day comes when death disappears forever and G-d wipes the tears of all faces.

But what does one do when an entire community is totally destroyed everywhere, namely in ghettoes, concentrations camps, forests, fields, gas chambers and all sorts of places by all means that Satan has invented.

Who is going to tend to the community of three thousand souls?

Who is going to erect a tombstone?

Where will it be erected when the bones of the inhabitants of Jaslo are scattered all over.

What memorial will be erected to memorialize their spirit?

Where will we meet to memorialize our dear ones that were killed by the Germans and their helpers in such tragic manner?

Where will we pay respect to their souls?

Who will understand the depth of our pain?

Who will comprehend the great disaster, the destruction and the shoa?

For there will be no eulogy, no consolation, no respect for the death, no writer or teacher to draw the necessary rules of conduct.

Jaslo, Jaslo! What can I tell about you, how many tears can I shed for you my distinguished community?

Who can I compare to you and how can I console you, city of Israel?

Where is your lost crown?

As one of the survivors of the Jewish community I assumed the responsibility to create a memorial that will serve as a spiritual monument to the memory of the saintly people of Jaslo.

The well of tears will always be with us as we reminisce of the tragic events by reading the book that was written in tears.

May G-d avenge the innocent blood that was spilled.

[Page 7]

Jaslo

Meir Mohar

Jaslo was a Jewish religious traditional city that lived quietly in the serenity of the faith and the topography of mountains. The city observed the Jewish laws and gave charity to the needy. The Jewish history of Jaslo was rather short but full of scholarship and education as most of the Jewish communities of the period. It distinguished itself in the pleasant synagogue services. The synagogue was a beautiful building built on top of a hill with a great view of the entire area. The mountains seemed to bow to the magnificent building. The services were inspiring and refreshing to all those that attended them, especially on Shabbath and Holidays.

The city is precious to me for I took my first steps in it as a teacher of Hebrew, bible, and Hebrew grammar at the local "Talmud Torah". The latter was well organized and paid well the staff and on time, a rare thing in those days. The principal, Mr. Diller, and the teachers received me nicely and helped me in my first steps in the teaching career with the necessary advice and guidance that a young teacher needs. The surrounding hills fascinated me and I was impressed by the concern that the well to do Jewish families had for the rest of the Jewish population. The serenity of the place really impressed me. Jaslo was the first place that I started my first step in my career. The reception that the place gave to my family really impressed me, for we just started our conjugal life in the big city. The year was 1913, prior to World War I, the place was peaceful, the world was at peace and so was this distant corner.

Then the tragic events followed
And embittered the days
And the saintly inheritance of generations
Drowned in blood.
Jaslo- stands for May G-d Remember her Sufferings forever!

[Page 8]

In Memory of the Jaslo community
Piercing disabled voices emerge from the ruins
The soul is mercilessly affected by the manner of the slaughter:
Why not come to the mass grave of your parents and relatives,

To say "Kadish" on the spot where they were removed from this earth?
A cruel death and a wasted mourning lead to the city,
Where is the prophecy of the bloody city, the hill of sacrifices!
The road is closed before us to visit our buried family,
To shed tears for the loss of dear father,
And sweet mother in the tremors of death, her soul left her.

May the firmament shine for the saints on their memorial stone!
May the perpetrators of these acts suffer eternal damnation!

[Page 9]

Memories

by Rabbi Dr. Itzhak Rappoport, Melbourne, Australia

This book on Jaslo will serve as a tombstone for the Jewish residents of the city, it is difficult to write as memories suddenly race through the brain regarding Jewish Jaslo. Here we were born and played in our childhood. We grew to manhood and absorbed the spiritual values of the place. All this was destroyed, gone forever, never to return again. Our parents and families that sacrificed themselves for us, the teachers and friends that gave us their best efforts, the religious and secular leaders of the community that guided us, all of them are gone, destroyed in the shoah without rhyme or reason.

Indeed man is a like a tree in the field. Seeds are planted and saplings grow. Saplings are planted; they blossom into trees and provide fruits. As long as nature follows its curse, the roots spread and reach deeper into the ground while the foliage spreads overhead providing great shade and beauty. But in our generation bad weeds have taken over the land and we became stepchildren. We are refused to be granted what we are entitled according to the law of nature. Our livelihood is reduced to the minimum. You, Jew have no right to exist here nor do you have the right to hope for better future, states the adopted country. The water wells and the forests are not for your use.

Great is the sadness and even greater the embarrassment to have to leave the place of birth and look for a new place. Some of us went all over the globe. Our attachment to the soil and place of birth slowly weakened until we lost all feeling for them. At first our footing in the new place was shaky as every beginning but with time it became sturdier, it offered new vistas, new connections, new attachments and a new way of life. New language, customs and manners had to be acquired.

[Page 10]

Technical difficulties and many changes had to be overcome by man. The latter had to adopt since he could not change his body or soul overnight to suit the situation. Some of us found peace of mind but not tranquility of the soul. Still, we found our rights and the right to live. The place where the writer lives you see Jews standing tall. He walks freely and nobody will push him of the sidewalk, as is the custom in many East European countries. The daily life struggle is difficult but the Jew is given the same right as everybody else.

Following two years of life in Australia, I returned to my native city to visit my dear parents. I was full of joy and happiness to see them but not for too long. Every moment became fearful. One evening, my dear parents, my small brother and I walked towards their home when we were accosted by a gentile who hit my brother without cause. I hit the man on the chin whereupon he began to pull from his boot a sharp metal instrument. My father pleaded with me to leave the scene by stating: remember what happened in the shtetl of Pszytik...(Jews defended themselves against the Polish attackers and were later accused of killing Poles, translator). I stepped aside. As I left Poland, I kept saying to myself, where am I leaving my parents? With whom? With a country that denies them the basic rights and a population that is willing to devour them? And the world could not care in the least; all the entrance gates were closed. Meanwhile dark clouds closed in and the evil destruction will soon begin. The prophecy soon fulfilled itself with great speed; the roots of Jewish life were soon totally uprooted in a sea of tears and blood.

No one can console us; our eyes have seen the worst, the deep pains and the loneliness of our people. No one can ease the burden of sadness, no written page can calm our broken spirit. Perhaps the erection of " Yad Vashem" will provide a memorial for our victims and the eternal light there will memorialize the souls of the perished victims.

[Page 11]

The nations of the world have sinned against the people of Israel and continue do to so presently. Maybe Israel will remember that nothing can destroy the Jewish people. The great religious leaders sinned by refusing to accept the holy land as the home of the Jews while the secular leaders have refused to accept the sanctity of the torah. Between the two camps there were constantly battles. Good news to one was immediately decried as evil by the other side and vice-versa. The divisions within the Jewish people reached such high level of animosity that it was very difficult to find a common ground amongst the leaders. Different leaders, different ideas that divided and confused the people until they were all destroyed.

Very little can be done for what happened but we must be forewarned that division merely serves to weaken the unity of the people, brotherly hatred merely serves to create animosity and disunion and irresponsible leadership leads to destruction.

"And what does G-d ask of you now etc... To serve him with all your heart and with all your soul, this is your reward, for he is G-d that created all the great things before you" With this spirit, our ancestors kept their land and so will we. Witness the constant growth of Israel.

[Page 12]

At the initiative of Moshe Nathan Even Chaim (Rapoport) a meeting of former Jaslo Jews was called at his house on January 22ⁿᵈ 1951. This was the constituent meeting to create a Jaslo landesmanschaft in Israel. Present at the meeting were Mr. and Mrs. Zeev Eintziger, Moshe Goldschmidt, Awraham and Hawa Hoffert, Rachel Weinstein (Rapaport), Leibish Thaler, Israel Just, Bracha Katz, Kalmen Tzuckerman, Shlomo Krisher, Naphtali Shochet, Genia Schochet, Shalom Shtams, Meir Shilat, Dawid Shpirer, and his sister, and Meir H. Rota from Jerusalem.

The host of the meeting proposed to the assembled people to create a committee of Jewish survivors of Jaslo that will group all former residents of this city, newcomers to Israel and old residents. The aim of the committee was to perpetuate the Jewish memory of the city of Jaslo that was totally destroyed. The host further explained the goals of the society in the future and related that the meeting was being held on Tu-bishvat or 15 days in Shvat, the holiday of tree planting in Israel, symbolizing the renewal of Jewish life in the homeland. He further stressed that he hoped that all former residents of Jaslo in Israel and abroad would join the association. The participants of the meeting were highly motivated and elected a temporary committee of seven people to organize the future annual meeting of former Jaslo residents. Letters were sent to all people to attend the first general meeting on March 25ᵗʰ, 1951 where the foundations for the national association of former Jaslo Jews will be officially formulated and presented.

The general meeting took place at the " Beiti" hall in Tel Aviv, 14 Dizzengoff Square, and approximately 200 people attended the event.

The assembly opened with a moment of silence in memory of the Jews of Jaslo that perished in the shoa. Further eulogies were held in memory of the victims. Then, Moshe Nathan Even Chaim addressed the assembled people and stressed the importance of this meeting and the establishment of this organization of former Jaslo residents in Israel. He also outlined future activities for the association namely the creation of a mutual financial fund to help publish the book on" The History of Jewish Jaslo" and to create a fund that will help build 'The Jaslo house" where needy former Jaslo residents will be able to live.

[Page 13]

He was followed at the podium by Dr.Miriam Hoffert, Dr. Israel Plotzker, Shlomo Krisher and Yerachmiel Zakal who happened to be visiting Israel. The latter mesmerized the assembled audience with his stories. He also promised to provide the paper for the book.

Committee of former Jaslo residents in Israel.
First meeting in Tel Aviv

A committee of 12 members was chosen to represent the central organization in Tel Aviv. Branch committees consisting of three officers were also established in Haifa and Jerusalem.

The central elected committee then met at the house of Even-Chaim and decided to send a bulletin of activities to all former Jaslo residents in Israel and throughout the world. The main topic of the bulleting dealt with selecting a fitting memorial day for the Jewish community of Jaslo. A day that will be devoted to the memory of the perished Jews of Jaslo. Yerachmiel Zakal also participated at the meeting and was unanimously awarded honorary membership in the association and was presented with a certificate that was signed by all the members of the Jaslo Association Committee.

[Page 12]

The year 1865

[Page 13]

Chapter 1

The Jewish community of Jaslo numbered about 3,000 souls at the outbreak of World War II (1939); it started to grow and develop from the small suburb of Ulaszowice. This quarter was located on the other side of the Wislowa River, and continued from the Ulaszowice Bridge in the direction of the villages of Guriowic, Koblow, Podzamci etc...

The elder residents of Jaslo told us that the "Tehum" (limit for walking on Shabbat) was the village of Ulaszowice for the Jews of Jaslo until the sixties and seventies of the previous century, although the village itself belonged to the district of the Koblow village.

In the village of Ulaszowice we found the core of the first Jewish families that will settle in Jaslo, in the lower part of the city next to the bridge. Here they will organize the main Jewish trading and workshop center. We have to remember that Jews were forbidden to live in the city of Jaslo proper since time immemorial.

A small synagogue was established in the village of Ulaszowice behind the homes of Wagshal and Kornreich near the Czerwonka (the red house), the house was built with red bricks. Here the Jews met daily for morning and evening prayers.

A.M. Mohar writes in his book "Shvilei Olam"- the paths of the world printed in 1864 in the city of Lemberg as follows: Jaslo has 2500 people, the courtyards are empty and few people are found in the streets, there are no Jews because the inhabitants refuse to admit them to live in the city. Thus the city is similar to a desert where there is no commercial intercourse."

It seems that until 1864, there were no Jews in Jaslo. The first Jews seem to appear about 1865-1867. We also have no documentary evidence of a Jewish community life before this date.

The city of Jaslo did not distinguish itself in any particular historical manner, although the city is mentioned in Polish history as being conquered hundreds of years ago and destroyed twice by fire. However these items did not in themselves attribute exceptional factors to the history of the city. The name of Jaslo is derived from the small river named Jasiolka that begins its flow in the vicinity of Jasliska, continues lazily to of Niglowic then to Koczerow where it joins the Wislowa River (There is another version for the name of Jaslo).

[Page 14]

Kosciusko Street. Building of the Oszcindenosci Bank

Building of Bank Polski

[Page 15]

The Wislowa River flows slowly in a snakelike fashion northeast of the city that creates a green bluish carpet of greenery around three sides of the city. The river contours the city, flows under the railway bridge and along the Targowica near the Christian cemetery of Ulaszowice, and passes Oczerow where it meets the Jasiolka River. The stream continues eastward and merges with the larger Wisla River near the city of Mielec.

On occasion, during a cloudburst, or during the melting of the snows, the Wislowa River overflows its banks and floods the area of Hiclowka and the waves even reach the homes of Nahum Shochet, Meir Berish, the religious slaughterer, and Moshe Margolies on one side. It also floods Ulaszowice and reaches the hills of Koblow near the house of Palik on the other side. The waters flood the Targowica from the house of Moshe Wolf and Elimelech Thaler to the homes of Abba Hollander, Moshali Haber and the Targowica well at the bottom of the hill, (known today as the tastiest and coldest water). This forced the residence of Targowica to organize water transportation by means of boats to get from place to place.

Near Niglowic streamed a small rivulet called "Ropa" (named for the burning material found in the area and called Ropa) that blackened after it passed the Niglowic Bridge. For all the pollutants of the oil refinery "Gertenberg and Shriar" built in 1889 streamed into this small river. Bright colored spots appeared on the water body and frequently emitted all kinds of colorful rays especially during the summer days and very pungent odors. This rivulet also joined the Wisloka.

History of the Jews of Jaslo

Chapter 2

About 1870, the veto on Jewish life in Jaslo was abolished. The city adopted the slogan of "Jaslo the free City" and all municipal papers were signed with this slogan.

Who was the first Jew to enter and live in Jaslo? There are different opinions. Some say that the first Jew to settle in Jaslo was Leibish Winfeld while others say that it was Chaim Steinhaus, both are originally from Zmigrod.

We are told that a Jew from Ulaszowice bought a piece of land in the city of Jaslo, not too far from the Ulaszowice Bridge. The seller received a down payment and set the date for the necessary land sale transaction. When the Christian population heard about the deal they decided to take steps to prevent the completion of the transaction. The seller suddenly claimed that there was a statue of Jesus on the land and the Jew would remove the statue, therefore he cannot sell the land.

When the news reached Chaim Steinhaus he decided to help the Jew by intervening with the authorities. The case went to the courts, to the courts of appeal and finally reached the highest legal authority in Vienna. The transaction was upheld as legal and binding and the land was granted to the Jew. With this decision, the municipal ban on Jews living in the city of Jaslo was cancelled.

Chapter 3

Jaslo later served as a district city for the smaller communities of Zmigrod, Osiek, as well as Dukla, Koloszyce, Fristig and Brzostek. These small towns provided the Jewish population for the city of Jaslo. There was also a second version that stated that Chaim Steinhaus and his family settled in the city. Being a rich man, he received permission from the Austrian Emperor Franz Joseph I, to settle in Jaslo and to open his business in the city.

[Page 17]

Indeed Chaim Steinhaus settled on the other side of the bridge. The house was soon sold to Eliezer Brenner. Steinhaus then built his home in the market square, between the house of the mayor and the pharmacy. Here he opened a restaurant and a bar where the local Christian intelligentsia met. (In later years the restaurant was leased by the descendant Bogusz Steinhaus, to Max Koegel.)

Steinhaus used his connections to help other Jews move to Jaslo proper and thus fell the anti-Semitic barrier that prevented Jews from entering the city. Jews began to move from the limited space of Ulaszowice to Jaslo. The first Jews settlers in the city feared to distance themselves from the old Jewish section on the village of Ulaszowice. Therefore they concentrated in the Targowica Square where they bought some wooden huts and built new wooden homes. Later with years to come, the Jews will move closer to the city center and built homes.

Leibish Winfeld, an entrepreneur, was the first to open a general store in the market square. The Christian youths refused to acknowledge this fact and created many disturbances around the store. Legally they could not prevent the opening of the store so they frequently resorted to smashing the front windows or stealing the merchandise, thus hoping that the storeowner will close the place. But Leibish Winfeld did not capitulate and kept his business going. With his death, the store passed into the hands of his son-in-laws: Molduar and Shendel. For many years there was a big sign above the store stating in bold gold letters that this store belonged to Moldaur and Shedel, originally established by L. Winfeld (Following W.W.I, the store passed into the hands of Yehoshua Krisher)

[Page 18]

The climate of the city was pleasant and plenty of greenery. There were many trees and shrubbery. Cool winds frequently blew in the summer from the mountains of Guriowic and the forests of Koblow located in the north of the city. There were also pleasant and gentle breezes from the fields of Sowiniow, Wrocenko, and Hankowka from other side of the city. From the fields of Morikim on the outskirts of the city, one could smell the sweet scent of the freshly cut hay, and see the first stalks of the new grain. Furthermore, the city was surrounded by three rivers that cooled it and provided a pleasant atmosphere to the city in the summer days.

Market square of Jaslo

The city distinguished itself by its cleanliness; the streets were always swept and clean. The residents observed the cleanliness of the city and did not litter the streets, as was the case in other Galician cities. The streets were broad and long, the houses were two and three stories tall. The gentile homes were built in the Renaissance style ornamented with decorations, balconies and columns of various natures. The Jews built their homes simple and efficient. Amongst the nicest buildings in the city were the building of Bank Oszcindenosci, bank Polski and lately the municipal building.

The 3ʳᵈ May Street in Jaslo

[Page 19]

Chapter 5

The first Jewish settlers set the spiritual imprint on the Jewish community and they were: Wolf and Menachem Eintzigers, brothers, Awraham Meir Orenstein, Elimelech Goldstein, Leibish Winfeld, Naphtali Winfeld, Libtchie Werner, Elimelech Teller, Yaakow Freund, who lived all his life in Ulaszowice, Simche Bunim, Tzimet and his sons, Lib Citronenboim and his son in law Yaakow Pinhas Krisher, Chaim Steinhaus, and Bril Stilman, who bought the land for the cemetery from the landowner who was

embittered when he found out the purpose for the purchase); we can also add the Yehoshua Altman family, Yoel Mendel Beck, Amer, Hirshel Korzenik and his sons, and Zelig Miller, the slaughterer in the Jewish community of Jaslo. The most active communal and enterprising person was Naphtali Winfeld, who was later selected to head the Jewish community. Elimelech Teller and Yaakow Freund dealt mainly with the religious issues of the community.

With the growth of the community, new families arrived who opened all kinds of businesses including stores, workshops, and small plants. Some of the enterprises were very successful. Jews began also to build two story houses in the market square called the " ring square" and three story houses along the main streets of the city, namely Kosciusko and third May streets and also along the side streets such as Nowa, Korlewskino, Karzimiez Wielkiego, Igielna, Sokol, Czickiego etc...

[Page 20]

The center of the religious life was mainly concentrated along Shajnochy Street (named for a Polish writer). The Rabbi lived here, as did the cantors, the slaughterers, the Hebrew teachers, the beadle, the Hebrew teacher helpers, and the book dealer Shlomole Hakatan. Here was built the first study center and next to it the bath house with the mikveh. Opposite was the slaughterhouse from where one could hear constantly the voices of the animals that were being led to the slaughter. These noises frequently interfered with the synagogue prayers or with the studies at the study center. The crowing of the roosters carried to the slaughter could be heard all along the street.

The street was not paved and did not even have sidewalks. After a rain, there was mud and people walked in the mud that reached their ankles. But this was the religious and spiritual street of the Jews in the city.

The Hebrew teachers first settled in Targowica square. Here the first generation of Jews received their instruction from childhood to maturity in the "heders" led by Israel Melamed, Yudel Melamed, Moshe Yukel, Yudli Gorlitzer, Awraham Ressler, etc... If my memory serves me right, many of the homeowners told me that they attended the first heder in Targowice Square that was taught by Israel Melamed. Years later, a "Talmud Torah" was built in Shajnochy Street by the famous donor Itzhak Yehuda Rubel. Thus, the street became the center of Jewish education. All along the street one could hear the voices of Jewish children studying the torah. Their teachers were Shimshon-li Melamed, Baruch-li Melamed, Shmuel Mendel, Nathan-L Melamed and Nehemiah, etc...

[Page 21]

With time other institutions were established: "Haknesset Kalah" or association to help wed the poor girls, " Bikur cholim" the association to assist the sick, Talmud Torahs, kloizim- or small congregational prayer rooms and a " Chevrah Kadisha" or burial society. The old timers assumed leading roles in the various societies and they soon became entrenched in the leadership of the various communal activities. It soon became a tradition that these people or their descendants would usually be appointed to head these institutions.

The Rabbi of Jaslo was Yona Tzanger who came from the area of Brzostek. He was the son in law of Elimelech Teller and Awraham Hirsh Brenner.

Chapter 6

In 1869-1870, the Jewish community of Jaslo consisted of about 30 Jewish families, the population increased steadily with new arrivals from the vicinity. The new arrivals were primarily concerned with the available religious facilities. They laid the cornerstone for the erection of a larger synagogue, a bathhouse and mikveh and to purchase land to erect a cemetery. Until this day, Jaslo did not have a Jewish cemetery and the deceased were transported to the Jewish cemetery in Zmigrod. The problem assumed serious proportions when the Rabbi of Jaslo, Rabbi Yona Tzanger died relatively young, he was Rabbi of Jaslo for more than two years, but could not be buried in Jaslo where there was no Jewish cemetery. The problem of selecting a new rabbi, cantors and slaughterers also arose and needed solutions.

During this period, a serious epidemic started in the hamlet of Sokolow near Rzeszow. Many Jews including the Rabbi and his family left the place and started to wander. They went from place to place, frequently the Rabbi prayed near caves or forests in isolation until he and his family reached the area of Jaslo. The Jewish community of Jaslo decided to appoint a committee to greet and invite the rabbi to become Rabbi. The latter accepted and became the spiritual leader of the relatively young Jewish community of Jaslo.

The Rabbi of Sokolow, Rabbi Awraham Yehoshua Heshil Rubin, grandson of the famous Hassidic Rabbi Asher from Ropczyce who was the son-in-law of the great Hassidic Rabbi, Naftali Ropczitzer. Rabbi Rubin became the new Rabbi of the community.

[Page 22]

Chapter 7

I will digress somewhat and take the liberty to devote a few lines to the Rubin family, especially to the founder of the dynasty. Here is what my grand father Rabbi Shalom Lieberman, brother of the late Rabbi of Tuporow who was the son-in-law of the first Rabbi of Jaslo had to say:

Rabbi Naphtali from Ropczyce used to visit small hamlets in the vicinity of Warsaw. As usual he would start his visit by attending service at the local synagogue. As he approached the synagogue, his eyes caught sight of a young group of students sitting in front of their open Talmudic books and arguing points of "Halacha" or Jewish theological laws. Amongst them he noticed a bright redheaded youngster who agued his points with great conviction, depth and logical reasoning.

The Rabbi remained standing and amazed, fascinated by the handsome lad who continued to argue in his pleasant voice. He was practically mesmerized by the youngster. He began to think seriously about marrying his oldest daughter to the young scholar. He approached the young student and asked him, his name. My name is Asher Yeshayahu but they call me Asheril. Who is your father? I have no father, answered the lad.

Do you have relatives? Asked the Rabbi? Yes, my mother sits amongst the stands in the market. The Rabbi hurriedly left the synagogue. He asked for directions to locate the widow of the boy. He located her and approached her.

[Page 23]

She was sitting near her stand, pale, wrapped in a sweater. She had an innocent and modest look.

The Rabbi said hello and informed her that he was visiting the synagogue and saw her son and was impressed with him. Furthermore, I would like to marry my daughter to your son.

The mother was stunned, who?, what?, what are you talking about said the woman?

The Rabbi again repeated, I would like to marry my daughter to your son Asheril!

The woman was still in a daze and did not grasp the situation. She said that Asheril was young a mere baby, and dismissed the proposal. She begged him to drop the issue but the Rabbi refused. Still the woman kept repeating that her son was very young.

Time passed and the Rabbi again visited the area and arrived at the particular hamlet. He remembered the youngster and again saw him in the synagogue. He was determined to get him to be his son-in-law. He decided to approach again the mother for her consent.

He explained to the mother the situation and furthermore pointed out to her that her son must continue his studies, which he guaranteed to implement. He even named the place where her son will continue his studies, namely with the "Hose of Lublin" or the famous Rabbi of Lublin. Both parties traveled to Lublin where they met the great Rabbi. On seeing the youngster, the Rabbi stated (you have received a nice Pessah sacrifice) you have acquired a bargain or a jewel for your family. Rabbi Asheril indeed passed away on the eve of Pessah but one of his descendants, Rabbi Elimelech, was the father of Rabbi Awraham Yehoshua Heshil Rubin (redhead), the first Rabbi of the Jaslo Jewish community.

History of the Jews of Jaslo

Chapter 8

1871

With the appointment of the Rabbi, the community proceeded to search for purchasable land on the other side of the Wisloka River near the Ulaszowica Bridge, for the construction of a synagogue and a home for the rabbi. Indeed in the year of 1871, the study center and the home for the Rabbi were built. Years later two more houses will be built on this land for Rabbi Tzvi Yossef, who will become the second Rabbi of Jaslo.

[Page 24]

The only study center in the city was too small for the congregation that constantly grew therefore the leaders of the community decided to build a bigger study center that will provide room for all the congregants of the community.

My grandfather, Rabbi Pinhas Eliezer Halevi Liberman from Tyczyn, brother of the above, son of the late Rabbi Mordechai from Toporow, told me that as a young boy he traveled to the wedding of his brother, Dov Issachar, who married the daughter of Rabbi Rubin from Jaslo in 1881. They traveled by train from Lemberg to Zagorz where the tracks ended. They then proceeded by cart to Jaslo.

They attended services at the old synagogue that was packed with people. He heard someone say that the new community of Jaslo had between 60 and 70 Jewish families. The community coffers were empty. Still the community decided to proceed with the project of a new study center.

On the other side of the old and small study center, on the left, leading to the village of Hiclowka, stood an abandoned building that belonged to a gentile. News soon reached the community that the building and the land were for sale and negotiations began. Finally the estate was purchased.

The old building was fixed and repaired and in 1883 was opened as a synagogue. The eastern wall contained a beautiful holy arc that was decorated with flowers and garlands. Three steps led to the holy arc. Next to it stood a large column dominated by a copper "menorah" with many branches protruding. In the middle of the hall was the wooden bima; copper alloyed chandeliers were suspended from the ceiling, four big oil lamps in the corners of the synagogue. Several small flats were also built, namely for the beadle and the slaughterer. The next section was devoted to the women. Nearby was built a bathhouse with two mikvot; one had heated water and the other one cold water. The latter shared its space with the steam room.

The synagogue remained standing until 1914 when the Russian army entered the city and destroyed it. The only items left standing were the walls and some roof rafters.

[Page 25]

Only with the end of World War I, in 1918, will the synagogue be repaired and restored. The initiative for the project was undertaken by a few well-to-do Jews, including my late father. Some changes were also made during the repairs and the synagogue began to service the Jewish community.

During the holiday of Sukkoth in 1934, a fire started in the bathhouse and soon spread to the study center. Only the charred walls remained standing of the synagogue. Again the Jews of Jaslo were left without a place to worship. It took a group of Jaslo Jews one to two years to prepare a new blueprint and to rebuild the synagogue accordingly. The construction was finished in 1939. The synagogue was totally destroyed during World War II.

Chapter 9
1888-1889

I already mentioned above that when the committee decided to build the synagogue the communal treasury was empty. Therefore, the leaders decided to take a mortgage in the bank. The money was issued to the association that was formed to build the synagogue. 32 people counter signed the mortgage on behalf of the association. The latter however could not keep up the payments due to the poor economic situation of the Jewish community. The banks that underwrote the mortgage had difficulty suing 32 people. They therefore decided to seize the land, the synagogue and the Rabbi's house as escrow. The entire estate was recorded in the association books as the property of one or two old Jewish residents of the city of Jaslo. The Rabbi was deeply shocked by the entire story. For he had prayed in this synagogue for 19 years and now it will be auctioned off at the block and some stranger may buy it. He called his son, Itzhak Yossef who lived in Sanok and was the son in law of the famous financier Avishel Kanner that also lived in Sanok. The latter was one of the richest merchants in the city of Sanok. The son came and paid the debts. He also registered the estate to his name. He will later become Rabbi of Jaslo.

Due to the financial problems around the synagogue, personal disputes arose between various members of the congregation. The Rabbi seeing the effects of the disputes, decided to retire and leave Jaslo for Palestine.

[Page 26]

On a Friday in 1888, the Rabbi announced to the congregation that he was leaving the community and urged that it appoint his son to succeed him as Rabbi. He pointed out to the community that his son settled the debts of the community. He then bid farewell and left for Rzeszow where he spent Saturday.

The Rabbi's decision shocked the entire community. The people did not know what to make of the strange decision. They could not accept the fact that the Rabbi would leave them. The obvious question that everybody faced was what will happen to the community. Should they react and in what manner? Should they follow the suggestion of the outgoing Rabbi and appoint his son as Rabbi? The community was at a loss.

The Rabbi's oldest son-in-law, Rabbi Issachar Dov Lieberman, wanted the post but did not have enough local support. He was certain that his brother-in-law, Rabbi Tzvi Yossef, who resided in Sanok and had opened a private bank and conducted extensive business of managing estates, timber, and forests, would not be interested in the position of Rabbi of Jaslo. He therefore decided to leave Jaslo temporarily and accept the position of Rabbi of Toporow where his father, Rabbi Mordechai Yaakow just passed away.

There were some leaders that suggested that Jaslo invite Rabbi Menachem Mandil, (related to the Raduszitz and Sandz Rabbinical dynasty), the second son-in-law of the Rabbi. But the majority of the community favored the selection of Tzvi Yossef as Rabbi of Jaslo. Meanwhile his father left Rzeszow and headed to Palestine. The new appointed Rabbi received the blessing of the saintly Rabbi Yehezkel from Siniawa, the son-in-law of the Rabbi Avishel Kanner, who came with hundreds of Hassidim for Shabbat to Jaslo to honor the new appointed young Rabbi.

Chapter 10

Rabbi Rubin left the city of Rzeszow with his young son Itzchakel and reached Palestine where he settled in Jerusalem. He remained in the city for one year and felt that the city was not religious enough. He left the city and headed to the hills of the Galilee where he spent time in communion with nature and finally reached the city of Tzefat in 1890.

[Page 27]

He was accepted as Rabbi in this mystical and Kabala city. For 19 years he remained at this post. He prayed at the Sandzer study center in Tzefat. His grandchildren tell us that their grandfather Rabbi Awraham Yehoshua Heshil Rubin served as Rabbi in three different places and in each place he was 19 years, namely Sokolow, Jaslo and Tzefat.

He passed away on the first day of Cheshvan 1908 in Tzefat and was buried there near the graves of Talmudic scholars.

The gravesite of Rabbi Awraham Yehoshua Heshil near Tzefat

The Rabbi had three sons and three daughters, namely; Rabbi TzviYossef, the oldest son, Rabbi of Jaslo and a leading rabbinical figure in Galicia. The second son Asher was a scholar and was fluent in several languages. He married to Rozwadow where he was involved in commerce and was also the chairman of the first Jewish bank in Rozwadow. He left the place with his wife and daughters and headed to the USA in the early twenties of the 20th century. The third son Itzhakel, was an ascetic and possessed a sensitive soul, he devoted himself to the study of the Torah. He frequently kept himself in isolation and concentrated on the Talmud. He became a Talmudic scholar in his own right. He succeeded his father as Rabbi of Tzefat. He remained Rabbi for 7 years and then passed away the first day of Cheshvan, 1915. He is buried in Tzefat next the grave of the son of Rabbi Hershele of Tarnow.

[Page 28]

Rabbi Rubin's oldest daughter, Dina, married a perpetual student related to one of the wealthy families, who owned a large estate in Eastern Galicia. The husband soon died and she was widowed. She eventually left Poland with her two daughters and settled in Palestine (one of the daughters named Reisil married Shimon Gelbstein from Jerusalem. They live in Tel Aviv).

The second daughter Rizli married Rabbi Issachar Dov, the son of Rabbi of Toporow who was the son in law of the Rabbi Hirshali of Tarnow and the brother in law of the famous Rabbi Chaim of Sandz. The Rabbi of Toporow died relatively young and left a young son who was married to the daughter of the Rabbi of Biecz, the son in law of the late great Rabbi Chaim Liberman who died in Buokahara (Russia). His son, Yehoshua Heshil married the sister of Meir Moshel and lives in Tel Aviv.

The third daughter was Primitel and she married Rabbi Menachem Mandil (grand son to the Rabbi Ber Maradoshitz and Rabbi Chaim of Sandz). He was a personality and familiar with the mystical scholarly world. He bought the land from the inheritors of Israel Melamed and built a study center and a dormitory for students. Many Hassidim from Jaslo prayed at the study center that was located at Targowica Square. In later years, Rabbi Menachem Mandil slowly distanced himself from people, avoided conversation and devoted himself to study. The family had one son named Yona and a daughter named Yutali. The son, Rabbi Yona Mandil was the son in law of the Rabbi Eliezer from Oshpitzin that resided many years in Jerusalem. Rabbi Yona Mandil was a Talmudic scholar devoted himself to the study of the torah and was very observant. He lived in Jaslo.

A few years after his marriage, his wife died and left him with a daughter and two boy infants. The daughter grew up with her maternal grandfather in Oshpitzin and the sons lived with their paternal grandfather. Chaim and Awraham Yehoshua attended the Bobowa Yeshiva. The younger one then went to Palestine where he continued his studies in Jerusalem. He married well and devoted himself to the study of the torah.

Yutali, the daughter of Rabbi Mandil, was a sensitive and intelligent woman. She married Moshale the son of Rabbi Itzhak Tuvia Rubin from Sandz. He was a very hospitable person, very active in communal affairs, familiar with the general population and well connected with the authorities. Although he was a candidate for the post of Rabbi, he devoted his free time to the well being of the community and needy individual Jews.

Suddenly, disaster struck, his wife died and left him with an infant son named Eliezer Yerucham. The tragedy caused him a severe shock and it took him sometime to recover. He moved from Jaslo to Sandz. He later became military chaplain in the Polish Army and was very active on behalf of Jewish soldiers in the army. With the fall of Poland, he managed to reach Russia but soon became ill and passed away. His son Eliezer Yerucham managed to reach Palestine, settled in Jerusalem where he continued his studies. He eventually left for the States.

[Page 29]

Chapter 11

Rabbi Tzvi Yossef was appointed Rabbi of Jaslo and immediately started to build two houses on the estate of the synagogue. After all, the place was registered in his name. He built for himself a magnificent villa covered in greenery. The outside was covered with greenery and plant climbers. Balconies protruded from many places and flowerbeds were everywhere. The entrance columns were covered with greenery. Next to the house, he built a large "sukkah" with a slanted roof that was divided into two parts so that the roof could be closed when it rained. The house itself was the residence of the Rabbi and it contained a large reception hall where the judicial rabbinical council met. The next house faced the road and was allocated for his sons and his father in law Rabbi Hirshele.

During his stay as spiritual leader, the community grew and contained hundreds of families. They opened businesses, workshops and small industrial plants. He administered the needs of his flock with kindness and perseverance. Fifteen years after his appointment as Rabbi, the famous synagogue was completed. He was considered one of the richest Rabbis in Western Galicia. He combined Torah and guidance. His straight posture, noble face with two eyes emitting warmth and purity, attributed to him charm and kindness. He visited Palestine prior to World War I and maintained extensive contacts with his family and friends.

[Page 30]

Many Jews left Jaslo when World War I started but the Rabbi remained to guide and protect his flock. This stand will cost him dearly later on during the Russian occupation of the city. As Rabbi he was often called by the military commandant of the city to explain all kinds of problems and situations that involved Jews. The interrogators were not the friendliest people, certainly not the Rabbi, and frequently threatened him. Still he stood his ground and defended his flock with sheer determination and bravery.

I still remember the bitter winter of 1914 following the Russian occupation. Military chaos ruled the city; the soldiers went on a rampage, especially against Jews. Some Russian officers and soldiers seized the Rabbi and led him to the synagogue where they abused him and accused him of having committed crimes against the Russians. They threatened to shoot him on the spot if he did not admit to the charges. Of course, the Rabbi refused to confess. They then abandoned the synagogue and left him inside with the doors locked. The Rabbi tried to leave but could not for he did not have the keys. For hours the Jewish population did not know what happened to the Rabbi and there were serious fears for his life. By accident someone discovered that the Rabbi was locked in the synagogue and freed him.

The Russians eventually retreated from Jaslo and decided to take hostages with them. They selected the Rabbi and a few other well-placed Jews with them. The Jews of Jaslo paid the ransom of 600 rubles that was imposed on these hostages. The Russians took the hostage money, bought spirits and consumed them; eventually they released some Jews and the Rabbi but soon rearrested him and other hostages. He was sent from place to place and eventually reached the city of Kiev, Ukraine.

The writer Sh. Ansky wrote in his book entitled " Hurban Hayehudim" – or destruction of the Jews"...in this room were seated 17 Rabbis, ten of them were very old, suddenly I saw in the room the Jaslo Rabbi, he looked at me with his childish eyes that emitted rays of warmth and a doze of spirit. He told me that during Passover, the Russians decided to arrest him a second time. He decided to pay them 600 rubles as ransom money, whereupon they left him alone. Within a week they returned and arrested him as a war hostage.

He remained in Russia for four years. He returned a broken man. His spirit was destroyed. Signs of depression affected him and he lacked energy. The sparks in his eyes were gone, instead hollowness appeared. His body weakened by the day and he became gravely ill. Then one day in Hannukah of 1928, he passed away. He was Rabbi of Jaslo for 40 years.

[Page 31]

The funeral took place in the evening and almost the entire Jewish population partook in the funeral. All those involved with the arrangements for the funereal went to the mikveh to ritually cleanse themselves. The water was heated for the occasion. The rabbis of the neighboring communities came to pay their respects. Amongst the Rabbis that eulogized the Jaslo Rabbi was Rabbi, Shmuel Fuhrer, the Krosner Rabbi. He began his eulogy at the great synagogue of Jaslo by quoting a line from the torah section of the week" ...and Yossef—Reb Tzvi

Yossef – he is the ruler of the country, he is the provider for the country, the entire nation bows to him."

He left two sons and four daughters. Rabbi Eklimelech assumed the post of Rabbi of Jaslo. The second son Aaron (the young Mandli) died as a young man. The daughters were named Mirci, Dinaci, Rizi and Pesia. (The daughter Shasha died after a short illness while being engaged)

Chapter 12

The oldest son, Rabbi Elimelech was the son in law of Rabbi Awraham Chaim of Flantsch - the grandson of the Rabbi Eliezer of Dzikow and the Rabbanit Margalia.

The Rabbi of Jaslo awaiting the arrival of the President of Poland

[Page 32]

Following his marriage, he devoted himself to studying and teaching torah. The religious youth of Jaslo flocked to his lectures including the author. He assumed the post of Rabbi of the city following the passing of his father. He was also appointed to head the religious judicial council of Jaslo.

Like his late father, he too was very distinguished looking and emitted a ray of nobility; his large yellow beard covered his face. He remained at his post for ten years.

He escaped to Tarnow with the outbreak of World War II, remained there for a while, and then returned to Jaslo to be with his younger brother in time of need. He was soon seized by the Germans along with my father and a few other influential Jews in the city. They underwent terrible tortures and died with the famous line "Shema Israel"- or hear Israel on their lips.

He had two daughters, Rachelci and Donaci, both well natured and graceful. The oldest was known as an educated woman and was involved in social work. She married Dovidl Halbershtam- grandson of the famous dynasty of Sandz, who was a perpetual torah student He was maintained by his father law while he continued his studies. They had two children, Awraham Chaim, a genius, and Tziporale. The former was soon accepted as Rabbi of Dobri in Czechoslovakia and left Jaslo.

The younger daughter, Dinahci, was known for her kindness and sensitivity. She married Rabbi Yoel Hilperin, the son of the Rabbi of Dubshitz-descendant of the Yachish dynasty- grandson of Rabbi Feibish Brezner. The latter was the descendant of 14 generations of Rabbis. Indeed the study of the torah returned full cycle for Rabbi Yoel Hilperin proved to be a great Talmudic scholar as well as knowledgeable in general education. He resided in Jaslo with his in laws and devoted himself fully to the study of the torah. They had two daughters and a son.

With the outbreak of World War II, he managed to flee to the Russian sector but was arrested on crossing the border. Eventually managed to reach the city of Boukhara where he helped Jews in need. He is well remembered by the Jews of the city for his devotion to their cause.

[Page 33]

Following the war, he managed to reach the D.P. (displaced persons) camp of Bergen Belsen (in the British sector of Germany, translator). He was appointed Rabbi of the camp and became very active in helping the surviving Jews. He was involved in many social organizations. He also worked very closely with Rabbi Shlomo Kahana, head of the judicial council of Warsaw-presently in Jerusalem- on behalf of the women whose husbands were missing. He published a special book entitled "Osef Takanot Agunot" or collection of rules regarding married women whose husbands disappeared. With the closure of the camp he left for the USA and settled in Brooklyn.

The Rabbanit Dina Hilperin

Rabbi Aaron Rubin, the second son of Rabbi Tzvi Yossef was a Hassid and strictly observant Jew. He kept himself in isolation and led an ascetic life. Following his marriage, he taught of starting a business but soon gave up the idea. With the establishment of Independent Poland, he left Jaslo and settled in Czechoslovakia, I think in the city of Bardejow where his wife's family lived. There he became a Rabbi with a sizable following.

[Page 34]

The third son of Rabbi Elimelech, Mandli, had a pleasant disposition, smart and intelligent, married to Lemberg where he resided until he left for the USA where he assumed the title of Rabbi of Jaslo. In the prime of his life, he fell ill and soon passed away. He left a wife and an infant son. The wife remarried Rabbi Moshale Rubin from Sandz.

Mirci, the oldest daughter married Rabbi Hershli Rubin, the famous scholar known as " from the Kloiz" of Tarnow. He was an erudite Talmudic scholar. He resided in Jaslo with his father in law and refused to assume a rabbinical position. He devoted his life to the study of the Talmud. He barely consented to lead the services on Saturdays and holidays at the synagogue (He visited Palestine prior to World War I.)

He had four sons and two daughters. The oldest son Asher was a torah scholar and devoted himself to the study of the torah. He married Ressler's daughter. His father in law was wealthy resident of Frysztak and this is where the couple lived for many years until they decided to return to Jaslo. He tried business ventures but failed. He then received a job in the kehilla.

The second son was Ephraim also a devoted student to the studies of the torah. He was a pleasant person, very familiar with the Talmud and rabbinical literature. He married the daughter of Rabbi Feivel Zak from Bardajew and the young family moved there. Several years prior to World War II, he moved to Belgium where he was appointed to head the " Reish Mesivta"- or Yeshiva in Antwerp.

The two younger sons were yeshiva students and were known for their fanatical religious views. The two daughters were named Rivali and Sarci. Both were pleasant and sensitive women. The younger one was a teacher at the "Beit Yaakow" school for girls.

The second daughter of Rabbi Tzvi Yossef Rubin, Dinahci, married Rabbi Chaim Baruch, head of the religious judicial council of Wisnic.

Rizi, the third daughter of the Rabbi married a descendant of a famous Rabbi and moved to Lodz. The fourth daughter, Pessia, well read, intelligent and possessed a modern outlook on life. She married Rabbi Dudil Horowitz, son of the Rabbi of Mielec in Galicia.

Dudil was an intelligent, educated and well-versed individual. Familiar with the Talmud and with general events. Observed strictly the commandments but was aware of the new winds in the air. Being the son of a Rabbi, he was familiar with the burning issues of the day for the Jews. He sincerely hoped for the fulfillments of the prophecies for Israel via the hands of the Zionists. His visions and thoughts were not understood or accepted by these contemporaries. He showed that torah observance and education could mix.

He left Poland and settled in Vienna and then in Berlin. Although he was involved in business, he still devoted time to the communal affairs. He was well liked by the community. In the twenties he left for the USA with his family. His youngest daughter, Sarah is in Israel, she holds an important position in the foreign office.

[Page 35]

History of the Jews of Jaslo - Continued

Chapter 14

Map of Galicia, Poland
Jaslo in the foreground

The railway station in Jaslo was opened between 1888 and 1890. The station was along the Lemberg-Krakow line. Three trains passed daily along that line and stopped in Jaslo. There was also an express train. Several years later, a side line was opened linking Jaslo to Rzeszow. During the same period, a high school was built in the city. In the Niglowic section an oil refinery was established along the Wisloka River. Near the bridge, they built a hydroelectric power plant between the years 1892-1894. The power plant moved to a new building in 1913, near Czackiego Street.

[Page 36]

Jaslo was also the district city, thus it had the judicial court center in the city. The courthouse was big and next to it was the business center. Many lawyers, amongst them Jewish lawyers, began to settle in the city, mostly along Kosciusko and May Third streets. Many new building arose along these streets that offered residences and offices to doctors and lawyers. All these tenants attracted many other people, especially Jews from the nearby small communities like Zmigrod, Dukla, Koloczic, Brzostek, Frysztak and Trzciano. The growth of the population also increased the Jewish population.

The core of the Jewish intelligentsia consisted of Hebrew teachers, doctors, lawyers, engineers, managers and higher officials at the refinery in Niglowice. A large segment of these people tended to assimilate very rapidly; but the Zionist reawakening stopped this tendency. The driving force behind Zionism was the able orator, the lawyer Awraham Kornhauser. He had a substantial following that joined him in the Zionist movement. (Doctor Kornhauser settled in Jaslo in the 1900, he stems from the Tarnow area where he finished high school.) He was a friend of Shtand and Zalc, leaders of Western Galician Zionism in those days. He was very impressive; tall, his black beard gave him the appearance of another Doctor Herzl. He was nicknamed the second Doctor Herzl.

His office was the first office of the Zionist movement in Jaslo and his home served as a meeting place for Zionist leaders.

I already mentioned that the Jaslo Jewish community was relatively young and did not have many established traditions or old established leading families or leaders. Most of the leaders of the community were people that came from middle class families; they did not belong to the Hassidic movement nor did they travel to Hassidic courts. Very few Jaslo Jews were Hassidim and the majority of them followed the Rymanow Hassidic court.

The number of Hassidic Jews increased at the beginning of the 20th century and we already see the appearance of Tchortkower and Sadigora Hassidim. For a while there was even a "shtibel" , a small congregational one-room synagogue, named the Tchortkow-Boyan synagogue. Occasionally the Rabbi of Rymanow came for Shabbat to Jaslo. Most of the Jews of Jaslo were basically religious people that followed the religion as their fathers.

[Page 37]

The lack of Hassidic tradition, the cleanliness of the city, the imposed modest dress code that the Jaslo Jews observed and the large number of educated Jews, gave the Jews the feeling of living in a modern city and sometimes the city was referred to as "the gentile city" or "the assimilated city"; the moderate Jews called the city "a modern and clean city". The large public garden added a certain environmental charm. The garden stretched from May 3rd street to the courthouse on Chelmska Street and in the width from Czackiego Street on the right to Sobieski Street. The garden was opened to the public in 1900 during the Imperial maneuvers. (The Emperor Frantz Joseph and his family participated in the war games and also visited Jaslo and vicinity). Various trees were planted in the garden; greenery paths interlaced the park that had a line of green benches for people to rest. For the benefit of the strollers there were colorful circular beds of various flowers that emitted floral scents. The roses, lilies, carnations and other flowers were in great abundance. Three main alleys bordered by green shrubs, white birch and chestnut trees were here. There was also a tennis court. In one of the little squares stood a green house with a slanted roof surmounted by a copper snake holding in his mouth a long trumpet. During the summer a band would be seated in the green house and play music for the strollers. In another square there was a huge statue, several meters high, dedicated to the great Polish fighter Kosciuszko, head high in the air, chest exposed and a sword in his arm. The statue was surrounded by a heavy copper metal chain supported by small columns.

The third square consisted of a circle of grass bordered by shrubs and concentric circles of different colored flowers.

The streets of Kosciuszko and 3rd May led to the park and were the main strolling streets in the city. The road to Guriowic and Koblow near the rock quarry and the surrounding mountains was the favorite strolling place on Shabbat and holidays. During the summer, many people went

[Page 38]

along the road to Hiclowka to swim in the river near Koczerow. This place served for many years as a "beach" for Jaslo. For a time, Targowica also served as a swimming place. The final swimming place however was the area under the metal bridge. The local beach area changed according to the season and the security of the place because frequently the swimmers were stoned by gentile youths.

Chapter 15
1898 - The Torching Of The Distillery

The Jewish community of Jaslo grew and developed when suddenly out of blue it was shocked beyond wildest imagination. An anti-Semitic campaign was launched by the priest Stoilowski, who represented the "Peasant Party" and wanted to be elected to the Imperial Assembly in Vienna (see the item of Yaakow Freund). The new Jewish settlers dreamed of a safe place where they could work and live in peace. Suddenly there were anti-Jewish outbursts throughout the area of Jaslo. The priest Stoilowski was busy inciting the farmers throughout the district against the Jews. He wanted to represent the Jaslo-Sanok district and spread the worst poison against the Jews in the area. He openly called on the farmers to take matters in their hands against the Jews. He even preached to the farmers that they should evict the Jewish farmers from their villages.

In 1898, the Jews began to feel that the Christian population was slowly avoiding contact with them. As the year advanced, less and less contact occurred between the populations. The farmers began to avoid entering the city. Tensions rose by the day. Then it happened, the church bells began to peel longer than usual. This seemed to be the signal for the event.

The Jews from Ulaszowice and nearby villages abandoned their homes and everything in them to the incited mobs of the priest Stoilowski. The frenzied mob destroyed every Jewish property it encountered. This was the moment that the farmer Jeworski from the village of Koblow waited for. He led a large incited mob to the farm of Naphtali Shmuel Solomon. The latter was a well to do farmer in the village of Podzamci near Koblow. Jeworski decided to exploit the situation and settle personal accounts with the Jewish farmer. The Solomon family decided to leave the farm and seek protection. It left their son Yehiel to protect the farm. The latter saw the menacing advancing mob led by Jeworski, and realized that his life was in danger and the situation was hopeless. He disguised himself as a farmer with a white shirt in the style of the peasants in the area and headed away from the farm. He hoped to make his way to the city of Jaslo. Jeworski recognized him from a distance as the son of the Shmuel Naphtali Solomon and began to chase after him. All the farmers joined the race. As he was running, the fringes began to emerge from under his shirt and now everybody saw that he was a Jew. The chase was on and Yehiel Solomon kept loosing ground. He knew that he was not going to make it to the city. So he decided to seek refuge at the distillery of Yaakow Freund in Ulaszowice. He was certain that the mob will not dare to enter the place. The mob surrounded the estate of Freund and demanded the body of Yehiel Solomon.

[Page 39]

Freund was certain that if the boy steps out of his place, the enraged mob would kill him. Thus he could not agree to the demands of the mob. He tried to explain to some of the farmers that the boy was his guest and he must protect his guest. The farmers insisted that he deliver Yehiel and then they would leave him alone. When the enraged mob saw that Freund would not surrender the boy, they began to attack the house, smashed the windows, destroyed everything in sight, and one farmer managed to break into the courtyard and toss a burning torch between the barrels of spirit. A fire started and soon spread through the area and the house.

The mayor of Jaslo was at that time, Grabowski, the son of a poor shoemaker who worked as a youngster in Freund's distillery. Grabowski was a smart fellow and excelled in his studies; he finished law school and was appointed to this high office. He befriended the local Count Riegers that resided in Guriowic. He also knew that the Count objected vociferously to the building of the distillery next to his estate but could not stop the process. He therefore decided to show the Count his loyalty and refused to give the order to extinguish the fire at the distillery. The place burned down to the ground while the fireman stood by and the mob was having a field day. The army arrived the next day from Rzeszow and established order. Nothing remained from the burned places. The smoke columns could be seen as far as Frysztak and Zmigrod.

Property worth 80,000 silver Rheinish went down the drain. He could not get a penny from the insurance since the policy lapsed two weeks ago and he did not renew it in time. He lost everything but he saved a soul of Israel, Yehiel Solomon (who lives in Jerusalem today).

[Page 40]

Chapter 16
Dr. Herzl on the Jaslo disturbances

The wanton destructive behavior of Stoilowski's followers soon reached the capital city of the Empire, where Dr. Herzl resided. He was shocked by the events that took place in the province of Galicia where many Jews lived without the slightest protection from the state.

Dr. Herzl had just established the platform for Political Zionism at the first Congress in Basle, Switzerland in 1897. He barely had time to rest when the news reached him. He still had not developed a solution for the Jewish problem but this incident in Jaslo provoked his anger and fueled his energy in building the Zionist Organization and organizing future congresses that would meet in 1898, 1899, 1900 and so on. The incident of Jaslo fired the fury of the Zionists who pointed out the hopeless situation of the Jew. Dr Herzl wrote an article entitled "Fire in Galicia" in 1898 (the complete article appears in "the book of Zionism" published in 1950). We will merely present some excerpts from the article.

"The priest Stoilowski misled his people. In a modern state no one has the right to start fires, to kill and rob people. The minister of the region may publish official statements that minimize and ridicule the event as though someone gave permission to rob and violate a certain section of the population.

[Page 41]

These rumors emerge from sources that are close to the priest Stoilowski as the facts indicate. In the district of Sanok, elections are to be held and in order to gain popularity amongst the masses, the Stoilowski party decided to terrorize the Jewish population and gain the favor of the peasants by instigating this pogrom. The poor and primitive peasants are easily instigated to attack the Jews. These acts that the government permits to occur from time to time have tragic consequences as Jaslo proves. These events frequently go out of control and the government is forced to send large troops to restore order. No wonder that Grabowski can then minimize or ridicule the situation by claiming that the whole thing was blown out of proportion and order has been restored. We had no doubts about the outcome of the event, it was not minimal, ridiculous but terribly brutal.

All parties that want to maintain order and peace in the country must sooner or later fight anti-Semitism. The Jew must be able to sleep in peace. And if a fire starts, the fireman will have to rush to the place to extinguish it and not sit on the sidelines. Government forces must remain at the fire until it is brought under control.

We live in solid homes in the midst of civilized society and expect the night watchers to see to it that fires should not start and sparks would not blaze. Besides we pay punctually our fire insurance to protect ourselves against fire, this is the least that the father can do for his family. Thus the need for a night watchman is essential. But the Jewish people which has produced so many great leaders and scholars throughout its long and famous history, failed in this respect. Furthermore we do not think in advance of the possibility of fire or the wisdom of prevention of fires. When the fires do take place, we do not know who to blame or where to get restitution for the damages. And whoever comes and demands to change the situation is ridiculed."

[Page 42]

We do not want to play politics with the incident of Galicia but it does provide us with serious information. Who were the casualties of the pogrom in Jaslo? Again the poor, helpless, and oppressed Jews. We who stand at the helm of the Zionist movement receive daily reports of the terrible situation of the Jews in Galicia. One can even consider them tragic.

Many Jewish children will remain scarred for life from the horror of the Sanok-Jaslo pogrom. The imprint will remain for ever. Therefore, we strive with all out heart and with all our forces to achieve security for our people in our own land."

Chapter 17

Dr. Herzl, who appeared at all the Zionist congresses, slowly awakened the Jewish people from its lethargy and attracted it to the cause of Zionism. Zionist groups or branches were formed in almost every city, by the intellectual or well to do Jewish elites. In Jaslo the Zionist "Yeshuron" club was formed in 1905-6. It was popularly called the "Tzionistiche Farein" or Zionist Club. This club attracted Jewish Zionists in the city and was the nucleus of the Zionist movement in Jaslo. The driving force was Dr. Kornhauser and friends. They organized discussion panels and conferences that were addressed by capable speakers, notably Meshulem Davidson who lived in Rzeszow. He was a talented organizer and helped launch the club in the city. (He now lives in Tel Aviv and has been living in Israel for the last 45 years.)

Amongst the founding members of the club were: Naphtali Hoffert, Eliezer Hoffman, Awraham Werner (Omik), Naphtali Menashe, and

Awraham Thaler. They were the first subscribers to the club and helped to popularize it in Jaslo and vicinity. The club was located at the house of Alexandrowicz. (The distillery and the house was later sold to Amer and Kornfeld). The club had at first a few dozen members. It even published for a time the magazine entitled "The Dawn" under the editorship of Berish Meller (today Dov Kimchi). The publication ceased when the editor left for Palestine in 1908.

[Page 43]

The city was visited on occasion by Zionist speakers including Yossef Shprincak, Berl Locker and others who spoke Hebrew. The idea caught on and pretty soon Hebrew teachers were brought to the city to teach the language with the Sephardi pronunciation. The first Hebrew teacher at the "Talmud Torah" was Mr. Karmerish, followed by Meir Mohar

(Presently, supervisor of Hebrew teaching of in the evening schools in Israel). During the same period, an association of "Poalei Tzion" was established in the city by young artisans, apprentices and store helpers. The two Zionist organizations occasionally sponsored social parties and cultural events. Similar to the "Poalei Tzion" association was the "Yad Harutzim" association, also established during this period. This organization consisted primarily of older artisans. The driving personality of the association was Asher Tzweig. At the end of Nowa Street, next to the corner of Wisoka street, was the synagogue of the association (it was destroyed by the Russians during W.W.I).

Several years later, a film about Jewish life in Palestine was shown at the "Sokol" movie house that made a great and lasting impression on the audiences (Mendel Meller was seen in the movie since he was there during the filming of the movie).

Chapter 18

As the Jewish population grew, there was a need for more places to worship. The first addition was the "kloiz", or praying room, at the house of Zelig Miller, the ritual slaughterer; another worship place was organized at the home of Mordechai Getzler; also the "Talmud Torah" had services prior to the opening for instruction. The building was a one-story house and still not finished. Many Hassidim that lived along Targowica or in the vicinity prayed at the synagogue of Rabbi Mandil.

All of these worship places were insufficient to accommodate all the worshippers whose numbers steadily increased. Most of them were accustomed to pray in comfortable synagogues at home and expected the same thing in Jaslo,. Therefore, the community decided to build a big synagogue that will seat several hundreds worshippers, male and female.

[Page 44]

To implement the order, land was needed. That was located on top of the hill with a view in several directions. The hill was called "Kuci Zamek" or cat castle and was purchased from the local count by the community. There was an old dilapidated barn on the estate that was repaired and services began there.

The Synagogue

Architects were hired to draw up the blueprints for the synagogue. Builders were brought from Hungary and artistic painters were brought from Italy to paint the interiors of the synagogue. An official ceremony took place with the placing of the first brick of the building. City officials were invited to partake in the festivity. The leader of the Jewish community spoke in Polish and concluded by stating "Thank G-d, here will be a synagogue. The phrase was catchy in Polish and was very popular with the attendants.

The construction of the building cost about a quarter of million thalers or krowns and was officially opened for services on Rosh Hashana 1905/1906. The community was very pleased with the building.

The building was impressive and imposing on the outside as well as on the inside. It received great publicity by its unique style in Galicia.

Blessed are those that managed to see the building in its full splendor as it dominated the city skyline. Many people including Christians came to see the building and appreciate its beauty. Unfortunately the Germans blew up the building in 1939 and destroyed the Jewish community. The building was blown up on the first Yom Kippur under German Occupation, a few days after the Germans entered the city.

I will try to describe from memory the building as I remember it so that the readers can get a good picture. I hope I will do justice to the synagogue. The hill was exposed to several air currents and a stonewall surrounded the estate. The wall faced the Rabbi's house and the study center, and was somewhat similar to the Western Wall in Jerusalem. The building reached

20 meters in height. The roof was covered with tin metal sheets and sloped down to about a third of the height of the building. The windows were also arched and resembled the tablets of the commandments. The glass was tinted artistically.

[Page 45]

The entrance to the synagogue was from the west. Seven stone steps led to the entrance of the hallway. The entrance gate was tall, wide, heavy and arched. The door handles were made of copper, large and heavy. The north side also had three entrance gates. The middle was wide and the two extremes were narrow. The gate to the women's section was from the south.

The synagogue of Jaslo
(The east-north side)

[Page 46]

The three northern gates were opened to the public during the high holidays, special days, birthdays of kings or presidents, and on the special occasions.

The interior walls were painted with oil paint. The lower parts of the walls were painted in a light color while the upper parts were decorated with a rich floral pattern. Between the flowers were inserted gilded and silver colored stars, as well as multicolored Stars of David. In the background were pinkish columns wrapped in floral garlands.

The large and tall Holy Arc was made from nut wood. The carpenters shaved it and decorated it with many gilded Stars of David. The velvet curtain of the arc was long and wide. A great deal of embroidery was crafted on to it as well as gold colored letters and precious stones. The curtain reached the floor and by pushing a button, the curtain would slowly rise. The curtains were often changed and they always looked new.

Four marble steps led to the holy arc. The steps were covered with a red carpet. On either side of the steps was a metal column headed by an electric lamp. Above the arc there was an angled wood panel painted in deep blue to resemble the sky. It also contained gold painted stars that reflected light on to the hall.

On the right side of the arc stood the large box and on top of it rested the great prayer book bound in an artistic manner. The pages were written in manuscript form and on parchment. Above the box, stood the large sign

" I have set the Lord before me" (hand-made by the artistic Menashe Weinstein). Next to it stood the large silver candelabra with many branches protruding from it.

To the left side of the arc was the honor seat that was usually reserved for the rabbi of the city. Above was the exit of the women's section; there was a three frontal breeze in the shape of the Hebrew letter "Het" and everything was supported by metal beams that were silver colored.

Above the bima, or reading table, was a giant copper chandelier with many light bulbs. The bima was surrounded with four columns, each corner had one, and each column had six electric light bulbs. Friday night or prior to a holiday, people lit many candles that gave the place a special air of light. The reflection of the light on the colored stars of the ceiling created the impression that the worshipers were really in the house of G-d.

[Page 47]

The bima was covered with a velvet cloth that was embroidered with gold letters. Next to it stood the famous beadle as though he was conductor, Yaakov Shames, looking at the large number of worshippers.

On the right side of the hall, was a small prayer room that was called "kahal shtibel" – small prayer room that was used for morning and evening services during week days, especially during the winter.

I will not exaggerate by saying that whoever did not see the Jaslo synagogue in its heyday missed seeing a great and beautiful building.

During the first year of the existence of the synagogue, a young cantor from Krakow conducted the services. The next year, the famous cantor Turbowski, nephew of the famous cantor Zidel Rubner was hired to conduct services. The latter came especially to Jaslo when the newly appointed cantor started to officiate services. Turbowsky was born in Russia; he was a baritone and had a choir to assist him. The choir consisted of Bliman, Lipczer, Nussbaum, Fridman, Raab, Schmidt, Shpringer, and others. Berish Baron was invited from Nowy Sacz to be the bass. The cantor dressed on Saturdays and holidays in formal clothing or a three quarter tuxedo, as was the custom in Russia and also wore a Galician shtreimel, a Hassidic fur hat. Lately he lived in the house of Mendel Gross. With the outbreak of W.W.I., he was given the keys to the synagogue. He left the city when the Russian Army retreated from Jaslo and with him left all the religious objects of the synagogue. (The famous cantor Yossele Rosenblat conducted the Shabbat services in the Jaslo synagogue during one of his tours of the area in 1894)

The Study Center

Next to the beautiful tall building of the synagogue, stood a small building that predated the synagogue by twenty years. It was built of wood with long wood beams. The worshippers of the study center were well to do people that did not want to leave it for the new synagogue. New arrivals who were not interested in cantorial music, but wanted to pray in a very traditional manner, also joined the services of the study center.

[Page 48]

Reb Asher or Asher Shames was the main beadle of this synagogue (he used to be a Hebrew teacher in his younger days); a particular type with a good sense of humor, strictly observant, very poor, a talmudic scholar very familiar with the history of the Hassidic families and their interrelationships, and had a large repertoire of stories and sayings. He never wavered from the truth and this caused him many problems that eventually forced him to resign prior to W.W.I. His replacement was Awraham Hirsh.

There was no electricity in the study center. Oil burners and chandeliers with paraffin lit the place. Following the war, with expansion of the electrification of the city, electricity reached the study center.

Chapter 19
1914

Most Jews of Jaslo dressed traditionally until 1914. On Saturday and holidays they wore silk coats and shtreimels. More modern Jews used to abandon the traditional dress for the evening Shabbat services and dress modern clothing. The elderly Jews grew beards and payot. The children were sent to the "heders" and then to the "Talmud torah". The younger fellows studied Talmud at the study center and continued the ways of their fathers.

World War I

On the ninth day of Ab, 1914, World War I started and in strides followed total chaos. The Russian Army conquered Eastern Galicia and even advanced to Western Galicia. As usual, the first victims were Jews.

The Austrians abandoned the city. Many officials and Jews left Jaslo. The Russians occupied the city for 4 days and suddenly withdrew. During the Yom Kippur services, the Russians hastily retreated and left a great deal of military equipment. Although the Austrians returned to the city, the feeling was that the front was not stabilized and the battle could go either way. There was a general feeling of unease and silently in the background the Austrians prepared to abandon the city again.

[Page 49]

Rumors began to circulate that the battles did not go according to plan; wild stories made the rounds of the town and as the city panicked many Jews began to pack. The retreat began. All official institutions were abandoned, the high officials left town, the trains became reserved for the army. Despair ruled the city. Everybody who could leave Jaslo packed their belongings and left; my father also packed and looked for a cart but could not find a coachman so he remained in Jaslo. A few days later, the Russians marched into the city. The retreating Austrian Army torched the Ulaszowice Bridge and the smoke covered the city. This did not prevent the Russians from crossing the Wisloka River and seizing every section of the city. They soon began to raid homes in search of vodka, the favorite Russian drink.

The Citronenbaum bar and distillery was located in our house. Thus we were the first victims of the Russian Army. The retreating Austrian Army ordered that all sharp spirits be spilled into the sewer. But the scent lingered on for days and attracted hordes of Russian soldiers to the place to search for vodka. They were certain that the spirit was stashed away. As a matter of fact, almost every Russian regiment that passed the area visited our house, resulting in constant harassment of the tenants of the building.

The soldiers also began to break into apartments and stores that were boarded up by their owners when they left the city. The local non-Jewish population joined the Russian soldiers in the looting feast. Everything that could be carried was removed from the homes and stores. The rest was smashed, trampled beyond recognition. Wherever they visited, there was destruction and desolation. Winter was approaching and there was a shortage of fuel. The Russian Army also needed fuel, so they decided to dismantle one by one the wooden Jewish homes in order to heat their places.

[Page 50]

The Russian cruelties to the population became increasingly harsh and Jewish sufferings increased by the day. A Jew that stepped out of the house and was recognized as such was immediately grabbed for some hard or debasing work detail that consisted of cleaning streets, or sweeping mud or debris and so on. The Jews also received bloody whippings from the Russians on the way to work. Sometimes they seized Jews in the street to abuse them, kick them about with their spiked boots, "in order to remember forever he heel of Esau...". The health situation was very poor. Many people had small pox and typhus resulting in many deaths. The lack of proper nutrition increased the despair and hopelessness.

The study center was converted into a stable. The holy arc, the benches, the tables, the doors and the windows were pulled out, broken and used for heating. The roof rafters were pulled down and only the empty walls remained standing.

The Russians advanced as far as the Carpathian Mountains, and even took the hamlet of Gorlice but they could not break through the mountain passes. Meanwhile German reinforcements arrived and stopped the Russian offensive. Bitter and bloody fighting ensued around Gorlice.

All Jews were forced to leave Gorlice which became the battle zone. Even the sick people had to leave for Jaslo where all the Jews of Gorlice managed to arrive. Many of the Jews of Gorlice were sick due to the red beets that they ate during the siege of the hamlet that lasted some time. They could not leave their homes and had to eat what was available namely beets. Jaslo also received many Jews from other towns in Eastern Galicia that were stranded on their way and remained in the city. Food and room shortages resulted from the influx. The medical situation fell on the shoulders of the few Jaslo

Jews that remained in the city. Of course the local Jewish population did everything possible to help the poor refugees.

During the Russian occupation of the city, the general headquarters was located in the city. In effect they requisitioned many private homes and the military medical facilities requisitioned many public buildings. Jaslo served as the main rear supply base for the Russian Army in the Carpathian Mountains.

The Jews from the nearby hamlets tried to bring some food to the city but it was very dangerous. The Russians were merciless with those caught in smuggling food. Once, Henech Berger, the brother in law of Leibish Tzimet, from Zmigrod brought a cart of loaves of bread to Jaslo. The Russians detected the merchandise and viciously attacked him with their

whips and batons. The loaves of bread were tossed into the mud and trampled.

Shimshon Melamed once stepped out into his courtyard where he met some Russian soldiers. They asked him; "Hey Jew what time is it?' he innocently pulled out his watch from his pocket to tell them the time. They grabbed the watch before he could even look at it, and cursed him while disappearing.

[Page 51]

Next to the mayor's office Russian soldiers attacked the Polish letter carrier because they liked his boots. They laid him out on the sidewalk and removed his footwear. The irony of the situation was that the mailman looked Jewish since he had a thick beard and a moustache. The poor man had to walk home barefooted.

Chapter 20
1915

Austrian planes flew daily over the city and occasionally bombed it. The bombs caused a great deal of human and property damage. The Russians mounted an anti-aircraft gun on the roof of the municipal building that would begin to fire with the arrival of the planes. Unfortunately, their aim was poor and the planes always escaped safely back to their base.

With the arrival of Passover, the Jews faced a serious problem, namely where to get matzoth, wine and other necessary needs for the holiday. The popular saying is that the food angel never sleeps certainly applied to us. For we soon received flour to bake matzoth, raisins for wine, potatoes and of course bitters of which we had plenty. We also managed to obtain other necessary items and began to prepare for the holiday of freedom. We certainly could use this freedom in the years 1914/1915. Together with our worries for holidays needs we also began to worry about the holiday needs of the Jewish soldiers that were stationed in the city.

[Page 52]

My father immersed himself in the work of organizing a Seder place for the soldiers. He went from house to house and collected matzoth, wine and other items needed for the Seder. He asked Mrs. Lambik to prepare warm meals for the Seder. He purchased the necessary "haggadah" pamphlets for the soldiers and collected glasses for the Seder. He then began to decorate the large hall on the second floor of the "Talmud Torah" where the Seder for the soldiers would take place. The eve of Pessah arrived. We were ready for the holiday when suddenly about ten Cossacks burst into our place and seated themselves at the table. Those that could not find a seat, sat on the floor. They opened their bags removed bread, pork meat and vodka and began to eat. We were all in despair..." what do we do now? hametz in the house on Pessah, pork meat in the home, suddenly we had an idea. A high ranking Russian officer stayed at the other end of the house so we approached him and explained the situation to him. Indeed he was understanding and ordered the soldiers to leave the place. We began immediately to clean the house again. And towards the evening, the place was clean of hametz.

With the closing of the prayers, my father rushed to the hall of where the Seder for the soldiers would take place to see that everything was in order. The soldiers thanked him profusely for the wonderful evening and then my father returned home at midnight to start our own Seder.

Sometime later, the German spring offensive under the command of Von Mackenson began in full force. All Russian counter attacks failed, and the first signs of hope appeared. Howitzer artillery constantly bombarded the Russian positions and soon the German advance began in earnest and a few days before Shavuot, the Russian high command began to pack. The Russian retreat had began.

In the morning of the first day of the holiday, we saw the Ulaszowice bridge on fire. The Russians had repaired the bridge after they occupied the city and now they set it on fire. This did not prevent the appearance of a German patrol; the patrol consisted of two riders in the afternoon at the entrance of the city, from the direction of the village of Naglowice.

[Page 53]

Some Russian units dug in at the hills of Guriowice and continued to shell the city. One shell hit the outside wall of the synagogue and remained stuck in the wall. The synagogue was already damaged from previous shelling. During the day, cavalry units arrived in the city followed by the infantry that crossed the Wisloka River. Further Russian attacks were repulsed and they left the area in great haste leaving a great deal of material and soldiers that were taken prisoners.

The sun shone brightly during the holiday of Shavuot; the inhabitants of the city were happy and enjoyed their liberation when suddenly the news reached them that the German Emperor Wilhelm is arriving. Indeed the Emperor with his generals Von Mackenson and Hindenburg and their military entourage made their appearance and were received warmly and enthusiastically by the city population.

With all the joy amongst the Jewish population of the city of Jaslo, there was sadness in their midst. For the cruel Russians took with them several Jewish hostages namely the Rabbi, Mendel Meller, Menashe Weinstein, Abba Altman, Israel Haber, and others when retreating from the city. Their fate and destination was unknown. Slowly, life began to resume, stores were opened although they were at first empty. The farmers began to bring daily small quantities of produce to the city. The Jewish population began to feel a bit safer in their daily life after nine months of terrible and cruel Russian occupation. The city was still under military rule but the atmosphere improved. Shimkale the policeman, and the fat policeman, together with military police, maintained order in the city.

Among the military police there was also a Jewish soldier with a long beard from the vicinity of Zabno near Tarnow. The Jews of Jaslo were happy to meet him and talk to him about the situation. A Jewish military policeman, what do you know, wonders never cease.

The first swallows appeared in the city. Individual Jewish families that left the city for fear of the Russians began to return to the city. The Jewish refugees in the city began to leave for home.

History of the Jews of Jaslo

Chapter 21

The fact that the battle zone moved further east did not immediately remove all problems. After all, the war continued and the government banned all free trade. Everything needed a permit. Bread and sugar was distributed by coupons and the lines for bread extended for tens of meters and frequently the bullies received the bread while the rest of the people did not. (In those days people were not accustomed to stand on line and proceeded to shove and push and the strongest managed to push their way to the head of the line). The government appointed a commissioner to supervise trade and commerce in Jaslo. He was named Kamitzky and he hated Jews with a passion and merely sought excuses to raid Jewish stores to confiscate goods; he even searched private homes and confiscated flour.

Despite the hardships, the authorities launched festivities with the capture of the city of Przemysl from the Russians.

Processions marched along the streets with Polish flags weaving and bands playing dancing music. The organizer and mover of the event was the son of Bliach.

The second grand celebration took place on the 85th birthday of the Austrian Emperor Frantz Joseph. A large military parade was held, bands played and Suris, the Christian cook, set off fire crackers. A special service was also held at the synagogue, and the cantor and his choir conducted special prayers for the Emperor and all the important guests.

Most of the Jews of Gorlice returned home. The hamlet was almost totally destroyed and the Jews had to rebuild it slowly. Most of the Jews of Jaslo also began to return home. Some of them found their places destroyed. All the wooden homes were dismantled. A few Jewish families from Jaslo remained in Vienna and other cities where they found refuge and some families left for Germany or the United States.

[Page 55]

World War I left serious problems in its wake among the Jewish population. The first signs of serious changes were evident in the behavior of the people towards customs and leaders. In this short period of time long established traditions began to feel the challenge of the time. Changes were in the air. People began to moderate their adherence to the ways their fathers practiced religion. They began to doubt and question, new winds appeared on the horizon. What represents two or three years in human history that consists of generations? Still the relative short period of time was enough to weaken and change the social structure and to give new spiritual dimensions for life.

More people began to wear more modern clothes like the three quarter outfits; they trimmed their beards; they curled their payot or side curls; and some even abandoned the traditional Shabbat dress.

I still remember Karp, Goldstein and other home owners who, prior to the war, wore the traditional silk coats and shtreimels. When they returned from their place of refuge, they adopted the bright tall cylinders or tuxedos or modern suits.

The worshippers at the study center and at Rabbi Mandil's synagogue continued with their traditional dress but amongst the worshippers at the synagogue there was a handful of people that continued to dress traditionally, including Nahum Shochet, Berish Bron, David Eliash, David Wilkport, Yehoshua Kippel.

Education also underwent a radical change. People that hesitated before the war to send their children to high school, now encouraged them to study, claiming that it was not a violation of the Shabbat. This conduct infuriated the very orthodox Jews but they could not stop the trend. They withdraw to the home. Jewish society slowly became polarized between very orthodox and religious Jews on one hand and secular, enlightened and Zionist Jews on the other.

[Page 56]

Education presented a special problem for there was no proper schooling for small children during the Russian occupation of Jaslo. All governmental schools, "heders" and "Talmud torahs" were closed. The children were roaming the streets and causing all kinds of problems. The teachers and Hebrew teachers had been drafted in the army. The problem of education was very serious and demanded action.

A few well to do Jews met and discussed the serious situation and they decided to appeal for help amongst the capable people of the city. They urged them to begin voluntary instruction to the children. An educational committee was formed to implement the resolution. The committee consisted of Chaim Rapaport (father of the author of this book), Eisik Dintenfas, and Moshe Eder.

The selected teachers devoted themselves daily to their tasks and began to teach bible, Talmud, and Hebrew. There were several teachers that came to Jaslo during the war and they joined this educational program, including Elikum Gorlitzer and Chaim Trzicicer (Wekselbaum) from the hamlet of (Trzcicina). The number of students who received a basic education was very small and did not affect the great majority of Jewish students who still needed and education. A committee was formed to reestablish the "Talmud Torah" chaired by Chaim Rapaport and nominally headed by Rabbi Elimelech Rubin.

The committee soon published ads for teachers listing the requirements. The response was positive and the first teachers accepted the paid positions in Jaslo. They were David Stratiner from Korczyna, Yossef Bendit Akselrad from Krosno, and later Yerachmiel Lipschitz nicknamed the "Pariser Hebrew teacher" and a few others. The educational committee consisted of Chaim Rapaport (father of the author of this book), Eisik Dintenfas, and Mordechai Drenger.

Chapter 22
1916-1918

During this time, the scout movement made its appearance and called itself "Hashomer", the guard, or the shomrim (guards), as they called themselves. They paraded in the streets or went on hikes in the country always dressed with large brim hats and wooden sticks in their hands.

The Hebrew songs they sang along their marches popularized the idea of Zionism and the return to the homeland. The white blue flag carried high

[Page 57]

by the youngsters gave the Jewish population a warm and national feeling.

This movement attracted many Zionist youths in the city including some of the best students, namely the Domb brothers, Miriam and Awraham Hoffert, Wistrich, Israel Plotzker, Kramer, Beni Karp, Rubel. The community suffered a great loss with the death of Awraham Werner, the son of Lipcze Werner, who fell in the line of duty with the Austrian Army where he served as a high ranking officer. Awraham was very capable, educated, and a leader who helped the Zionist cause in the city. His loss was felt throughout the community. His body was brought to the city of Jaslo to be buried. He was brought to the synagogue where he was eulogized by many speakers including Dr. Thon, who came especially from Krakow to eulogize the young Werner who defended his country. The synagogue was packed with people who were moved to tears.

Chapter 23

Writing these lines on a day in Chanukah, I am reminded of an incident that took place in our town which shook me beyond description. It affected a young student that was studying at the synagogue. He was insulted and lost face in the synagogue. I feel the need to record this unpleasant event in this book, for to this day I feel repulsed by the event that took place in Chanukah of 1917, following the Balfour Declaration. The young Zionist movement decided to launch a party in honor of Hanukah or as it was then called "A Maccabi Party" in the "Yeshuron Hall" in the house of Amer and Kornfeld on Kazimierz Street. A young student from the study center also attended the party to express his support for the Zionist movement or to see what was going on.

The visit soon became known amongst the student body of the study center. When the young student entered the study center the next morning, and sat down at his usual place, another student approached him and told him: you were at the Zionist party and therefore you have no place here; get up and leave the place instantly. The innocent student was at a loss and did not know how to react. Do they want me to leave the place or are they just jesting? The spokesman then grabbed the student in question by the neck and threw him out from the study center. No one reacted or protested the bully's actions. The young ejected student stood and begged, felt dejected, white as the wall, tears in his eyes, pleaded his case but to no avail. He was forced to leave. He returned the next day, thinking that the incident was forgotten, but the enforcer again took matters in his hands and approached the student and screamed at him: again you are here! I will not permit you to study here! Get lost and don't come back! He was not permitted to continue his studies. He was beaten and dragged away from his study place in a shameful manner. The case went to the courts and litigation started that did not bring great honor to the community and eventually the innocent youngster left Jaslo.

The lawless behavior of one of the beadles and the overcrowded conditions of the synagogue on Shabbat and holidays led many of the worshippers to the conclusion that a new place is needed to worship. They began to search for a permanent place. They decided to refurbish the old study center that has been empty for four years. The place was restored and services for several dozen worshippers began there.

[Page 55]

Chapter 24

The war continued in Europe. Hunger embittered the people. The mob was angry due to the terrible conditions that never seemed to end. Suddenly an outlet was found in the pogrom of Targowica and the side streets. A mob of Christian youngsters emerged from the small streets of the Targowica area and began to smash windows of Jewish stores and apartments. They were also screaming abusive language towards the Jews, namely: "The Jews started the war and they are responsible for the hunger and shortages in the city".

Night after night bands of underworld people, amongst whom one could see the anti-Semitic agitators, attacked and molested the Jews of the city. Stones were aimed at Jews, specifically at the bakery of Zelig Korzenik . First the mob stoned the place then broke the doors and practically dismantled the house.

On the third day of the disturbances, the Jewish youth decided to react. They decided to infiltrate the bands of hooligans and when the latter start to throw stones, they will also threw stones but at the Christian homes and windows; what is good for the goose is good for the gander.

The nightly attack repeated itself but this time there were also broken gentile windows and homes, for the Jewish youth decided to visit the gentile streets and do what was being done in Jewish streets. The reaction was one of amazement at what the Jews did but it had a sobering effect on the city and soon the Army made its appearance. There were still a few protests against the government with sign calling "Bread for the People, An End to the War". (The Jewish wholesale dealer, Benjamin Kramer, of flour and fuel was detained for a few hours). However these events soon ended and the city calm was restored.

During these days, the Joint Committee opened a public soup kitchen to provide meals to the needy. Nuta Maltz's daughter and few other people devoted themselves to this project.

[Page 59]

Chapter 25

Three years of war and the occasional Austrian victories left their impressions on the children. The fighting spirit affected all their games which now consisted of war games. The hill at the top of Shajnochy Street, near the destroyed blacksmith's place, gained prominence. It was called Trzicicir Mountain because the Hebrew teacher from the hamlet of Trzciana lived there.

[Page 60]

Brutal fights took place at the top of this hill between groups of children. Stones were thrown at each other. Some gentile children also participated in these war games including Winicki, Loch and Nimcinski. Many fights also took place in the hills of Guriowic that resulted in injuries and prisoners. It is important to add that the "Trzicicir" Mountain also served as the main skating place and the center of sled rides during the winter. The sleds consisted of simple wood planks, boards, boxes, broken chairs, etc. Those children that did not have sleds, or were afraid to use them, used pots, pans or large bowls. These were the so-called winter sports of Jaslo. During the winter months, Shajnochy and Widok streets were especially noisy since this was the central skating section of the city and most of the Jewish youth came to practice this sport here. The starting skating line was next to the synagogue and downwards. To this place streamed the youth from the "Talmud Torah" and the "Heders" in the area. They used skates or horseshoes mounted on pieces of wood and small sleds. The place was active from morning to evening. The inhabitants of the area disliked the noise but when they tried to protest, they were chased away by snowballs fired by the youngsters. (Even passerby pedestrians often received snowballs). The screams and shouts that the children emitted when somebody slipped or fell on the snow could be heard throughout the neighborhood.

The Year 1918

The fall winds blew away the last leaves on the trees and they also foretold changes in the air. The large ethnic minorities within the Austrian Empire became restless in spite of the Austrian and German victories. These populations wanted their national and cultural independence that was inculcated amongst them for some time.

Emperor Karl the first was crowned in 1916 and managed to visit many imperial cities including the city of Jaslo. He stayed at the home of P. Karp. These visits however could not stop the disintegration of the

Austrian Hungarian Empire. The process went rapidly down hill and the State of Poland emerged with its capital in Warsaw. Overnight, the Galician Jews who were Austrian citizens became Polish citizens.

[Page 61]

The Poles who were subjugated for about 140 years soon began to act like lord and masters over their minorities, especially the Jews.

Pogroms aimed at Jews occurred everywhere, led by ant-Semitic students who also incited the peasants, the discharged soldiers and the mobs to attack Jews and attack they did throughout Poland. A wave of bloody pogroms rocked the country.

Jewish life was in danger everywhere. Jews that lived in farming villages were robbed and then their places were burned; this forced them to flee to the nearby cities for protection. It was very dangerous to travel on the railroads because the anti-Jewish elements would toss Jews out of moving trains. The Jewish market stands were constantly attacked and robbed of their goods. The Polish police played stupid and did not interfere with the mobs that attacked the Jews and their property. The terror gained the upper hand and ruled the country inflicting heavy physical and financial damages to the Jewish population. The newly gained Polish State thus showed its attitude to the Jewish people of the country.

During these bloody days, Dawid Furman was killed in the city. He was a quiet person. The tragic incident shocked the entire Jewish population in the city that attended en masse the funeral at the synagogue. The wounds barely healed when another incident took place; Dawid Mergalit, the son of Abtche Margalit, was tossed out of a moving train heading to Bochnia from Krakow. His body was found along the railroad tracks. Dark clouds overcast Jewish life in Poland. The pogrom epidemic spread throughout Poland. No place was safe. The dangerous road situation meant that Jews from nearby cities like Krosno, Rymanow, Dukla, Frysztak, Zmigrod and Brzostek stopped coming to Jaslo to trade. The bigger cities were a bit safer and thus attracted many Jews who sought safety.

Zmigrod suffered greatly from pogroms that occurred occasionally. The Rabbi of Zmigrod, Rabbi Sinai Halbershtam then left the hamlet and settled in Jaslo. Eisik Ditenfas placed his apartment at the Rabbi's disposal. (The Rabbi of Zmigrod was a grandson of Rabbi Chaim of Sandz, the author of "Divrei Chaim". He was one of the great and well known Hassidic Rabbis in Galicia. He was a great Talmudic scholar and a capable speaker and attracted many people to his speeches. His great knowledge profoundly influenced the Hassidic movement. With the outbreak of World War II, he managed to reach Russia and there he passed away. His oldest son, the Rabbi of

Sczekowa resided for many years in Jerusalem. His youngest son reached Palestine during the war period. He resided for many years in Petach Tikva and is now Rabbi in Jaffa.

[Page 62]

Chapter 26

The pogroms aimed at the Jews continued unabated and forced the Jews to organize a self defense force called the Jewish Police to protect the Jews and their homes. Practically every city organized such a force which consisted of local Jewish youngsters. The Jewish police in Jaslo began to train with live ammunition and some non-Jews joined the ranks. I still remember Pinhas Shwimer dressed in civilian clothes armed with a rifle patrolling the city streets with an entire backup group which included Abish Eliahash. As a result of these actions the situation in the city began to improve.

The disintegration of the Austrian Empire released thousands of Polish soldiers who returned home; amongst them some real troublemakers including Tcharni Frank and Stashek Beitluk who would always start a commotion on Friday, the day of the market in Jaslo. They would drink with the farmers and then proceed to attack Jews, Jewish property, windows were smashed etc. The peasants took advantage of the lawless street and began to break into stores with their wooden sticks that they

[Page 63]

brought with them. Any Jewish store that was not closed hastily was vandalized by the mob.

The Jewish institutions appealed for help from the government and the later promised to restore order but did very little besides paying lip service. The police began to appear at the scene of the riots but always a day late. The fear was so real that frequently people did not attend Shabbat services for fear of being attacked and on a few occasions the services were halted when the news reached that a mob was assembling at the entrance of the city.

I remember one Friday evening when Naphtali Mahler was leading the services, since this was the memorial day of the passing of his parents. Suddenly there was noise outside, it sounded as though a mob was approaching the synagogue. Fear gripped the worshippers and they began to escape. The leader of the service took of his praying shawl and joined the escapees.

The Polish anti-Semitic behavior reached new heights when the Poles attacked the Ukrainians in Eastern Galicia. The Poles entered the city of Lemberg and immediately organized a terrible slaughter of Jews. They looted Jewish homes and then burned them. Synagogues were torched including the famous synagogue of the author of "Hatori Hazahaw" or the golden column. Religious books and torah scrolls were desecrated. The despair reached many Jews. The question was on everybody's lips "what will be?" "Will there be a possibility of living in Poland for Jews?" Is everything lost in Poland? The heart foretold destruction and desolation but no one knew how close these feelings were to reality.

1919-1921

The injured Jews barely recovered from their wounds when a new wave of terror was unleashed on them in the form of the demobilized soldiers of Hallerczik. They wore the blue uniforms of the Polish Army and whenever they encountered Jews, especially religious Jews, they attacked viciously. Their favorite sport consisted of grabbing Jews on the train, molesting them and brutally cutting their beards and side curls. The cutting frequently resulted in deep flesh wounds for it was done very sadistically.

[Page 64]

Amongst the Jews of Jaslo that experienced such event was Leibish Hass, who had a full grown lengthy beard and was caught on the train. They not only clipped his beard but also part of his chin so that he had to wear a handkerchief as a partial face mask to hide the injury. The same fate befell Elimelech Shochat on the train.

The armies of General Haller, or rather the soldiers that served with General Haller in the fight of Poland against Ukraine, distinguished themselves in attacking helpless and defenseless Jews by torturing, disemboweling them and finally killing them. Blood libels against Jews also began to make their appearances. A Polish maid disappeared in the hamlet of Stzyzow on the eve of Passover and immediately the accusation was made that she was abducted by Jews. Luckily, the maid was found in time.

I remember that one late Yom Kippur evening; a few people were sitting in the study center and noticed a wrapped bundle near the building. Fear instantly seized the worshippers that this was a provocation. They feared that the bundle contained a child that someone intentionally placed there in order to accuse the Jews of kidnapping a child. The panic ended merely in fears and shattered nerves.

The study center along the Koczerow Road and the big synagogue were frequently stoned, resulting in broken windows. Eventually the windows were protected by shutters. Along the railway line Krakow-Jaslo, there was a station called Biecz (a small hamlet, translator). The

Jews that traveled along this road frequently huddled amongst themselves when they entered the station, for the name is pronounced just like the Polish word to hit, meaning or alluding, you can hit here Jews.

I frequently digress from the main topic of Jews in Jaslo but I think that these unrelated events influenced greatly the life of the Jews of Jaslo, many of whom left for the USA or other countries. These events also affected the growth of the Jewish community of Jaslo, which stopped expanding. The pogroms continued until the elections for Parliament in 1921.

[Page 65]
Chapter 27
The Polish anti-Semitic parties launched their election campaigns with bitter attacks on the Polish Jews. The most rabid anti-Jewish party was of course the party called the "Endek" or the "Endejca" party, which openly called for the economic destruction of the Jews of Poland.

The Polish government based itself on so-called democratic principles that promised equal rights to all citizens of the country including the Jews. The government did little except for issuing oral promises to the Jews. The latter also feverishly involved themselves in the elections.

Many speakers and representatives appeared in Jaslo where there was only one big hall, namely the study center that could accommodate a large crowd. Appearing on behalf of the Zionist cause were Dr. Yehosua Thon (also spoke in the synagogue), Dr. Schwartzbard, Chaim Nigger and others. Their appearances were very impressive and dignified.

Dr. Thon mesmerized the audience at the synagogue when he said that the Jewish people must appear on the world stage as a people with a country. The Jews must know what lies ahead and take, demand or insist on the necessary steps in that direction. The Jews must concentrate more on their future. Settling and building Palestine should not only be a commandment that is spoken in religious circles, it must become a real goal, and not a mere paraphrase that is exchanged superficially. This is similar to the student that hears his teacher explain a sentence and then combines the word to mean something else. The Jewish people as a nation must think a bit and understand that it is like other nations!

The successful placement of Zionist candidates on the parliamentary list can be attributed to the following people, namely Dr. L. Oberlander, Dr. Naphtali Menashe, Yossef Frumowicz, Dr.

Awraham Kornhauser, Dr. Shtin and others. Amongst the Mizrahi party activists we have to mention Mendel Meller, Shlomo Schmidt and others. Indeed the Zionist cause was victorious and elected forty Jewish candidates to the Polish House and Senate.

[Page 66]

The Jewish elected officials immediately began to protest against the anti-Jewish behavior of the government. The Endekes and their supporters protested and frequently shouted down the Jewish speakers or threw stones at them when they left parliament. Still the Jewish representatives kept up the pressure which was supported throughout the world. Finally, the government began to act and slowly the pogrom atmosphere began to decline until it eventually disappeared, and life returned to normalcy.

A spark of hope did appear on the horizon that promised hope and fulfillment for Jewish life in Poland, namely two charming words that had one purpose: to unite and to organize for the movement to Palestine.

Rabbi Groibard from the town of Staszow appeared at a packed study center on behalf of the "Mizrahi" Zionist party (in his retiring years he will be chief rabbi of Toronto, Canada). He exposed the idea of the religious Zionist party and intertwined Talmudic scholarship with Jewish reality and was very successful. Hundreds of shkalim (membership cards for the forthcoming Zionist Congress elections, translator) were sold that evening. The same evening a reception was held in his honor at the home of Abraham Schecht. The "crème" of the Jaslo Jewish society was there and the Mizrahi Zionist branch of Jaslo was established. Founding members of the branch were: Chaim Rapaport zal., Motel Beck, Naphtali Hupperrt, Israel Wilner, Mendel Meller, Awigdor Kilig, Awraham Schecht, Shlomo Schmidt, Tzwi Tzimet, Yaakow Miller, Ozer and Moshe Engel and others. The Engels were brothers and came from the small hamlet of Nowy Zmigrod where they absorbed hassidic tradition and acquired an erudite contemporary Hebrew literary knowledge as well as Talmudic scholarship. Both spoke fluently Modern Hebrew. Moshe later left for Palestine with his wife but due to his state of health had to leave the country and return to his native land but years later returned.

[Page 67]

The branch office was located at the house of Yaakow Will on Nowa Street that also served as praying hall and an occasional assembly hall.

Members of the " Mizrahi " movement branch in Jaslo

The worshippers of the new study center decided to name the place the "Mizrahi Study Center". There was some objections from the very religious worshippers that called the place the "Bolshevik Study Center but they had to acquiesce in view of the large majority in favor of the name.

Jaslo was frequently visited by distinguished speakers namely Wolf Getzler, the son of Mordechai Getzler, who appealed to the audience to support the national feelings of the Jewish people. These lines strengthened the inner feelings of the listeners. M. Kamelhar, the son of Yekutiel Kamalhar of Sanok, presented lectures that dealt with Jewish scholarship and intertwined it with religious scholarship that mesmerized the audiences.

The free discussion of ideas did not last too long in the city of Jaslo before the Zionist opponents begun to vociferously attack the concept of religious Zionism. I remember the following incident that was very upsetting and angered the Jewish population. The Rabbi of Kolo, near Lodz, was once invited to speak on the ideology of the religious Zionist movement of Mizrahi. A libel was spread to the effect that the rabbi's beard and payot were on to pretend. A series of ugly incidents followed, namely, the night before a speaker was to address an assembly at the study center, someone entered the hall and placed paper wrappers in the electric sockets so that the hall would be dark. The meeting was cancelled. The sabotage was discovered later. The Rabbi Yehezkel Levine (the son of the Rabbi Cohen of Rzeszow, later Rabbi of Lemberg) visited Jaslo once to speak about Zion. The meeting was disrupted by bullies that screamed, shouted and prevented the audience from hearing the speaker resulting in the suspension of the session.

[Page 68]

Another serious incident occurred when the Rabbi Tzwi Hirshhorn (later Rabbi of Jaworzne) came to Jaslo to organize the branch of the very religious political party "Agudat Israel". His speech was full of venom directed at the religious Zionist leaders of the Mizrahi movement. He used lines from King Solomon's trial and, most importantly, insisted that the movement disappear. Tempers flared and threats and insults were hurled at each other and at the speaker. Mendel Meller, one of the leaders of the local Mizrahi movement, challenged the Rabbi. The discussion became vociferous and personal with innuendos being flung by both sides. The noises and the fights spread to the Jewish community that was now divided between Zionists, Assimilationists, Religious Zionists and very orthodox Jews.

The study of a daily page of the Talmud was then introduced to many Jewish communities in Poland, including Jaslo, in spite of the political divisions within the Jewish community. The organizer of the event was Rabbi Meir Shapiro of Sanok, later Piotrikow and Lublin. He was later a member of the Polish parliament. He also established the famous "Yeshiva Chachmei Lublin". The main reader of the program was Rabbi Yehiel Engel.

Rabbi Meir Shapiro once visited the city and paid a visit to the local Rabbi. He discussed with him the need for a Yeshiva of a high standard that would be based on a religious foundation.

At one of the talks, he described a so-called great "learner" that was asked to conduct the services. During the service, the man had an inspiration and barely finished the "Amidah" prayer of the service. The Rabbi insisted on finding the identity of the party and it was soon revealed to be that of Nachman Krochmal. The great Rabbi then said that the great ideas of Nachman Krochmal merely confuse individuals as well as the leader of the service. The Rabbi further added that the scholar that has solid ideas based on scholarship does not confuse the worshipper; what does confuse him are the inspirations of so-called torah scholars of the Nachman Krochmal type.

[Page 69]

Chapter 28
1928

During these days Jaslo experienced a so called golden period of life for the Jewish community. Life was rather pleasant and undisturbed. The economic situation was flourishing and steadily improving. The atmosphere was pleasant and people could begin to breathe the air of tranquility. The President of Poland, Professor Ignace Moscicki visited many cities including the city of Jaslo.

Prior to the visit, the home owners along the presidential route had to paint and clean the homes along the reception road. The President was to tour the market and several streets of the city. All the stores and workshops were ordered closed during the day. The streets were to be decorated with the national flag and the day of the visit would be declared a national holiday. Many people were expected to visit the city on this day. Amongst the many delegations that lined up to receive the President was the delegation of the Jewish community council with the rabbi amongst them, sitting with a torah scroll in his hands under a bridal canopy. A large crowd of people stood behind them. The Rabbi greeted the President with the traditional blessing: Blessed be for honoring us!

We must not forget the fear that remained within the hearts of many Jews. They remembered the insinuations that he uttered in 1925 in Lemberg to the effect that the Jews were somewhat involved with the plan to blow up the former president of Poland, namely Woijciechowski.

[Page 70]

Dr. Wilusz and his wife were the official hosts of the President and sponsored a festive evening for the honored guests at the municipality. Hundreds of people gathered about the building during the evening. The next morning, the President with his entourage headed for church. The sidewalks along the route were full of spectators that came to greet the President. As the entourage left the market, a woman pushed her way through the crowd and handed the President a personal closed letter. Mrs. Alter Shulem Bialiwloss refused to divulge the content of the letter and the President accepted the item and continued his procession. For a moment it seemed like an explosion will take place but the event resolved itself in thin air.

Chapter 29
Gleaning and Summary

The Jewish community of Jaslo existed for about 70 years. It represented 25% of the city population. The community was lead by 7 presidents that were elected by the Jews of the city. The first president, Naphtali Walfeld, was also the founder of the community, and was followed for many years by Lipcze Werner, and then Dr. Shtin followed by attorney Awraham Kornhauser. The fifth president was Wolf Kornefeld, followed by Dr. Shtin and finally Israel Silbershtein. As temporary fill ins included Wolf Tzimet, Elimelech Goldshtein, Mordechai Karp, attorney Fishel Walfeld, Benyamin Goldshtein and, for very short period of time due to the sickness of the presiding officer, Leib Tzimet.

* * *

The city of Jaslo was known as a modern city and in spite of its small size served as a sort of minor center of the area. The city produced many religious scholars, writers, Zionist leaders and pioneers that left for Palestine.

* * *

[Page 71]

A group of active civic leaders gathered and decided to purchase a house that will serve as a community center for lectures, conferences, shows and meetings. Thanks to the efforts of I.Igler, St. Wistrich, Yossef Karp and Benyamin Kramer property was acquired from a Polish major. The estate was rather large; it consisted of about 50 acres, and was located in Kriowic. A section of the place would serve as a training place for pioneers who will receive agricultural training before leaving for Palestine.

* * *

The first child to be born and circumcised in Jaslo was that of Meir FeldBrand.

* * *

Despite the accepted version that the first Jews in town were either Chaim Steinhaus or Leibish Winfeld, there was still a third version that a doctor named Tzuderrer was the first Jew in town and served as a medical doctor.

* * *

The families Weil, Winfeld, Welfeld, and Werner considered themselves as one family.

* * *

Above the "Talmud Torah" lived Ben Tzion Shames since World War I. He had two daughters and barely managed to make a living. His main joy was selling small blankets with the inscriptions: "Blessed be

He", "Blessed is his Name", and "Amen". (He used to give the children a penny to recite the blessings so that he could answer them). One day the community was astounded to learn that he bought one of the buildings in the city.

* * *

We must stress the fact that Jaslo did not have the large array of beggars who would collect handouts and food from passersby, as was the case in many Galician cities and hamlets. The synagogue entrance had Friday and holiday beggars that waited to be asked to share a meal, but most of them were not from the city of Jaslo proper.

* * *

In 1928 an association for the help of the poor "Tomchei Aniim" was established in Jaslo. It collected money on a weekly basis from the Jewish inhabitants in order to provide care for the poor people from out of town so that they should not have to go from house to house. They received individually a note with the amount that they collected at the treasury of the association. (The initiators of the project were Ben Tzion Hacohen Gutwirt and the author, who were always available in the study center to interview the needy).

[Page 72]

* * *

A school for girls was established in the twenties. The teachers were graduates of the various "Beit Yaakov" seminars. The wife of the rabbi headed the institution that became popular with time amongst religious families.

The "Beit Yaakow" school for girls

* * *

The Jewish bank "Bank Ludowy" existed for almost twenty years and conducted extensive business deals. The executive officer of the bank was Kalman Raab (today in the USA) and his assistant was Shwartzman who was also the accountant.

* * *

During the existence of the Jewish community of Jaslo there were ups and downs. There were bright lights and dark shadows as well as some sensational stories. One of them consisted of an attempt by Polish farmers to create a monopoly over the sale of geese. This took place during the height of the anti-Semitic campaign aimed at the Jews. The farmers demanded outrageous prices for the fowl that were purchased primarily by Jews. The Rabbinate decided to take steps against this policy and insisted that the purchase price will be 18 guilden. No Jew is to purchase a goose above that price. The penalty for violation this ordinance was excommunication.

A few days following the publication of the order, a Jewish resident of Jaslo came to the rabbi and told him that he bought a few geese before the ban and paid more than 20 guilden per goose. He bought them for Passover and left them with the farmer to fatten them. He would like to know whether he could eat them now?!!!

[Page 73]

* * *

During a winter day, a Jewish farmer brought a dying calf to the animal market. He could not sell it and took it back to his village of Osobnica. He decided to slaughter it himself and two days later brought the meat to sell in the city. When the butchers discovered that he sold meat in the city they insisted that he tell them where he got the meat. It soon became apparent that he killed the calf and sold the unkosher meat to the people. The rabbi was informed of the situation and immediately placed the seller in a state of excommunication for his sinful act. Saturday morning the proclamation was read in all the synagogues that on Sunday the excommunication will take place for the sinful act that the party committed. A large crowd assembled on Sunday to see the villager that was specially brought to face the excommunication. Those that purchased meat from him spat on him and cursed him for what he did to them. There were also some that were about to take pity on him. In the meantime a discussion began regarding the implementation of the excommunication with regards to the state law. The villager cried and begged mercy for his sinful behavior; he abjured his act and the act of excommunication was not imposed.

* * *

In the year... a well known Jew passed away after a long illness, on the eve of the Shemini Atzeret holiday. The funeral was scheduled for the evening of Simchat Torah. Before the dancing with the torah, a large crowd came to pay their last respects to the deceased and to escort the funeral in order to pay back the man for all he did for the community. He had collected money for charities, contributed to weddings, circumcisions, and "Jahrzeits" or anniversary of the departed.

[Page 74]

Suddenly, the crowd was informed that the Hevra Kadisha or burial society was demanding instant payment for the service in spite of the holiday. The people were angry or rather furious. How is this possible on a holiday and to a person that did so much? This is a mere sacrilege!

Those responsible for the burial disappeared so there was no one to talk to. The shouts and screams of the crowd did not help the matter, finally the widow brought her silver candle sticks as deposit and the burial proceeded.

* * *

The compulsory school education laws in Poland meant that thousands of Jewish children rushed each morning to the Polish school that started at 8 A.M. in the morning. They sat hatless in the classrooms and faced a crucifix on the wall. Here they were exposed to Polish culture and environment.

Most of the Jewish youth of Jaslo belonged to the various Zionist youth movements. Dozens of students left for agricultural training farms and later left for Palestine. Some of them joined kibbutzim and moshavim – or farm villages, and attached themselves to the land. Others settled in the cities and small hamlets. Some of the parents joined their children in Palestine.

The youth organizations had clubs and meeting places where the youth was inculcated with Zionist ideas. The stress was not only in education but also in physical development namely sports. Within the Zionist groups the sport association named "Maccabi" was formed; it organized a soccer team with the same name. The driving force of the sport organization was Wilk (Wolf) Eintziger. He pushed the sport activities and insisted that the soccer team enter the competing games with the white and blue flag. The "Maccabi" soccer club played with nearby Jewish soccer clubs and on occasion played against the local non-Jewish team, "Tcharni" on their grounds called "Agzacirka" in Ulaszowice.

* * *

[Page 75]

The hall of the study center resounded with the voices of the young Talmudic students that sat and studied the Talmud between 16-18 hours a day. The place had some dark and unclean places but the special tune used in studying the Talmud could be heard a distance away. Tens of students sat in close proximity on the hard benches and studied the Talmud in depth. Some of them would emerge as great scholars in Jewish law. Amongst the better students at the study center prior to World War I were: Dawid Ullman, the Katz brothers, Moshe Nussbaum, Yudel Rota, Simcha Beer Rinhald, the brothers Yehoshe and Hirsch Reich (today in the USA), Tzwi Tzimet, Motil Citronenboim (today in Jerusalem), Shulem Shtams (today in Tel Aviv) and Yehoshua Appel (today in Paris).

* * *

The author of these lines organized in 1924 the young men of the "Mizrahi" movement. Many students of the study center joined the group. The meeting place was at Elimelech Teller's place in the Targowica which was rented as a permanent meeting place. Mendel Zilber arranged the furniture of the meeting hall and Moshe Meir Getzler delivered daily lectures in the Talmud. Hebrew lessons were also offered there as well as a daily prayer service. The active members of the organization were Awraham Korman, Shlomo Krisher (today in Tel Aviv) and Mendel Zilber.

Mendel Beck, a member of the "Mizrahi youth movement, left for Warsaw to study at the "Tachkomoni" school. The Zionist spirit even penetrated the walls of the study center in Jaslo; one day six students left together to continue their studies in the Polish capital. Two of them were Dr. Meir Tzukerman and Shlomo Krisher (live today in Israel). They were followed by Dr. Itzhak Rapoport, my brother (today chief Rabbi of Melbourne, Australia), Yaakov Drenger (today in Paris), Fishel Krisher (Rabbi in Warsaw) and others.

* * *

The Talmudic studies in the city continued to attract many youngsters and some of them even distinguished themselves in religious scholastic, namely Shmuel Bilt, Ben Tzion Gutwirt, and Yehoshua Horowitz.

* * *

[Page 76]

With expansion of the Jewish community also grew the hassidic movement in the city, especially the following of the Bobower Rabbi. The adherents of this Rabbi dominated the Jaslo Jewish scene and gained momentum amongst the very pious youths of the city. The latter found great inspiration in the words and deeds of the rabbi who was one of the great Hassidic rabbis in Galicia prior to World War II.

The Rabbi of Dukla

The followers of the Rabbi of Bobowa were numerous in Jaslo but another rabbi rapidly gained ground in attracting followers in the city, namely the Dukla Rabbi, Rabbi Menachem Mendel Hilperin. In the early thirties the rabbi left his home in Dukla and took up residence in Jaslo. He built a home with a study center on land that was bought from Dawid Denner near the big study center. His philosophy summarized itself in three words: "Hessed" or mercy, "Gvurah" or strength, and "Tifereth" or splendor. He lived his life as close as anyone could to these three symbols. He carried the concept of mercy to the furthest point particularly in regards to his fellow Jews. He had a feeling and understanding of the painful miseries that Jews felt. His deep penetration into the souls of Jews gave him a good understanding of the pains and his soft and comforting speech gave reassurance to the people. His deep attachment to the individual could be felt when he recited the line "Nishmat kol Chai" or the soul of everything alive of the Sabbath and holiday prayers. He enunciated these words with clarity and emphasis so that everybody could hear; and tremors went through the worshippers as they heard these words.

Strength he showed when he buried his only son, a student devoted to the study of the Talmud. He faced his son in silence, his eyes aflame but no tear. He accepted the heavenly decision and stated the accepted sentence "G-d gives and G-d takes".

His adherence to splendor expressed itself in the way he conducted himself and the way he looked at individuals. A certain warmth radiated from this tall Rabbi that towered above his Hassidim and penetrated the onlookers. His exceedingly long beard further added rabbinical stature.

He resided in Jaslo until the outbreak of World War II and with the advancing cruel enemy managed to flee to Bezon where he remained for some time. His trace then disappeared.

[Page 77]

The last community council of Jaslo consisted of:

Israel Silberstein, president, Chaim Shlapf vice-president, Eisik Dintefas, Benyamin Denner, Dr. Naphtali Menashe, Betzalel Kriszwirt, Elimelech Krisher, Yaakow Shturch.

The Mai 3rd Street in Jaslo

The September winds were blowing above the mountains; thick black clouds were blocking the skies and obscuring the sun rays which allowed red stars to appear on the horizon. What do they have in store for us? Who can read the future? Who can tell us what awaits us at the next day? The month of Elul, the month prior to the high holidays, the blowing of the shofar... and nobody knows the future.

On the Polish borders are poised Hitler's forces ready to launch a total destructive war that will destroy the world. The "Hun" presents all kinds of claims and revendications of the Polish government. He demands some sort of referendum with regards to the corridor of Danzig. The Germans want to annex the city of Danzig but they must obtain a piece of Polish territory.

[Page 78]

The tensions mount by the hour and the responses seem to ignore reality for the skies are already darkened and on the morning of September 1st 1939, the Germans launch their massive air attack. The flood gates of destruction have been opened with the first bombs that our city received.

A terrifying panic seized the citizens and the destruction also added to the frenzy. The German beasts attack Poland and blood is spilled all over.

The Jaslo Jewish community will be destroyed with all other Jewish communities.

People
(In Alphabetical order according to the letter A in Yiddish)

Alef א

Betzalel Adler

He was a man of few words and believed in the saying that silence was golden. He was a modest man and barely managed to earn a living. He was in charge of the public bath for a while, then he was a religious trustee of the kosher butchers to see that everything is kosher in spite of the fact that they had kashrut certificates. Before Passover he would start to bake matzot and also bake "Shmira Matzot" or special prepared matzot. He also baked on the eve of Passover special light matzot for that day and also sold slivovitz brandy (brandy made from plums) kosher for Passover. He also helped his sons in the book binding business. Lately he lived along Florianski Street. He had several sons that received a traditional religious education and were members of the young Mizrahi club. His oldest son Mordechai Dawid was a typical youngster in the city. He was well read, loved to research material, familiar with Jewish Talmudic scholarship, and a well balanced mind. He sold books to the religious youth in the city. His brother worked for Rubel at the distillery in Siowniow.

P. Adler

Elimelech Goldstein's son-in-law; he lived for a few years in Jaslo.

Chanoch Chenech Adler

Mishket Miller's son-in-law (See Zelig Miller)

Oberlander family

The father of the brothers Nathan and Ludwig Oberlander, who were attorneys, settled in Jaslo when the oil refinery was built in Niglowic. The father worked there as a clerk. His two sons distinguished themselves as lawyers due to their excellent logic, deep penetration of cases and manner of presentation.

[Page 82]

Nathan Oberlander, doctor of law, was not pleased with his stay in Jaslo. He left the city for Krakow with the declaration of Polish independence. He was considered one of the best lawyers in the country. He distanced himself from any contact with the Jewish community.

Ludwig Oberlander, doctor of law. Contrary to his brother's philosophy, he was devoted to Zionism and gave a great deal to this cause until his dying day. He was always ready to battle for the cause whether it involved communal, municipal or national elections. He spoke well and to the point. He spoke with devotion and bluntness about his Zionist feelings and was always ready to defend the cause. I still remember the national elections and the electoral campaign between the "B.B" (or the ' Pilsudski Party) that was represented by the number 1, the Zionist Party by the number 17 and the "Agudath Israel" by the number 33. It was a bitter campaign and Oberlander devoted all his energies to the Zionist cause neglecting his office and his clients. He appeared everywhere, even amongst very religious people although he knew in advance that they would not support him. Still he went on Sabbath to the study center to try to reason and to appeal to all the worshippers to support the cause. His face was white, his forehead sweated, and the voice uttered logical and cool reasons for his cause. He attempted to penetrate the religious crowd.

He influenced the Polish author and statesman Kasori Pruszinski to visit Palestine and familiarize himself with the Zionist movements in

[Page 83]

Palestine He wrote many articles in the newspapers on Jewish topics and problems as well as on Zionism. He published a booklet entitled "Judeous Propanos" before Hitler became master of Germany and described the shoah that will take place in Europe...

Dawid Oliner

He was quiet person who had liberal opinions. He was a wood merchant. His two daughters received a high school education. One of his daughters married the attorney Schnep and they lived on Kosciusko Street.

Chaim Reuven Ullman

He was the brother-in-law of Leibish Roth. He was a Hassid and knowledgeable individual as well as G-d fearing person. He was an easy going person and had a pretty good voice in conducting services, was familiar with musical instruments and most important of all prayed with feeling. He was well connected with the Rabbi's court. He lived in Karp's house where he also had a store that sold animal skins. Later on he moved to Florianski Street. Following World War I, he was discharged from the Austrian Army and began to reorganize his life. Suddenly he fell ill. He fought the disease but failed and died in the prime of his life. He left a wife, four daughters and a son named Dawid. The latter was a smart fellow, full of life and sympathetic to Zionism. He left Poland with his older sister Hannah for the USA with the independence of Poland. He and his family visited the Holy Land twice. He spent a few weeks in Tel Aviv and decided to settle in the country but due to the crisis at the time he was forced to return to the States. He was the head of the Jaslo landsmanshaft in New York.

Another daughter named Riwka, a member of the Zionist movement in Jaslo, left for Palestine in the thirties and settled in Tel Aviv. Following her marriage, she opened a leather workshop along Ben Yehuda Street in Tel Aviv. Meantime, another sister named Sarah also left for Palestine with her husband and two daughters and settled in Jaffa.

[Page 84]

Kopil Ullman

Kopil Ullman was the the son-in-law of the Hebrew teacher Ressler, in Targowica. He lived on Nowa Street in a wooden hut that was destroyed during World War I. He was very pious. He dealt with geese and feathers. He left Jaslo prior to World War I and settled in Germany.

Benyamin Unger Halevi

A wealthy individual and greatly respected. He was a follower of the Belzer Rabbi and belonged to an old established family in the city. He was an important figure in the study center and as the name indicates was also a Levi. He built for himself a one story house on the corner of Florianska and Sokolow. His store of kitchenware, glass and ceramics was also a workshop to cut glass for windows. In the twenties he fell ill and suffered for a long time. He had three sons that received a traditional education and two daughters. His oldest son Elisha lived in Tarnow and was considered a well-to-do person. The second son also lived in Tarnow while the third son lived in Krakow.

The two daughters were married to people devoted to the study of torah. One was named Yakili Cichanowski and the second one Shalom Shikler. Both were well respected in the city. Eventually Shalom Shikler and his family left for Belgium. His third son, Itzhak Unger that resided in Krakow recently arrived in Israel and settled in Haifa.

Eliezer Austro Halevi

He was born Szandiszow. He was the son-in-law of the well-to-do Awraham Shapiro of Gorlice. He was a wheat wholesaler in his house in the marketplace. The house would later be sold to Feivel Kleinman. His beard covered his face and his eyes revealed a clear thinking man.

He married to Jaslo in the nineties of the previous century. He and his father- in-law left Gorlice after the big fire in the shtetl. He was very pious and helped socially the needy. He was a good natured and congenial person.

He started in the wheat business in Jaslo but later opened a grocery and a dairy store on Florianska Street in Branstadter's house. He was one of the most active people in the restoration of the destroyed old study center during World War I. He was appointed to be one of the beadles. With the establishment of the new Polish state he left for Germany with his family.

He settled in Palestine in 1935 and resided in Tel Aviv. He then took ill and died. He left a wife, four married daughters and a son named Moshe. The latter was a member of the study center in Jaslo but presently he employed as a clerk in his brother-in-law's shoe store named "Phil" in Tel Aviv. The owner of the store is Tzvi Tzichner who is the largest shoe dealer in the city and he is the youngest son-in-law of Eliezer Austro. Israel Austro, oldest son of the family, died in the shoa; he was an excellent student in the study center and was a founder of the association of "Shlomei Amunei Israel", a forerunner of the "Agudath Israel party. Following his marriage he settled in Oswiecim. In writing these lines an incident comes to mind of a political fight that I had with him when I was about eleven or twelve. When the "Mizrahi" organization in Jaslo opened its branch office, some of the best students at the study center joined the group. Some of the opponents decided to form their own group namely the "Shlomei Amunei Israel" to oppose the Mizrahi movement as well as the idea of Zionism. Israel Austro was one of the organizers of the group. In spite of my young age, I already realized that the main reason for the organization was his bitter opposition to the movement and to the idea of Zionism.

[Page 86]

On the eve of the Shavuot holiday, a poster was placed on the bulletin board of the great synagogue that the association of "Shlomei Amunei Israel" is organizing a branch in the city and asking people to join it.

When I came to the synagogue to pray and saw the big poster along the southern wall of the study center, I was furious and decided to rip it off, tear it and to leave the place in haste. Israel saw the entire incident from a distance and began to chase me. I managed to escape but did not return to the study center. During the holiday I no longer prayed there for fear of creating antagonism. From that day onward I avoided him and always managed to avoid meeting him.

Berthold, Oczart,

He was an engineer who recently settled in Jaslo. He lived on Kosciusko Street. As an assimilated Jew he kept his distance from Jews and the Jewish community. During World War II his daughter came to Palestine with many Polish emigrants and resided here with a non-Jew. Eventually they left the country.

Yaakow Orgal

A pious Jew adopted by Eisik Dietenfas. He was a member of the study center. He had neurological problems but was cured. The effects of the disease depressed him and remained with him forever. He became weak and lifeless. Following his marriage he entered commerce but did not last long in trade. A job was found for him as the sexton of the study center instead of Awraham Hersh.

Awraham Meir Orenstein

He was one of oldest member of the Jewish community in the city. He had the stature and allure of an important person. He was the son-in-law of Leibish Winfeld, the first Jew to establish his home in Jaslo. He was very active in communal affairs of the Jewish community. He was one of the first beadles in the study center that was built during the period. He was a

wine and spirit merchant at his home along Kazimierz Street, opposite the mayor's office and opposite the eastern wall of the synagogue, close to the holy arc. He had two sons and a daughter.
With his death at the outset of World War I, the family sold their assets in Jaslo and moved to Krakow.

[Page 87]
Chaim Shaul Orszicer
He was one of the sons-in-laws of Yaakow Freund. He was a Hassid and very pious man. He was a gentle person who lived along Mai 3rd Street in the house of Shochet. With the establishment of the new Polish state, he left Jaslo and settled in Rzeszow.

Israel Igler
He was one of the dedicated and devoted Zionists in the city of Jaslo. He arrived in the city from Sambor in the thirties and became very involved in the Zionist cause as well as the in the social affairs of the community. As a Zionist visionary and clearly dedicated to the Zionist cause he not only supported morally the cause but also contributed financially to various Zionist campaigns. During the struggle in Palestine between the years 1936-1939, he headed the campaign to raise money for Jewish emigration to the holy land. During his brief stay in the city, he managed to acquire a large following and gained prominence in the Jewish community. He was also appointed to important positions namely the financial committee of the municipality of Jaslo and its leading spokesman. He was manager of the "Oscindonosci Bank" and a member of various boards in various Jewish organizations. He was well placed in the Jewish community but refused to run for office. He had many business interests in the city and was a partner in the oil drilling company in the area of Borislaw Drohobicz. He received a gold medal from the Polish government for his contribution to Polish commerce. In 1934 he helped acquire a large farm from a Polish major and together with three other partners they ran the farm of about 50 acres. The farm was located in Kriowic and had about 30 cows. This is where Zionist youth acquired agricultural training before they left for Palestine.
[Page 88]
In spite of his busy financial schedule, he never refused individual requests for help and enjoyed helping people. His wife was also very busy with social work especially amongst the Zionist women organizations. She was known as a large financial contributor to the Zionist feminine causes. She visited Palestine in 1935 and bought an orchard so that Jews should have a place to work. With the outbreak of World War II, the entire family managed to leave Poland and reach Palestine. Israel Igler was a member of the Revisionist party and supported the underground group in their war against the British. Lately he established a metal and a plumbing factory that provides many jobs.

Alter Chaim Eisenberg
He was the son of Yaakow Eisenberg and the brother-in-law of Moshe Zilbershtein. He was an honest and pious man. One of the founders and builders of the synagogue in the city and his seat was along the eastern wall and lived in Targowica. Prior to World War I he left for Germany.

Chaim Eisenberg
He was a very modest man and kept to himself. He observed strictly the commandments. He was the son-in-law of Baldengrin and lived along Kazimerz Street and later moved to the market square where he rented a place from Eliezer Rosner. He dealt with animal skins and barely managed to make a living. He recently sold his business to a shoemaker by the name of Kaplan.
Itzhak Eichler

He was called Itzik Haker. He was a butcher along Kazimierz Street in Orenstein's house. He lived in the Targowica next to the animal market. The business was neglected for many reasons and eventually failed. It was finally liquidated. He was sick for a long period of time that resulted in his death. He left a wife and several daughters. Their financial condition was very poor. They were expelled from the apartment for lack of rent money, so they decided to settle in the study center and refused to budge. They lived there for a while until the daughters began to work and earn some money. They then left the synagogue and became independent.
[Page 89]

Awraham Ingber

He was one of the more educated and well read people in the city. Well behaved, avoided involvements, and refused to be drawn into community participation. He was a teacher. He became ill prior to World War I and the disease dragged on until he passed away. He left a wife and small children who managed with time to get a decent education and even reach high academic teaching institutions.

The oldest son, the son-in-law of Israel Moshe Blum, was a teacher at a high school in Krakow. He was in Russia during World War II and returned to Poland where he died. His sister came to Palestine as a Halutza in the thirties and married a grandson of Baruch Ganger and settled in Tel Aviv. Another sister is in a kibbutz. The mother came to Palestine after the war with a son Monik, who lives in Hertzlia.

Moshe Einhorn

He was a modest man who knew his limitations and was pleased with them. He was very observant person. He was the torah reader at the study center of the rabbi until his last day. He lived for many years at the house of Feivil Klinman. He dealt with yeast. His younger son Motele, a member of the study center left Jaslo following his marriage. Another son lived in Krakow.

Awraham Einhorn

He was the son of Moshe. He was familiar with the scriptures and tended to read but was basically dedicated to the Hassidic movement. He dealt with kitchen ware and pottery at the house of Feivil Klinman. Lately his business was in decline and had to struggle for every customer. He had two daughters and a son. They all received a traditional education.

Zeev Wold Eintziger

The old timers of Jaslo used to say that he was the eighth man for the minyan and his brother Menachem Man was the ninth man in the new
[Page 90]
place of their residence. There were missing a tenth man to complete a minyan that requires ten men. Bogusz Steinhaus was already thirteen years old but refused to go to services. Thus they frequently were forced to pray as individuals unless somebody from Ulaszewice joined them for minyan. (The family name means "one" or "unique" in Yiddish). The name stems from one of the many visits that the Austrian Emperor, Joseph the second, made during his reign. During one of his visits in the area of Nowy Sacz, he lodged at the home of the Eintzigers and stated to one of their forefathers while shaking his hand "You are the first Jew that I slept in his house". The family then adopted the family name of Eintziger.

Reb Zeev or Wolf Eintziger as he was called, to be distinguished from Wolf Tzimet, who was his friend and shared his age. The former was a respected member of the Jaslo Jewish community that he helped to establish. He was deeply involved in communal affairs. He never acquired a technical education yet was authorized to deal with architectural and engineering building plans. He built most of the Jewish houses in the city and was rather a successful builder. He had six daughters and a son. His sons-in-law were observant and well read. Four of them resided in Jaslo and were engaged in commerce; they were: Yehoshua Kipel, Yehoshua Lempel, Chaim Feber, and Shulem Kuntz. The fifth son-in-law moved to Tarnow with the outbreak of World War I.

His sixth son-in-law, Rosentzweig L. owner of a candy store in the market square died at a very young age. He left a son and a daughter. (The daughter later left for Palestine as a pioneer and is a member of kibbutz Dan). His son Nathan recently reached Israel with his wife, the daughter of Eliezer Gorzik. They were first on the kibbutz with their sister-in-law but later settled in Haifa.

[Page 91]

Pinhas Eintziger

He was the son of Wolf Eintziger and the son-in-law of Shlomo Berger. He was well read in Jewish studies and was very religious. Still there was in him a flair of European knowledge and outlook as he expressed himself. He was always polite. He resided in Jaslo until 1913 and then moved to Brzeszow. He had a crystal and porcelain store. He had three sons and three daughters. They all received a higher education and all managed to reach Palestine. Yaakow Nathan Or (Eintziger), the oldest son of the family, finished the polititechnikum in Lemberg. He was very active amongst the Jewish academicians and was even elected president of the academic house in Lemberg. As a result of his efforts, the student building was enlarged and additional floor was added for Jewish students at the institution. He left Poland and reached Palestine where he received a good position with the Tel Aviv municipality. He was an excellent worker but soon left and opened an engineering office,

The second son, Moshe finished as an attorney and reached Palestine following the war. He settled in Tel Aviv. The third son, Yehoshua settled in Kfar Yehoshua. One daughter is married to a clerk in the Tel Aviv municipality. The second daughter, Esther, is a teacher and married to Mr. Ein Sela. The third daughter, Yaffa, works for the tnuva dairy organization.

Pinhas Eintziger left Poland to settle in Palestine. He returned to Poland to liquidate his business affairs in Poland where World War II caught him. He shared the fate of the Jews of Jaslo.

Menachem Man Eintziger

In the city he was known and called by the name of Mani Eintziger. He was involved with many activities and was very active in the community. He was very familiar with the municipality and community board. He was one of the movers behind the building of the big study center. He was later a member of the committee to build the large synagogue and was one of its first beadles.

[Page 92]

He was a tall man with a certain personal charm. He had an opinion on everything and expressed it everywhere. He lived in a house on Nowa Street. He was a wholesaler of animal skins. He kept his mother in his house until she died in 1916. Recently he rented his store and managed to live until World War II

Pessah Eintziger

He was a brother of Wolf and Mani. He was a modern person that you rarely encountered in Jaslo prior to World War I. He owned the hotel "Victoria" on Iglena Street. This was the first elegant Jewish hotel in the city. The first Zionist meeting in Jaslo took place at this hotel. When he left the city the hotel was converted to a residential building and was sold to Moshe Foist.

Zeev (Wilik) Eintziger (Libler)

He was the son of a brother in Sands, son-in-law of Shlomo Berger of Koblow. He studied as a youngster in Jaslo and later at the Yeshiva in Unsdorf in Hungary. He settled in Jaslo following his marriage. He opened a luxury shoe store in the market square and was rather successful. But with time he started to neglect his business and devoted himself to social communal affairs. These activities demanded time that he had to take from his business.

In spite of his youth, he excelled in public activities and was a well known figure in the city. He became a well known communal leader full of energy and leadership. He was elected to the municipality on the Zionist ticket in 1920 and will retain his seat until 1931. He was also a member of the community board during the period of Dr. Kornhauser. He was one of the organizers of the soccer club " Maccabi" and as its presiding officer insisted that they enter the competing field of sport with the white and blue flag.

[Page 93]

He left Jaslo in 1934 and settled in Sanok. As a high government official he used his connections on behalf of the Jewish community in Sanok. With the outbreak of World War II, he managed to reach Russia where he was also involved in helping people. Following the war, he reached Palestine with his wife and two daughters. His only son remained in Poland where he obtained a high government position. The father was the founder of the Jaslo landesmanshaft in Israel.

P. Altholtz

A quiet person devoted to his commerce and livelihood.

Yehoshu Altman

He was one of the first settlers in Jaslo. He was a Hassid of the old tradition. He had several sons and daughters that resided in the city and carried on the Jewish life.

Berish Altman

He was Yehoshua's son and a Shiniawer Hassid. He was very pious and prayed regularly in the study center. He was a wood merchant. He owned a big house on Kosciuszko Street. He was considered one of the rich people in the city. His oldest son Shlomo left the city with the outbreak of World War I and settled in Vienna. His two younger sons and daughters remained in the Jaslo.

Yossil Altman

The second son of Yehoshua Altman was a devoted follower of the study circles at the study center. He was immersed in the study of Talmud. He had a grocery store on Florianska Street. He made a nice living. He had two sons. The younger one Moshe distanced himself from his father's ways and became influenced by modern trends. He became a member of the Maccabi soccer team.

[Page 94]

Yehoshua Altman

He was the older son of Yossel Altman. He was a quiet person and familiar with Jewish literature. He was follower of the Hassidic movement and prayed regularly at the study center of the Rabbi. His father also attended the same synagogue. He was a merchant and lived in his father's house.

Abba Altman

The third son of Yehoshua Altman had a short red beard. He prayed at the big synagogue. He dealt with eggs and also exported them with Hollander, Korzenik and Karp. He was an expert in incubating the eggs during the summer for the winter season when there is a shortage of eggs.

He was amongst the hostages that Russians took in 1915 when they retreated from Jaslo; he returned four years later, an exhausted man. He lived on Shaynochy Street. He had several sons; the oldest was called Zeev or Wilk who settled at kibbutz Gath.

Blumcze Altman
Daughter-in-law of Yehoshua Altman. Following her widowhood, she opened a grocery store in the Targowica area and there she also lived.

Chaim Altman
He was Blumcze Altman's son. He was very pious and studied in Sandz. He returned to Jaslo in the twenties. He was an egg merchant and lived in the Targowica.

Hersh Altman
He was Blumcze Altman's second son. He lived with his mother and helped her with the business. He was a member of the Zionist organization and of the "Maccabi" sport club

Meir Elliowicz
Very pious person, son-in-law of Moshe Tzimet

Yaakow Alexandrowicz
He belonged to one of the oldest Jewish families in the city. He runs the distillery for years after he obtained the license from Yaakow Freund of Ulaszoeice.
[Page 95]
He also owned two houses on the corner of Kazimierza and Nowa Streets, opposite the mayor's office. Both properties were later acquired by Amer and Kornfeld. Next to the house on Kazimerza Street there was an orchard and a vacant piece of land that reached the house of Shmuel Lehr. The plot belonged to Adamski who sold to a builder that built on it the homes of Eliasz, Kramer and Karp.
He was considered a very modern person in Jaslo. His three sons sold all the properties and the business and left the city of Jaslo. The distillery was acquired by Mordechai Anisfeld who owned it until 1939.

Meir Ament
He was an extremely orthodox Jew who worked in his tin workshop that belonged to Amer and Kornfeld on Nowa Street. He was known in the city as Meir Koler since he came from Koloczyc. He had two sons and five daughters who received a very religious education.

Shmuel Ament
Meir Ament's oldest son was well read in Jewish knowledge. He studied in his youth at the study center. He learned the trade from his father. He was very skillful and specialized in the production of tin ovens for gas. He worked with his father.

Moshe Ament
Meir Ament's second son was very smart and well read. With Polish independence, he left for Hungary to study in a Yeshiva. Later he told stories about Jewish life in Hungary. Married to Sokol but later returned to Jaslo and opened a grocery along the Przedmiace where he bought the house that he lived in.

Yehiel Engel

Following World War I, he left Zmigrod and settled in Jaslo. He was scholarly and behaved accordingly. He was considered one of the sharp Talmudic minds in Jaslo and his Talmudic interpretations and explanations were well received by those that attended the lectures. He avoided all glorifications and stressed his privacy. His children were raised in the Hassidic spirit and were all torah students. His first son-in-law, Reuven Eisenberg, was a Talmudic scholar of the first grade. He was very pious and learned. Recently he served as dayan in Zmigrod. The second son-in-law, Shmuel Bilt, born in Frysztak was a well-to-do person and soon left Jaslo. The third son-in-law was a merchant but studied daily at the study center in Jaslo.

Ozer and Moshe Engel absorbed knowledge at their home and both were well spoken and spoke several languages. (While writing these lines I am told that Ozer Engel managed to survive the shoah and reached the USA.)

[Page 96]

Itzhak Engel was basically very depressed due to the loss of many of his children in childbirth but he did not let this factor influence his dealings with people. He settled in a small house along Wisoka Street on reaching Jaslo. The place was near the Yad Charutzim synagogue. He started to trade with yeast and then opened a kitchen ware store in Rosner's house.

Mordechai Engel

He was also a native of Zmigrod. A Hassidic Jew that dealt in wheat. He used to come to Jaslo and stay for the week and returned for the Shabbat home to Zmigrod. Several years prior to World War II, he stopped commuting and settled in Jaslo and began building a house along Korlowski street that was finished with the outbreak of the war. He managed to reach Russia in 1940. There he took ill and died as did one of his sons. His wife and two sons managed to reach Israel. One of them, Yehoshua, lives in Holon.

[Page 97]

Chaim Englander

Prior to World War I, he had one of the finest reputations in town as a scholar. He was descendant of a privileged and well known family namely Chaim Hacohen Englander, the son of Rabbi Israel Aaron from Frysztak and the son-in-law of the well-to-do Naphtali Shmuel Salomon from Koblow and Podzamci.

Chaim Englander was known as a smart person, well educated, loved to study, and connected with rabbis, pleasant and sensitive human being. His language was interlaced with sayings of the sages and quotes from the original sources. While still a young man he cultivated a beard that was well trimmed and gave him a stature of a learned man. He built the "Grand" hotel next to the railway station and managed it for many years. A year prior to the outbreak of World War I, he left Jaslo, sold his estate and settled in Tarnow. His sons received a religious and general education. One of his sons owned a toy factory and later left for Palestine in the thirties. Recently his wife and daughter joined him after they survived the shoah. They reside in Tel Aviv.

Awraham Engelhardt

He was born in Rymanow and settled in Jaslo with Polish Independence. During the war he lived in Czechoslovakia. He was a pleasant person, fair and wise. He had a pleasant appearance and gentle manners. His language was well mannered and polished. He had a pleasant voice and conducted services in the evening. He was known for his cantorial rendition of the priestly blessing during the holidays, the omer prayer and services in general. He was a wine merchant and lived in Podzamci. He had six daughters; all were members of the Zionist movement. Two of them left for Palestine as pioneers. One of them is at kibbutz Dan and the second one Rishka Shtern lives in Tel Aviv. (She is a member of the Jaslo landesmanshaft committee.)

[Page 98]

Dawid Antner

He had three last names namely Dawid Antener, Dawid Zommer and Dawid Stolar. The last name reflected his trade, a carpenter. He was a carpenter and managed to make a living. He lived simply with what he could afford but was always content with life. Lately, his carpentry extended to building caskets. He lived all his life at the Targowica. He had three sons. (According to rumors, one son survived and managed to reach the USA)

Mordechai Anisfeld

He originates from Krakow. He was a quiet person with a good temperament. In spite of his education he kept away from political and communal life. His outlook was extremely modern for his days. He supported the Zionist movement and its activities. He was the son-in-law of Alter Tzucker. During the two great wars, he run the distillery and had the exclusive monopoly on the sale of "Okuczim" beer. He reached Russia during World War II with his family. He suffered a great deal and passed away in Uzbekistan in 1942. His son Yonathan received an academic education and married the daughter of Shlomo Elias of Jaslo. They both reached Palestine. He received a job with the electric company in Tel Aviv. They live in Tel Itzhak. Recently his wife and daughter managed with great difficulty to reach these shores and settled in Ramat Hachail.

Nahum Shochet

I must devote some time to this noble figure that I admired in my youth. He was admired by the community. His deeds and manners were highly praised. He was born in Maden, near Przemysl. With the development of Jaslo, he reached the city and was accepted as conductor of the services and a ritual slaughterer.

[Page 99]

Prior to the existence of the great synagogue, the modern worshippers and those that liked cantorial prayers attended the services at the Getzler house. Here Nahum was the main attraction of the "mussaf service" – or second half of the service during the high holidays. (Awraham Piar was his main assistant. He later became a known cantor and left for Vienna).

Nahum Shochet later conducted the first half of the High Holiday service when the great synagogue was opened with the regular cantor and the choir. He also conducted services twice a month at the synagogue. Frequently the beadle urged him to conduct the services, especially for the "Neila service" on Yom Kippur. He distinguished himself in conducting his services in a moderate tone. He prayed in the traditional emotional style of the cantorial school. His service was emotionally inspiring. His two sons Eliyahu and Yeshayahu were members of the choir. Lately he was assisted by his son Awraham Itche and his grandsons, Simcha Rothfeld, and the sons of Eliezer Weitzman.

He was a Hassid of Bluzow and was familiar with the court of the Rabbi, when he visited the Rabbi on a Shabbat, he was asked to conduct the services which the Rabbi and his Hassidim enjoyed immensely. In spite of the fact that the Rabbi had an excellent voice and also conducted services. Whenever famous rabbis visited Jaslo, he was always asked to conduct services.

He was known to have a great deal of medical knowledge without ever having attended medical school or any school. The story is as follows: while still a young resident in the city, he lived next to the Tzinglewicz family – a non Jewish family- and made the acquaintance of one of their sons that just finished his medical studies and was granted the medical degree. This doctor influenced Shochet to study and develop an interest in medicine. The student showed aptitude and before long even acquired a rudimentary knowledge of Latin in order to read prescriptions. Word spread that Nahum Shochet was a doctor . He took excellent care of his Jewish patients and saved them lots of money. (We do not have records to show the amount of savings but they amounted to a large sum over the years). He conducted services and was a ritual slaughterer for over 50 years in the community. Each day, he used to visit the sick people in town from 10-12 in the morning and 4-6 in the afternoon.

[Page 100]

On his visits, he was always dressed, his shoes were polished and his medical bag in his hand. He even had some tools to perform superficial surgery. He was a doctor to the full extent of the word. He diagnosed the person and prescribed medications with instructions for their use. He was pleasant and wished the patients good luck. He soaped and washed his hands on finishing the examination. Spoke to the patient and encouraged him to take care of himself and to the family told to carry out the instructions. If the disease was serious, he urged that another doctor be called in. The latter would always ask has Nahum been called, regardless whether it was a Jewish or Gentile doctor. This indicates the respect that the doctors had for Nahum Shochet and the work he carried on for years without looking for rewards.

He had four sons and four daughters. His first son-in-law was Hertzel Rothfeld, the second was Wachner (Apfel), the third son-in-law was Eliezer Weitzman and the fourth Avishai Naman. His oldest son Eliyahu lived in Pilzno near Tarnow and was a cantor and a ritual slaughterer. Kalman was the second son who studied at the study center. He was the sales representative of rubber stamps and grinders. He married to Przemysl and opened a successful business.

Yehoshua Apfel

Nahum's third son was a studious Hassid. He studied at the study center. He resided in Jaslo and worshipped regularly at the great study center and conducted services there. He dealt with money exchanges and made a pleasant living. With the outbreak of World War II he reached Russia. Following the war the family reached Paris France

Awraham Itche Apfel

The youngest son of Nahum was a studious member of the study center. He was a follower of the Hassidic court and observed every minute command. He was greatly influenced by his brother-in-law Naman. He married to Dukla and resided there for a while but soon returned to Jaslo and studied slaughtering but soon left it for commerce.

Shragai Feivel Apfel

He was Nahum's brother. He was a fine and gentle man. He was respected in the city and in the community. He also conducted services and followed the cantorial pattern of Bluzow of which he was a Hassid. He had a workshop in the market and sometime between 1908-1910 he left for Germany.

Yudel Meir Apfel (Horowitz)

A scholarly student of the Talmud, son-in-law of Yaakow Freund, he owned a paper and toy store in the market. He left for Austria prior to World War I. and settled in Vienna. The business was assumed by Gittel Apfel (Nahum's daughter).

P. Apfel

A very gentle person who avoided all involvement. He was a clerk at the flour mill in Pocholenko, outside the city. His son finished legal studies and opened a law office in the city.

Shmuel Wolf Ehrlich

He was very religious and pious man, straight in his dealings with other people. Brother-in-law of Yakel Kalb. He always worked as a glazier. Since 1914 he lived in the house of Amer and Kornfeld on Nowa St. He passed away in the twenties following a prolonged disease
He left a wife and two sons Leibish and Naphtali and five daughters; Raala, Rachel, Roza, Neche, and Zlata (a son named Mendel died as a youngster).
Following his death, his wife opened a grocery store in the same house. Two of his sons-in-law lived in the city of Jaslo. One of them Yerachmiel Tevel who owned a grocery on Florianska St. next to Kalszturna. The oldest son Leibish left Germany and settled in Petach Tikva, Palestine. He was a very religious man and worked for a living. His son fell in the independence war. The fourth daughter Neche left Poland as a pioneer of the Mizrahi women organization and settled in Petach Tikvah and following her marriage moved to Tel Aviv. Shortly, thereafter, she took ill with a terminal disease and soon passed away, leaving a young child.

Akiva Arman
He was known in the city as Akiva Podzamci since he had a farm in the village by that name near Jaslo. He was a kind person, nice mannerisms, and an excellent host. He was also generous. He reached the ripe old age and used to tell stories about the old days.
He once told the following story. I received the order to appear before the draft board in 1928 in the village. He then went to visit the old Rabbi Tzvi Hersh Hacohen of Rymanow and he gave him the following blessing "You will live a long live". Indeed the blessing fulfilled itself since he managed to see many grandchildren.

Yaakov Ehrinfreund
He was the son-in-law of Israel Meir Kornreich. He was well read and involved in the community. He lived in the Elias house on Kazimierz Street where he had his store of spirits. He reached Russia with the outbreak of World War II and passed away there following a disease.

Hertzel Ashkenazi
He was the son-in-law of Leib Tzimet. Well educated and student of the torah.

[Page 103]

Bet ב

Mandil, Baron, Rabbi
He was the son in law of Rabbi Awraham Yehoshua Heshil Rubin, the first head of the judicial rabbinical council in Jaslo.

Yona, Baron, Rabbi
He was the son of Mandil Baron.

Berish Baron
His last and first name were unknown to the Jews of Jaslo. He was known by his nickname, "the bass". He held this post with the choir of the synagogue. He helped the dynasty of Jaslo cantors in their cantorial performances. He was brought especially for this post from the city of Sandz. He also traded in the market. He barely scraped a living from both occupations. He was a tall man with a big yellow beard that reached his shoulders and chest.

He had a son named Yaakow and a daughter that died as a youngster. Lately he stopped singing in the synagogue and prayed in the study center. When the Rabbi of Dukla opened his study center, Berish Baron joined him there.

[Page 104]
Yudel Bodner

He was a Hassidic Jew and each day partook in the lecture sessions dealing with the Talmud. He distributed charity and received guests warmly. He helped to rebuild the study center and was one of the first beadles.

Saturdays he was busy arranging the third meal of the day namely the "Shalishides". He joined the Rabbi of Dukla when the later opened the new place and became a regular worshiper at the center.

He started out as a yeast merchant prior to World War I but then rented a store on Kosciuszko Street where he opened a grocery. He was a successful businessman and became one of the big sugar wholesalers in the city. He had five daughters and two sons that received a very religious education.

Mendel Bodner

He was the son of Yudel Bodner and was a member of the study center. He was well read in Hebrew and general literature. He married the sister of his brother in law, Reuven Kliman. The couple managed successfully the family business, specializing in importing wheat and sugar.

Baruch Bodner

He was the son of Yudel Bodner and was a member of the study center. He was also a member of the "Young Mizrahi Movement". Following his marriage, he devoted himself to commerce. (According to rumors he managed to survive the war and reach the USA.)

Leibish Bodner

He owned a farm in the village of Sowionow where he lived. He led a traditional religious life. He would occasionally come to the city to pray. Besides the farm he also dealt in commerce. His children received a general education in the city school system.
(I am informed that one of his sons reached Israel).

Nathan Boim

He was one of the first settlers of Ulaszewice between the years 1850-1860. He drowned in the river when he went to wash himself at a relatively young age

[Page 105]
Zeelig Boim

He was the son of Nathan Boim, one of the early Jewish children of Ulaszowice. He was very religious, charitable and highly respectable. He sold building materials.

He had two sons and two daughters. One daughter married Dawid Schwartzman and one son named Nathan left Jaslo in 1895 for Vienna and much later reached Israel and settled in Tel Aviv. One son and a daughter live in the States.

Shmuel Buch

He was the son of the ritual slaughterer from Koloczyc and the son in law of Moshe Margolies. He was a very smart individual and familiar with the environment. Interjected jokes in his discussions and conversations. He was a sympathizer of the Zionist movement. Always spoke the truth and disliked hypocrisy. He was a regular worshipper at reb. Mandil's minyan.

He started by selling grocery products, wrapping paper and paper bags, then shifted to candy production. His venture was not successful. He had an only son Naphtali who tried to enter

Palestine but could not make it because the British would not let him enter. Meantime the war started and he disappeared.

Tzwi Hersh Baumring

He was one of the oldest homeowners in Jaslo. He was the largest wholesaler and retailer of grocery goods in the city. He was a very representative person, and observed his religion and its customs. He always lived along Kosciuszko Street in his own house. He had three sons and four daughters. One of the latter was married to a member of the Shochet family. This family escaped to Russia with the outbreak of World War II where the husband died and the wife survived and presently resides in Tel Aviv with the Shochet family. Another son, Doctor Yaakow Baumring studied at the Yeshiva and received a general education where he excelled. He presented himself to the external examinations for the university and was accepted as a student. He later became a well known doctor in Krosno.

Leibish Baumring

He was the oldest son of Tzwi Hersh Baumring He owned a flour mill in Jaslo. He was modern in outlook and well read. He was one of the dedicated Zionist members in the city. With the outbreak of World War II he left everything and escaped to Russia. He and a son reached Palestine.

[Page 106]
Itzhak Baumring, doctor

The youngest son of Tzwi Hersh Baumring completed high school and graduated from dental school. He managed to reach London.

Buksbaum, the widow

She lived all her life in Kornfeld's house on Kazimierz Street. She sold items in the market on the down payment system. She had a son in Germany and a younger son at home in Jaslo.

Shlomo Bezner and doctor Itzhak Bezner

Meir Batman

He was the son in law of Mendel Meller. He was short and had large spectacles. He was familiar with the Hebrew literature. He prayed daily and then reviewed the available reading materials. He was a quiet person and somewhat withdrawn but very polite. He was a very good member of the Mizrahi Zionist movement in Jaslo while he resided in the city. He was a businessman.

Alter Shulem Bialywloss

He was a Hassidic Jew and a Cohen. He was the son in law of Mordechai Getzler and was considered one of the great scholars of the Jewish community. In spite of his lack of showmanship and young age, he was selected to be one of the beadles in the big study center up to World War I. Lately, he was a regular worshipper at the study center of the Rabbi and was the regular Torah reader there. His son Henech was raised in the Hassidic tradition. He lived in Rubel's house along May 3rd Street and there was his shop.

[Page 107]
Shlomo Biar

He was a quiet and withdrawn person. He observed the Jewish traditions and was the son in law of Ephraim Brick. He earned his living from the bar that was located downhill from the Targowice opposite the well. He had three sons and three daughters. They were all members of the Young Zionist movement. The youngest son Yaakow was very active in the pioneer movement and in the thirties left for Palestine. Another son, Shulem, was shot by the Germans on entering Bochnia. The eldest son supposedly survived and reached the USA.

Eliezer Bider

He was from Gorlice and came to Jaslo with the Gorlice Jews that were expulsed from their place because it became a battle scene in World War I. He was a quiet and well mannered individual. He was well read and fluent in several languages. He gave private lessons in accounting. He prayed at the big study center where he had a seat near the southern wall. Here he revealed his inner most thoughts.

He had three sons and two daughters. The oldest son Ori was a member of the Mizrahi movement. All the children were active Zionists and were the first pioneers to reach Palestine from Jaslo. Ori was killed in 1921 in Jerusalem during the riots. His brother Shmuel joined the Communist party in Palestine and then left the country. The daughters also left the country and one is supposedly in the USA.

Shmuel Bilt

(See Yehiel Engel)

Hershel Bindiger

He was a Hassid of the court of Lejansk and was greatly involved with this dynasty. He was a simple man and contented himself with the bare minimum as was the aspiration of the Hassidic world that rejected luxury. He was a yeast merchant. His wife Sheindil was born into the Handel family. In the twenties, his daughter Feiga opened a candy and fruit store at Mendel Meller's place. She was married to a religious student named Yaakow Hanoch Rosen. They had a nice income.

Lately he lived in Shmuel Stillman's place in the market. He had three sons and three daughters. One of the sons left Jaslo in the early twenties. The younger son Ezriel managed to survive the Germans and reached Israel where he settled in Jerusalem.

[Page 108]

Zinwil Bindiger

He was the son of Hershel Bindiger. He was very religious and strictly observant. Lately he became a follower of the Dukler Rabbi. He was the son in law of Menashe Shtern. He married Shosha Shtern. Following the marriage, he became a partner in the haberdashery store of his brother in law on Kazimierz Street.

Itzhak Binder

He was well read and familiar with religious literature. He was the brother in law of Awraham Shecht. He produced vinegar but was not very successful. His economic situation kept declining and lately it was very bad. He had a few sons. One of them was born with six fingers on his hands and toes. The family left the city in the twenties. The mother of the family helped out in the Rabbi's house until she passed away.

Elimelech Bikower

The Jews in Jaslo did not know the family name. He was known as Elimelech Bikower since he came from the village of Bikowa near Brzostek where he had a large farm. He was a Hassid and follower of the Rabbi of Willipoli. He was a simple person and highly respected educated people. He contributed largely to the special "Shmira" matzo fund.

He was a tall man and always looked down. His beard was disheveled and the side curls reached the beard. He wore a large woolen belt when he came to the city to visit his in laws.

Just as the child bestows credit on the father, sometimes, the son in law bestows credit on his father in law as was the case in point. He had one daughter named Frida Leah for whom he selected a an excellent husband namely Ben Tzion Gutwirt. The latter was a Cohen and an excellent yeshiva student. The supporter of the marriage was the Rabbi of Willipoli. The marriage gave Elimelech a great deal of prestige

[Page 109]

Elimelech Bikower made no secrets of his status and behaved as a simple farmer. He even said himself that he was a simple person and should be accepted as such. He had two sons that helped him on the farm. They behaved in a similar manner.

Shlomo Bildengrin

He was a butcher and lived in the Targowice. He was a quiet and easy going person. He was a Hassid that followed the Rabbi of Rymanow and later became a follower of the Dukler Rabbi, He had several daughters.

Chaim Shlomo Blut

He was born in the village of Pezatzlew and was the son in law of Treitel. He was one of the partners of the non-Jewish Polish printing company named "Wisloka" located in the Targowica square. His family was very interesting and he was a peculiar type of person. He was a sympathizer of the Zionist movement and the Mizrachi Movement. He was a strong supporter of the Polish Worker Party (P.P.S.) in Jaslo. He observed tradition and the religious aspects of Judaism but also celebrated the workers holiday of May first and participated in all labor manifestations with the red flag flattering above his head. He was the only bearded Jew that participated in the May celebrations in the city. As a student at the study center in his youth he acquired a large Jewish religious education and he loved to quote from the sources. He had comments on everything and made frequent interesting observations. He was in general contemptuous of events and situations. His trimmed beard covered his bespectacled face. He wore large gold rimmed glasses that gave the impression of a writer or a poet of the Jewish enlightenment. Indeed he was well read and familiar with many books. His Hebrew was fluent and he loved to read Hebrew papers.

His children received a general education and were influenced by left wing ideas and ideologies. They all belonged to extreme left wing parties and rumor has it that one of his sons was killed in the Spanish civil war fighting for the Republican forces.

Eliezer Blum

One of Zeelig Miller's son in laws. He was very involved in the community and was beadle for many years in the big synagogue. Things that did not suit him were highly criticized and explained but were never accepted by the leaders of the community.

He was very influential in establishing the prayer house of the "Hevra Kadisha" on Sokola Street, next to the house of Benyamin Unger. He had a haberdashery store on Kosciuszko Street that also sold items of the latest fashions, especially lady hats. He had three sons and four daughters.

[Page 110]

Israel Moshe Blum

He was one of Eliezer Blum's sons. He had a haberdashery store in the market square.

Eliezer Blum

He was always called "Der blinder Eliezer" – the blind Eliezer since he had limited vision. Still he studied daily the Talmud wrapped in his praying shawl and phylacteries at the synagogue. He prayed along the suggested lines of the mystic of Tzefat, Itzhak Arieh Luria, and was deeply influenced by Jewish mysticism and Kabbala books. He was always studying texts and next to him was always his sniff box.

He sold the items used for Sukkoth namely the etrog, the lulav, the myrtle and the willow branches. In order to obtain most of these items, he traveled yearly to Italy and other places where he purchased them.

His wife Sheindel sat daily in the market until 1914 and sold oriental fruits and sweets. Lately he lived in Feivel Kliman's house. He had one son that left for Germany where he was very successful businessman. He also had a daughter that opened lately a candy store.

Yermiyahu Blum

He was a watchmaker and a jeweler. He was a quiet person and lived on Florianska Street. He died in 1914 with the outbreak of World War I.

P. Blum

He was an enlightened person and a member of the Zionist movement in the city. He owned for many years the pharmacy called "Pod Gwiazdon" – or under the star along Kosciuszko Street.

[Page 111]

Adam Blumental

He was an engineer that worked in the technical department of the oil refinery in Niglowic. With the outbreak of World War II he left Jaslo and wandered about until he reached Palestine where he settled in Haifa. Sometimes later he left for the USA.

Feiwil Blonder

He was a typical type but very interesting. In his youth he was a member of the "Poalei Tzion" movement and later became very religious. He worshipped at the Rabbi's study center. He had progressive ideas but adhered strictly to his Hassidic concepts of life. His beard was well kept and trimmed in the shape of a square. He wore a large "yarmulke" of velvet that was tall and broad. He also wore a three quarter coat and a large silk band around his waist.

He was busy as a matchmaker and opened a centrally located kiosk next to the movie house "Sokol". He barely made a living but was always happy.

He was very involved in communal affairs, especially social affairs. He was very active in the association of "Hachnesset Kalah" – or support for the unmarried girls. He was the band leader of the orchestra that entertained at weddings. He always carried in his hand a baton with a silver ball at the top that was the tone giver for the band. He used this position to visit prenuptial couples and their families with requests for donations for the various charity funds Feiwil was also a member of the ' Bikur Cholim" society to help the sick where he called the doctors and took care of the patients. He also preceded the funeral cortege with a charity box in his hand asking for donations. He was active in the Talmud torah group to raise money for charity and was also responsible to receive guests in the city.

He made several statements against Zionism and was very active during the elections to the kehilla board. All these jobs that he performed did not help his income. Lately he received a job on behalf of the association for the poor or "Tomchei Aniim" to distribute the coupons for the needy or poor people that came to the city of Jaslo. This job kept him fully occupied. (In writing these lines, I am informed that one of his sons reached the USA).

Moshe Balzam

He was the son in law of the widow Keller who operated the kiosk near the municipal court house along the road to the railway station. With his marriage he took possession of the kiosk. He also took over the job of Moshe Winkler who ran the bathhouse. He made several changes and his income increased. Then in 1934, a fire started in the boiler room that soon spread to the study center. The latter building was burned, luckily the bathhouse was lightly damaged and he continued to operate it.

[Page 112]

Israel Eliyahu Belzer

He was the owner of a large store that dealt with animal skins and shoes on Kosciuszko Street. He was a good man and very honest. He was observant and was one of the first worshippers at the big synagogue.

He took ill at a relative young age and the best doctors of Krakow and Vienna could not help him. He died on the tenth of the month of Elul in 1924 in Bad-Neuheim. His body was brought to Jaslo where he was buried.

He left a wife and two sons; Shachne and Feiwil. He also left three daughters. With time the business flourished and they received the exclusive representation rights of the "Wudetta" rubber factory. The family also bought shares in the oil drillings in Poland and Rumania that were successful. The family became one of the richest families in the city and distributed charity on a wide basis.

The widow sends daily food to the poor people and to the Jewish prisoners at the jail. She also tried to help the latter with whatever she could.

Shachne was one of the soccer players of Maccabi as well as an enterprising young businessman. He managed large business affairs in Warsaw and Lemberg until the outbreak of the war. He managed to reach Russia and then with the Polish Army he reached Palestine. He settled in Tel Aviv where he opened an electrical plant.

Benyamin Bliman

He lived at the top of Florianska Street. He was nicknamed Yemin the grave digger". He used to walk daily the streets of Jaslo with a bag under his arms and a broken umbrella. These symbols served to advertise that he repaired umbrellas, bought and sold rags and bought antics. He had two sons.

[Page 114]

Leibish and Michael Bliman

Leibish was the oldest son. He was a quiet person and was a tenor in the synagogue choir. He assisted all the cantors in Jaslo that prayed at the synagogue. Singing was his source of income. The second son worked with his father.

Aaron Blank

He lived in Dembowce near Jaslo. He was the son in law of Mordechai Ris. He dealt in commerce and was a fine host and very observant.

He had two sons and four daughters that were educated in the city. The oldest daughter settled in Zmigrod following her marriage.

The family left Dembowce in the thirties and settled in Jaslo.

One son named Yossef managed to survive the Germans and after many detours managed to reach Israel. He settled in Tel Aviv and works in the printing shop of Shochet.

Tzwi Benet

He settled in Jaslo in the thirties, He was a modern minded person. He was a partner in the glass factory in Jaslo.

Joel Menachem Beck

He was nicknamed Joel Mendel. He was a native of Trziciano near Jaslo, He settled in Jaslo in the seventies and was one of the first people to have their homes in the city.

He was a moderate person and avoided involvement. He concentrated on his business that consisted of timber, coal, chalk etc... He was the only one to sell these items in the city.

Dawid Beck

He was the oldest son of Joel Menachem Beck. He was highly respected in the community. He dealt with the same items that his father. He lived all the years on Florianska Street. He had two son in laws; Saphir and Segal. Both were quiet, concentrated on the business and lived in Jaslo. His oldest son Herman left the city for the USA.

Motel Beck

He was the youngest son of Joel Mendel Beck who was born in Jaslo. In his youth he studied at the study enter daily until he was married. He remained in Jaslo and conducted his business of building materials and heating implements. He was aware of the environment and was interested in activities in communal activities as well as Jewish Zionist affairs. He was active in the municipal sphere as well as one of the founders of the local Mizrahi branch movement in the city. Motel also partook in the creation of the "bank ludowy". He was the presiding officer of the of the mutual charity fund "Gmilat Hessed". He was a devoted Zionist and defended the movement everywhere. He was a steady reader of the Hebrew Press namely "Hatzfira" and "Hamitzphe" and others. He was a friend of doctor Kornhauser and the other older Zionists in the city. He was elected to the community council on the Mizrahi election ticket.

He was an honest man, avoided combinations and shortcuts and always expressed his true feelings. Near the stores of Moshe Tudor and Chaim Krisher in the corner between Kosciusko and Iglena, was the political center where he expressed himself in public

He had four sons and two daughters. All received a religious and Zionist education. Mendel the oldest son was one of the first to leave Jaslo and study at the "Tachcomani School" in Warsaw. He completed his studies and graduated from law school and became a lawyer in the Polish capital. He was also secretary of the lawyers association. With the outbreak of the war , he escaped to Russia and nothing was heard of him.

Genia, his daughter left for Palestine in 1933 and married Npahtali Shochet. She was one of the founders of the former residents of Jaslo. The oldest daughter Itka and her family perished in the shoa. One son fell in the battle of 1939 as a Polish soldier. Two sons; Romek and Zeelig survived the war and reside in Toulouse France where they have a clothing factory.

Following the war, he and his wife managed to leave Russia and reached Israel. He was very happy that finally his youthful dream was realized. These were difficult days for the country just received its independence. He settled in Jaffa and was about to open a store when he suddenly fell ill and passed away within a few days.

[Page 115]
Moshe Beck

He was Dawid's son and observant. He sold timber, coal and chalk at the bottom of Targowice next to the well. He lived in his apartment on Korlowskiego Street.

He was blessed with sons for he had thirteen of them. All of them were strong and played soccer. Some of them left the city in the twenties for Belgium. According to rumors only two children survived the war, one of them is in London and a daughter.

Tzwi Bergman

The family was originally from Gorlice but settled in Jaslo during World War I. He lived all his life in Targowice. Lived a simple life and avoided extravagance as befits a Hassidic Jew. He introduced the Shabbat and havdala wax candles. He had two sons and three daughters. The latter were known as excellent seamstresses and were nicknamed the "Gorlitziankes" to indicate the place of origin. The youngest daughter was married to A. Rosenfeld. She and her husband managed to reach Israel and settle in Kfar Saba.

Shlomo Berger

Almost everybody knew Shlomo Berger in Jaslo. He lived for many years in the village of Koblow near Jaslo. He left the village in the twenties and settled in the city. He was rather known by the name of the village were he used to live.

Following his marriage while still being a yeshiva student, he settled in the village of Dembowce. He became a timber and forest merchant. He succeeded rather well in business and began to purchase real estate. He also bought the big quarry near Griowic and owned a large brick factory. His latest acquisition was the famous Koblow estate.

Most of the parcels of land among Kosciuszko Street near the railway belonged to him. He was forced to sell the three story house opposite the court house because he signed as a guarantor for friends and they could not pay. So he had to bail them out fore as a Hassid of Rymanow how could he leave someone in debt.

[Page 116]

Mr. Shlomo Berger and wife

He gave charity and was an excellent host. He was friendly with the Rabbis and was on very good terms with Rabbi Mandil .

Daily he came to the city with his horse driven cart. Two beautiful and well groomed horses drove the cart. He himself was dressed in fine Hassidic clothes. He had in his hand a black cane with a silverized handle. Slowly he walked and distributed food and dairy products from his farm for the needy. He called the action my "anonymous" charity. He always provided the synagogues with greens for the Shavuot holiday.

He left for Sanok where he lived a full and long life. He even managed to celebrate the golden wedding ceremony. He had seven daughters and two sons. He married his daughters to educated men from good families. His first son in law was Chaim .Zilber from Sanok. The son in law of Dr. Israel Plotzker (two of Ch.Zilber's sons are in Israel). His second son in law was Pinhas Eintziger the son of Wolf Eintziger from Jaslo, the father of the engineer Yaakow Or (Eintziger). The third son in law was Yehoshua Gutwin the son of Wolf, the shochet from Trziciano near Rzeszow. He lives today in kibbutz Gever-Am with his daughter and son in law (one of his sons serves as police officer in Tiberius). The forth son in law was Zeev (Wilik) Eintziger of Sandz. He lives in Tel Aviv. The fifth son in law was Emanuel Kronenthal from

Bezun. The sixth son in law was Kopil (Hans) Kamnitzer. He was the owner of the famous pension "Kamnitzer" in Hertzlia.

[Page 117]

The seventh son in law was Tzwi Hersh Langsam of Bokowsk. The oldest son Dawid received a religious and general education. He left Jaslo and settled in Germany but lives today in London. He visited Israel several times. The second son Mendel settled in the USA.

Hersh Yaakow Berger

He was the brother of Shlomo Berger. He was a Hassidic Jew. He lived many years in the village of Koblow and then moved to Ulaszowice and then to the village of Blaszkowa near Brzostek.

He had five sons and the oldest left for the USA where he was very successful. He sends tickets for the entire family and they all left for the USA.

Meir Berger

He was the son in law of Moshe Dam from the Targowice. He was a student and devoted himself to the study of torah. Together with this author they fixed and restored many of the books at the big study center.

He was a disabled person; he had poor vision as a result of World War I. On his discharge from the Polish Army he received a license to deal in sprits from the Polish government.

During the thirties he started to build a five story house on a plot that belonged to his father in law at the end of the Targowice square next to the well. But he could not finish it due to the deterioration of his health. He himself lived all his years in a poor flat that belonged to Weinberg next to the synagogue. With the building of the house, he moved there although the place was not ready.

He had several sons, the oldest escaped from Poland where he faced a jail sentence for belonging to the Communist party.

Dawid Berger

He owned a chocolate and fruit store in Leibish Amer's house along the Iglena Street. He was successful in business and moved to May 3ʳᵈ Street where he opened a large store that sold candy , fruits and soda.

He was the son in law of Israel Haber. He was a quiet businessman. His son reached Palestine after many tortuous roads. He lives in the Sheik Mounis section near Tel Aviv.

[Page 118]

Zishe Bruder

He observed tradition and was very familiar with the surroundings. He was a member of the 'Yad Harutzim "association from the first day of its inception. He was also a member of the community board and a member of many other organizations. He owned a house on Badanarska Street where he lived.

He had five sons and four daughters. All the children received a general education. His sons helped in the business. Three of them are presently in Australia and one in England one daughter lives in the USA. The youngest daughter left for Palestine and following her marriage, she settled in Tel Aviv.

Yaakow Bruder

He was the brother of Zishe. He was an old member of the Zionist party as well as an old member of "Yad Harutzim". He was quiet but very efficient in his work. He was modern in his thinking and rose early each morning to attend services at the synagogue.

He had a house on Nowa Street where he lived all his life. His workshop was located in Yossef Manashe's place. He had two sons and two daughters. His oldest son, Michael left Jaslo in the twenties and settled in Danzig where he opened a business. His second son was a dentist and the youngest daughter left for Palestine as a pioneer and settled in the village of Ness Tziona.

Ephraim Brick

He was an old timer in Jaslo. He was very presentable and easy going person. His had one of the first butcher stores in Jaslo. He was a founding member of the "Yad Harutzim Association" and was the beadle of their synagogue for many years.

He lived his life in his house that was surrounded by greenery and trees. To reach his house you needed to go down the stairs that paralleled the road to Ulaszowice and faced Shanojchy Street.

He had two daughters; one was married to Shlomo Biar and the second one to Chaim Goldblat and an only son.

[Page 119]

Michael Brick

He was the son of Ephraim Brick. He was a modest and shy person. He also opened a butcher store in the market square. He lived in Branstadter's place next to the municipal building. He devoted himself to business.

He died after a prolonged disease while still a relatively young person. He left a wife, a son named Libik and a daughter named Idela. In the early thirties, the daughter left for Palestine as a pioneer and married there Israel Shtoier. The son was a dentist and lived in Krakow.

Shlomo Brand

In Jaslo he was nicknamed "Der Kleiner Shlomale" – or the small Shlomo. He lived in a small wooden barrack near the study center, a few yards from the holy place where he spent most of the time as some other idlers. In the winter he used to sit next to the burning oven, his hands behind his back or they were tucked in the long sleeves of his coat. He sat next to the small table that was placed near the stove and the Talmud book open.

He was a book binder but not terribly successful. He was a crude worker and used primitive binding materials that stained the pages or threads that were visible to the naked eye.

He had many jobs but little income. He also sold books, religious articles and haberdashery items. Every Friday he and his wife Ita Neche opened their stand at the market. On occasion he even traveled to other markets nearby.

He always begrudged the book salesmen that came from other cities and sold their merchandise in Jaslo. He considered them to be competitors that cut into his business. He observed with anger as the city residents approached these merchants. In general however, he was a pleasant man and the students at the study center liked to hear his opinions on different matters since he considered himself a scholar, a businessman and a fine binder.

[Page 120]

In spite of the numerous complaints about the foreign competition, he sold many books. I personally bought books from him and a large part of my library was purchased in his stand. I also gave him many books to rebind and some of these were from the study center. When I bought the Talmud edition in 1928 for the study center and wanted that he should rebind it, however the membership decided otherwise and gave the job to Shlomo Goldfaden. He did not protest since he knew that he could not do the job.

He lived all his life in the wooden barrack. He never wore glasses and was always healthy. On returning one evening from the study center, he went to sleep and passed away. He left a wife, a son and a daughter.

Awraham Hersh Brenner

He was born in Dembice and was the son in law of Rabbi Yona Tzanger that was Rabbi of Jaslo. He did not assume airs or behave with arrogance; on the contrary, his manners were simple. He told stories about the Hassidic saints of Dzikow, Rozwadow, and especially of the Rabbi of Dembice.

Following the resignation of Asher the sexton he assumed the position at the study center that lasted almost twenty years.

Lately his economic situation improved as a result of his business dealings and he resigned his position. He always lived in the Amer and Kornfeld house. He had five daughters and two sons. Two of his daughters left for the USA, and one son left for Belgium.

Yona Brenner
He was the oldest son of Awraham Hersh Brenner and was a member of study group at the study center. He studied tailoring and returned to Jaslo in 1918 where he opened his workshop that employed many workers and trained many religious workers to be tailors. He left for Antwerp.

[Page 121]
Eliezer Brenner
He was born in Pezatzlew and was the son in law of Dawid Elias. He was well read and an excellent businessman. He had a large house and a big store where he sold timber. The place was located near the Ulaszowice Bridge.

Two of his sons received higher education; one Mendel became a lawyer and practiced law in Krosno. The second son Abish reached Israel and settled in Jaffa.

Henryk Brenner
He was the owner of a store that sold books and office supplies. It was located in Dr. Willush's place in the market. Lately, he kept open his business on Saturday in spite of the protests of some religious Jews.

He was of an assimilationist inclination but he still kept an active interest in the Jewish community. His wife was very active in the Zionist movement, in " Wizo" and in other social Jewish organizations.

He had two daughters and a son that received a general education and continued their studies, The son was killed trying to escape the Germans by crossing the river.

Wolf Brandstadter
He was one of the early settlers in the city and one of the richest property owners. He owned a private bank as well as a large knitting store. The store was located in his house on the corner of Florianska Street opposite the municipal building, prior to World War I. He was not a religious person and was a descendant of Mordechai Dawid Brandstadter from Tarnow. We are told that he avoided all public contact in order to avoid giving charity.

There was a story that circulated in the city to the effect that a poor person once came to his store to ask for a donation. The owner dismissed him and even insulted him. The poor man left and wished him a "Zakana". The owner was under the impression that he received a blessing and rushed to the door where he asked the beggar why did you bless me when I refused to give you a donation. The poor man answered, you are an educated man that avoids giving contributions so you should also know the meanings of the initials of the word Zakana: Ziftzen-to sigh, krechtzen-to groan, Nissen-to sneeze, and Hissen- to caugh. The store owner understood the meaning of the word and felt a bit humiliated but still gave the poor man a donation.

He had one son that was married to the daughter of Shingel from Sczenica. He lived in Dantzig and had a private bank.

Dawid Berenstein

He was a progressive man. He was a violin teacher and also played at weddings. He was also an accountant. He lived in Targowice and later moved near the post office. His sons received a general education. His son Moshe excelled in music and left Jaslo for Krakow.

His old mother used to live opposite the synagogue and gave Yiddish lessons. She lived to a ripe old age.

Yehoshua Bresman

He resided in Jarniowka near Koczerow and was traditional. He led a simple farmer's life. He had a small farm and was also involved in business. Two of his sons are in the USA. One is named Awraham and the second one Itzhak

Yossef Berkowicz

He was a barber. He was the son in law of Yaakow Bruder. He was a pleasant and kind person. He was progressive in outlook. Following his discharge from the Austrian Army, he became ill and passed away. He left a wife and small children. The widow remarried another barber. The children left Jaslo as they became older.

[Page 123]

Gimel ג

Elimelech Gutwin

Polish Independence brought with it a wave of pogroms and anti-Jewish riots that forced many Jews to leave their homes, especially in rural areas. Elimelech Gutwin or as he was called "uncle Elimelech" was no exception and forced to leave his residence in Omshitz village near Targowice. He lived there for thirty years and left for Jaslo where he started everything anew.

He was a wise and careful man that explained to everybody his opinions. He was happy with his lot and expressed it in his talks. As a Hassidic follower of the Rabbi of Dzikow, he visited the Rabbi frequently in order to be inspired. He always used to preface his sayings by the expression: In the name of the Rabbi that gave him the opportunity to repeat or introduce something that he heard the Rabbi state. Of course, this enabled him also to describe the customs and ways of the rabbi.

He opened an inn in the Targowice with his arrival to Jaslo. The atmosphere of the place was very homey. His wife Towa, a modest and observant woman gave birth to four sons and four daughters. All the children received a traditional education. The oldest son Awraham left Jaslo for the USA prior to World War I. He enlisted in the Jewish legion and fought in Palestine in World War I. With the end of the war he returned to the USA. The second son Shmuel Leib, very likeable person, settled in Zmigrod following his marriage. The third son, Eliezer, left Jaslo and settled in Germany, later he moved to Palestine and settled in Haifa where he was a member of the "Shahar" cooperative. The youngest son, Nathan, run a tailor workshop. The oldest daughter was married to Gedalia Lefelholtz, a student at the study enter of Dukla. The second daughter, Tzirel, settled in Krakow following her marriage. The third daughter married Eliezer Gisser. The fourth daughter, Nechi, owned a workshop for underwear.

Moshe Nathan Gutwin

He headed the Hassidic group in the city. He was the son of reb Asher Gad Gutwin of Korczyna near Krosno who was the son of the Hassid Yaakow Itzhak. He was very familiar with the Talmud and Talmudic literature.
[Page 124]
Yaakow Yitzhak had five sons; Zeew was the oldest and was the ritual slaughterer for Trzicina. Gad Eliyahu who claimed to have had 'contact with Eliyahu', Aaron the preacher of Korczyna

Yehiel Michael of Sandz also called Mechel the white one on account of the white long beard. The fifth was the above named Elimelech. (One daughter Channah Liba was married to Pinhas Dim in Krakow a scholar and a Hassid of Belz. The second one Sarah was married to Naphtali Hertz of Frysztak)

Gad Asher the father of Moshe Nathan was known for his honesty and correctness. He was always involved in communal affairs and was the collector for the fund of Rabbi Meir Baal Haness charity organization. He held this position for life. As a sign of respect and affection he was nicknamed reb Gdali. He expressed the highest form of charity and devotion to social causes. He fasted on Mondays and Thursdays and never ate before midday.

According to his story, the prophet Eliyahu came to him in a dream and offered him a bag of gold coins so that he will be able to concentrate in his studies without the need to worry about an income. However GadAsher refused to accept insisting that he can only accept money that he earned himself. He reached a very ripe old age and on the holiest day of the year in 1938 standing on the bima platform where the torah is read, after reciting the " "neila " prayer, he set his arm on the table and then rested his head on the arm and thus passed away.

His wife Sarah was modest and noble. She was one of the pious women in the city. She was the daughter of Nathan Rozner who was killed in Hungary by robbers while on a wine business trip. He was still a young merchant. He was descendant of Rabbi Eliezer Lippa, the father of the saints Rabbi Elimelech of Lejansk and Rabbi Zishe of Honipoli. Prior to the marriage, she paid a visit to the Sandzer Rabbi, Rabbi Chaim. He stood up and walked towards her. He tended her a gold coin as befits "Doron Drisha" an important person in Israel.

He was called in the city, Moshe Gitche's on behalf of his wife's name Gitche. She was an excellent business woman. He hardly spoke and let his wife manage the finances. He was a friend of Rabbi Mandil and prayed at the study center.

He had a shop in the market and was considered well to do. He had four daughters; Esther, Reisil, Leah, and Tzirel. They were all raised in the traditional way. The youngest son was named Dudel,

[Page 125]

The first daughter married Yaakow Shturech from Gorlice. The second daughter married Itzhak Sheingut from Sandz. And the third daughter married M. Shendorf from Krenica. The husband of the fourth daughter is unknown to us. Who did not envy Moshe Nathan as he walked with his son in laws dressed with "Shtreimelech and silk capotes" to the synagogue on Saturdays and Holidays. This was a pure delight watching the group walking. The Germans took care of this for they were all killed. Gitche was killed on the way to the cemetery for she could not keep pace with the column. She fell to the ground covered with blood.

Ben Tzion Hacohen, Gutwirt

His name alone gives the party some deserved credit for he was the symbol of dedication to study, self deprivation to the end degree, and a great deal of naïveté in the positive sense. All these contradictory elements managed to coexist within this personality. All these descriptions fitted him and he could have served as a role model for each of these characteristics.

He studied in various Yeshivas especially in Unsdorf in Hungary. He concentrated on his studies until he married. He was considered an exceptional student and was also a good looking fellow.

On reaching Jaslo following his marriage, he was assigned a seat near the western wall downstairs in the study center. He prayed standing facing the wall. He prayed with great dedication and concentration as though he committed many sins.

He was a first rate Talmudic scholar and continued his studies day and night. The father in law, Elimelech Bikowsky provided all the expenses.

Throughout life he regretted the fact that he was supported by others namely his in laws. When his first son was born he stated that he would like to support himself. Indeed, he started to

produce paper bags for various stores and also sold wrapping paper. The business did not last long for he had difficulty concentrating on business matters and the ethics involved in commerce. He changed jobs and began to teach at the Talmud torah the older students.
He lived at the house of Rachel Margolies near the study center.

[Page 126]
S. Gottlieb, doctor.
He was a well known attorney. He was a serious personality in the city and was a devoted Zionist that contributed to Zionist causes. He represented legally the firm "Gartenberg at Shreier". He had a son and a daughter that received an academic education. He lived on Koscuiszko Street.

Zalman Gottlieb
He was a well mannered person and extremely polite. He came from Eastern Galicia and settled in Jaslo in the twenties following his marriage to the Rosentzweig widow, daughter of Wolf Eintziger. They made a nice living from their grocery store in the market square.

Yehoshua Gottfreund
He was the brother of Chaim Gotfreund. He left London where he resided for a number of years to return to Jaslo. He was an insurance agent for chemical Laundromats, the owner of a soda kiosk at the corner of Skola and Kosciuszko Streets, and was also a matchmaker. He barely made a living from all these occupations.

Chaim Gottfreund
He was the son in law of Liebe Citronenbaum. He opened a pub in moving to Jaslo. The pub was located in A. Goldstein's house. He was the leading figure of the local followers of the Rabbi of Bobowa. He assumed a position of Hassidic leader and tried to teach everybody about Hassidism and everything else. Still he was a pleasant person and managed to get along with everybody. He was a steady member of the daily group that studied a page of the Talmud and prayed at the study center of the Rabbi. He also liked to conduct services. He had sons that were raised in the traditional Hassidic manner.

Nathan Gewirtz
He was a Hebrew teacher that taught young children the rudiments of Hebrew prayers. He was deeply immersed in Hebrew literature and insisted on adhering to Hebrew grammar. He also stressed the need to enounce the Hebrew words when praying before the congregation. He showed everybody the codex book that stressed that the leader of the services must pronounce the words correctly and stress the rhythm of the sentence and the words. This was a problem since few people were familiar with Hebrew phonetics.
With Polish independence, he left in the twenties Jaslo for the USA where his sons had established their residence years ago, namely prior to World War I.

[Page 127]
Asher (Shamesh) Gold
He was the first beadle of the great study center. He had three sons and six daughters. His oldest son was a fine Talmudic student and later studied with Rabbi Shlomo of Bobow. One of his son in laws lives in Tel Aviv.

Leibish Goldblat

He was the son in law of Ephraim Brick. He was a moderate person with a fine head on his shoulders. He was a refined and kind torah person. He was considered to be a leading merchant of Jaslo. He lived all his life in his own house near the Ulaszowice Bridge and his timber warehouse.

He had six daughters that received a general education. One of his daughters managed to survive and reach Palestine

Chaim Goldblat
He was a brother of Leibish Goldblat. He lived in Siobniow

Adolph Goldner
In the twenties he returned to Jaslo and opened an elegant store. The store was located in Dr. Willush's house on Kosciuszko Street. The store catered to the latest fashions.

He was a modern person and dedicated to his business. He was very successful and built up the store where he received the well to do clients.

[Page 128]
Itzhak Meir Goldfaden
This was a Hassidic family that could serve as an example of a fine religious family in Jaslo. He was a very religious Jew and followed the precepts of the rabbi of Bobow. His entire household followed his example. The children received a religious Hassidic education and dressed in the rabbinical garb in imitation of the rabbinical children. He prayed with other Hassidim of Bobow at the study center of Rabbi Mandil and was a close follower of the latter.

He lived in his private house on Nowa Street and had a fine income. Only one son named Nachman managed to survive the war and reach Palestine. Five sons and a daughter perished in the shoa.

Michael Goldfluss
He was an influential person in the city. He was an old Zionist and considered one of the richest men in town. He owned a flour mill near the railway station where he employed a number of Jewish workers.

Elimelech Goldstein
He was one of the people that established the pattern of Jewish behavior in the city of Jaslo. He was born in Dembice to a Hassidic family of well to do standing. He received a good religious education but also managed to acquire contemporary manners since he dealt with estate owners, princes and feudal lords. With time he became very wealthy and purchased all the land along the Wisloka River near the Ulaszowica Bridge. He also purchased the house that he lived in opposite the district court house of Jaslo. He continued to amass real estate and opened a private bank. He dealt in real estate on a large scale. He also found time to study and to devote time to the communal affairs. He was active in building the study center and later the synagogue where he became a beadle. He was also elected to the municipality and to the community board.

While presiding as beadle of the synagogue, he managed to antagonize a good part of the worshippers when he decided to distribute the "kaphot" on Simhat Torah amongst the poor worshippers.

[Page 129]
On Saturdays and holidays he wore a wide shtreimel sobol and in the winter he wore an expensive silk fur hat. He had four sons and three daughters. One son left Jaslo for Venezuela prior to World War I where he worked for an oil company. The second son Yossef worked with his father. He was an early Zionist and had a fine education.

Benyamin Goldstein

He was the oldest son of Elimelech Goldstein. He was familiar with religious literature. He was well mannered and presentable. He was a Zionist in his youth and became the leader of them in Jaslo. He was also elected to the kehilla board on the Zionist ticket and later also served as the head of the Jewish community.

Until 1914 he wore a shtreimel and silk traditional clothing. He dealt with real estate and forests. He was partner to wood mill and exported timber. The children received a traditional education and continued their studies.

Wolf Goldschlag

He was one of the partners of the oil distillery "Gertenberg and Shreier. He was a modern person and actually managed the refinery until World War II.

One of his sons fell with the Polish Legion during World War I. His second son, Ludwig managed to escape to Australia where he was sick and died.

Maurice Goldschlag

He worked as a salesman for the refinery and with the outbreak of World War II; he managed to reach Lemebrg where the Germans killed him

Tzwi Goldschmidt

He was a tall erect man with a black beard. He was very active in the "Yad Harutzim" Association. He headed the organization for many years. He was the son in law of Mordechai (a very observant and pious Jew that descending to the mikvah fell and several days later passed away).

[Page 130]

Following the destruction of the synagogue of the "Yad Harutzim" association by the Russians during World War I, he was the driving force in rebuilding the place. Indeed the synagogue was rebuilt and he took care of all the details.

I remember how he dragged wood and coal during the harsh winter of 1928 to provide the necessary heat for the synagogue. He was overjoyed when he saw new faces in the synagogue during these bitter cold days.

He was a partner of a small plant to produce brooms and made a nice income. He had two sons and three daughters. His oldest son, Israel was killed in 1921 in Budapest during the Bela Kuhn revolution.

The second son, Moshe headed the "Shomer Hatzair" organization in Jaslo. He later left as pioneer for Palestine and eventually settled in el Aviv. The oldest daughter Esther is in the USA and is very active in the field of social work. She is also active in the Jaslo landesmanshaft in New York. The second daughter married was married to Benyamin Denner in Jaslo.

Mendel Gorgel

He was a simple and quiet Jew. He was the son in law of Nute Maltz. He conducted business and was also a partner in a soap factory. He lived all his life in the house of Feiwil Klinman in the market square.

He died relatively young following a prolonged disease and left a widow and children. His oldest son Yerucham started to work and the second son Shamai was finishing dental school. He later left in the twenties for the USA.

Elazar Guzik

He lived all his life along the Kowalowy road and was a merchant. He was known as a kind and modest person and kept the Jewish traditions along the orthodox manner. He came on Saturdays to the study center of the rabbi,

[Page 131]

He had several sons that received a traditional upbringing. Some of his sons left Jaslo for the USA in the twenties following Polish Independence. His wife was tragically killed by a car. His daughter was married to Nathan Rosenzweig and they both reached the shores of the land of Israel where they settled in kibbutz Dan.

Wolf Gintzig

His was one of the families that left Gorlice during World War I and remained in Jaslo. He was a very religious Jew and was well acquainted with the Talmud. He was a modest and quiet person. He was one of the first to join the *Beit Ha'midrash* of the Rabbi and was a devotee of Rabbi Mandil. Each day he prayed at the *Beit Ha'midrash*.

He lived in the house of Berish Altman on Kosciuszko Street and was a merchant. His sons received a religious education. The younger children were members of the Mizrahi Hatzair movement- or youth movement of the Mizrahi movement.

P. Gisser

He was a modest person. He was a tailor and lived all his life at the Targowica. He was drafted to the Austrian Army during World War 1and following his discharge became ill. The sickness progressed and caused is death. He left a wife and son named Eliezer. The financial situation in the house was very poor but with time, Eliezer started to help out by working and the situation improved. They opened a business of clothing and things picked up. Eliezer was a member of the young mizrahi movement and was very active.

Leibish Glassman

He owned a carpentry shop along Tzickiego Street near the public garden. He was a religious person but tended to follow the modern trend of life. He was active in the Yad Harutzim movement. He was involved in the life of the community and was very active prior to elections. He defended the interests of the Jewish population. He gave charity generously to individuals and organizations. He lived in a simple apartment and was content with the simple life.

I. Glassman

He lived for years in Koblow and was busy trading. Lately he left the place.

Shimshon Glazer

Very few people in Jaslo knew his true name, he was known as Shimshon-la Hebrew teacher. He was one of the old elementary teachers in Jaslo. Hundreds of mall children passed through his classroom in spite f the fact that he had a speech impediment that prevented him from speaking clearly. Still he taught the alphabet and punctuation and stressed Hebrew phonics. His problems were known and still he was a very good teacher. He traveled every year to the Carlsbad spa to recuperate mentally and physically from the strain.

He lived most of his lie on Chajnochy in a wooden barrack opposite the Talmud torah. In the thirties he moved to a private house that he bought on Iglena Street. He began to write a torah scroll and finished writing it on the eve of Hoshana Rabba in 1933. The same evening he was escorted to the study center under a canopy with chants.

P. Glicher

He was originally from Korczyna and settled in Jaslo in the twenties following his marriage to the widow of Shmuel Stillman. He was a modern person but kept distance from people and was practically unknown.

Yehoshua Geller

He was an enlightened person. He was the accountant for the timber saw mill firm of Sh.Z. Wistrich. His children received a general education and continued their studies.

His daughter Adzia worked in the pharmacy Pod Gwizdon on Kosciuszko Street and she was considerate a beautiful girl. One day she suddenly took ill and passed away a few weeks after she became engaged to be married. The event shook the community especially the people that knew her. Her family suffered greatly since they could not accept the bitter fate that was dealt them.

[Page 133]
Shlomo Geminder

He was one of the active members of Yad Harutzim, Bikur Holim and other social organizations. He was one of the first Zionists in the city. He was the owner of the broom factory that was very successful. Many years he lived in the house of Eliezer Brenner near the Ulaszowice Bridge and later moved to the house of Elimelech Krisher on Asnika Street. His oldest daughter married a yeshiva student named Rachmil from Tarnow. They later left for Palestine and settled in Tel Aviv. Lately they opened a delicatessen store. The second daughter married Leibish Raab and they lived in Tarnow. Following World War II, their son Arieh managed to reach Israel and works for the electric company (his granddaughter Shoshana Rachmil is a famous singer in Israel)

Baruch Ganger

He was one of the elderly Hassidim of Bobow. He was born in Bobow and visited the house of Rabbi Shlomele and remained loyal to the dynasty of Bobow. His sons followed in his footsteps and did not budge from the main line.

He was known to enjoy comedy and interlaced jokes in his conversations. In the worst moments of his life he would interject some joke or comical comment that would end the sadness and self pity of the moment.

Most of his life he lived in the house of Feiwil Klinman in the market square. He had a shop and sold merchandise. He died suddenly in his elder years and left two sons; one lived in Jaslo and the second one in Piwniczna near Krenica. He also had two daughters; one lived in Berlin and the second one married Eliezer Bransdorfer that resided some time in Jaslo and then moved to Milowka where he was accepted a s ritual slaughterer (the son of the above named married Bronka Ingber from Jaslo and they live in Tel Aviv).

Yehoshua Ganger

He was the son of Baruch Ganger. He was a serious minded individual with set ideas. He was a tall person and had distinguished features. He sold manufactured items in the square market near the municipality. He loved to dress in the manner of the rich people but avoided public recognition. He observed Jewish religious laws and raised his children in his footsteps. Like his father, he too was a follower of Bobow. He was a steady member of the study center of the Rabbi and a loyal supporter.

[Page 134]
He had two sons; Yehezkel and Yossef. The latter one was a member of the young mizrahi movement and presently resides in the USA. He also had two daughters; the older one married a yeshiva student named Li. Kaplener. He was a strong Talmudic student and was also able to lead the congregation in services. Lately he lived in Jaslo and was involved in business. The

second daughter Bronka was married to Pinhas Shtrum. During World War II she remained with a daughter and a son in Jaslo and perished in the Jaslo ghetto.

Aaron Dawid Ganz
He was one of the oldest Jewish resident in the city and owned the only Jewish fish store in town. He had a special place near the river under the Ulaszowice Bridge where he kept his fish. He kept the place until World War I. He was a pleasant person and tried to satisfy his customers. His two sons worked as painters and one of them Naphtali left for the USA prior to World War I.

Israel Ganz
He was the son of Aaron Dawid Ganz and he was a painter. He was a member of the Yad Harutzim association and also a member of the Zionist movement. He was elected to the community board on the workshop owners ticket. Often he abandoned his business in order to tend to municipal or communal affairs or parliamentary elections. During these activities he was full of anger and fury and defended the rights of the workshop owners and workers to best of his ability.

Mordechai Getzler
He was one of the old timers and a scholar in Jaslo. The city benefited immensely by his presence and his ideas. He was born in Zmigrod and left it with the development of Jaslo. He bought a wooden barrack on Chajnochy Street that will serve him as residence for life.
[Page 135]
According to my memory, there was a wooden barrack that stood at the lower range of the hill between the Talmud torah and the synagogue near the house of the rabbi and the study center. Four wooden steps led from the street to the barrack. The steps were always shaky and had the impression that with each step they will give away and the person will fall into the mud.(Most of the year, Chajnochy street was covered with mud and any person that walked on it had mud on his legs that sometimes passed the ankles). For many years he rented part of the barrack as a synagogue or as a study center.
With his passing away at an old age, he left behind five sons and three daughters. Two of his sons and two of his daughters lived in the city. Dawid was the oldest and lived in Tarnow where he was an esteemed member of the community. He was one of the bigger merchants of herrings and marinated fish. He gave his sons a traditional and general education. His second son Yehoshua was educated and made a nice impression. He resided in Lemberg and was well established within the community. Wolf was the third son and lived in Tarnow. He was very active in community affairs as well as a devoted follower of the mizrahi movement. He was a paper wholesaler but gave priority to the Zionist cause and frequently left his business to tour the area in order to spread religious Zionism. His campaigns led him to fight the orthodox world and made an impression on the listeners.
He was a steady worshipper at the Sandzer kloiz- or small Sandzer synagogue in Tarnow where he led a vociferous Zionist campaign amongst the worshippers. He hoped to lead them to accept the new movement as a revelation for the Jew in exile. But he was disappointed for his efforts did not succeed and he left the kloiz.
Wolf Getzler combined the torah spirit and the general spirit. His house served as a meeting place, especially for mizrahi people. He was very friendly and in the thirties visited Palestine and considered to settle there but the plans did not fulfill themselves in time and the Germans cancelled all further plans. (While writing these lines I am informed that one educated son and a daughter survived the war and reached Palestine,)

[Page 136]
Yossef Getzler and Moshe and Meir Getzler

While the older children Dawid, Yehoshua and Wolf were ambitious and enterprising businessman and civic minded leaders, the younger children were the complete opposite. However they were excellent students and they received a reputation as potential scholars. Indeed they continued with their studies and acquired mastery in Talmudic scholarship; they refused public receptions but dedicated themselves to study.

Moshe Meir Getzler did not hide his Zionist sympathies in spite of the fact the he was a very pious person. He lectured on the Talmud at the young mizrahi movement center for years in the city. They lived with their parents and helped in the paper business.

Moshe Meir Getzler

He settled in the twenties in Jaslo. He was a native of Zmigrod. He was well read in Jewish and general knowledge. In spite of his modern outlook, he was a regular member of the Rabbi's minyan and a steady visitor to his home.

He opened a chocolate and fruit store in Jaslo along May 3rd street. His wife tended to the store and he was busy exchanging foreign monies and discount notes. He succeeded well for he was soon considered a well to do person in the city and in the thirties he bought a section of Leib Amer's lot on Kosciuszko Street and then build a three story house on the plot.

I met him on several occasions and tried to influence him towards Zionism or rather to invest in Palestine some of his monies but to no avail. On the contrary, he tried to convince me to abandon the idea of Zionism. I remember we once walked for some time and he asked me why I hesitate to move to Palestine. He then explained to me that Jewish life goes on even in Jaslo in spite of the fact that it is part of the exile. Furthermore, life was worth living even in Jaslo. One did not have to live in Palestine to enjoy Jewish living; this goal could be achieved in exile. My reply to him was that indeed Jewish life continues in the exile but it is still part of the non- Jewish world. One never knows when the wheel will turn and the Jew will lose his footing, for our senses have not yet developed a scale for measuring rapid changes. True we study torah here but it is the torah of exile. To fulfill the commandments in accordance with the torah we must live in the holy land amongst the Jewish people. Only this environment can grant us the spiritual freedom that is needed to fulfill the command.

I do not know whether he was influenced by my points but the fact remains that he used young pioneers from Jaslo in the construction of his home in Jaslo. Apparently, he was moved by some of my points.

With the outbreak of World War II, he managed to reach Lemebrg with his family and then continued to Russia where he became ill and died. A son of his also died there. (I heard that his wife survived the war and reached Europe)

Dawid Gerber

He settled in Jaslo following Polish independence. He opened a bakery on Korlewski Street. His bread soon received an excellent name and he was a very successful. He acquired many properties.

Yaakow Grabshrift

He was an enlightened and moderate person. He worshipped at the great synagogue. He provided his children with a higher education. He was an old hand at real estate especially forested areas. He lived on the way to the railway.

Herman Grabeshrift

He was the son of Yaakow Gerbertshrift. He was a dentist. He was a Zionist from his youth and was devoted to the cause. He was a pleasant person.

Yaakow Grubtuch

He was the son in law of Mendel Kinstler and was native to the city of Tarnow. He was an engineer and served in the Austrian army during World War I as an officer. After his marriage in 12919, he settled in Jaslo and was active in commerce. He was a member of the Zionist movement and with the purchase of the farm in Kraiowicz, devoted to pioneer training, he became very involved in the project. With the outbreak of World War II, he and his son managed to reach Palestine. His wife died in the ghetto of Jaslo with many other Jews. His son continued his studies and then left for Australia where he has a respected position at one of the universities in Melbourne.

[Page 138]

Mendel Gross

He was an old timer in Jaslo. He was a religious and smart Jew. He loved to express his political views on municipal matters and was keenly aware of the political situation in the country.

He had a store that sold kitchen ware and wooden furniture. His store specialized in woven baskets and suitcases. He lived all his life in his house on Korlowski Street. He had three sons and three daughters who received a general education. One of his sons finished the school of commerce and settled in Krakow. Two of his daughters reside in Israel and one in the USA.

Leib (Leon) Gross

He was the son in law Yaakow Kalb. He was a modern Jew and dealt in timber. His sons received a higher education and were members of the Zionist movement.

Ignac Gertenberg

He was one of the partners of the oil refinery named Gertenberg and Shreier" in Niglowic. With the out break of World War II he managed to reach Ankara in Turkey where he fell ill and died.

Dawid Grin

I have my doubts whether most of the Jews of Jaslo knew his name. He was known as Dawid Gorlicer since he came from Gorlice. He was also known by several other nicknames namely ' the star gazer", the numerical man, and the distributor of notes for Sabbath for every eve of Sabbath he made the rounds of the city and distributed leaflets announcing the schedules of candle lighting. He was very familiar with the Jewish calendar and Jewish dates of configuration of high holidays. He remembered the memorial day of each person that passed away in Jaslo and so informed the parties in advance. He even notified people years in advance when the actual date of the Memorial Day will be in any given year according to the Jewish or Gregorian calendar. All these calculations were done instantly.

It is a pity that this mathematical wizard did not put his ability to better use for with all his knowledge about stars and astrological symbols he personally had little luck. He was always poor and depressed. An occasional drink helped soften his bitterness.

Yossef Grinfeld

The residents of Jaslo called him Yossef Dukler for he came from the shtetl of Dukla He was a follower of the Rabbi of Dukla. He gave his son a very religious education in the Bobow tradition. His son was a devoted student. Also his daughters received a traditional religious education and attended various "Bnot Yaakow" religious schools for girls that were established by the Agudath Israel.

He was a poor tailor but loved to involve himself in communal affairs in order to show off. He was a member of the 'Hevra Kadisha and other societies.

Yehoshua Grinfeld

He was the son in law of Yekil Kalb who also came from Dukla. He was well read, tall and had a yellowish sparse beard that covered his face. He leaned to the Bobower Hassidic court and visited the Rabbi on occasions. He prayed together with his father in law at the study center of Rabbi Mandil. He had a haberdashery store on Floriasnska Street

Tzwi Hersh Grinshpan
He worked together with his brother in law Moshe Fass passed the road to the sport stadium. They had a big warehouse of fertilizers that emitted terrible odors. The place was far from their residence and they were far from the city thus they were hardly known. They made nice living

Gernik family
The family lived in Pszedmishce. They left Jaslo with the outbreak of the World War I.

[Page 140]

Dalet ד

Dawid, (Edmond) Domb
He was an educated and enlightened person. He came from Rymanow and worked as a cashier at Menashe Margolies' place, whose father was Adolph Margolies. He was an old time Zionist and was highly respected in the commercial milieu. The store carried a large selection of agricultural implements namely harvesters, plows, containers for building materials and was located along Kochanowski Street at the edge of Kosciuszko Street. There was also a store that sold metal products and household goods at the market.

He had three sons that were the first to join the Zionist movement in the city of Jaslo. They organized the local scout Shomer Hatzair branch in Jaslo and later devoted themselves to the organization. They finished high school and continued their studies. The oldest finished medical school and became well known doctor in Jaslo

P. Domb
He was the brother of Dawid Domb and was a tinsmith. He lived in the house of Elimelech Goldstein near the bridge. He led a simple life. Following Polish Independence, he left Jaslo with his family and headed for Belgium.

Michael. Dorsht
He was a very pious Jew and the son in law of Berish Altman. He came from Gorlice and worshipped steadily at the study center of Rabbi Mandil. He lived all his life on Florianska Street where he had a small grocery.

Lately he expanded his business and became a wholesaler. Rumors had it that he received an inheritance from overseas, apparently the USA. He indeed became a wealthy person. He had one son and a daughter.

[Page 141]
Chaim, Diller
This personality influenced the life of the Jewish community for almost fifty years. He behaved in a patriarchal and respectful manner

He was born in Zatur near Krakow to a family of rabbis and the grand son of the head of the judicial council of Zatur. He started his studies in the heder as was the custom in those days, and later studied at the kloiz and at the Presburg Yeshiva.

Reb Chaim Diller

He presented himself as an external student and received the certificate to teach Jewish studies at the high school and other governmental schools in Jaslo, The Polish government bestowed this certificate on him in 1908 .

[Page 142]

He represented a fine synthesis between Jewish and general education namely quotes from the "Maharasha", answers from Akiva Iger and the Hatam Sofer on one hand and the poems of Kochanowski, Mickewicz, Schiller and Heine on the other hand. His knowledge and fluency were extraordinary and flowed with ease.

As a teacher in the school system, he of course prepared his work for the day but at the same time did not neglect his religious studies and one could always find on his desk Talmudic books or commentaries.

He was the head of the "Talmud Torah" until World War I and was also involved in other social organizations. With the outbreak of the war, he was drafted as a military chaplain and devoted himself to the soldiers needs. He was taken prisoner by the Russians in the attack on Przemysl.

(In his absence from Jaslo, his position was assumed by the religious teachers Hoffman and Tratkower). With the signing of a truce between Russia and Austria, the prisoners of war were exchanged and Rabbi Chaim Diller came back and assumed his previous position. He continued to teach as he did before the war.

He helped greatly the mizrahi movement in the organization of the branch. He gave lectures to the members on current events, and the Talmud. He urged the creation of Hebrew schools and was one of the first to join the "Mizrahi" synagogue.

Suddenly, Rabbi Chaim Diller passed away. He suffered a heart attack on the night of Purim in 1932. Almost the entire Jewish population escorted the funerary cortège to pay their final respect to the man. He was carried to the "Mizrahi" synagogue where he laid in state for a while, no eulogies due to the holiday. But one close sympathizer, Yossef Frumowicz, could not restrain himself since he was emotionally affected by the tragedy, burst out by making a very touchy statement namely; "Look and see if there is a pain that is more painful to the one that we just received". The emotional outburst affected all those present at the funereal.

He left a wife, three daughters and a son. They all received a general education and continued their studies. One daughter left for Palestine as a pioneer in the thirties and lives in Hertzlia, Another daughter escaped the ghetto and managed to survive. She presently teaches at women teacher seminary in Tel Aviv. The son Israel works with the Jewish Agency as an engineer. The youngest daughter lives next to Ramat Itzhak.

[Page 143]
Eisik, Ditenfas
He was one of the great Talmudic scholars in Jaslo. He really understood the religious texts. He was a religious extremist and was involved in charity work but foremost he was the speaker of the most extreme religious followers. He was one of the heads of the "Agudath Israel" and a founding member of the local branch in Jaslo. He conducted for years the daily lectures for the members of the synagogue. He was a member of the community board representing the religious voters and was an official of the Hevra Kadisha and other organizations.

He was a closed friend of the Rabbi and a regular worshipper at his study center. He lived in Kornfeld and Amer's house along Kazimierz Street where he had a small grocery store. He did not have sons but adopted Yaakow Gorgal.

Moshe, Dam
He was a very nice and decent person. He lived in the Targowice and had a butcher store that provided him with a nice income. Prior to World War I he fell ill and never recovered. He died and left a wife and two sons; Nathan Awraham and Yehoshua. Both sons continued their religious studies at the study center. He also had four daughters. His first son in law was Meir Berger. The family dealt in geese and their oil especially in the winter. One of the daughters was very talented and drew models.

Zeew, Damask
He was a Hassid but enlightened with broad visions. He was a member of the Mizrahi and a regular worshipper at their service. He had many plans regarding settling in Palestine but they remained wishful dreams for he never implemented them.

He lived with his father in law Awraham Amer on Florianska Street. He was a partner to the soap factory. His only son was a member of the Zionist youth organization. He finished medical school and did his medical stage at the Jaslo hospital.

[Page 144]
Israel, Dan
He was a quiet introverted Jew. He was straight and honest in dealing with people. He tried to observe punctually all the commandments. He insisted on buying every year the honor of raising and dressing the torah after reading the section of Genesis on Shabbat at the big synagogue. He was a merchant and lived all his life in Hiclowka

Dawid, Denner
He owned a butcher store on Iglena Street. He was very religious and observant. He was also known to give charity. He was one of the first Hassidim of the Rabbi of Dukla,

He lived all his life in his own house next to the great study center. His place was surrounded with a large tract of land. A section of this plot was purchased by the Hassidim of the Dukler Rabbi and they built a home and a study center for the Rabbi on it.

Benyamin, Denner

He was the son of Benyamin Denner. In his youth, he was a member of the Poalei Tzion. He was smart and familiar with the surroundings and gave easily charity. He married Tzwi Goldstein's daughter.

He devoted himself to Yad Harutzim and was very familiar with municipal politics. He was elected to the community board by the Yad Harutzim members. He remained a member of the board until World War II when the Jewish community was destroyed

Shmuel, Der

He arrived to Jaslo with the Polish Independence. He opened a bakery and a cake place in the red house near the "Betuniarnia" not far from the Ulaszowice Bridge. But the business did not succeed and the family left for Antwerp.

Mordechai, Dranger

He was a well known personality amongst the religious and general population. He was a sympathetic individual at home with the general intelligentsia. He was very influential in Jewish life. He never forcefully imposed his views but discussed and debated in a gentle way his opinions. He was a follower of the Tchortkower Hassidic court. He gave charity and dressed impeccably as befits a scholar.

[Page 145]

He lived on Kosciuszko in the house of Dawid Wilchport. His haberdashery was neatly and tastily arranged. The color arrangement between of white the inside the store and the outside where the expensive latest style items were on display and the various perfumes were his specialty. He attracted a well to do clientele with fixed prices and special individual care. He was very successful.

But is man protected for ever and from everything? Can man live for ever happy in his wealth? The answer is obviously no in the case of Mordechai Drenger. He took ill in the morning and was immediately advised by the local doctors to travel to Krakow to visit medical specialists.

At that time Poland was undergoing a turmoil of pogroms and military riots that affected the mood of the population. Still the people of Jaslo were concerned about the fate of Mordechai Drenger. His situation deteriorated from day to day and the people of Jaslo became alarmed by the progression of the disease. The medical specialists gave no hope; he finally passed away and the city went into deep mourning.

He left a wife and three sons and two daughters. Elchanan was the oldest son and he left Jaslo for France where he settled in Lille. The second son Yaakow was an excellent student at the study center but decided to leave for Wilno to study general studies but later left Poland and settled in Paris, France. The third son Menashe left Jaslo for Palestine as a pioneer and settled in Haifa. The youngest daughter also left Palestine as a pioneer and also settled in Haifa. The oldest daughter died in the ghetto of Jaslo.

[Page 146]

Hey ה

Dawid Halbershtam, Rabbi
He was the groom of the Rabbi of Jaslo, see origins of the Rabbi's house

Moshe Haber

He was a quiet and modest man. He was a tailor of ladies coats and prayed at the "kahal shtibel" that was located in the big synagogue. He was happy with his lot and did not have great ambitions. He lived all his life at the Targowica. During World War I, his son was drafted and in 1915 he was taken prisoner by the Russians and all traces of him vanished.

Israel Haber

He was the only Jew in town to work as a builder. He lived in his own house at the Targowica. When the Russians retreated from Jaslo during World War I they took him as a hostage with other Jews but he managed to escape in Lemberg returned home. Shortly thereafter, he took ill and passed away. He left a wife and several small children. When the oldest son matured, he bought a horse and a cart and started to transport people and goods from and to the railway station. The second son Itzhak was the first one in Jaslo to learn to drive and was the first cab driver in the city. He reached Palestine with the Polish Army and later left the country for Holland.

Hersh Chaim Hegel

He was a merchant and lived his entire life in the market square. He observed traditions and worshipped regularly at the big synagogue. He was considered a smart and reasonable person. Every social activity or action that did not receive the support of the community aroused his fury.

He had three sons; Dow, Mordechai or Motik, a student of the municipal high school, Baruch and a daughter named Sheindil.

[Page 147]

The oldest son left Jaslo in the early twenties and following his marriage, they managed to escape the Germans and reached Palestine with the outbreak of World War II. They settled in Jaffa where he worked for the municipality and then opened his business.

Yossef Holoshitzer

He really deserved to be called the "Hassid". He was known as Yossef Holoshitzer of Gorlice or Yossele shtriker for he was a weaver and he represented honesty, piety and integrity. He was an early walker to serve G-d. He would speed to the study center with his large bag under his arm that contained his prayer shawl, his phylacteries, his big prayer book that also included the psalms, the law book of Israel and the book of "Mishnayot". The routine was the same, winter or summer, he would reach the place and go straight to the mikvah to immerse himself before the morning service. He would then proceed to his regular place along the south side of the bima. Here he would stand and read completely the book "Hokla Israel". He then wrapped himself in the prayer shawl and placed the phylacteries and devoted himself to praying. He did not indulge in small talk or hearsay but concentrated his energies in devotion to the creator.

Yossef Holoshitzer and his wife Nehema

[Page 148]

He merely answered "Amen" where he was required by ritual otherwise he concentrated on his prayers. He was an excellent host and tried to accommodate people. He worked all his life at his trade, especially in preparing silk belts for the synagogue. His work was very precise and he took great pride in these belts and they became famous for their beauty and dedicated work. These silk belts were known as "Jaslo belts" and those that wore them took great pride in them. He observed strictly the rules pertaining to Shabbat and did not want to accept any easements of these rules. He was the only one in town that wore white socks on Shabbat and holidays. He had three sons and two daughters. His oldest daughter Matil left for Palestine as a pioneer in the thirties and following her marriage settled in Tel Aviv. Many of the Jaslo Jews that reached Palestine found a place in her home. The second daughter Hannah and a son Yehhezkel left for Palestine and settled in Tel Aviv.

Abba Hollander

He was an old timer in the city and lived in his private one story home at the Targowica. He was far removed from the city noise and considered well to do. He exported eggs and had large warehouse of fertilizers that he sold to the farmers in the area. He was a Rymanower Hassid and met the Rabbi of Rymanow in person. Thus his residence was the place where the famous rabbis would stay on their visit to Jaslo. Some of the Rabbis were well known namely Rabbi Aarale of Krosno, Rabbi Hershele of Rymanow, Rabbi Moshele, the son of the Rabbi of Krosno and the brother in law of the Rabbi of Rozwadow. He prayed at the big synagogue next to the eastern wall. He headed many appeals for various social needs and especially devoted time to the campaign for matzoth for the poor. A fire started in his house on Yom Kippur eve at the beginning of the century. The fire resulted from a lit memorial candle that fell. The people had to run from the synagogue to extinguish the fire before it reached the wooden houses of the neighbors.

[Page 149]

He had four sons that received a traditional and religious education. His oldest son Leibish left Jaslo for Germany and two married daughters lived in Jaslo.

Yehezkel Hollander

He was the son of Abba Hollander and was very pious. He was a merchant and lately acquired an inn. He was a regular member of the study center of the rabbi and loved to conduct services in spite of his slight speech impediment. He was always given to conduct the afternoon "Minha" service of the Yom Kippur day.

Moshe and Shimon Hollander

They were the younger sons of Abba Hollander. They both studied at the study center. Shimon even studied at the "Tachkamoni" school in Warsaw. He was one of the organizers of the Mizrahi youth wing within the movement and later became the leader of the group.

With the outbreak of World War II, they managed to reach Russia and then left for France where they reside in Paris.

Akiva Hoffman

He was born in Butchac. He was first a teacher in one of Baron Hirsh's schools and then was the official Jewish teacher in the Jaslo school system. He belonged to old guard Zionists in the city. He wore a black beard similar to Hertzel's beard. He helped establish the "Yeshuron" club and was also involved in social affairs. He was an effective speaker and was a member of the "Joint Organization committee" in Jaslo with the establishment of Polish independence. His sons received a high school education and continued their studies. One of his sons joined the Polish legion during World War I and was killed in action. He became depressed due to petty rivalries and left the city for Krakow. But here too he could not find himself and took his life.

[Page 150]

Naphtali Hoffert

Naphtali Hoffert

He was one of Zelig Miller's sons in laws. He came from a well known Hassidic family in Rozwadow. He was knowledgeable in Torah and was also well read. He was one of the first readers of the Hebrew press in Jaslo. He also participated in the founding of the Yeshuron club and the Mizrahi branch in the city. He was also involved in the community, and was the beadle of the synagogue for many years.

[Page 151]

He owned a factory for bottling mineral and seltzer water. He lived all his life in the house of Mordechai Karp and was his friend.

He had two sons and two daughters. His oldest daughter was Miriam Hoffert a doctor. She was active in the Zionist youth movement and left for Berlin. She then left Germany and reached Palestine. She is presently the head of social services at the ministry of welfare. She is known to devote herself to her work. She was selected by the UN social committee to study in the USA various aspects of social work.

She greatly assisted new immigrants from Jaslo in Palestine.

Awraham Hoffert

Hoffert the older son planned to settle in Palestine as a pioneer in the twenties but there were disturbances and he postponed the trip. Meanwhile he left for Germany where he stayed until 1933 and then reached Palestine.

Awraham Hoffert was the son in law of Moshe Yaakow Yerachmish of Jaslo. He was a pleasant and soft spoken man. Former residents of Jaslo found in him a person ready to listen to their problems. His wife Hawa was an excellent host with a great deal of understanding.

They had two daughters; Chaya and Shulamit. Both played piano. The older one worked as a clerk in the city of Tel Aviv and the second one studies at the Hebrew University in Jerusalem. Hawa Hoffert was one of the founders of the Jaslo landesmanschaft in Israel.

Chaim Hoffert

He also came from Rozwadow. He was the son in law of Abba Hollander . He was a yeshiva student and well read. He was a regular member of the Rabbi's minyan at the study center. His children received a religious education.

He had a paint store in M. Karp's house along Kazimierz Street and he made a nice living.

Yoel Horowitz

He was a Talmudic scholar and knew a large part of the material by heart. He constantly devoted himself to the study of the Talmud and was at home in the field. When challenged on halachic points, he would immediately reach the library shelf and select the appropriate text that pointed out the problem, the discussions and solutions to the problem.

He frequently had Talmudic disputations with other students and frequently with my father. The debates raged but in the end the arguments were settled in accordance with the truth of the matter. The fights never became personal, literary fights always resolved themselves in greater understanding of the concerned parties. They remained friends in spite if the disputations.

[Page 152]

He was a Hassid and a very observant Jew. He was a Belzer Hassid and never tried to cut corners when it came to religious matters.

He was a merchant and sold head kerchiefs. He lived in Shmuel Cisser's house. He had one son named Yehoshua in memory of the old Belzer Rabbi. He was a member of the study center group and left Jaslo following his marriage. They also had a daughter named Beila.

Yehoshua Horowicz

He was not related to Yoel Horowitz. I mentioned him in a previous chapter as a scholar in the city.

I would like to acquaint the reader with some aspects of this scholarly student as I remember them;

He was the son of the head of judicial 1 council of Frysztak that was received by that community during World War I and following his marriage of the daughter of Shmuel Mendel Ross he settled in Jaslo.

He was an exceptional student with a fine mind that grasped every nuance of a debate. He was fluent in the Talmud and its commentaries. He was master of all four books of the "Shulchan Aruch codex" - or Jewish rule books. He knew his Hebrew grammar and was fluent in modern Hebrew, bible, and the latest literary Hebrew works. The best part of his study was the fact that he remembered everything that he studied and knew where to look for it in case of doubt. His intellectual ability to grasp ideas and knowledge soon introduced him to the intellectual Talmudic elite in the city. He was totally immersed in his studies and in books. He read the latest Talmudic books and was familiar with the great halacha questions and answers. He wrapped his talit about himself and sat in the study center to the side and faced the front. You never saw his face except when he was called to the torah. Many communities wanted him as Rabbi but the family and his wife objected. He eventually left for the USA where he became a Rabbi of a congregation in Brooklyn.

Elisha Hazelnuss

The people of Jaslo did not know his name. He was always called the Linsker shoemaker since he came from Lesko. He barely made a living for he was a poor craftsman. He was also a sick person that was tended by his small children. He was a non-talker and lived in the house of Elimelech Goldstein.

[Page 153]
Menachem Mendel Hilperin, Rabbi
(Hassidic Rabbi of Dukla, see previous chapter)

Yoel Hilperin

The son in law of the Rabbi, see chapter dealing with the history of the rabbi's house

Shulem Hiller

He was known in the city as Shulem Tupoliner since he came from the village of Tupolina near Sczenica where he had a large farm and an inn.

He was a kind person that continued to follow the old tradition. He had a well kept long beard that gave him a patriarchal appearance. He was well acquainted with the rabbinical world and dressed like one of them. By tradition he conducted the prayers on "Yom Kippur Katan" before the holy arc on the eve of the new month of Elul and also the "shachrit" service or morning service of the high holidays in the great study center. On reaching a ripe old age he became ill and passed away on Passover in 1928. Due to the big distance from the city only the strong young fellows that were about to be drafted went to the home of the death party and carried him in the direction of the city. When they reached the city limits near May 3rd Street, the Hevra Kadisha members were waiting to take the body. The initial porters refused to hand over the body and stated that they started a mitzvah and will finish it. Indeed they continued to carry the body to the entrance of the cemetery and then let the burial party take over.

He left four married daughters and a son. One daughter that was married to Feiwil Ris of Dembowce left for Palestine in the early thirties and settled in Haifa. Four grandchildren from two older daughters are in Israel. One grand son, the son of Shmuel Wolker fell in the independence war of Israel.

[Page 154]

Kalman Hirsch

He came to Siwionow from Mielec in the twenties and was a clerk in the spirit distillery of Rubel. He was a well mannered person and versed in the Torah. He also knew Hebrew grammar. Each Saturday he came from Siwionow to the study center to pray with the community. He enjoyed immensely conducting religious conversations and interpretations of various religious texts. He frequently stayed long after the services were finished to conduct his torah discussions.

He had two daughters that were members of the youth Zionist group. They received a high school education. One of them Riwka left for Palestine as a pioneer in the thirties and eventually settled in Rehovot. Her husband worked at the Weitzman institute where he was instantly killed by an explosion. His wife continued to work at the institute.

Yaakow Hirshfeld

He came from Sandz and was immediately installed as the beadle in the synagogue of Jaslo. He was known in the city as Yekil the beadle. He was not the usual small town beadle that feared every strong voice in the community. On the contrary, he had a knack for navigating his ship and soon gained tremendous strength in the community and his position became impregnable. He lorded over the synagogue and gained the respect of the worshippers.

M.Kipnis who wrote for the Yiddish paper "Haint" in Warsaw traveled extensively throughout the cities of Poland and visited once Jaslo. He of course went to visit the Jewish Street namely Chajnochy Street to get the feel of the place. When he reached the gate of the synagogue the place was locked. He sent someone to ask the beadle to open the synagogue. Soon enough he heard the noise of keys and indeed the beadle was here and opened the gate. The beadle gave the visitor a guided tour of the place and answered all the questions as well as various pertinent comments.

[Page 155]

On leaving the synagogue M. Kipnis stated that he has visited many places, has spoken to many important people like presidents, directors, managers, community leaders, beadles that wore top hats, bowlers, shtreimels, hats of various kinds, cantorial hats, no hats, but has never had such a fine tour as the one that Yekil the beadle gave him in the synagogue of Jaslo. Indeed Kipnis did no exaggerate. I still remember him standing on the bima glancing across the faces of the worshippers and checking every corner of the place, On occasion he would strike the table and ask for silence.

What silence reigned at the synagogue on Saturday and Holiday nights when Yekil took the Kiddush cup to recite the blessing over the wine. He decided who should get an alyah to the torah this Saturday or next Saturday, He would also give instructions to his two assistants that usually agreed with his decisions. I still hear his voice intoning, Mr. so and so is called to the torah... and later... will make the following contribution ... Amen.

His voice had a special intonation when announcing special events relating to the community. Who could at those moments compare himself to his eloquence.

[Page 156]

He also used to appear at the study center and announce special announcements. His appearance usually indicated that an important matter was about to be discussed. He would enter the study center at a slow peace, his hands behind his back, the golden chain on his chest, the lips ready to speak and at the same time a bit of a smile.

The audience started to whisper, Yekil the shames is here, it must be important. He headed to he bima, took a deep breath, pounds the table for silence and begins to announce his statement. Of course, the audience demands explanations and begins to discuss the implications of the statement.

He was highly respected in the city by the entire community, those that were close to him even permitted themselves to call him reb Yekil and the more modern elements in the city called him Mister Hirschfeld.

He even influenced the behavior of the youngsters at the synagogue. His look told the youngsters to behave and stay close to their father.

He was well off especially in later years when he started to deal with money exchanges and discount notes. He was also connected to the authorities and helped people that needed assistance.

He had three sons and two daughters. The two younger ones Zelka and Yehoshua were modern in outlook and left Jaslo for Germany and later reached the USA. Zelka became very active in the Jaslo landesmanscheft in New York. The older daughter married Yehoshua Chop of Dukla and the second daughter married Zelig Shpirer.

Chaim Hirschfeld

He was the oldest son of Yekil Hirschfeld and was the son in law of Dawid Lipcer. He was a yeshiva student and very pious and observant. He was an outspoken Hassid of Bobowa. He had a grocery in the house of Dawid Elias. He once traveled to see the rabbi of Bobow and felt ill at ease. He became ill and passed away within the day of Rosh Hashana. He left a wife and several small children. The latter grew up and learned trades. They followed their father's footsteps and were also Bobower Hassidim. Two of his sons are in Melbourne Australia.

[Page 157]
Ben Tzion Hirshkowicz

He was the son in law of Asher shames and was known as one of the most dedicated students of the study group. Following his marriage, he taught youngsters Talmud and commentaries but later left everything for the business world.

He was a true Hassidic Jew with a large wavy yellow beard and two long side curls that practically covered his face. He was a close follower of the rabbis, especially reb. Baruch of Gorlice and Rabbi Yossele of Rymanow. His Hassidic manners and behavior were worthy of a deeply religious person.

Following Polish Independence, he took his brother in law's advice and left for Germany. His brother in law was Dawid Shindler who lived in Germany. He had three daughters and a son. One of the daughters lives in Jerusalem.

Dawid Helman

He was a short person and owned an inn for many years on Florianska Street. He was a sick person and suffered for a long time until he passed away prior to World War I. His wife, (the sister of Zeelig Korzenk) continued the business.

They had two children that received a general education and continued their studies that led them to high positions on graduating from their studies.

Mordechai and Yaakow Heller

They were brothers and traded horses. One of them lived on Korlowski Street and one behind the municipal building. They died one after the other following illness and left wives and small children. They are today in the US

A Heller

He settled in Jaslo in the twenties. He had a hat store and lived with his brother that also came to the city to help him with the business.

Dawid Hemm

He was a typical enlightened person of the old school. With age he became more observant and began to attend Saturday services at the study center he usually told the listeners his youthful stories mixed with the sayings of the sages and even boasted a bit that he studied with Rabbi Naphtali Pessah and Rabbi Moshele of Tarnow, two well known giants of the Talmud who headed yeshivas.

He took a great deal of liberties with his religion at the time namely he shaved his beard and curled his side curls. He was called at the study center the one that lost a bit his way, in other words a lost sheep.

[Page 158]

He owned a big house on Kosciuszko Street near the municipal court house. He belonged to the Yeshuron club and later joined the mizrahi movement. The Ludowy Bank had their office in his house until they moved to the new place in Lipa Tzimet's house. He had no sons but only daughters that received a good education

Dawid Hemel

He was a very pious Jew that was familiar with torah literature. He was clever and sharp, aware of all things that were happening in the city. He was familiar with the religious and general population. He always had a comment and always expressed his opinion.

He lived in Pozdamcze where he had a grocery store. With the outbreak of World War I he left Jaslo.

Israel Hendler

He was the owner of an inn at the end of Floriasnka Street near the municipal building. There was an artistic poster of a cluster of grapes at the entrance to the inn. He was modest and moderate, followed with the prevailing mood of the population. His daughters received a high school education.

Leibish Hess

He was an old timer in the city of Jaslo and had a large timber business. Yom Tov Leibish Hess was a tall man and wore a long beard as he walked at a leisurely peace in town.

Until 1914 he worshipped at the great study center near the eastern wall. He was even the beadle for several years but avoided publicity and public attention.

[Page 159]

He had four sons that lived in Jaslo and were all influenced by the new Zionist winds for they were all members of the Zionist movements. They lived in a house on Florianska Street.

Shlomo Zalman Hess

He was the oldest son of Leibish Hess. He was educated and a member of the Mizrahi movement and the head of the local branch for many years.

His three story house on Florianska Street he acquired in 1914 with the outbreak of World War I. He also had there a large warehouse of construction materials and metals.

Eli Hess

He was the brother of Leibish Hess and was also a businessman. He was a quiet and fair person. He had business relations with timber importers of foreign countries.

He married off his daughters with educated husbands that were members of the mizrahi movement. One of them was Lauffer and the other one was Rapoport. Both worshipped at the mizrahi study center.

His young son Itzhak, a high school student, drooped from school and began to learn a trade. He also devoted himself to the Pioneer Zionist movement in Jaslo and headed the group for many years. He left Jaslo in the thirties for Palestine. He lives and works presently as a locksmith in Kiriat Borochow

Israel Hefner

He was from the area of Tarnowci. He was a coachman and hauled merchandise to and from the railway station. On Saturdays and Holidays he used to dress as a very pious Hassid and listened to all pulpit preachers. He loved to fulfill good deeds. Gave charity and was a good host. He traveled to holy rabbis and was particularly attached to the Rabbi Shlomo Libli of Tyczin.

He lived all his live in Hiclowka. He had three sons and two daughters. The oldest Awraham left Jaslo in the early twenties and settled in Argentina.

With the end of World War II the younger son reached Palestine and settled in Tel Aviv. According to rumors he later left for Canada.

Israel Hefner had a brother that lived in Tarnowci and was involved in business.

[Page 160]
Hannah Herbst

With the death of her husband who was a cattle dealer, she left the village near Jaslo and settled in the city. She sold fish in the corner of the market.

She was left with two sons, three daughters and life was difficult. The boys learned tailoring as they grew up and the girls learned to be seamstresses. They boys excelled in their studies and had excellent relations with their clients.

The youngest son reached Palestine with the Polish Army in the forties. He works today in the municipality of Tel Aviv.

Manes Hertz

He was a refined and cultered man. He suffered frequently from a sore throat and one could barely hear what he had to say. It was a pleasure to speak to him on various topics. He was familiar with international as well as local politics. He also expressed himself on matters that he felt were incorrect. He sold wines and spirits in the house of Stillman in the market square, in the court yard. He lived in Kornfeld's house on Kazimerz Street. He had only daughters.

Israel Hertz

He was a shoemaker and had a bit of a strange appearance. He was short, pudgy and limped. He spoke Yiddish with a German accent. He lived in Israel Haber's house in the Targowica

Yaakow Hertzig, attorney

He settled in Jaslo in the twenties after he married the granddaughter of Itchi Yehuda Rubel. He was one of the best attorneys in town. He was a Zionist and very respected. He managed to escape the Germans and lives presently with his family in Paris.

[Page 161]

Vav ו

Tzadok Weber

The family was a very colorful family. Tzadok Weber was a butcher. Due to a disease he lost his hair and had no beard. He died prior to World War I and left a wife and five sons; Lipcze, Motil, Itzik, Hershel, Yekil and four daughters.

With regards to charity, the Weber house took the first row in town. The house was open to every poor person in the city and the widow treated them with respect and helped them. She dressed in old style rabbanit clothing. She did an excellent job of hosting the poor and the down trodden people in the city

Leib Weber

He was nicknamed Lipcze Weber in his youth while a student at the study center. Later he joined the workers association named Poalei Tzion that was established in Jaslo at the time. He delved into the activities of the association and became very politically very active.

He was busy in the butcher shop but still read a great deal and there were always books in the store as well as newspapers and magazines. In effect he was acquiring an education.

The political situation in Poland following World War I. was in turmoil. In Russia the communist party seized power and turmoil prevailed in many other places. All these events influenced Leib Weber who was already familiar with the writings of La Salle, Luxemburg and Lenin. He was looking forward to the future, to the fulfillment of the social objective of the "Jewish working masses" together with other workers. Hunger and lack of work embittered the general population as well as the Jewish population. Thus he received the opportunity to speak everywhere on behalf of the Jewish worker. The various community officials that presented reports about the need for more help from the "Joint Organization" usually met Lipcze who criticized them for their behavior and demanded their immediate resignation.

[Page 162]

The electoral campaign for community leadership began and . Lipcze appeared everywhere and spoke on behalf of the Jewish working masses. His words are like sparks of fire directed at the leaders of the community that tried to hide behind the veneer of respectability. They have no right to speak on behalf of the community for they do not represent it. The elections to the community board were finished then came the elections for the Polish parliament. Again the speeches and rallies. Almost every Sunday there were mass rallies at the big study center where the speakers were Hoffman, Dr. Korhauser, Mendel Meller, Dr. Naphtali Menashe etc…

But Lipcze Weber attacked them all and addressed himself to the audience " Jewish brothers, the united Jewish masses can not permit themselves to be led by these people… We are from the masses that have a clear conscience shaped by the Jewish proletariat that will only vote for this list…" And I suggest these candidates and only these candidates are fit.

Mendel Meller replied to Lipcze's oratory and managed to silence him by referring to a particular personal incident in which he was involved.

We must admit that Lipcze Weber was an honest man that truly represented the worker and their interests. He personally had no gains. He was a good speaker and used a great deal of reason and persuasion. Even the opponents admitted that he was a fine speaker.

He was elected to the community board as representative of the Yad Harutzim Society. He also represented this organization in other social institutions in the city.

All the members of this family used a particular manner of speech to distinguish themselves from each other whether in the speech pattern of the guttural letters or in the rolling of the letter "R" to create the impression of a Russian accent.

In the thirties, he was already an elderly and sickly man who decided to get married and ceased all political work.

[Page 163]
Motil Weber

He was the main bread winner of the family. He traded cattle and was also a butcher. He was assisted by Lipcze and Yekil. He was a religious fellow with a trimmed beard and was also known to be a charitable person. He was not known to be involved in politics and rarely expressed his opinions. He was a bachelor.

Itzik Weber

He resided many years in Germany. On returning to Jaslo in the twenties he married the daughter of Awraham Schecht. In the evenings he used to sing German, Yiddish and Polish folk songs.

Hershel Weber

He was a gifted child and showed great promise at an early age. The teachers predicted a great future for him. There was no subject that Hershel did not master. Students were jealous and envious of his great ability. There were no difficult problems for this student who was also very helpful to other students by explaining them the problem and the solution.

He graduated school with honors and prepared to enter high school as an extern. He continued his studies and also continued his Talmudic studies. He once encountered a serious problem that was beyond his comprehension. He went to the Rabbi's study center and met Ephraim Rubin who was a great Talmudic scholar and he explained him the question and the answer. He graduated with honors from the University of Krakow and the Academy of Arts in the same city. His vast knowledge of literature, mathematics, physics, astronomy, philosophy and art did not enable him to get a befitting position in the country. He wrote articles and literary reviews in Polish newspapers but nothing concrete.

[Page 164]
Only in 1940, with the occupation of Lemberg by the Russians was he appointed to the chair of mathematics at the University of Lemberg. The appointments lasted for a short time since he decided to visit his family in Jaslo. On his return trip he was stopped and shot by the Germans. They kept firing until he collapsed to the ground. Thus was lost a fine and distinguished soul in this period of chaos in the twentieth century.

Yekil Weber

He was the youngest son of the family. He was tall and large boned. Like his brothers he also song Yiddish and Polish folk songs. He had a beautiful tenor voice. At first he started as a supporter of Yiddish and soon joined the ranks of the communist party and became a very active member. He also enlisted his sisters in these efforts.

The Polish authorities soon received information about them and they were all arrested for illegal activities. The communist party was forbidden in Poland. Yekil and his sisters went to jail where they remained for several years.

Brili Weber

He was a short person with a sparse yellowish beard. He lived all his life at the Targowica. He was a simple tailor and lately began to sell ready made clothing.

He was modest and quiet. He prayed at the study center of Rabbi Mandil. He had two daughters and a son named Hershel. They all worked earning a living

Zeew Wagshal

He had an estate in Worzic near Jaslo. His brother, Moti Wagshal was the dayan- or religious judge of the city of Biecz. Zeew Wagshal was a very pious and honest person.

He moved to Jaslo and settled in Ulaszowica near the bridge where he opened a store. He had four sons and four daughters. He had three sons in laws namely Michael Platner, Yossef Mate, and Yehoshua Guttman. They all resided in Jaslo. One of his sons, Israel married to the daughter of Awraham Schecht and opened the transportation line from Jaslo to Tarnow. First by cab and later by bus. The line continued to operate until World War II. The second son Leibish was a businessman.

[Page 165]
Moshe Wolf

Everybody knew Moshe Wolf in Jaslo if not by his name then by his nickname from the Targowica. He was a very intelligent and a highly rational thinker that could tackle difficult problems and solve them for people.

He was very familiar with the law especially the financial aspect of laws. He could interpret every new financial regulation or law and was also called the "iron head". He was referred to as the lawyer when it came to financial laws.

Jews with serious problems or dilemmas would frequently come to Moshe Wolf for help and he would drop whatever he did and sit with the party to help. He checked and on occasion criticized the community leadership when they tried to pull a fast one. He was always reading or checking references. As soon as he reached the study center he would pull out the book "Questions and Answers" or similar books and browse standing with one foot on the bench. He also had a peculiar habit when someone talked to him, he always reached for his beard and then dropped his arm. This habit repeated itself constantly in the conversation. He lived all his life at the Targowica. He had a grocery store. He had no sons.

Eisik Wolf

He was the first son in law of Yudel Budner. He was a yeshiva student and very religious. Lately lived at the Targowica. He had a nice income as a merchant.

[Page 166]
Eliezer Wiser

He was a modest and quiet person. He observed his religion and tradition. He produced vinegar and made a nice living from it. He lived in his brother in law's house, Yehiel Rosner, in the market. He had a son Pinhas and a daughter. The son was also a quiet person and kept his distance from activities. He worked with his father.

Chaim Wechselbaum

He settled in Jaslo with the outbreak of World War I and was known in the city as Chaim Trzcicer since he came from the shtetl of Trzcicer.

He was a god fearing Jew and a follower of the Rabbi of Bluzow. Subsequently he traveled to visit his son, Rabbi of Bribitic. He also owed allegiance to the Hassidic court of Trzcicer since Rabbi Shlomo Libli of Tyczyn was his uncle. On Saturdays and Holidays he would hardly talk except to murmur short Hebrew words. He prayed with a great deal of devotion, crying, begging and asking for mercy.

Friday nights he prayed at the big study center near the northern wall facing the wall and on Saturday he used to pray at the study center of the Rabbi.

He was a Hebrew teacher and had between 10 and 15 students. This provided his income. He lived all his life in the court yard of Yaakow Bruder where he had two dark rooms. His three sons were businessman and also studied at the study center. The oldest Yehoshua left Jaslo for Lejansk following his marriage. The second son Reuven left for Belgium in the twenties. The third son Shlomo was very active in the mizrahi youth movement. He then married and settled in Jaslo. He also had two daughters. One of them was Mirele active in the Zionist youth organization. She married Yehezkel Pnichel on his return from Palestine. The second daughter Chaya was also involved in the Zionist youth movement.

[Page 167]
Yaakow Wechselbaum
He was the son in law of Wolf Stillman. He was traditional and a member of the Zionist movement. He worshipped at the great synagogue where he had a seat in front to the holy arc. He had a haberdashery in his father in laws house on Kosciuszko Street. His son left for Palestine after World War II and received a job as a clerk but soon left to be independent.

Yaakow Weil
He had a friendly facial disposition to people. His friends loved him. He was known as a Zionist and a religious Jew. He prayed at the big synagogue. When the Mizrahi organization established itself in the city, they rented a big room in his house that was used as a meeting and assembly hall for the party. He dealt all his life with animal skins and lived on Nowa Street. He had two sons and several daughters. One daughter married Moshe Meir Freifeld and they left Jaslo prior to World War I. The second daughter married a yeshiva student named Rubel, the couple resided in Jaslo.

Awraham Weitz
He was originally from Koloczyc and settled in Jaslo during World War I. He was a Hassidic Jew and thanked the creator for everything that was bestowed on him. In conversation, he always had a smile as if he really enjoyed small talk. He also kidded with the youngsters on occasion.
He dealt with animal skins and had a house on Iglena Street. He had three sons; Yaakow, Asher, and Dawid and two daughters. The youngest son settled in Stryzow following his marriage.

Yenkil Weitz
He was the oldest son of Awraham Weitz. He was very religious and attached to the Rabbi of Bobow. He also dealt in animal skins and lived at the Targowica.
[Page 168]
Lately he took ill and recovered but only temporarily. He became ill again and soon passed away.
Hershel, the oldest son that was raised at the yeshiva in Bobow was familiar with all the Bobower Hassidic tunes and spread them through Jaslo. Following his marriage, he left for Stryzow then for Krakow. Another son named **Asher** managed to survive World War II and resided in Silesia Poland. One daughter managed to reach Palestine and settled in Hertzlia.

Asher Weitz
He was the second son of Awraham Weitz and made a nice living as an expediter of goods. He was a quiet person and followed the community. He had three sons and three daughters. One son Mendel Reached Palestine following World War II and settled in Tel Aviv.

Mendel Weitz
He lived all his life in Worzic (I have little information about him). As I am writing these lines I am informed that he returned to Jaslo after World War II and lived in Wagshal's house near the bridge. He is the only Jew to live in the city following World War II.

Eliezer Weitzman

He was originally from the small hamlet of Flanch. He was the third son in law of Nahum Schochet and was recognized as a scholar by the local leadership. He was capable of explaining very difficult passages in in the halacha. He also had a very good tenor's voice and the news spread through the city. He followed the traditional frame of cantorial music but kept musical time.

Lately he began to travel each year to Czenstochowa for the High Holidays where he conducted the mussaf service at the study center of the Rabbi of Trisk (a grandson of the famous pulpit speaker of Trisk) who lived in the city. As cantorial understudies he took with him Simche Ruthfeld and Betzalell Lipczer. The Hassidim that came to the rabbi's court for the holidays loved his spirituality in the services. (I met in Israel with some of the Czenstochowa residents that heard him pray and they had nothing but the highest praise for the cantor from Jaslo.

[Page 169]

He was also an excellent torah reader and knew where to place the stress and was extremely familiar with the cantilation of the reading.(He read all the years at the study center and when he was absent, I, the author. assumed the role).

He lived on a small street named Karmelicka near the market where he had a grocery. His children received a very religious education. One of them was named Chaim and the kids nicknamed him Chaim Weitzman number two... An allusion to Chaim Weitzman who was president of the World Zionist Organization.

He also tried his hand at medicine as did his father in law. He read up some material and acquired some rudimentary medical knowledge but he never made a go of it. He barely made a living.

Awraham Wildstein

He was the owner of a butcher store in P. Klinman's house in the market and also dealt with animals. He was very traditional and observed strictly the commandments. He was a member of Yad Harutzim.

Yudel Wildstein

A very religious Jew. He had a long black beard and sidecurls. He dealt with animals and lived in Feiwil Klinman's house. He suddenly fell ill in the prime of his life and never managed to recover. He passed away a few months later and left a wife and several small children.
(According to rumors, his son is today a leading military figure in the Red Army)

Awigdor Wildstein

He was the brother of Yudel Wildstein and was also involved in cattle trading. He was a religious and active in Yad Harutzim. Loved to hear himself talk especially prior to election times, regardless of what elections were to be held. He lived on Nowa Street next to the synagogue. He had a son and a daughter that received a high school education and continued their studies.

Shmuel Wildenstein

He was a small individual and his bent skinny body made him even shorter. He was nicknamed Cilkala after his wife who name was Cilka. He and his wife sold fruits at the market all their life. Their economic situation was rather poor. In the twenties, he became ill and passed away leaving several sons.

Itzhak Wildenstein

He was the son of Shmuel Wildenstein and was nicknamed "Itzikel". He was also skinny with an unkempt yellowish beard. He was always in hurry, always angry, always involved in many activities namely selling fruits, waiting at weddings and official dinners thus the nickname Itzikel the waiter, he also sold religious items, assisted sick people, slept at the home of deceased people, collected contributions at funerals and many more chores. But from all these activities he barely earned his daily bread. He lived at the hill top behind the municipality.

Dawid Wilchfort

He was one of the fairest people in town. He was kind and a gentle person. He was a Bobower Hassid and sold wholesale chocolates, candies and tropical fruits. On the eve of Rosh Hashana, he used to provide the Jews of Jaslo and vicinity with fresh Palestinian fruits namely, grapes, figs, dates, and boxers to make the blessing of the new fruit for the new year.

He was known as a man of charity but avoided publicity. He did not look for special honors but his influence was felt in the Jewish community as well as in the general society in the city. I remember a particular incident that occurred in Jaslo. The draft commission appeared in Jaslo on Saturday and had ordered many Jews to appear before it. The commission was known to be very strict and drafted every body including people that were border line cases and even below the usual medical standard. When the news reached Dawid Wilchfort. He changed his Shabbath clothing on coming home from the synagogue and put on his regular clothing and went to visit Dr. Tzol, the mayor of the city, regarding the strict line adopted by the commission. His intervention bore fruit, the commission began to behave in a more human manner with regards to Jewish draftees. He had four sons and two daughters. His oldest son Aaron drowned during a summer when he went to the river to wash on Friday. He was swept away by a river wave past the Agazacirka park. The tragic news upset the entire Jewish community. The second son Awraham studied for a while at the study center and also Hebrew and finished high school.(He is presently in Germany). The daughter Leah (Lonka) is in Paris and the youngest son Hanoch managed to reach the USA according to rumors

[Page 171]
Israel Wilner

He had a store of animal skins and all kinds of materials for shoemakers. His store was located in M. Karp's house. He was a Sadigore Hassid and well versed in the Torah. When he had the time, he sat with his pipe and read the mishnayot book or the "Irin Kedishin" book written by the saintly Rabbi of Rezin. From his first marriage, he had two daughters. The oldest daughter married a yeshiva student named Nathanel Klinman who lived in the house of Eliyahu Lehrer. Rather early in life he became ill and passed away. The second daughter lived in Lisko and had a son named Dawid who drowned in the mikvah on the eve of the Shabbath. The entire community was shocked by the tragic event. The daughter Mindel married a yeshiva student. They managed to flee from the Germans and survived the war. They reached Israel and settled in Ness Tziona.

Leibish Weinberger

He lived all his life along Korlowski Street. He was a wine and spirit merchant. He was the son in law of Leibish Hess and was well read and expressed often his opinions regarding public matters. He inherited a seat at the eastern wall in the study center when his father in law stopped praying there.
[Page 172]
His two sons dealt with timber and later left Jaslo in the early twenties.

Shmuel Weinberger

He was a quiet person. He was a tailor and had a small house opposite the synagogue. He left for the USA prior to World War I and left his wife and son in Jaslo.

With Polish Indepenedence he returned to Jaslo with several thousand dollars in his pocket and began several business ventures. First he started a business with Moshe reb Mandili's and Moshe Wolf to import sugar and sell it wholesale. But the partnership soon dissolved. Then he went into partnership with Leib Shperling to sell ready made clothing. This venture also finished rapidly and Shmuel Weinberger sold his properties and returned to the USA with his family.

Shlomo Weingarten

He settled in Jaslo following World War I when he sold his estate near Biecz. He was always involved in the sale of timber. However he started out as a manufacturer of bone flour, glue and organic manure in Gorlice. He also owned a saw mill and a flour mill in Biecz that provided Jaslo, Gorlice, and Biecz with flour for matzot on Peassah.

He was known as an observant person and gave lots of charity. He was known to distribute potatoes and dairy products to the poor people of Biecz. The reputation followed him to Jaslo for here he continued to provide charity for the needy. He imposed himself on the people and was elected to be beadle of the synagogue and remained at the post until he left the city. He was known to give praise to people for their work or suggestions. When his daughter came to the study center on Rosh Hashana and saw the women section she was appalled. The place was of course devastated by the Russian in 1914. There was no roof and there was not much of a floor. She was wondering whether this was indeed a place of God. When her father heard the daughter's complaints he stated that he will provide all the lumber to fix he place. Indeed, the materials were provided and the women section was restored.

[Page 173]

He had four daughters and two sons. One daughter married a yeshiva student that was already ordained to become a rabbi. He was from Rzeszow and belonged to the Yaari family. A second daughter married the son of M.A. Werner of Jaslo.

Shlomo Weingarten has been living in Tel Aviv for 18 years. He opened a weaving place and succeeded. He built himself a nice house in Ramat Gan. Life has been good to him. One son married the daughter of Lipa Tzimet and two daughters live in Paris and one daughter lives in Israel.

Dawid Weintraub

He was a person with a modern outlook on life and worked for a living. Lately he rented a big place in Iwonic and rented rooms to the people that came for spa treatments to Iwonicz. He lived all his life at the house of Weinberger opposite the synagogue . He had several sons that left Jaslo after they graduated from school.

Leibish Winfeld

He was the first Jew to step on the ground in Jaslo. He also opened the first Jewish store in the city. The store sold retail and wholesale goods. The Jaslo gentiles resented the store and did everything in their power to close the place but they failed. They rightfully saw in him the gate crasher for the Jews. The store windows were smashed time and again but this did not stop Leibish Winfeld. He was determined to continue his business and so he did.

He came from Zmigrod. He was a Hassidic Jew and a very respectable person. He was a doer and was very involved in the community. He recited the first prayers on opening the holy arc on the eve of the Simchat Torah Holiday. This tradition continued for life. He greatly influenced and shaped the Jaslo Jewish community. He helped the needy and forwarded loans to those that needed a bit of a push.

[Page 174]

Awraham Meir Orenstein and and Eisik Moldauer were his first son in laws. The first one dealt with wines. The second received the store that he ran with his brother in law Shadel (that died as a young person) until 1914. Both families left Jaslo with the outbreak of World War I.

Pinhas Winfeld

He was born in Zmigrod and settled in Jaslo in the twenties. He lived in A. Goldstein's house and was nicknamed Pinale. He was a very fanatical religious person. He was active in the "Agudah Israel party and volunteered for all kinds of jobs on behalf of the party. He pushed himself into all kinds of activities and was always involved with the extreme religious group. He bitterly contested Zionism and did everything in his power to annoy them. The Zionists paid him back when they became the majority in the community. He was always appealing the voting results in order to cancel the elections.

He had some very religious friends but they distanced themselves from him when the tide turned. He had no sons but daughters that received a "Beit Yaakow" education. Some years later, he left Jaslo and bought a house in Krakow where he settled.

Moshe Winkler

He stems from eastern Galicia and settled in Jaslo following World War I. He lived on Florianska Street He was a builder and continued the work of Israel Haber when the later died. He did not work steadily at the job.

He run the bath house for many years and tried to please the public. He received a small salary but contented himself with the sum.

He later left the bath house and Jaslo to try his luck elsewhere.

[Page 175]

D. Winkler, engineer

He was a devoted, loyal and hard working Zionist. He lived all his life on Kosciuszko Street and his office was in Altman's house.

He took his Zionism seriously and decided to implement his beliefs. He made alyiah and left Jaslo in the thirties. He settled in Haifa.

Yossef Elazar Wiener

He lived in the market square until the outbreak of World War I. He had a store that sold elegant ready to wear clothes.

He was an educated person, well mannered with a certain personal charm. He dressed in a Hassidic manner.

When he left Jaslo, his store remained empty for a number of years until his brother in law, Moshe Warsher, took it over. He had four sons and a daughter. All received an academic education in Vienna. His oldest son, Dr, Michael Wiener left for Palestine in the thirties and settled in Haifa. His daughter lived in Tel Aviv.

When the Germans entered Vienna, Yossef Elazar Wiener left Austria for the USA and settled in Brooklyn

Menashe Weinstein

He was something special in Jaslo. He was well educated and behaved in an aristocratic manner. He was well read in classical German literature and was interested in international politics. He frequently quoted "Die Neue Frie Press" newspaper. He had an excellent hand writing and was a good accountant, draftsman and artist. He designed the two posters in the synagogue and the study center that faced the leader of the services. He worshipped every morning in the kahal stibel and participated every evening at the mishnayaot sessions but was also a Zionist and highly enlightened individual

With the establishment of Polish independence, he headed the grocery cooperative "Oscino" at the house of Man Eintziger. The venture soon collapsed.

[Page 176]

He lived all his live on the Targowica in the house of his father in law Skowlewski and was a copper welder by trade. His sons received a high school education. His oldest son continued his studies and was about to be appointed judge in the city but an unfortunate accident occurred that affected his vision and finished his legal career.

Chaim Weinstein

He was one of the refugees of Gorlice during World War I that decided to settle in Jaslo. He was nicknamed Chaim Schochet since he started out as a ritual slaughterer in the city. He was a Hassidic Jew but moderate n his behavior and pleasant to talk to. He worshipped at the study center of the rabbi and participated daily in his lectures.

He had two sons and several daughters. The oldest son Yehezkel who lost an arm during the war left for Vienna where he studied at the teacher seminary and obtained a teaching post following his graduation in the capital. The second son Heshil who studied at the study center and was a Bobower Hassid,was a businessman. He was very active in the young mizrahi movement.

He lived all his life in Zanwil's house on Iglene Street. Lately he opened a store in the market square,

Hersh Weinstein

He settled in Jaslo during the twenties. Hersh Hacohen Weinstein was a well to do Jew who left Zmigrod for Jaslo. His beard and side curls gave him the look of a great rabbi or scholar. He was one of the great merchants but with his arrival to Jaslo he withdrew from commerce. He had views and frequently expressed it. He liked to tell stories of the past that he himself witnessed or experience. They were told in a pleasant manner.

He had two son in laws in Jaslo namely; Yeshayahu Cylinder and Hersh Elimelech Stein.

Eliezer Weinstein

He was one of the older residents in the city but was hardly known. He was a simple and quiet person. He revolved around his family and business. He lived in Podzamce where he had a grocery and an inn.

[Page 177]

Nathan Weinstein

He was the son in law of Moshe Margolies that left for America. He was a scholarly type and familiar with books. He represented many manufacturers. He lived in Podzamce (according to rumors, his son managed to save himself from the Germans).

Eliezer Weiss

He resided but a few years in Jaslo but made a name for himself amongst the yeshiva students. In spite of the fact that he was busy with his daily work, he managed to find time for the various Zionist organizations namely the "Mizrahi" movement. He decided to leave Poland and settle in Palestine with the young pioneers.

He fulfilled his dream and joined an illegal ship that carried illegal immigrants to Palestine for the British severely curtailed the number of certificates given to Jewish immigrants.

For many weeks they traveled aboard the illegal ship "Velos" but had to return to Greece and then to Poland. He later managed to get a certificate and settled in Haifa. His parents Leibish and Bat Sheva remained in Jaslo and shared the fate of the Jewish community of the city.

Shlomo Zalman Weistreich

He stems from Zmigrod. He had a modern outlook on life. In his youth he studied at the study center and wore a kolpack- a special shtreimel - on Saturdays and Holidays.

His home was a very religious and traditional. Still, the atmosphere was one where Zionism penetrated. He had four sons and two daughters that received a modern religious education and a high general education. He was considered one of the well to do people in the city. He contributed heavily to Zionist causes. He dealt in timber, real estate, and owned a saw mill near the railway station and a flour mill.

Two of his sons that were members of the Maccabi sport club helped him run the business.

Dawid Gutwein worked as an accountant for him and when he moved to Krakow so did the accountant who remained there until the outbreak of the World War II.

[Page 178]

S. Westreich

He was the son in law of Yossef Manshe. He was an attorney and very involved in the Zionist movement.

Mendel Westreich

He was a very quiet and modest person. He was familiar with the surroundings and was also familiar with literature. He distanced himself from the public in spite of the fact that he lived near the center of political life in the city on the Iglena – Kosciuszko Streets. A place where there was always people discussing political events.

He was a wine and spirit merchant. His wife Esther was a sister of Tzwi Shtoyar.

Mrs Weistreich (widow)

She lived in Hiclowka and was a middleman. She was nicknamed Jentchowa. Following the death of her husband she raised three daughters and two sons.

The oldest son Monek distinguished himself as an excellent student and later worked as a clerk at the refinery in Niglowic. He hoped to reach Palestine. He studied Hebrew and waited for a certificate that never came since the war put an end to his dream.

Dr. Philip Wachtel

The only Jew to serve in Jaslo as a district judge. He had practically no contact with the Jewish population of Jaslo. He had a small circle of friends that consisted of assimilated Jews. He showed up once at year at the synagogue to partake in the recital of Yizkor for the death.

Yossef Wachner

Few people knew him by that name in the city. He was well known as Yossele Apfel. Apfel was the last name of the wife who was the daughter of Nahum Apfel (the slaughterer) and the sign above the house still carried the name of Gitele Apfel. The previous store owner was also Apfel, thus the nickname remained with him.

He was also the son of a slaughterer from from a place I believe to be Nardimo or that area. He followed the Hassidic world and always attended the study center for prayers.

[Page 179]

His business succeeded well, he sold writing material, toys and gifts. He had the biggest store in town. As things began to improve financially he shortened his religious garb and began to dress as a member of the enlightenment. He spoke gently and had manners. He gave charity and had twin daughters.

Dawid Waldhorn

He was an old Sadigora Hassid, a bit naïve but very familiar with Torah scholarship. He studied daily at home and was not interested in public affairs but helped out people in his own way. He was a merchant and had a store on Kosciuszko Street but in general his wife handled the business. He suddenly became sick and passed away in 1920 and left a wife, named Braindil, four daughters and three sons. (His wife was the sister of the Teller brothers, she died ten years later in 1930)

The children received a general education and continued their studies. The oldest daughter Rachel left for Palestine and settled in Tel Aviv. The son of the second daughter, Sarah Pearlberg also reached Palestine and settled in Tel Aviv. Two daughters Chaya and Yetta and three sons Yossef, Eliezer that were married and Israel the bachelor perished in the shoah.

Naphtali Walfeld

He was an old-timer at Jaslo and was one of the oldest activists in the community. One can say that he laid the foundation for the Jewish community in Jaslo and was the official head of the community for many years.

He was one of the undertakers to build the great synagogue after so many failed in this effort to acquire the hill from the owner of the building. Thanks to his persistence and stubbornness was the building completed.

Naphtali earned the right that his name be remembered with respect by the Jewish community in Jaslo and indeed his name has always been remembered with reverence.

[Page 180]

As a sign of recognition and honor a portrait of him was hung in the community hall of Jaslo. The portrait was two meters tall and rather artistic.

Even the authorities entrusted him with all kinds of public works as a builder and supplier. His sons received a high technical education. One of his sons became the head of the railway station in Rzeszow.

Fishel Waldfeld, Dr.

He was the nephew of Naphtali Walfeld. He lived all his life along May 3rd Street. For a short period of time he involved himself in public life but soon gave it up and devoted himself to law.

His wife was devoted member of the PPS or Polish labor party. She was very active and on May the first paraded with the red flag.

Their daughter reached Israel following the war and settled in Holon

Shmuel Walfeld

He was a brother of Fishel Waldfeld. He was an educated person and served as a Hebrew teacher in the regular public schools in the 19th century. His predecessors were Diller and Hoffman. When he passed away, his wife became the secretary of the community. They had two daughters; one of them was a doctor and lived on Railway Street.

Eliezer Walker

He was the brother in law of Leibish Hess and lived on Florianska Street. He was a quiet person and revolved around his business as an inn keeper and the owner of a grocery. He had three sons, one of them worked at the refinery at Niglowic. The second one, the son in law of Wolf Stillman, lived in Jerusalem and worked at the potash plant at the Dead Sea (Writing these lines, I am told that he passed away while still relatively young)

[Page 181]

Shmuel Walker
He comes originally from Frysztak. He was a very gentle and friendly man. He dressed well and was very active in various communal social institutions namely "Tomchei Aniim" - or help the poor association, "Bikur Cholim" or assist medically the needy and others. He was selected to be the beadle at the great study center for a while. He was a devoted follower of the Rabbi of Dukla and spent a great deal of time in his courtyard. He was a merchant.

Dow Walker
Hero of the War of Independence

His son Dow reached Palestine and was drafted. He fell in the battle for Tarshicha in the Upper Galilee fell on the 29th of October 1948

Leibish Wax
He lived on Florianska Street in Shpringer's house and was the only Jewish locksmith in town.
[Page 182]
He had three daughters and one son. With the German entry to Jaslo, he escaped with his family to the area of Sambor where he and one of his daughters were killed by the Germans

Shmuel Wrocenker
(See Shmuel Jakubowic)

Mordechai Werzicer (Fichter)
He was known in the city as Mordechai Werzicer. His family name was unknown but he came from the village of Werzitch. He settled in Jaslo somewhere between 1917/1918.
He was a very religious Jew but was also involved in social work. He collected money for all kinds of social assistance programs. He himself was a legless person yet he attended every function, winter and summer, where he could expect to collect some pennies for the various charities in the city. He even managed to reach villages if he knew there was money to be had. After a prolonged illness he passed away on the eight day of Shemini Atzeret. He had no sons. We have to admit that little was done for him for all the services that he did for the city. May he be recompensed in the heavenly world.
Lipcze Werner

Like his predecessor Naphtali Walfeld also Lipcze was a central personality in Jaslo He also headed the community for many years.

He was one of the first Jewish settlers in Jaslo. He stems from Lapigus near Sowiniow. During his administration the Jewish community expanded and he became a well known leader. He devoted a great deal of energy to the well being of the community. He had a successful inn and was later the owner of quarries in the vicinity of Rzeszow. He was also a builder. He had five daughters and a son. The latter was named Awraham Chaim (Omek).

While still a student, the son was already affected by Zionism that began to make its appearance in Jaslo through the efforts of the Jewish intelligentia. He laid the foundations for the Zionist Jewish Youth and also played a role in the creation of the Yeshuron club in the city. He was selected as a representative to the Zionist congress and was a Zionist delegate to Zionist Congresses.

[Page 183]

He was drafted during World War I and reached the rank of officer. During the bloody battles of 1916 he fell on the battlefield. His body was brought to be buried in Jaslo. Almost the entire city participated at the funeral and Dr. Thon from Karkow arrived to eulogize him.

He was engaged to marry Dawid Hersh Kornfeld's daughter.

Moshe Aaron Werner

He was the brother in law of Lipce Werner. He was a traditional Jew and wore a shtreimel on Shabat and Holidays. He was a quiet person with a set mind. He lived first in Noah Melink's place and then in Podzamce. He had an inn in his private garden. He was not seen often in the city, thus he was not familiar to the population especially to the newcomers.

He had four daughters and three sons. One daughter married Moshe Weingarten's son who was a dentist and lived in Jaslo. Another daughter named lady Rip lived in Tel Aviv.

Moshe Warsher

He was the brother in law of Yossef Eliezer Wiener. He settled in Jaslo about 1919-1920. He was originally from Lesko. He was considered one of the great scholars of the city and was a real Hassid that followed the Baluzer Hassidic court. He traveled often to visit his rabbi regardless of the business consequences.

I still remember that in 1932 or 1933 the Baluzr Rabbi passed Jaslo on his way to Kroscenko. He remained standing at the railway station due to a train delay. He was the happiest man that he could stand in the company of the rabbi for a few more moments until the Rabbi was escorted to Tarnowci.

Moshe was also known as leader of services and prayed in the traditional manner without missing a note. He led the services regularly at the study center of the rabbi and during the high holidays he led the mussaf services.

He lived all his life at the market and sold ready made clothing. He later opened a grocery. He had a few sons. His oldest son Yossef was a member of the study center and devoted his time to torah study and the Talmud The second son Mendel left Jaslo and settled in Holland in the twenties. In 1952 he came to Israel with his family.

[Page 184]

Zayin ז

Dawid Zommer
(See Dawid Antner)

Sh. Zommer

He was a traditional Jew with modern tendencies. He was the son in law of Abcze Margolies and had a stationary n Reuven Rubles' house along May 3rd Street.

Nathan Ziegfried

He was from the hamlet of Kolaczyce and settled in Jaslo following World War I. He was always jovial and took great pleasure in fulfilling the commandments. He wanted to provide his sons with a very religious education and brought to Kolaczyce a Hebrew teacher called "Pariser" to instruct his sons. The instruction lasted for several years and the expenses were paid by Nathan Ziegfried He prayed regularly at the study center where he had the privilege of requesting and getting the honor of lifting the torah after the reading of the section of Genesis on Shabbath.

He traded in cattle and was well to do. His sons were also in the business. Two of his sons left for Palestine following a long stay in Russia during World War II. They settled in Haifa four years ago and are did rather well but lately left for the USA where they brothers lived.

Awraham Zidrowic

He was a religious and quiet person. He was a tailor and barely made a living. He lived all his life in Bransdadter's house in the market square. He took ill at a young age and and subsequently passed away leaving a wife and several young children. (While writing these lines I received information that some members of the family survived and reached the USA.)

Naphtali Zilber

He was the son in law of Shalom Topoliner and came from a respected and distinguished family. He was raised in a traditional religious manner and his free time was spent studying the Talmud and references. The family used to live behind the municipality and then moved to Nowa Strreet. They were merchants and had three sons who received a very religious education. The oldest son Yehoshua devoted himself to studying and was considered an upcoming young scholar. He also read many books on Hebrew grammar and books in general. He settled in Zmigrod following his marriage. His father in law H. Ginzburg resided in Zmigrod where Naphtali Zilber opened a shoe store.

The second son Mendel was a student of the study center. He was one of the founder of the young Mizrahi movement branch in the city and was a very active member. He was a scholarly type and dreamt of moving to Palestine to help build the country in the spirit of labor and the torah. He therefore decided to learn a trade. Meanwhile he was accepted as a teacher at the Mizrahi Hebrew school in Sandz. He later moved to Krakow and started a billfold workshop. He never realized his dream of settling in the Holy Land for World War II started and dashed his hopes.

The third son Tzwi Dawid started out as a student at the study center but later left for Warsaw to continue his studies as a teacher at the teacher institute named Poznanski. Upon completing his studies he remained in Warsaw and received a teaching position that he held until 1939. He managed to leave Warsaw and returned to Jaslo when the Germans occupied the Polish capital to see his parents and family. He then left the city and headed for the Russian controlled part of Poland. He later joined the Polish Army that was created in Russia as an officer. He fought with the Polish Army until the defeat of Germany and received several medals for distinguished service.

Following World War II he left Poland and headed for Palestine on an illegal ship that was intercepted by the British navy and sent to a detention camp in Cyprus. He finally received a certificate and entered Palestine. He is presently a teacher at the general school of Nachlat Itzhak.

One daughter also left Jaslo for Palestine in the thirties and lives in Nathanyia.

Chaim Zilber

He was a known timber merchant. He was fair and honest in business and very observant. He prayed at the synagogue and lived all his life on Kosciuszko Street.
[Page 186]
He also devoted time to the community in spite of the fact that he managed a big glass factory. He was very active in the community and assisted various charitable institutions. He was elected to the community council prior to World War II on the Zionist ticket. The council selected him to be the head of the community a position he held until the Germans entered the city.
He managed to leave the city at the last moment with his wife Julia, (Hamershlag from home in Nowy Targ) and daughters. They reached the city of Lemberg where all died as a result of infectious diseases in 1942 .

Shmuel Zilfan
He was the son in law of Leibish Kinstler and was born in Siniawa. He lived on Sokol Street and was a merchant and a representative of a beer company. He established a cold storage warehouse near his house but struggled for a living. He had no sons.

Dawid Seinwel
His father Simcha Seinwil came from England and settled in Gorlice where they found oil deposits (Emanuel Shinwell who was Minister of Defense in Britain was his nephew).
He married Gitcha Miller who was the daughter of the ritual slaughterer. He was an educated person and had a fine background. He led the services and also read the torah at the study center and later at the synagogue.
He joined the early winds of Zionism as a lover of Zion. He was a very religious man and the son in law of Zelig Miller the schochet, still he decided to send his son in 1917 to the municipal High School. This was then considered a breach in the religious community and arose the enmity of many religious Jews against him. A delegation of rabbis was sent to his house to try to alter his position but it failed to budge him. The delegation consisted of Reb Hirshale, Reb Elimelech, the judicial rabbi of Jaslo, Aaron Rubin, and was headed by Rabbi Mandil.
We have to add that he was the only student that did not write on Saturday in order to keep the promise he made to his grand father Zelig who did not like the idea of the high school. The son Shmuel graduated high school and became a lawyer. He has an office in Tel Aviv.
[Page 187]
He also devioted time to thew community in spite of the fact that he managed a big glass factory. He was very active in the community and assisted various charitable institutions. He was elected to the community council prior to World War II on the Zionist ticket. The council selected him to be the head of the community a position he held until the Germans enetered the city.
He managed to leave the city in the last moment with his wife Julia, (Hamershlag from home in Nowy Targ) and daughters. They reached the city of Lemberg where they all died as a result of infectious diseases in 1942.

Shmuel Zilfan
He was the son in law of Leibish Kinstler. He was born in Siniawa. He loived on Sokol Street. He was a merchant and a representative of a beer company. He established a cold storage warehouse near the his house. He was not very successful. He had no sons.

Dawid Zinwel

His father Simcha Zeinwil came from England and settled in Gorlice where they found oil deposits (Emanuel Shiwell who was minster of Defense in Britain was his nephew).

He married Gitcha Miller and was an educated person as well as a fine background. He led the services and also read the torah at the study center and later at the synagogue.

He joined the early winds of zionisam as a lover of zion. He was a very religious man and the son in law of Zelig Miller the schochet, still he decided to send his son in 1917 to the municipal High School. This was then considered a breach in the religious community and arose the enemity of many religious Jews against hi,m. A delegation of rabies was sent to his house to try to influence him to alter his position. The delegation consisted of Reb Hirshale, Reb Elimelech, the juduicial rabbi of Jaslo, Aaron Rubin, and headed by Rabbi Mandil. The delegation did mnot change the situation.

We have to add that he was the only student that did not write on Saturday in order to keep the promise he made to his grand father Zelig who did not like the idea of the high school.

The son Shmuel graduated high school and became a lwayer. He has an office in Tel Aviv.
[Page 188]
He had a big house on Iglena Street and a store in the market. In the thirties he sold his business and gave his store to Yossef Pearlberger.

Dawid Zinwel and his wife

He had five sons and three daughters and was lucky that four of his sons and one daughter managed to leave for Palestine. The daughter was the first women pioneer in Jaslo. Two sons live in Haifa, one in Raanna and the fourth one, is a lawyer, in Tel Aviv. The daughter is a member of kibbutz Mizra .

One of the daughters lived in Karakow and an other one married Menashe Weissberg of Tarnow. He was a pleasant person and a well educated young man who opened a wholesale haberdashery store on Walowa Street. Suddenly, he took ill and passed away in 1938 in the prime of his life.

Shmuel Seinwel
He was the oldest son of Dawid Seinwel and the son in law of Eliezer Raab. He was modern in his outlook but observed tradition. He was very active in the Zionist movement and later became an influential Zionist leader in the city. He was also the secretary and later president of the local Keren Kayemet and Keren Hayesiod chapters in the city.
He remained in Jaslo with his family and perished in the shoa.

[Page 189]
Mrs. Zifman
She was a member of the Wolf Bransdadter family and was a partner of the big house in the corner between the market square and Florianska Street near the municipality.

Michael Zakal
He was one of the old timers of the city. He was a quiet person and had great deal of patience in dealing with people. He stressed Hassidut and was a regular member of the mishnayot group under the leadership of Shlomo Schmidt and participated in these lessons till his dying days.
He came from Drohobicz as a specialist of mineral, seltzer and soda waters to the factory of Moldauer. As manager of the place he made a salary that modestly provided for his family. When the factory closed, he and his wife began to sell geese and their feathers.
He had seven happy go lucky sons that received their education in the Talmud torah as was then the custom. His oldest son presently in Tel Aviv, worked for a short period prior to World War I as a printer in the Schochet printing place.
During World War I. another son died of small pox in 1915.
On reaching old age in 1927, he became ill and was taken to the hospital in Krakow but the medical efforts failed and he was buried in the city.
His oldest son Arieh- Leon- lived for some time in Bydgoscz where he was a substantial and respected merchant. He represented the large chocolate factory "Zet" and was also the assistant manager of the local Jewish bank.
Yerachmiel- Milik-Emil, the second son was also a very successful merchant in the coastal area of Poland.
[Page 190]
With the outbreak of the war, the brothers managed to reach Russia and then Leon reached Palestine and settled in Ramat Gan. He opened in Tel Aviv a furniture store called "Eilat". Emil lives in Vienna where he has a factory. He is known to support charity. He visited Israel several times. Two of his sons are still known to be in Russia.

Chet ח

Baruch Chayot
He was a teacher of small children for years in Jaslo. He suffered for years from his stomach and was forced to travel each year to Karlsbad for medical treatments. In spite of these medical problems, he was devoted to his job and hundreds of young students learned through him the Hebrew alphabet and elementary Hebrew reading.
He had several sons and daughters but luck avoided him. One of his young daughters drowned at Koczerow. His oldest son was injured and died from the wounds. One daughter left for the USA. Only Tziporah, the oldest daughter was very ambitious and managed to open a haberdashery stand in the market and following her marriage to a yeshiva student named Sheffel opened a chocolate, fruit and seltzer store in the market in the house of Stillman. She

was very successful and their economic situation improved . One son an apprentice at Unger's glass workshop and remained there as a worker.

[Page 191]

Yerachmiel Tevel
He was the son in law of Shmuel Wolf Ehrlich and lived on Florianska Street. He had a grocery store on the same street and made a nice living.
He was very religious and worshipped at the study center

Elimelech Thaler
He was born in Zmigrod and was one of the old timers in the city of Jaslo. He was one of the first to own their homes in Jaslo. He was one of the people that established Jewish life in the city and shaped it. He was a honest and straight. He was also known to be a scholar and student of the first rabbi of Jaslo, the late Yona Tzanger.

[Page 192]

Elimelech Thaler

He was a very active person and under his guidance the community bought land. He was the initiator of the building of the study center and the public bathhouse and was one of the first to sign the so called consensus paper or invitation to the first official rabbi of Jaslo, Rabbi Awraham Yehoshua Heshil Rubin.

He built his home in the Targowica near the home of Rabbi Mandil. Those that visited Jaslo in the thirties saw a patriarchal figure with a very long beard who promenaded along the sidewalk next to his one story house . This was the elderly reb Elimelech Thaler.

Most of his life he dealt with grains andwell off. His sons received a religious and traditional education. His first son in law was Feiwil Klinman.

Awraham Thaler

The oldest son of Elimelech Thaler was an original student at the study center when it just started to function. He devoted himself to his studies. Already as a youngster he was attracted to the Zionist movement in the city and was one of the five original members of the Yeshuron club.

He left Jaslo with the outbreak of World War I. and settled in Holland. He used to visit annually his family in Jaslo. He was in hiding during World War II, survived the war and then left for Belgium but soon returned to Holland. He visited Israel in 1951 with his wife and participated at the meeting of the Jaslo association in Tel Aviv, Israel.

Shmuel Thaler

A brother of Awraham Thaler. He was a student at the study center and was very well educated. He left Jaslo and lives today in London

Mordechai Dawid Thaler

One of the first Hassidic Jews in Jaslo. In the prime of his life he took ill and passed away. He left a wife, four daughters and a son. The oldest daughter married Moshale Eder (see later).

The daughters received from Shmuel Hankower the right to distribute the milk from his farm in the city. The lease provided jobs to the girls for many years.

One of the girls named Hendel Weber left Jaslo in the twenties and settled in the USA with her children. Another daughter was married to Tzwi Teitelbaum of Frysztak.

[Page 193]
Ber Thaler

The son of Mordechai Dawid Thaler was a non talker and hardly uttered a word. He was a merchant and also worked with egg exporters. He placed the eggs in a chalk solution during the summer when there was an abundance of eggs and then took them out in the winter and crated them for export. He lived all his life in the house that belonged to Bransdadter-Zifman in the market square. He had two sons.

Naphtali Thaler

He was very familiar with books, kept his Jewish tradition and observed the religious traditions. He dealt with grains and imported sugar and flour for retailers. He had a small house near Zelig Korrzenik on a side street of Nowa Street. (The house was demolished during World War I by the Russians). His wife Miriam Shifra managed a modest home. They had five sons and two daughters. One daughter was named Zelda and the other one Henia.

**Naphtali and Naala Rechfeld
(children of Zelde Thaler)**

Brili Thaler was the third son in the family and he suddenly died at the age of two. The sister Henia also died at a very young age.

[Page 194]

When the fourth son was born, a large circumcision party was held. Indeed many guests were invited and it was a lavish affair. The circumcision finished, he was given the name of Dawid. The baby was handed to his mother who began to feed him. The guests sat down to partake in the meal when suddenly they heard a piercing scream from the mother of the baby. The latter fell asleep in the hands of the mother and did not awake. The shock was beyond description. Minutes ago, the blessing was made over the circumcision of a Jewish child and minutes later everybody was uttering condolences.

The daughter Zelde, an intelligent girl, left Jaslo for the USA and later returned to marry Yehezkel Rechfeld. They had a son Naphtali and a daughter Naala. When the war started, Yehezkel Rechfeld and the children disappeared. Zelde returned alone to the USA.

Leibish Thaler, the younger son of Naphtali Thaler was the owner of haberdashery store for many years. He was a member of the Zionist movement and left for Palestine as a pioneer in the thirties. He settled in Tel Aviv.

Yaakow Thaler

He was a brother of Naphtali Thaler and an old grocery merchant that also dealt in sugar and flour on a retail and wholesale basis. He was extremely religious and lived on Kazimeirz Street. He had five sons that received a very religious education. Three of the sons are in the USA. One of the sons named Awraham was wounded on the Austrian-Russian front and his legs had to be amputated.

Due to the serious injury, Awraham received from the Polish government an exclusive license to sell tobacco in Jaroslaw where he settled and married the daughter of the religious slaughterer.

Yossil Thaler

He was the only one amongst the brothers to learn a trade namely hat making. He was a quiet person but had a great deal of drive and sold all kinds of hats besides taking orders for custom made hats.

Like his brother, he too was religious. He lived in one of the Amar-Kornfeld houses on Kazimierz Street. He had four sons and three daughters. The oldest son left for Germany in the twenties. The second one left for the USA. The third son Tzwi was very active in the Zionist youth movement and for a while was the official secretary. He then left Jaslo for Palestine in the thirties and lives presently in Kfar Ata.

[Page 195]

Yaakow Thaler

The oldest son of Naphtali Thaler studied at the study center in his youth. He was busy selling haberdashery items in his stand at the market. He had no sons.

Betzalel Thaler

He was the second son of Naphtali Thaler. He also studied in his youth but later had a haberdashery business and made a nice living. He had three daughters; Leah, Rachel and Haya Beila and one son named Hershale who died as a child. The family lived all their life on Nowa Street.

Btzalel Thaler's daughters

Awraham Yaakow Thaler

He was a native of Frysztak and the son in law D. Mandel who was nicknamed the redheaded teacher. He had a bakery on Iglena Street and was a devoted Hassidic follower who often traveled to visit his rabbi. He gave lots of charity.

His only son managed to survive the war and reached Palestine where he settled in Haifa.

[Page 196]
Moshe Tudor

He was one of the old time merchants of ready made clothing on Kosciuszko Street. He was a very respected individual and spoke with great authority. His house was open to all needy, and he supported the poor people and the needy institutions n the city.

He lived in the Amar-Kornfedl house since 1914. He had a spacious apartment that he placed at the disposal of various groups where they could meet and discuss their situation. Amongst his visitors was the saintly Rabbi Shlomo Libli of Tyczin. He himself was a follower of the Rabbi of Rymanow.

He headed the Association of " Yad Charutzim" for many years. He tended to the maintenance of the building that contained the synagogue, especially the outside appearance. He also prayed daily, at the synagogue morning and evening.

He had six sons and three daughters. All received a religious education as well as a general education. Two of his sons and a daughter died during his life time.

His oldest son Dawid and the second son Shimshon- a son in law of Yoel Margulies and the third son Reuven lived in Tarnow and sold ready made clothing and sweaters. The fourth son Israel studied engineering and worked at Bilitz.

He escaped to Eastern Galicia with the outbreak of World War II and from there reached Russia where he died. Two years ago, his widow reached Israel with three sons. Dawid settled in Haifa, Reuven in Petach Tikvah, and Israel resided in one of the reception centers but he later left the country. Lately, Shimshon and his daughter left Paris, France, and came to Israel.

P. Turbowsky

He was the main cantor in the great synagogue until World War I. He was from Russia and descendant of the Zeidel Rubner family. He was a a talented musical baritone. He conducted the services at the great synagogue with an excellent choir.

When the Russians retreated from Jaslo during World War I. in 1915 he also left the city. Nothing was heard of him again. (See chapter 18)

L.Tigerman

He was a highly educated person and the son in law of Goldshlag. He was one of the managers of the oil refinery in Niglowic. He escaped to Stanislaw with the outbreak of World War II but there he was killed by the Germans. His wife survived the war and lives in Australia.

[Page 197]
Asher Yeshayahu Teitelbaum

He had a small grocery store behind the municipal building and was a very religious and G-d fearing individual. He worshipped regularly at the study center of Rabbi Mandil.

He was sick for a number of years until he passed away. He left a wife and some small children. His oldest son followed in the father's Hassidic footsteps and was named after the Rabbi of Bobowa where he studied at the Yeshiva

Moshe Teitelbaum

He was the brother in law of Shmuel Knobloch and resided in Rymanow. In the twenties he moved to Jaslo and opened a store that dealt with animal skins on Florianska Street.

He was of small statue with a full grown beard. He had excellent manners and was a capable conversationalist. He prayed regularly at the study center and daily studied the Talmud.

Awraham Teitelbaum

He was the son of Moshe Teitelbaum and a yeshiva student. He followed the Hassidim of Bobow. He loved books and enjoyed reading them. He had a shoe store on Florianska Street.

Benyamin Teitelbaum

He was the younger son of Moshe Teitelbaum. He was already influenced by modern ideas and was very alert and sharp. He resided for some time in Belgium. On his return to Jaslo, he married the daughter of Ephraim Teumim.

Following his marriage, he opened a shoe store. The couple managed to flee to Russia where both died in Russia during World War II.

Betzlel Teichler

He was a good natured individual and an old follower of the Rabbi of Gorlice. He dedicated himself to the prayers and held conversations with the creator. He was basically a happy person in spite of the fact that he had no sons. He accepted the good and the bad. He took care of a sick wife for many years and always tried to comfort her.

[Page 198]

He was always patient and explained to people the situation. He was always willing to help. With the reconstruction of the great synagogue, he was one of the ten worshippers who started the services. He prayed next to the holy ark.

He was a representative of a beer company and thus earned his living. He lived on Esnika Street.

Yehezkel Tepper

He was originally from Frysztak and moved in the twenties to Jaslo where he lived opposite the synagogue. He was a Hassidic follower that strictly observed all religious rules without deviation.

Each day he displayed his merchandise on the shelves of his stand in the market. He was pleased with life.

Yaakow Trencher

He was born in Krosno and worked for many years in Jaslo as a tailor. He was one of the original members of the "Poali Agudath Israel" in Jalso. He was a Hassidic Jew and loved to browse through books.

Following his marriage to Charna, the daughter of Ezriel Rosenwasser, he settled permanently in Jaslo and opened a tailor workshop on Widok Street.

Yehoshua Tschup

He was originally from Dukla and was the son in law of Yekil Hirshfeld. He dealt in money matters and was well known in the city. With the passing of his father in law he assumed his position as the beadle of the worship place.

He was always good humored and always had a joke or wisecrack for the people that he dealt with. He also continued with the job at the synagogue. He left Jaslo for Russia with the outbreak of World War II.

[Page 198]

Yod ‬י

Return

Dina Johans

The Johans family left Gorlice in 1915 following the heavy battles in the area and settled in Jaslo. Shortly thereafter, the father of the family took ill and soon passed away. He was a god fearing man and a scholar.

[Page 199]

He left a wife, two sons and two daughters. Dina Johans was a modest and heart warming woman. She accepted her faith as a religious person. She did not complain for she did not want to gossip or indulge in idle talk.

She continued to manage the family with the limited resources at her disposal. She received great satisfaction from the studies of her son Eliyahu who was a student of the Rabbi Shmuel Fuhrer from Krosno. He was an excellent student and capable of absorbing vast knowledge. He was soon considerate one of the great upcoming Talmudic scholars.

Rabbi Eliyahu Johans

Following his marriage to the daughter of the Rabbi of Luptin, he was appointed as Rabbi of Ozipoli (he perished in the shoah with his family). Her second son Dow was also a student with Rabbi Shmuel Fuhrer of Korsno and was also

an excellent Talmudic student familiar with Jewish law. He survived the war and reached Israel where he lives in Ramat Amidar in Ramat Gan.

Emallia Johans the oldest daughter married a yeshiva student named Chaim Zeew Kizelstein from Krosno. She, her husband and a daughter left for Palestine and settled in Tel Aviv. He is a clerk with the community council

The mother and the youngest daughter perished during the shoa.

[Page 200]
Israel Just
He was the son of Dow Beril Just from Zmigrod. Nobody knew his family name in Jaslo and he was known as Israel the teacher. He was one of the first "heder" or Hebrew teachers in Jaslo with the development of the Jaslo community. Many of the old time residents of Jaslo were proud students of Israel Just who gave them the first elementary Jewish education.
He lived in the Targowica as did most of the early Jewish settlers near Jaslo. When he passed away, they sold the plot on which stood the shaky hut of Israel Just to Mandil. He built on it a residence and a prayer house.

Baruch Just
He was a fine and gentle spirit. He was born in Jaslo and was consider red as one of the scholars of the Jewish community. He was well read and familiar with the enlightened literature as well as with the early Zionist literature namely Mapu's book "The Love of Zion" and Smolensky's "The Error in the Way of Life".
He grew with the community and frequently heard the complaints of the population against the actions of the community leaders. He joined the Zionist organization as soon as the first branch of the movement was opened in Jaslo. The blue collection box was always in his house. He was a jeweler and had a nice income. He lived all his life on Kosciuszko Street. He had three sons and four daughters who received a Jewish and national education.
His eldest son Berish organized the first Hebrew speaking club in town. He attended the Hebrew lectures given at the "Yeshuron" club. (He left Jaslo following his marriage)
[Page 201]
His second son Israel was the local reporter for the Hebrew press and organized the first Hebrew Dramatic group called the "Anski" group. He was an artist and had a sensitivity for artistic events and thus invited theater groups, artists and poets to the city to present their creations. He also took part in some of the theater presentations as an actor. He was the head of the "United" organization until he left. Following World War II, he reached Palestine after crossing the Hungarian forests. He settled in Jerusalem and later moved to Tel Aviv where he worked as a government clerk. His younger son Alter lives in Belgium.

Dawid Just
He was first son in law of Elimelech Freund and one of the leading religious intellectuals that were known to the community in Jaslo. He was the grandson of the ritual slaughterer of Tarnobrzeg and visited Palestine during the fourth Aliyah period. Following his engagement, he returned to Jaslo where he continued to support the building of a Jewish National Home.
Following his marriage he settled in Jaslo where he opened a shoe store and developed plans to settle in Palestine. Meanwhile he was very active in the Zionist movement and one of the most active in the Mizrahi movement and an active community leader.
In 1933 he left for Palestine again with his family and settled in Tel Aviv. He went into business and later became a builder. His only son Yaakow, born in Jaslo, was a very talented youngster who showed some writing abilities. He joined the "Hagana" or Jewish underground army prior to the establishment of Israel. He participated in several battles during the Independence War of Israel and distinguished himself in the military operation code named "Dawid" of clearing the approaches to Tel Aviv where he fell. He was killed on the third day of Adar, Tashah or the 13th of February 1948. He was still in the prime of his youth (see some of his writings).

A. Jortner
The family lived for many years on Iglena Street. All the neighbors knew old Jortkena who tried to earn a living by baking bread and cooking tcholent for people for Shabat

Her sons left Jaslo for the USA in the thirties and she died a lonely woman.

[Page 202]

Naphtali Imner

He was a serious and quiet person. He had modern and advanced views on life. He lived in the Targowica and his sons received a general education. His daughter was involved in the Zionist movement and left for Palestine as one of the early pioneers. She lives today at kibbutz Merchavia.

Elimelech Jawitz

He lived in one of the alleys of the Targowica, behind the Christian cemetery where he had a small house and a grocery.

He was a non talker and kept stayed clear of any involvment. He went daily to the prayer house and participated in the mishnayot study group. He had no children, and no other interests.

Shmuel Jakubowicz

He was known in the city as Shmuel Hankowker since he came from the village of Hankowka. He was a typical country type of person but good natured. He brought daily his dairy produce to the city and distributed it to his customers.

On the day when his parents passed away he used to go to pray at the synagogue. He then wore a green velvet hat, a long old coat and a multicolored kerchief at the waist. He would drive his cart into the courtyard of the synagogue and enter to pray. He stood at his place and did not budge, he recited the "Kaddish" and frequently distributed cheese and schnapps for the sake of the soul. He uttered good morning in Yiddish with a heavy accented r and left the place.

Zalman Jakubowicz

He was a brother of Shmuel Jakubowicz and was called Zalman Koczerower for he came from the village of Koczerow that was beyond the Joselka river. He observed strictly the religious laws. He was a merchant and had three daughters two of whom are in America. His only son was killed in World War I.

[Page 203]

Mordechai Itzhakowicz

He was one of the first Jewish residents in Ulaszowica. He was a good natured person and was a Hassidic Jew who followed the path of the righteous. He was a butcher and thus earned his livelihood.

P. Jeroslawsky

He was of Russian origin and lived in Jaslo for a number of years. He helped to establish the "Poalei Tzion" movement in Jaslo. He then disappeared from Jaslo without a trace; some people said that he returned to Russia.

Moshe Yaakow Jermiash

He was born in Jasinic and settled in Jaslo following his marriage at the beginning of the present century. In the city he was known as Moshe Yekil. He had good intentions, friendly, vivacious and liked to please his customers.

He was adored by the intelligentsia and the students at the study center and had devoted customers. He had friendly face and was well disposed to listen.

He lived all his life on Nowa Street near the great synagogue. He had two sons who were active in the Zionist youth groups; Berl and Nachman. The daughter Hawa married Awraham Hoffert and in 1934 left for Palestine and settled in Tel Aviv. Following World War II, the youngest son of the family also reached Palestine and settled in Rishon Letzion

Kaf כ

Mattityahu Katz

He belonged to the first group of Hassidim in the city. He was very close to the rabbi. He was tall and had large beard that gave him a splendid presentation He was a clerk at the spirit refinery from the days of Aleksandrowitch. He became ill in the twenties and soon passed away

[Page 204]

The family left for the USA. Simcha and Benyamin Katz, the sons of Mattityahu Katz, are strong supporters and contributors of the Zionists movement in the USA.

(Benyamin visited Israel two years ago.)

Lamed ל

Shmuel Lehr

He was an old-timer in Jaslo and had his own house on Kazimierz Street. Later he acquired another house on Chajnochy Street that bordered the first house. He was a furrier and a hat maker who also sold hats. He had a nice income and three sons. One of them lived in Munich and another one Moshe Lehr lived in Krakow. The family took great pride in the fact that he was the beadle at the famous "Rama Synagogue" in Krakow.

Eliyahu Lehr

He was the third son of the family. He was jovial, liked to joke and listened to stories. He continued his father's trades. He was also very handy in creating velvet gloves that were very elegant. The study center and the yeshiva students liked these gloves.

He was also the due collector for all those people that used the market. Every vendor, stand and cart had to pay a certain money tax for the use of the place. Frequently, peasants refused to pay or tried to vanish that resulted in fights but the dues were collected.

He had four daughters and a son who received a general education. Two of the daughters survived the war and the son is in the USA.

P. Laufer

He was the son in law of Eli Hass and was very familiar with torah literature. He was a member of the Mizrahi movement and a timber merchant who lived on Florianska Street.

[Page 205]

Mordechai Leizer

He had a haberdashery store on Kosciuszko Street. He followed the mood of the community. Sometimes he dressed modern, still he attended all the lectures at the "shtibel" and at the study center where he delved into the study of the Talmud. Lately he gave up his business and became an agent for many firms in Krakow, Rzeszow and Lemberg. He handled the purchasing and shipping by railway of the ordered merchandise. He had a son and a daughter who received a high school education.

Yossef Licht

He was an old haberdashery store owner and a pleasant and moderate person. He liked to listen to torah discussions and rabbinical interpretations and customs. He was always neatly dressed. As a religious person he distanced himself from every scandal. He concerned himself primarily with his business. But since he lived amongst people, he was once nominated on a party list for the community board and was elected.

He had two daughters.

Dawid Lipczer

He led a saintly and simple life. His outside appearance gave the impression of a great rabbi with his white beard that covered his face that was full of holes caused by years of work as a baker. All his life he lived in Elimelech Goldstein's house. He had one daughter that married Yekil Hirshfeld and three sons.

Itchi Lipczer

He was the son of Dawid Lipczer and he devoted himself to the study of the torah. He served as cantor for many years at the synagogue of "Yad Charutzim". Lately he received the job of collecting money for "Tomchei Aniyim" or the poor people association. He had several sons that received a traditional religious education in the spirit of Bobow.

Moshe Hersh Lipczer

He was the second son of Dawid Lipczer . He was religious and a baker like his father. He also sold bagels. He was a sick person

Betzalel Lipczer

He was the third son of of Dawid Lipczer and the son in law of Meir Felderbrand. He was one of the first to join the

"Poalei Tzion" or Jewish workers union branch in Jaslo. He tried to be modern and worked as a baker. He was disappointed with his achievements and left for Germany where he also failed to settle down and returned to Jaslo. He had a nice voice, he was a baritone and assisted all the city cantors. He was a member of the dramatic club that was organized by the Zionist youth movement.

Yehoshua Lipczer

He was a younger brother of Dawid Lipczer and was also pious and modest. He was a tailor and later opened a grocery and soft drink place when his daughters were a bit older. They even managed for a while a haberdashery store.

His life was very difficult, first his oldest son who used to study at the study center died as a result of a disease contracted during the prolonged battle of Gorlice in 1914. An engaged daughter died from a prolonged disease that drained her. His oldest son in law died of tuberculosis at the age if thirty and left a wife and small children. He continued his life in spite of all of these tragedies.

One of his sons Meir was active in the Zionist youth group and worked as an electrician although he never studied the trade.

Eliezer Lambig

He was the beadle of the "Yad Charutzim " synagogue and tried through this job to provide his family with food but was not terribly successful since he had a large family.

With the outbreak of the World War I, he became ill. He lived in a basement flat of the house the belonged to Lehr next to the "Talmud Torah". The disease progressed and the war prevented real treatment for the Russian occupied the city. He soon died and left a wife and several small sons.

Yehoshua Lempel

He was the son in law of Wolf Eintziger and came from old Sandz. He was a quiet and modest man. He was content with his lot and observed the religion. He prayed at the study venter.
[Page 207]
He was one of the first store owners to sell kitchen ware and later opened a haberdashery in Amer-Kornfeld's house.
His daughter who was a devoted member of the Zionist youth left for Palestine in the thirties and is a member of kibbutz Dan.

H. Langer, doctor.
He was a doctor and settled in Jaslo in the thirties. He lived on Kosciuszko Street. Only his daughter managed to survive World War II and reached Israel where she settled in Tel Aviv.

Yossef Lans, doctor.
He was one of the old doctors in the city and an original member of the Zionist movement in Jaslo. He lived all his life on May 3rd Street. During the summer season he opened a medical office and a rest home for children in Iwonicz.

Gedalia Lefelholtz
He was from Dukla and the son in law of Elimelech Gutwin. He was a Hassid and familiar with the torah. He was a regular worshipper at the study center of Rabbi Mandil and also partook in the daily lessons given there. He was a merchant and lived in the Targowica square. He was honest and strait. He married Sara Gutwin and they had several daughters.

Mem מ

P. Mager
He was one of the senior clerks at the refinery in Niglowic. He was an intelligent person and religious. He had a large and trimmed beard. One day while crossing Kosciuszko Street he had a stroke and died on the spot. His son left Jaslo and settled in Haifa.

[Page 208]
Eisik Moldauer
He was the son in law of Leibish Winfeld and was considered a modern person. At first he started the bottling of seltzer water and then took over the business of his father in law that was located in the market square. He continued with the business until 1914 when the war started he left for Vienna.

Meir Moshel
He was the second son in law of Moshe Tzimet. He was a student of Rabbi Shapiro of Lublin and was an active and very pleasant. Community leader (See Moshe Tzimet)

Simon Mata, Dr.
He was one of the first doctors in the city. He was very respected and lived on Kosciuszko Street. He died in the twenties and had only daughters.

Yossef Mata
He was a very modern person and had modern ideas. He was a Zionist and prayed at the big synagogue where he was elected as beadle. He was the son in law of Wolf Wagshal and lived in the corner of of the square where the busses parked and had had an inn there. He was doing

well and his children received a high school education. His oldest son left Jaslo with Polish Independence.

Zelig Miller
With the growth of the Jewish community in Ulaszowica, he was selected to be the religious representative of the Jewish community. He was appointed to organize the "Hevra Kadisha" and was also appointed as ritual slaughterer and performer of circumcisions.

He was a very popular figure in his time in Jaslo. He presented himself in a traditional pattern and was very scholarly. He devoted himself to piety and religious obligations. He was one of the first to arrive to serve G-d in the synagogue.

He lived in a wooden hut on Chajnochy Street near the house of the rabbi where he raised his family of nine children, six boys and three daughters. He contented himself with little and was very modest. One day he decided to abandon the slaughtering business and devoted himself to commerce.

[Page 209]
This was a very smart move to open a store in the market of Jaslo in spite of strong ant-Semitism. A liberal gentile named Brongliwicz rented him space to open the store. He managed the store for years with his son in law Eliezer Blum. The Polish noblemen of the area took a liking to him and spent hours talking to him about life and the purpose of life. He had excellent commercial contacts with the local gentry.

He lived a long life and at age 80 still led the congregation in the afternoon Minha service of Yom Kippur that was dedicated to his wife that passed away on this holy day some years ago.

His daughters married yeshiva students of respected families. Five of his son in laws lived in Jaslo; Eliezer Blum, Dawid Seinwel, Moshe Kalb, Moshe Margulies, Naphtali Hoffert, the sixth Itzhak Goldberg left for the USA.

Zelig Miller

[Page 210]
Two of his sons Chaim and Pinhas were affected by the enlightenment and became highly educated yeshiva students. Both left Jaslo prior to World War I; the first one settled in Koln, Germany and the second moved to Holland.

He was very happy at the marriage of his granddaughter to Dawid Seinwel and showed it while dancing the traditional ceremonial group dance with a bottle of spirit in his hands. A rapid body count indicated that he had about 109 members in his family. He passed away at the age of 87.

Moshe Miller
He was the oldest son of Zelig Miller and a scholarly type who devoted himself to study and meditation. He was a weak person yet did a great deal of penance and fasting. He encouraged his son Shmuel to study in group studies until the early morning hours. The son passed away while the father was still alive.
He traveled to visit the Rabbi of Siniawa and when the latter died he continued to travel to see his follower. Suddenly he became ill and was diagnosed as having intestinal inflammation. The doctors recommended immediate surgery and on Saturday he left for Vienna where the operation was performed but the patient died and was brought back to Jaslo to be buried.
He left a wife named Miszket, four sons and one daughter. Miszket Miller was a known merchant in the market and continued with the store until she passed away.
The daughter was married to Henech Adler who was a very pious and strictly observant yeshiva student. He participated in all the lectures at the shtibel synagogue and was a regular member of the study center of the rabbi. His flat was in the market and he sold goods. He had three sons who were raised in the Bobower Hassidic tradition and were students of the study center. He also had two daughters.
Gdelia Miller was the oldest son of Moshe Miller and he left Jaslo with the outbreak of the war and settled in Vienna. His son reached Palestine in the thirties and settled in Kfar Saba.
[Page 211]
The second son Yaakow, a member of the Mizrahi, settled in Tarnow following his marriage. Eliezer, the third son was a member of the Zionist movement and remained in Jaslo and helped his mother with the business. The fourth son Yehezkel was a lively fellow and loved in his youth to act as s a stand up comic. He left Jaslo with Polish Independence.

Moshe Mintz
He was a butcher and a very quiet person. His sons studied design and were excellent artists particularly artistic signs. One of his sons was killed by a co-worker while standing on a ladder at the work place. The other children left for Vienna.

Nute Maltz
He was one of the first cattle merchants and also had a butcher store in Jaslo. He was very well known amongst the artisans and devoted himself to the association of "Yad Charutzim" and to this end he dedicated his second home. His first home was destroyed by the Russians in 1914.
He had a few sons and daughters. Following World War I, his daughters became very active social workers in the city on behalf of the "American Joint". One of his daughters left for the USA in the twenties and while writing these lines I am informed that two of his daughters reached Israel and live in Haifa.

Zelig Maltz
He lived all his life in Tarnowica and was very religious. He strictly observed all the commandments and raised his sons in the same spirit. He brought a special teacher to provide his sons with a religious education. As a village Jew he also engaged in commerce and brought dairy products from the farm to the city. We are told that he observed the commandment of receiving graciously visitors and each visitor in the village found a place in his home. He also gave charity to the needy. One of his sons is in the USA.

Shlomo Maltz

He was the son of Zelig Maltz and settled in Jaslo behind the municipality. He was involved in many enterprises but basically devoted to visiting his Hassidic rabbi.
[Page 212]
He wore silk outfits and a shtreimel. He was the torah reader for years at the "Yad Charutzim" synagogue.

Mendel Meller

Everybody in Jaslo knew Mendel Meller and certainly heard of his sayings, jokes and innuendos. As a matter of fact, he was so popular that when people made a joke or stated a saying they would say that it is a quote from Mendel Meller.

I will be remiss if I did not mention some of his activities in Jaslo for he was a colorful and creative personality who enclosed contradictory characteristics in his personality.

Mendel Meller

He was a follower of the Hassidic Rabbi of Bluzow and absorbed the Zionist theory of Hertzel and one of the first Zionist members in the city while studying a page of the Talmud daily. He wore a large silk capote with an overcoat that had a velvet collar and a silk waistband. He walked with enlightened and non-religious people. He told stories about the famous saintly rabbis and their way of life. The grandchildren devoured the stories. Yet he is also well connected to the Rabbi and to the Tzimet family that is very conservative and traditional. He dreams of Zion and the Palestinian colonists that live in the colonies and build the country. He admires them and sanctifies Zionism for this achievement in spite of the mistakes.

One day, Mendel Meller left Jaslo and headed to Palestine to see for himself what is happening there, what is the reality of the situation. He remained in Jerusalem for several days and then visited each settlement and met the young pioneers. He is impressed with the achievements and is very pleased with his experiences. He even participated in a film that was being made in Palestine about Jewish life there. Indeed he appeared in the movie next to the bronzed young pioneers with their large straw hats that drained the swamps, tended to e wine and orange orchards. He was very pleased in the movie. (The movie was shown in Jaslo in 1913)

He built a large house on Main Street of Jaslo, Third May Street that contained stores on the ground floor. The house had large balconies and large rooms but he himself had a small store of leather and shoe maker supplies. On the long table in the store were always displayed books; Talmuds, newspapers, "Hatzfira" edited by (Nahum Sokolow, a Zionist) next to a Mishnayot, "Hamitzpe" of Lazar on top of an open Talmud book, and Rabbi Mendel wearing a large skullcap looks from under the pile of reading material and smiles. He draws from here and from there, always reading material in his hand. He had a phenomenal memory and one word would start him reciting entire lines in the Talmud. Indeed, I personally witnessed one evening as we sat in the shtibel synagogue when Mendel Meller recited entire pages of the Talmud.

[Page 214]

He was always the spokesman of the group and always had brilliant opening lines for the appropriate group. He would start a conversation by asking where the word was mentioned in the torah and most of the answers would be wrong. He then stated where it appears and in what context, all of this was done orally without notes or books.

The Russians took him as a Jewish hostage in 1915 during World War I when they retreated from Galicia. He spent his time writing a book on Hebrew grammar. He was musically talented and composed Yiddish songs that he sang at various occasions, namely "Nahmo, Nachmo Ami", "Juden Bnei Rachmanim", " Rishke".These songs were also sung at the Rabbi's Purim party. With his return from Russian captivity he wrote a song entitled "Hayev Adam Lebsumi Beboriah" with a special Purim tune.

He was sick as a child and his face remained marked with scars for the rest of his life. People asked him why he was punished in such manner. He answered as follows

"You know that when a child is conceived it absorbs knowledge for nine months and prior to birth an angel taps the lips of the soon to be born child that erases all knowledge, thus the child is born without knowledge. When the angel came to me and tried to eliminate my knowledge I resisted. The angel stated that he must carry out the order.

[Page 215]

I refused to budge and covered my face with both hands so that the angel will not be able to touch my lips. I refused to abandon my torah knowledge. We struggled back and forth until the angel managed to push away my hands and slapped me. You can see the results. Of course I resisted as much as I could but the angel overpowered me. On occasion he would ask the worshippers to pick a line from the torah section that was read and build on it a funny story or pun. These stories and puns circulated throughout the community and were always attributed to the author namely Mendel Meller. He once stated that he will break the record of speed-reading the " Mishne Torah" and he did it in fifty-five minutes flat. He read without mistakes and with the special tune appropriate for the Holiday of Hoshana Rabba.

He was also a very serious person in spite of his comical approach to things. He devoted himself to public affairs. At the community board he represented the Zionist cause and at the municipality the merchants interests.

He had four sons and four daughters. One of the sons was the famous Hebrew writer Dow Kimchi who resides in Jerusalem for about forty years. The young son of Dow Kimchi, Igal Kimchi, relates facts about his father's work as a secretary for the late Chaim Weitzman. Another son, Hersh Elimelech left for the USA in the twenties. The youngest son, Israel is presently in Paris. His first son in law was Yossef Frumowicz, the second one was Meir Batman, the third son in law was Pinhas Raab the owner of the the photo shop "Flora" on Kosciuszko Street. One of the daughters, Chaya, left for Palestine and lives in Jerusalem.

The Germans caught him but he managed to wrap himself in his prayer shawl and destroyed all real cherished items so that they should not fall into the bloody hands of the Germans. Mendel Meller thus sanctified the heavenly body on this day of destruction.

[Page 216]

Awraham Meller

He was the second son of Mendel Meller and was well read and educated. He always had a friendly smile on his lips and was close to the ideals of the Mizrahi movement. He was an active member of the movement and was one of the founders of the Mizrahi School. He prayed regularly at the Mizrahi synagogue and was a merchant. His son Elimelech survived the war and recently, arrived in Israel where he settled in Haifa.

Yossef Meller

Prior to World War I he became known as a benefactor of the needy and a provider for those that needed a place to sleep for the night. He was known to welcome guests especially out of town people. He also invited poor guests and fed them. On occasions there were as many as ten to fifteen people at his table. He dealt with cattle.

He was one of the founders of the association of "Hachnassat Kalah" or helping poor girls marry. In order to raise funds towards this end, he created a special band that wore blue bands and copper buttons on the jackets, red stripes along the pants and special hats with shining feathers. This band appeared at various functions namely weddings and all receipts went to the association. The band was well known in the city and existed until the outbreak of World War II.

Hersh Meller

He originates from the area of Brzezow and settled in Jaslo in the twenties. He lived all his life in Hiclowka. He was a tailor and a quiet sensitive person. He was very observant and helpful to the needy. He prayed at the big synagogue.

Dawid Mandel

He was nicknamed the red teacher. He lived many years at the Targowica. Lately he did nothing since he was sick. He had two sons, Yehezkel and Shlomo who were bakers and three daughters who married bakers

[Page 217]

Yehezkel Mandel

He leased the bakery from Zelig Korzenik. He was a working man and belonged to the Polei Tzion in his youth. His business picked up in later years.

Yossef Manashe

This was his German nickname from his younger days. He was actually from Tarnow and came to Jaslo as an assistant to the weaving store of Brandsdadter.

Following his marriage, having saved some money, he decided to open his own weaving store. With time his business expanded and he became one of the wealthiest Jews in town. He built a big house in the market facing Nowa Street opposite the mayor's office. His was the largest store of this type in Jaslo. He was really a self made man and had a modern outlook on life but observed tradition and prayed daily at the Yad Charutzim synagogue. He was not interested in politics or public affairs. He devoted himself to his business and his clients that earned him the reputation of an honest man. Customers trusted him and relayed on him to obtain the best woolens at the best price.

All his four sons and three daughters received an academic education. One daughter Miriam was married to Dr. Emanuel Tzuker, a children's doctor, son of Alter Tzuker of Rzerzin who was the son in law of attorney Naphtali Manashe.

Awraham, Manashe, doctor

He was the oldest son of Yossef Manaashe who was called Dolik in his youth. He was an attorney in Jaslo and known as Adolph Manasse. He tended to assimilation and kept his distance from public affairs. He lived on Kosciuszko Street.

Naphtali Manashe, doctor
The second son of Yossef Manashe was called as a youngster Tulik. He was also an attorney and considered one of the best in town.

[Page 218]

He joined the Zionist movement while a student at high school. He was one of the founders of the Yeshuron club in Jaslo between 1905/1906 and a friend of Dr. Kornhauser and Dr. Stein. Together they were very active on behalf of Zionism and spread the idea amongst their clients and the Jewish population at large.

He was elected to the community board along the Zionist list and protected adamantly these interests. He was also elected to the municipality and defended the Jewish interests and honor in Jaslo.

He was very soft spoken, lax in religious matters but attended the synagogue on high holidays in order to listen to the rabbi's "mussaf" or second half of the service. His only son was raised along Zionist lines.

The family managed to reach Russia with the outbreak of World War II where he and his son became ill and passed away. His wife returned and reached Israel where she settled in Ramat Hayil.

Zigmunt Menashe
He was an engineer and worked for a Dutch company in Sumatra. With the outbreak of World War II he was caught by the Germans and brought to Poland where he perished.

Michael Menashe, doctor
He was the fourth son of Yossef Menashe. He was a lawyer and left Jaslo for Lodz where he established a flourishing legal practice. The Germans caught him and brought him to Jaslo where his traces disappeared.

Giselle Menashe-Kagan
She was the oldest daughter of Yossef Menashe and finished as doctor of pharmacology. She never practiced her profession since she became involved in social work. She worked with several social institutions and dedicated herself specifically with sick orphaned children.

[Page 219]

Hanka Menashe-Westreich
She was the second daughter of Yossef Menashe and was also involved in social work and tried to help the needy. She was married to attorney Westreich who was a Zionist and active in the community. He supported his wife's activities. He was very active and was elected to the municipality on behalf of the merchant's ticket where he defended their interests.

St. Westreich did not practice law but managed with his father in law the family business. The firm was known as Yossef Menashe and son in law. He managed to escape with his wife and is presently in Paris with his family. His son visited Israel and worked on a kibbutz but later returned to Paris.

Moshe Margolies
He was one of the influential Jews of the city. He was highly respected as an individual and scholar. He was very familiar with the surrounding milieu and a very pleasant speaker. He dressed neatly and radiated warmth. He was also known to discreetly administer assistance to the needy.

He was a wood merchant and his house was near the study center on Chajnochy Street near the river, opposite the house of Meir Berish the slaughterer. Prior to World War I, he fell ill while on a business trip. On returning home the disease progressed, he suffered for a while and died. He left a wife named Hawa Rachel, two sons, and two married daughters. His young un-married son Sender, a student at the study center, was infected by a contagious disease in 1914 and died.

Hersh Margolies
He was the second son of Moshe Margolies and a student at the study center. He was a quiet and shy student who continued in his father's footsteps and observed religion and tradition. He was also a wood merchant and married the daughter of Berish Altman. The couple lived in his house on Kosciuszko Street.

Moshe Margolies
He was the son in law of Zelig Miller and very religious. He was well acquainted with the Talmud and dressed neatly. He prayed at the study center and had a store in the
Market. He had five daughters and a son named Hershel who left Jaslo for the USA. (According to rumors, his son did very well in the USA).
He did well and took the entire family to the USA following Polish Independence. Only one daughter remained in Jaslo.

[Page 220]
Abba Margolies
They were three brothers that came from Trzycic. The oldest was called Abtcze Margolies and owned an inn in the market place. He did very well and led a Hassidic life. He had a seat along the eastern wall and loved to hear himself sing in his younger days. He loved to conduct services or sing the songs during meal time. On occasion he would also read the torah when the regular reader was absent. Lately he became very close to the rabbi. He never expressed his own views in public but was always involved with the big study center where he was the beadle.
He had three daughters and one son named Dawid who was tossed out of a speeding moving train by anti-Semitic Poles. This occurred in 1919 after Poland received its independence. The train was coming from Krakow.

Baruch Margolies
The second brother was the son in law of Kornreich and a wood merchant. He was a fair man and presented a nice picture of himself. He distanced himself from all public activities but was a Zionist. He was influenced by modern trends. His sons received a general education. Nathan his second son married his cousin, Abcze's daughter. One of his daughters left for Palestine and settled on a kibbutz where she lives presently. He also visited Israel twenty years ago and hoped to settle in the country.
When his house near the Ulaszowica Bridge burned down prior to World War I he moved to Karp's house. (His oldest son is in America)

Yoel Margolies
The third brother was the son in law of Feiwil Klinman. He observed tradition and prayed at the big study center. He had a store that sold writing materials in the market square before the tobacco store of Frankel. He made a nice living and had two daughters and a son. The oldest daughter was married to Shimshon Tudor.

With the outbreak of the war he managed to flee and following the World War II he reached Israel where he lives today in Pardess Hanah.

Adolph Margolies

He inherited his father's store on the death of his father Menashe Margolies. It was a big store that sold building materials, electrical supplies, machines and fine metals in the market square. Adolph Margolies was not related to the other Margolies families in town. He was an educated person and tended to follow assimilation. His wife was a devoted member of the Zionist women organization and "Wizo" and took a sincere interest in these societies.

She was killed on the train by Polish anti-Semites during the first days of World War II and he managed to escape but remained in Poland.

Moshe Margolies

He lived but a few years in Jaslo and with Polish Independence moved to Przedmiscze. He then left Poland for the USA. He was the son in law of Fass, the barber.

Lewi Markowicz

He was an excellent host and gave a great deal of charity. He was very popular, especially his wife who was considered a Sainte for she gave generously charity and made no pretensions about it. Their house was open to all poor and needy people in the city. The indigenous were received with open arms. Both husband and wife traveled to visit the Rabbi of Dukla prior to his moving to Jaslo. While waiting for his place to be finished, the Rabbi stayed at their house. As a sign of a good host, he displayed a picture of Awraham receiving the three angels in the desert before his tent.

He lived all his life in Eliezer Brenner's house and made a living by preparing the ingredients for the salami industry.

[Page 222]

Nun נ

Leibish Nebentzahl

Leibish Hacohen Nebentzahl was from Kolaczyce and settled in Jaslo with Polish Independence. He lived in A. Goldstein' house and was a very pious Jew reciting constantly the psalms. He prayed daily at the study center and loved to listen to the torah discussions. He was always happy and content with life. He sold animal skins and I think that he had a son named Eli who was called in his youth Eli Hacohen.

P. Nagler

He was one of the clerks of Niglowic and escaped to Kolomyja in Eastern Galicia with the outbreak of World War II but his traces were lost.

Yehoshua Nutman

He was the son in law of Wolf Wagshall and very quiet. He was a glazier and lived all his life at Ulaszowica.

Yossef Leib Nussbaum

He was one of the more pleasant personalities in the city. He was known as a serious person with a head on his shoulders and was also known as Yossef Libli.

He was one of the old Wilipoler Hassidim that were God fearing and followed the commandments without the need to explain. They did as their parents did.

He was rather small with a large beard and two long side curls that covered most of his face. From the bushy eye brows shone two sharp eyes. He had a pleasant smile and dressed in the traditional manner. A red handkerchief was always in his back pocket. The four fringes of the "talit katan" or small prayer shawl were hanging below the knees and so he walked daily in the streets of the city and frequently visited his customers with whom he negotiated business and wished them good morning.

The city people respected him and I remember an event that occurred in my presence as Yossef Leib Nussbaum was walking he met the mayor of the city, Dr. Willusz.

[Page 223]

Good morning mister Orrzehowski? How are you? Greets him the mayor jovially and how is business today while he continued to walk. Yossef Leib Nussbaum raised his hat and nodded to the mayor as a sign of respect and answered something to the effect that everything is ok but deep inside he knew that the mayor was no great friend of the Jews.

The height of his joy he reached at the eve of the Shabbath, following the immersion in the mikvah and the preparation for the Sabbath. His eyes gleamed at the lights of the Shabbath candles. He packed his little pouch with sniff so that he has for two or three portions that will keep him going during the Shabbath services.

He was very close to the rabbi and one of his close associates. He was always in a hurry to be at the rabbi's table on Shabbath and holidays. Here he received a half a glass of beer that could not be refused. Then he began singing Shabbath songs that the crowd enjoyed. When he finished singing, he blessed the rabbi, the household and all the present people and sipped the remainder of the beer. He wiped the foam of his face and with a heavy heart bid farewell. He tied his red kerchief around his neck and began to head to the door where he was one of the last people to say Shabbath Shalom.

He was an excellent shofar blower and service leader. He loved to conduct services on Saturdays and Holidays. His service was sincere and pious. Particularly moving were his services during the high holidays when he shed tears and almost talked to the almighty.

He lived all his life in Lehr's house on Kazimierz Street. He reached old age and passed away leaving two sons and a daughter who did not live in Jaslo.

[Page 224]
Chaim Dawid Nussbaum

He was the oldest son of Yossef Leib Nussbaum and a Hassidic Jew who continued his religious studies. He observed with severity all religious instructions and was fanatic on religious matters. He remained in Jaslo following his marriage and lived in Lehr's house next to the Talmud Torah.

He was also a close follower of the rabbi as was his father. The rabbi's words were holy to him as though they came from Mount Sinai. He led the services at the study center. By tradition he led the morning service or "Shaharit" of the high holidays. His voice was a bit weak but he prayed with his heart.

He was a merchant and later became a teacher at the Talmud Torah. He had several sons but only his oldest daughter Tziporah managed to survive World War II and reached Israel where she married a member of "Hapoel Hamizrahi" and settled in Tel Aviv.

Moshe Nussbaum, the second son of Yossef Leib Nussbaum, was known in his youth as Moshale. He was a student at the study center and was considerate erudite in religious literature. He sat and studied the Talmud with a great deal of concentration in order to understand the profundities of the printed word. The page had to be crystal clear before he proceeded to the next page. He was a sympathetic person but followed the crowd and the time. He sung in the synagogue choir since he had a fine musical voice. He also used to sing Saturday evenings at the third meal the various appropriate songs. His favorite song was "Ein Keelokeinu" that was performed at the rabbi's study center.

He left for Vienna following his marriage and was ritual slaughterer and cantor in that city. He managed to flee Vienna for the USA with the arrival of the Germans. According to rumors he continued these activities in the USA.

Moshe Nibert

He settled in Jaslo in the twenties and was a modern Jew who belonged to the Zionist movement. He was a cattle merchant and a partner of Tzwi Elimelech Stein in the export of cattle. He was known as a charitable person.

[Page 225]

Abish Neiman

His whole face painted a picture of gentility covered by a long yellow beard. His large forehead, shiny bright eyes, and piercing glances made deep penetrations. Dressed in clean and neat clothing, a black walking cane, he used to walk several streets each day in the city. He used to develop bright ideas along these walks and confided them in Pinie Shtrum his long close friend. This was Abish Neiman the son in law of Nahum Shochet.

He was an understanding religious man and familiar with things. His serious approach and positive thinking led to his appointment as an inner member of the Rabbi's court. He became a close confidant of the saintly Bobower Rabbi. He was originally from Bobow where his father was the ritual slaughterer of the community. He was a witness to each word that the Rabbi uttered and became well associated with the Bobower Hassidic court.

When he reached Jaslo he continued his work on behalf of the Bobower Hassidut. It was not an easy job since Jaslo was a modern city but he soon found adherents and continued to expand the influence of the court of Bobow. He together with Pinie Shtrum managed to organize the religious youth under their wing. They organized short and long nature hikes for the youngsters and gained their adherence to Bobow. As an experienced cantor he was familiar with the latest tunes that came from Bobow and introduced them to Jaslo together with the Hassidism of Bobow. The tunes of Bobow became famous throughout Western Galicia and Jaslo. The music was indeed of a high musical caliber with fine soft tunes and laced with religious fervor created an attractive force. The musical services attracted many religious Jews to Bobow, especially the religious youth that embraced Bobow and was willing to follow the Rabbi at all costs

[Page 226]

Following his marriage he divided his time between popularizing Hassidism of Bobow and torah study. With his father in law he studied the rules pertaining to slaughtering of animals. Subsequently he was appointed assistant cantor in the big synagogue and the ritual slaughterer of the Jewish community in Jaslo.

Elimelech Nirenberg

He was a religious Jew familiar with religious and non religious literature. He was well versed in Jewish theological laws, especially with the "Even Ezra" book. He was readily accepted by the religious scholars in the city.

He settled in Jaslo in the twenties and rented a grocery from the previous owners at the Hess house on Kosciuszko Street. He prayed at the study center opposite the holy ark.

Dow Namer

He was a clerk for many years at the refinery in Niglowic and managed to escape to Russia with the outbreak of World War II where he took ill and died. His wife reached Israel and works as a secretary in the government.

Samech ס

Nathan Segal

He was the son in law of D.Beck and very religious. He received a fine education and was in close touch with the milieu. He was an old member of the Mizrahi and contributed to the establishment of the Mizrahi School and synagogue. He was also active in the community and expressed his ideas. He was a merchant and lived on Florianska Street.

Hanina Sokoler

He lived all his life in Sczenica near Jaslo and was acquainted with religious books. He was a very pleasant person who had long beard that covered his face and his tall erect bearing suggested a patriarchal figure. He had a big farm and also dealt in commerce.

[Page 227]
Naphtali Shmuel Solomon

He was considered one of the first Hassidim in Jaslo. He was a doer and his house was open to ideas of the torah. He was blessed with a deep understanding and the ability to befriend people with his words and money. Still he weighted carefully all his moves. He gave generously charity.

He had a large estate in Koblow-Podzamci in the district of Jaslo where many people were employed. As a merchant of wood and forests he came in contact with local gentry that led to good relations. These contacts did not prevent him from keeping his daily religious appearances.

He had four sons; Benyamin, Dawid, Awraham and Yehiel who received a very religious education. He also had three daughters who were married to well established and known families, namely Chaim Cohen Englander the son of the judicial rabbi of Frystak, the second son in law was Betzalel ben Wolf Tzimet Halevi from Jaslo and the third was Pinter from the saintly family of Rabbi of Bukowsk.

During the peasant uprisings in the district of Jaslo in1898 that were organized by anti-Semitic priests notably Stoialowski and are known as the "Disturbances of 1898" he suffered greatly and decide to sell the estate. (See chapter 16, 1898 "The torching of the spirit refinery").

He bought a house on Kosciuszko Street in Jaslo opposite the "The Bank of Oscidonowski" and settled in the city. He passed away at the right old age prior to World War I. His daughter Hancze Englander lived in Tarnow and managed to survive World War II. She reached Palestine with her young son Yehiel and settled in Jerusalem

Pinhas Solomon
(See **Wolf Eintziger**)

Leib Shmulewicz

He was an enlightened, pleasant and quiet Jew. He was a painter but was well accepted by the community. He was respected and lived on Iglena Street. They had only one son who received a general education.

[Page 228]
Mordechai Hacohen San

He was from Frysztak and the son in law of Tuvia Fabian. He was an honest and considerate man. He bought the "Grand "hotel near the railway station and settled in Jaslo.

He had three sons and two daughters. One of the daughters Sheindil was married to Awigdor Kilig when he later died she continued to manage the hotel. She was a fine and genteel woman who granted charity and sympathy. She and her sons Mendil and Chaim managed the hotel. Chaim San is today in Argentina. The sons were known as quiet and moderate people that gave charity discreetly.

Yaakow San

He was the oldest son of Mordechai San and was a torah student. He had fine manners and a member of Mizrahi. He was a supporter of all the institutions of the movement as well as other social institutions. He was one of the big apartment owners in the city.

He dealt with timber and forests and was one of the larger exporters of wooden building materials. His daughter married Porsher and lives in Argentina.

Nachman San

He was the first son in law of Mordechai San and lived all his life in Frysztak. He moved to Jaslo in the twenties. He was a very religious person and gave his children a very religious and general education. He had two sons and four daughters.

He was a successful timber merchant. His son Tzwi was a member of the young Mizrahi in Jaslo. He was a cultured person with a large torah background. He left for Palestine in the thirties and settled in Tel Aviv where he works for the insurance company "Hasneh"

P. Saphir
(See **Dawid Beck**)

A.Sokolowski

He was a copper artisan and lived in the Targowica. He was the son in law of Menashe Weinstein. Following his death, his wife rented the kiosk in the market that was empty for years.

[Page 229]

Ayin ע

Moshe Eder

He was a well-known individual in the city and very involved. He was a quiet moderate person familiar with the Torah and expressed himself clearly in a voice that was barely audible. He never involved himself with the burning issues of the day but was selected to head many social institutions. He was for many years the beadle at the study center synagogue and one of the leaders of the "Agudat Israel" branch in the city. He was very close to the rabbi and did his bidding. He had a clear conscience and acted accordingly.

He had a store and lately started as a wholesaler and did rather well. He had two sons and a daughter. The oldest son Nachman was a student at the study center and belonged to the youth branch of the Agudat Israel. He remained in Jaslo after his marriage and worked with his father. With the outbreak of World War II, the family managed to reach Russia. According to my information, some members of the family reached the USA.

Dawid Elias

He was an inspirational person and known as a wealthy individual. He had influence in at city hall. He frequently intervened on behalf of the community and himself with the authorities and the police.

In spite of the fact that he was known in the city, he did not to push his weight about. On the contrary, he avoided honorary jobs when offered. He was one of the first worshippers at the big synagogue but most of the time he prayed at the Yad Charutzim synagogue where he felt at home. He was a moderate Hassid and adhered closely to the Hassidic court of Rymanow. He was familiar with the great rabbis and some of them stayed in his house on visiting Jaslo.

He started as a poor worker and saved his pennies to begin a business. He succeeded as a timber, forest merchant, and then branched out to exports. With time, he built a big house with stores on Kazimeierz Street. He also had a house on Targowica Square and several lots in the city

[Page 230]

The residents considered him one of the richest people in the city. (In his old age, he lost most of his assets). For many years, he collected the parking fees for the stands in the market for the city. He also collected the fees for slaughtering chickens and cows on behalf of the community. These leases were sold at auctions by the municipality and the winner received the license. Of course, these licenses provided a nice income.

He had six sons and one daughter. One son left for the USA prior to World War I. Another son named Leibish lived in Przemysl where he was one of the well to do people in the city. He was a timber merchant and owned a sawmill and a flourmill. The youngest son Moniek, a member of the soccer clubs "Maccabi" distanced himself from tradition. He left in the twenties and returned to Jaslo. (According to rumors he survived and lives in Australia)

Shlomo Elias

He was the second son of Dawid Elias and studied at the study center. He was well educated and pious. He prayed at the synagogue and was an excellent torah reader. He wore a shtreimel on Saturdays and Holidays. He also dealt with timber and lived in his father's house. His wife was very active in community social affairs. His only daughter married Yonathan Anisfeld and the couple lives in Ramat Itzhak, Israel.

Abish Elias

He behaved in accordance with the time. He assisted his father in the business. He was the one who organized the Jewish self-defense group in Jaslo to act against the Polish hoodlums during the anti Jewish disturbances following Polish Independence.

Following his marriage, he remained in Jaslo and went into business partnership to open a seltzer bottling plant. His son recently arrived in Israel and lives in Tel Aviv.

The Elias family

I was not familiar with the family for they lived in Podzamcze and were involved in business.

Leibish Emer

He was an old timer in Jaslo and a rich merchant. He also owned several houses. He was a respected individual and presented himself well. He followed the times. His children received a general education. His oldest son managed for many years the "Fortuna" bank in his house. He lived many years in Krakow and dealt with ready made clothing. The younger son finished law school and opened an office in Zmigrod. Lately one of the daughters reached Israel and settled in the Petach Tikvah area. One of his sons lives in the USA according to rumors.. The attorney's son married the daughter of Awraham Englard.

[Page 231]

Awraham Emer

He was the brother of Leibish Emer and also an old timer in the city. He was a religious merchant. He owned a house on Florianska Street. His son opened a ready to wear store in his house. He liquidated the store after a few years and left the city. He was married to Zeev Damaszek's daughter.

[Page 231]

Peh פ

Tuvia Fabian

He was known in the city as old Tuviale or in Polish as "dziadek" – grandfather. He was born in the village of Odzikon near Korczyna. The village became rather famous due to stories based on the two tall rock outcrops that reach several hundred meters in height. Legend tells us that the peaks kept growing taller and taller; the local inhabitants became frightened and sought help from one of the saintly rabbis in the area. He came to the site and supposedly commanded nature to stop the growth process. Indeed, the picks stopped growing. In addition, an old destroyed Polish castle that belonged to one of the Polish kings was there. I myself saw the place when our class visited the area on a school trip.

Tuvia Fabian loved to tell stories about his youth and was fortunate to meet the old saintly Rabbi Itche of Rymanow who passed away in 1843. He was about one hundred years old when he passed away. His son from the USA once visited him. Rumors had it that he was a very wealthy person in New York and contributed

greatly to charity. His daughter Sheindel was married to Mordechai San whose father owned the "Grand" hotel

[Page 232]

Chaim Feber

He was a pleasant young man. He was the son in law of Wolf Eintziger and had a haberdashery store along May Third Street. Lately he left Jaslo for Tarnow.

Moshe Faust

One of the main suppliers of manufactured goods to the merchants in the city. He was very ambitious and lived in his house on Iglena Street. He followed tradition and had three daughters; the oldest married Yaakow Sheinberg (see previous chapters) and the second married Henoch Plotzker in Sanok (see previous chapters).

Pokoriles, magister

He came from Eastern Galicia and settled in Jaslo in the thirties. He leased the pharmacy "Under the Star" on Kosciuszko Street from the previous owners. He was an enlightened and pleasant person. He supported Zionism and other institutions in Jaslo. With the outbreak of World War II, he managed to reach London where he became ill and died.

Moshe Polaner

He was very modern in his outlook for the time. He was one of the first Jewish religious teachers in the Polish school system. He also kept the Jewish birth records for the Jewish community board. Two of his daughters are in Israel. One works for the medical insurance group called "Kupat Cholim" in Jerusalem and other one is in a kibbutz.

Michael Postiboler

He was an old village resident who followed the Jewish tradition of his fathers. He lived in the village of Postibola near Jaslo and went by the name of the village. No one knew his last name. He used to visit the city on business trips and to sell his dairy products from the farm,

[Page 233]

Dawid Forman

He was a quiet person who made a living by repairing umbrellas and lived on Korlowski Street. Polish hoodlums killed him in the streets of Jaslo during the turbulent year of 1919. They surrounded him while he was going about his business and opened his head with wooden sticks that resulted in his death.

The entire Jewish community in Jaslo went into deep mourning and participated in the huge funeral procession. He was eulogized at the synagogue. The comforting words remained with us for a long time.

P. Forshtehr
He was an excellent shoemaker and a serious person. He was very influential at the Yad Charutzim synagogue. When his sons left Jaslo and settled in Krakow, he followed them.

Yossef Forsher
He was born in Bobowa and his wife was a Stillman. He made a nice appearance and spoke predominantly German, as was the custom amongst the enlightened people during the Imperial Austrian days. He had a shoe polish factory called "Luna" that was successful. The product was popular. He had a son and a daughter both received an academic education. He lived all his life in his one story house on Nowa Street.
(Rumors have reached me to the effect that his wife and son live in Argentina.).

Yekutiel Peterfreund (Petrezil)
He was from Gorlice that he left during World War I for the hamlet became a battleground between the Austrian and Russian armies. He was as a very religious and G-d fearing Jew. He was a traditional service leader at the synagogue and dressed in the style of the rabbis. He was the kashrut supervisor of the salami preparations in Jaslo and sold the products. At first, he lived in Rudi the baker's house and then moved to Yehiel Rosner's house in the market square. He lived there for ten years and then left Jaslo.

[Page 234]
Yossef Peterfreund
He lived for years in the "sukkah" of the rabbi where he had a room. His wife and daughters sold geese and the fats of the geese. He barely made a living as a tailor but was well liked and very helpful especially to poor and needy people.
He was one of the few Jews in the city who really observed the custom of receiving guests in his home that happened to visit the small sukkah. People that had no place to spend the night found a place in his sukkah that sometimes had as many as ten people. Everybody knew that there is always room at Yossele's. He did not charge and even provided a slice of bread and vegetables.
He derived great pleasure from leading the Minha service on Saturdays and when he reached "Ata Ehad and Shimcha Ehad" or You are one and Your name is unique, he closed his eyes and lifted his head towards heaven as though imploring the almighty with the line "Mi caamcha Israel" or who is like the people of Israel. .
He always interpreted the line from Jeremaiah (sect;14) " Im Oneinu Anu Bnu" or if we sinned we are still your children and worthy of forgiveness.
He had two sons who became tailors and the younger one left for Palestine in 1937 and settled in Haifa.

Leibish Piar
He was born in Kolbasowa but reached Jaslo at an early stage of development. He lived in the Targowica and was one of the first workers at the alcohol refinery of Itzhak Yehuda Ruble in Subiniow.
He would rise while it was still dark and read the psalms, the "hakle" book, and then head to the synagogue to be among the first worshippers.

He was a Hassid in word and deed. The community entrusted him with the management of the bathouse where the mikva was located. They expected him to keep the place clean, and control the youngsters who tried to swim and carry on.

[Page 235]

Repeatedly he would urge them to leave the place. Other people have to immerse themselves, enough is enough he used to say to the youngsters. A special mention was given to his wife Malche who was the midwife in Jaslo. She was a wise and intelligent woman known by her own private name in town. She continued to work for almost fifty years and delivered the mothers, daughters and their grandchildren. She was frequently referred to as the midwife. She was fast, handy and loved by the population.

They had five sons and two daughters. The oldest was Awraham who was a Hassid. He was the cantor in Vienna of the "Poilishe Shul" or the Polish synagogue for many years. He sang at the meal songs of Shabbat and holidays amongst the very religious circles. He is now living in Jerusalem (His son Yossef is also a cantor in New York and published a book on the biographies of cantors and their musical creations.).

One of his sons named Benyamin died as a youngster while on a "Lag B'Omer" or 33 days in the Omer field trip excursion with his friends when gentile youngsters attacked them. One of the stones hit Benyamin on the head resulting in a serious head injury that led to his death.

Another son named Itzhak fell in battle while fighting with the Austrian Army in Italy. Two of his sons; Moshe and Yaakow are in the USA.

The daughter named Reisel married Moshe Unger who was very religious and lived in Jaslo. The family left for Vienna with the outbreak of World War I. Two of their sons had nice voices, one of them Benyamin Unger is the cantor of the "Central" synagogue in North Tel Aviv. The other son is a cantor in Philadelphia, USA. She died with her youngest daughter in the shoa,

The second daughter named Hanci married Eliezer Eichorn and they live in Raanana, in Israel. In the thirties Maltchi and Leibish Piar left Jaslo and settled in Vienna. The Germans deported them to the death camp of Therensdadt where they perished.

[Page 236]

Awraham Findling

The family lived in the village of Zilkow near Jaslo and dealt in commerce. They also had a farm. On Saturdays and Holidays the father and the sons used to stay in Jaslo to pray at the study center. They were of course dressed in the traditional Hassidic manner.

Itzhak Findling

He was born in Gorlice and settled in Jaslo during World War I. He was a religious person and knitted socks and sweaters for a living. His wife sold wigs. They lived all their life in the market and had a few sons. One of them was accused of belonging to the communist party and was sentenced to a few years in jail. He managed to escape from prison and left Poland

Eliezer Finder

He was of small statue, skinny and had a sparse beard on his chin. He lived on Sokolo Street. He was one of the early expeditors of goods in the city but later left Jaslo.

Ephraim Fish

He was a traditional Jew and owned a large bakery in the city at the house of Dawid Elias. His sons were all members of the Zionist youth movements. They were hard working children and assisted their father.

The oldest son left Jaslo prior to World War I for the USA. During the twenties, he visited his parents in Jaslo and shortly later sent them the necessary entrance papers to the USA and the family left Jaslo.

Shmuel Fish

He distinguished himself by his quiet behavior and good-natured manners. He was religious and lived in Hiclowka. In 1914 he was drafted to the Austrian army and
sent to the Italian front. During the great battles of 1915-1916, he fell and to this day no one knows the exact place of his burial. He left a wife, three sons and three daughters. They all made a living from the grocery in their house. The youngest son survived the war and is presently in Israel

[Page 237]
A. Fishbein

Nobody knew his first or last name. He was called "Der einbinder" – or the bookbinder. Indeed his work was very artistic. He lived all his life at the Targowica, barely made a living. He died because of a disease in 1914. His son was also sick during this period and died. One of his daughters owned a haberdashery stand in the market until the outbreak of World War II.

Meir Felderbrand

He was the first Jewish child to be born in Jaslo. He was a moderate person with a nice presentation. He was very active in public affairs and always defended the public. He prayed at the Yad Charutzim synagogue and a loyal friend of the association. He sold animal skins and shoemaker supplies in his store located in Kramer's house.
He had five daughters and two sons who were all members of the Zionist youth movements. One daughter reached Palestine in the thirties and a second daughter reached the country and settled first in Jerusalem and them in Tel Aviv.

Yossef Felderbrand

He was similar to his brother in appearance and had a long beard that covered the face. He was a gentle person that belonged to the regular membership of Yad Charutzim and prayed there regularly.
He lived behind the municipality on top of the hill. He had a haberdashery stand in the market square that was operated mainly by his son Yekil while he worked at odd jobs. He had four sons and four daughters. One of his sons was aboard the ship #147;Patria" that carried illegal Jews to Palestine and drowned near the shores of the destination. He left two young sons in Palestine.

[Page 238]
Henoch Plotzker

One of the big wood merchants and exporter in Jaslo, His brother was the well known rabbi Meir Dan Plotzker, the author of the book "Klei Hemda" who was a leading figure in the Agudath Israel and the chairman of the "Rabbinical Association" in Poland.
He was a distinguished personality, erudite and familiar with the world. He spoke well, had excellent manners and behaved in an aristocratic manner. His trimmed beard reminded one of the beard of Nahum Sokolow to whom he was related.
I still remember the discussions religious circles about the Plotzker brothers namely Rabbi Meir Dan and his brother Henoch Plotzker. One belonged to the Agudah and the other one to the Zionist movement. Their differences were not only political but also in their living styles, dressing, and thinking. Complete opposites in every sense of the word. Rabbi Meir Dan Plotzker participate at the wedding of Israel Plotzker the oldest son of Henoch Plotzker but did not stay at the home of the brother instead spent the night at the home of the local rabbi. The house of Henoch Plotzker was too Zionist for the brother. He had two sons and a daughter who received an academic education and continued their studies.

Israel Plotzker, attorney

He was the oldest son of Henoch Plotzker and graduated as one of the youngest and brightest lawyers. He was a very popular person and mingled with the people. He was a Zionist as a youngster and continued these activities. He organized the "Hashomer" youth organization in Jaslo and headed it for many years. He was also very active in communal affairs and participated in many fund drives notably for matzot for Pessah for the poor, and other needy causes.

He married the daughter of Chaim Zilber of Sanok who was wealthy and respected. The latter was also the son in law of Shlomo Berger. The family left Poland with the outbreak of World War II and reached Russia. Three years ago the family arrived in Palestine with their only son. They settled in Jaffa where he received a position in the tax department.

Eliezer Plotzker

He was the second son of Henoch Plotzker and Avery active Zionist since his youthful days. He finished the school for commerce. He was quiet and sensitive.

[Page 239]

He married Moshe Faust's daughter and the family settled in Sanok where he became a wood merchant. His wife and son Dan remained in Poland where they perished in the shoa. He managed to reach Russia and following World War II. Reached Israel where he worked in the accounting office at the ministry of defense. He became ill and passed away in 1953.

Michael Platner

He was a very intelligent and an intellectually gifted Torah scholar. He was from Brzostek and married the daughter of Zeew Wagshall who was a wealthy person and had a big farm in Worzic near Jaslo.

He settled in Jaslo and became a model of conduct and good deeds. He was fearful of G-d. His business venture did not bear fruit and was forced to ask the community to provide him with a job as the bookkeeper of the community. He was also the bookkeeper of Leibish Tzimet.

He had four sons and five daughters. His oldest son was sensitive and educated. He left for Germany with Polish Independence. A group of German bullies attacked him, robbed him and mercilessly beat him. He never recovered and passed away. His second son also lived in Germany. In 1935, He reached Palestine with his family and settled in Petach Tikvah. The third son Reuven lives presently in Bolivia and visited recently Israel. The fourth son Dawid survived the war and settled in Jaffa.

Chaim Flick

He was a traditional Jew as well as a Zionist. He was a moderate person. His appearance and presentation indicated respect and gentility.

He was a merchant and owned land along the road to Kobolow near the dense forest that contained different trees as a well as ancient sycamore trees. He had a large inn where the peasants of the area used to drink.

The Zionists used the forest for their summer camps and group meetings. Various societies met here to launch their fund raising campaigns. He had several sons. His daughter and a son live in the USA.

[Page 240]

P. Pelikan

He held a very high position in the Jaslo judiciary system. He belonged to the assimilationist elements in the city. He kept away from things Jewish. He was a serious and quiet person. Lately his daughter reached Israel and settled in Tel Aviv.

Awraham Feller

He was born in Osiek near Zmigrod and settled in Jaslo in the twenties. He was a modern Jew and devoted to the Zionist cause. He was as a charitable person. He built a special house on Asnika Street where he sold fish and sardines, wholesale and retail.

Moshe Feinchel

He was a very pious and observed strictly the commandments. He was tall and well built. For years, he read the torah at the Yad Charutzim synagogue and he had a powerful voice. He holed merchandise in the city. He managed to reach Russia with the outbreak of the war and died there. He had four daughters and a son. His daughter was the first one in Jaslo to open a photography studio in Stillman's courtyard in the market.

Yehezkel was his son and one of the first pioneers in Jaslo to reach Palestine where he remained for seven years. He returned to Jaslo and married Chaim Wechselbaum's daughter. They settled in Sandz where he acquired a truck. He soon left the city and returned to Jaslo.

He always dreamt of returning one day to Palestine but World War II disrupted the plan and he managed to reach Russia. He was arrested and almost shot but was reprieved at the last moment. His wife and daughter recently arrived I Israel and settled near Ramat Gan.

Israel Penczer

He was modest and observed tradition. He lived in the village Opczi near Koczerow. He was a merchant and had two sons and two daughters. One of the daughters managed to survive World War II and reached Israel where she lives in Tel Aviv.

[Page 241]
P. Fink

He settled in Jaslo in the twenties and was a merchant.

Moshe Fass

He was the brother in law of Hersh Grinspan and they worked together in the messenger business. He was discreet and lived outside the city, after the Ulaszowica Bridge.

A. Fass

He owned a barbershop along Kosciuszko Street. He used to be located along May 3rd Street near the park. He was very polite and well mannered. He was a member of the Zionist movement. His father was one of the old workers at the railroad station of Jaslo.

Yossef Pepfer

He was from Dembice and married the widow Ethel, daughter of Yossef Hacohen Rapaport. With the death of his mother in law Pearl Rapaport, he took over the grocery. He lived in Dawid Elias' house on Kazimierz Street. He prayed at the study center and loved to lead the service.

With the outbreak of the war, he managed to reach Lemberg and hence Russia where he died of starvation.

Yossef Frumowicz

He was a highly respected member of the Jaslo Jewish community. He was a scholar familiar with the bible and Hebrew grammar. He also had a broad knowledge of things and spoke several languages including a fluent and idiomatic Hebrew.

He was an excellent orator that intermingled biblical and torah sayings with every day issues. His speeches were always interesting.

He belonged to the Jewish aristocracy of Jaslo and on occasion published Hebrew and Polish articles in the Zionist press. The items had depth and common sense.

[Page 242]

He adhered to the Zionist movement in his youth and grew with the movement. He was inspired by the ideas of Jewish reawakening and devoted himself totally to the idea of Zionism. To this end, he used all his energies, fulfilled all the obligations imposed on him by the movement. He represented the movement and defended vehemently its interest's whether it implied running for local community, municipal or national elections. He was one of the major speakers on behalf of the Zionist party in Jaslo. He was elected chairperson of the local Zionist party. He was member of the Polish Zionist committee, member of the local Keren Kayemet and Keren Hayesod boards. He was also very active in selling "shekels" on behalf of the Zionist movement prior to Zionist congresses.

Yossef Frumowicz

He was a teacher and organized the bible study group. Lately he began to translate "the Babylonian Talmud" to Hebrew with his commetaries. The section of "Bracjhot" appeared in Warsaw published by the "Achiver" publishing house. The work was dotted and had commas and also question marks

He was an agent for the insurance company "Pheonix" in Vienna but lately opened a store for ladies clothing.on Kosciuszko Street. Two of his sons received a general education. He had the good fortune to see his sons and daughter Naomi, settle in Palestine. He unfortunately was caught by the Germans in one of their actions in Jaslo and shot.

[Page 243]

Lipa Proper

He was one of the old timber merchants and highly respected in the city. He was an easygoing person who did not look for attention but remained within the circle of Zionist friends. Prior to his settling in Jaslo he owned a farm, a flour and a sawmill near Biecz.

He followed the spirit of the time. He had four daughters and one son who received a general education and were members of the Zionist youth movement. He was one of the wealthy people in the city. He lived in his own house of five stories that was the tallest building along Kosciuszko Street.

Chaim Lipa Friedman

He recorded for the municipality all Jewish births in the city. He was a modern looking person and lived all his live at the Targowica. He had several sons and daughters who received a secular education. His son Moshe was one of the soccer players of Maccabi. When the father passed away, his oldest daughter continued the registration of Jewish children. The youngest son reached lately Israel and settled in Haifa.

H. Friedman

He was the son in law of Moshe Feinchel and worked at various jobs. He belonged to the Zionist movement in Jaslo. His wife continued to run the photography studio.

[Page 244]
Dawid Friedrich

He settled in Jaslo during World War I when the Gorlice area was the battleground between the Austrian and Russian armies. He was a very religious and G-d fearing. He was the regular mussaf or second part of the Morning Prayer leader at the study center of Rabbi Mandil.

He was a grain merchant and lived all his life at the Targowica. He had two sons who received a very religious education. The younger one was a tailor apprentice at Yonale and the son in law of Ben Tzwi Freund.

Lipa Prizner

He settled in Jaslo following Polish Independence and opened a cleaning store for hats at Seinwel's basement on Iglena Street. He was far from religion and adhered to the left, as was the case with workers. He was good natured and helped people. His hand was always open for charity.

He became seriously ill and remained bed ridden for several months. Suddenly he got better and left his bed. He suddenly returned to the faith and began to attend morning and evening services at the study center. He dressed in black and the fringes were hanging down from under his jacket. He grew a beard and side curls. He ended the prayers by reciting the psalms and joined the mishnayot group at the study center. He also attended various other lectures and listened to the stories about the famous rabbis and their deeds.

Yeruham Frei

He was very modest and avoided all contact with communal affairs. He feared the slightest public activity. He was an honest and fair man that could be immitated . He was always neatly dressed and had a pleasant walk. He spoke little and worked as an accountant at the spirit distillery.

[Page 245]
He was an old friend of the Rabbi Mandil and always prayed at his study center where he read the torah in a very peasant manner.

His son in law Moshale Reich, a serious torah student and well read. He was an intelligent person and served in the Austrian Army as an officer. He received a medal for distinguished military service. Until 1914, he had a n inn in Hiclowka opposite the house of Nahum Miller, the slaughterer. Following World War I, he settled in Przemysl where he opened a leather store. His son Motel was a good Talmudic student and was ordained rabbi. He was also an excellent violin musician. He was a devoted Hassid and loved to be near the rabbis.

Shevah Frei

He was the only son of of Yerucham Frei. He was a tall Hassid who studied diligently the Talmud. He was sensitive as his father and was also a devotee of Rabbi Mandil and prayed at his study center. He had a small grocery and dairy store at Tzimet's house on Iglena Street.

Elimelech Freund

He was a modest man and a non-talker. He instructed yeshiva students and was clean dressed. He was a good-natured person and avoided gossip. He kept his distance from community affairs. He was a follower of Rabbi Mandil and prayed at his study center,

Elimelech Freund and his family

[Page 246]

He lived on Karmelicka Street and had a leather and shoe store. He was well off. His wife was Chaya a native of Dembice. Her maiden name was Taub. They had six daughters and three managed to reach Palestine. The oldest Miriam was married to Dawid Just (Tzutzkenbaum and they left for Palestine in the thirties and live in Tel Aviv. The Third daughter Tzipora was a member of the Mizrahi daughters group in Jaslo and left for Palestine in 1933 when she married Meir Shilat (see previous chapters). The fourth daughter married LI.Grossman, from a Hassidic family, presently a builder and they live in Tel Aviv. The second daughter Esther married the son of Chaim Zilber. The two youngest daughters Bat Sheva and Riwkah shared the fate of the Jewish community of Jaslo,

Ben Tzion Freund

He was the brother in law of Elimelech Frei and quiet as his brother. He was religious and kept his distance from public activities. He prayed at the study center. He had a shoe store in the market square and had two daughters. One of them married Dawid Friedrich's son

Zinwel Frish

He was the son in law of Abba Hollander and a Hassidic Jew. He was familiar with the Talmud and prayed at the study center of the Rabbi. He was a member of the Agudath Israel and owned a store that sold crystal earthenware and glass on Kosciuszko Street,

Yossef Pearlberger

He was a genteel torah student and moderate in his opinions. He was the son in law of Leib Tzimet and was a wholesaler of haberdashery and writing materials in the market. His sons received a religious education in accordance with the Bobowa tradition. He himself leaned to the Agudath Israel party and prayed at the study center of the rabbi.

Pearlbergerg family

This family settled in the thirties in Jaslo and rented the store from Man Eintziger.

Yaakow Freund

His house was a pleasant mix of torah and gentility in Jaslo. He was born in Gorlice and married to Ulaszowica, the center of the first Jewish settlers in Jaslo.
[Page 247]
Here they found their way to make a living. Yaakow Freund was a gifted undertaker and had the determination to complete undertaken ventures. He opened the first pub in Ulaszowica that belonged to the judicial district of Koblow and maintained the liquor distillery in Jaslo. It took a great deal of effort to obtain the liquor license in Krakow and later in Vienna and still more effort to build the refinery adjoining the noble family of Rigers of Griowic. The later fought the factory but lost in the end.
(The estate was later acquired by count Roczinski) The distillery was one of the biggest in Galicia.
He was a very busy man yet found time to devote to organize Jewish institutions in the community. Due to his intervention, the community received permission to build the mikvah that was previously denied to Chaim Steinhaus. He was at heart a Hassid by his deeds and gave a great deal of charity. He was familiar with the religious figures as well as with the needy. He assisted secretly needy people. His place of residence was a minor fortified palace. It was always humming with people going and coming with many requests on their minds.
He was admired and respected. He led his life along the river Wisloka until one day it was attacked by anti-Semitic mobs that were enraged by the agitator and hate spreader, priest Stoilowsky. He was a fervent Jew hater and wanted to be elected to the chamber of representatives in Vienna on behalf of the peasant party in the Jaslo district.
During the period of 1898, there were anti Jewish outbursts and a mob of enraged peasants led by the farmer Jaworski attacked the home of Yaakow Freund. First they encircled the refinery and threw atones at the place. They then threw lit torches into the area and the fire spread through the refinery. The mayor of Jaslo did not permit the fire brigade to extinguish the fire (see chapter of events of 1898). Unfortunately, the insurance policy of the place had lapsed two weeks ago and the owner was unable to renew the policy due to a tragic event. Thus, the entire refinery estimated at 80,000 reinish went down the drain.
[Page 248]
Due to the great commotion of the fire, the family forgot about the youngest daughter aged 6 who was sleeping in one of the rooms of the house. Yaakow Freund grabbed a ladder and entered the house through the roof. He reached the child that was already choking of smoke

inhalation. He managed to save the daughter but she was barely breathing and it took some time for the doctor to restore her breathing.

(She lives presently with her husband Awraham Gelt from Jaroslaw and their family in Tel Aviv).

We can associate the rescue of the child with the rescue of the young Yoel Salomon who hid in Yaakow Freund's house. The latter refused to hand him over to the enraged mob that was chasing him from his home in Koblow.

He was very embittered when he appealed to the Emperor of Austria for damages and was replied in the negative. He tried to recover some of his losses but the event was too much for him. He became ill and passed away.

He left two sons Itzhak and Dawid. The first one left for Palestine via Berlin. The second one resided in Jaslo until the outbreak of World War II. He was a Talmudic scholar and had eight daughters who married very religious husbands. Some of them lived in Jaslo. These are the names of his son in laws; Awraham Shtier (he left for the USA. In the twenties), Chaim Shaul Orshitzzer, Yudah Meir Apfel-Horowitz who lived in Vienna, Menndel Shentzer, Chaim Fuhrer in Israel, Hersh Eder, Awraham Gelt from Jaroslaw. The later was a Rymanower Hassid who was very active in the Agudath Israel and represented the party at the community council of Jaroslaw. He reached Palestine where he lives in Tel Aviv.

[Page 249]

One of his granddaughters (the daughter of Itzhak Freund) is married to Rabbi Arieh Paris who is the head of the Yeshiva Tel Aviv named for Rabbi Ahrenson of Tel Aviv. One of his grandsons Menahem Freund, the son of Itzhak Freund, is one of the well to do people in Jerusalem and married his son to the daughter of the chief Rabbi of Tel Aviv, Rabbi Unterman. The second son of Awraham Freund was known as a charitable person and lives in Ahuza on the Carmel in Haifa. He sells car parts along King Street near the port of Haifa.

The second daughter Fanie is married to Noah Lewin, a community leader and secretary of the Afula area council. He was the son of Rabbi Lewisn who was the religious judge of Afula.

Israelke Freund

He was the first son in law of Mordechai Netzler. He was familiar with books and worldly affairs. He had a grocery and a paper store along Dzieckiego Street next to the high school and this is where he lived. He had a son and daughter. Moshe Meir was his son and he studied at the study center and acquired a general education. He was a member of the Agudath Israel. He married the daughter of the rabbi of Bilitz and lived in his father's house in Jaslo until the outbreak of World War II. He managed to escape the Germans but perished along the road. (His mother in law, the wife of Rabbi Shtern was the granddaughter of SH.B. Tzimet)

Wolf Franzbalau

He was a quiet person and one of the first Jewish settlers in the city. He was a merchant and owned a haberdashery store in the market square. He liquidated his business and took over the management of the bathhouse on behalf of the community prior to World War I. When he passed away, he left three daughters and two sons one of them Yaakow left for Germany.

Nathan Franzblau

He was the second son of Wolf Franzblau and was modern in outlook and leaned to the Zionist movement. He had a kiosk where he sold chocolate fruits and seltzer water along Kosciuszko Street. He was doing very well and lived in the house of Emer and Kornfiedl on Kazimierz Street. His oldest daughter was married to Chaim Ben Reuven Shilat

[Page 250]

Itzak Franzblau

He was an active community leader between the artisans and a member of Yad Charutzim. He was affected by the modern trends and was elected by the artisans to the municipality of Jaslo. He lived all his life on Florianska Street and was an excellent tailor. He became ill at the prime of his life and soon passed away. He left a wife and young children. One of his daughters managed to reach Palestine as a pioneer and settled at kibbutz Mizra.

Israel Frazblau

He was the brother of Itzhak Franzblau and was a successful painter. He lived all his life on Florianska Street. The father of both sons lived for some years in Niglowic where he had some minor position at the refinery.

Shulem Frankel

He was an enlightened Jew and very involved. He wore a shtreimel and silk clothes on Saturdays as did the the Hassidim. He sold tobacco and cigarettes at the house of Steinhaus in the market. He had a nice income. Following his discharge from the Army after World War I there was no tobacco and no business. He sold the place to Yoel Margolies.
He had five sons and the oldest received a religious education but the others received a general education. The youngest Yehoshua finished high school and continued his studies. One of his sons left for Germany and later reached Palestine in the thirties. He lived for some time in Tel Aviv but presently resides in Haifa.

Menachem Peretz

He was the son in law of Shulem Hiller from Topolini and was very religious. He was a good natured Hassid as well as merchant. He was drafted to the Austrian Army in the World War I but suddenly took ill. The disease terminated his life and he left a wife and sons.

[Page 251]

Tsadek צ

Return

Itzhak Tzahler

He settled in Jaslo in the early twenties following World War I. A well built man with a large beard that partially covered his face. He was the representative of the feudal lord of the village of Yaniv near Jaslo. He was very pious and had several sons, amongst them Gadl that studied at the Talmud Torah in Jaslo. He was tall and studied well.

Asher Tzweig

Brother in law of Nute Maltz. He was a businessman but was very involved with the workshop owners and artisans. He was one of the founders of the "Yad Charutzim" Synagogue. He left the city and headed for the USA. He donated part of his money to build the "Yad Charutz center" in the city.

David Tzutzkenboim (See Dawid Just)

Alter Tzuker

He was a very rich person and well known. He owned an estate and a beer brewery at Zarszin near the city of Sanok. He moved to Jaslo recently. He had five daughters and two sons. One of his sons, Shlomo Tzuker, lived in Sanok for many years. Two of his son-in-laws lived in Jaslo, namely M. Anisfeld, and Dr. Naphtali Menashe.

Emanuel Tzuker

He was the second son of Alter Tzuker. He was a pediatrician, married to Yossef Manashe's daughter. He was a member of the Zionist movement. Lived all his life along Czickiego Street in Jaslo

[Page 252]

Mendel Tzuker

He was a very experienced hand in the distillery business. He was seriously ill and as a result died at a very young age. He left three daughters and two sons namely Meir and Shlomo who were engaged in commerce and artisanship. They eventually purchased the house that they lived in. One of the daughters married in Krakow.

Shlomo Tzuker

The second son of Mendel Tzuker had a large sewing workshop that employed many workers. He was married to the daughter of the religious slaughterer of Miroslaw. He was a Hassid and prayed steadily at the synagogue of the Rabbi of Dukla. With the outbreak of World War II, he left the city of Jaslo and left his family behind. He wandered through many places in Russia and eventually made it to Palestine where he resides in Haifa. His family perished in the Shoa. One of his sisters also survived the war and reached Palestine with her husband aboard the famous ship "The Exodus". She also lives in Haifa.

Mrs. Shlomo Tzuker with sons

[Page 253]

Elimelech Tzukerman

The community of Jaslo was left without a cantor when Yossel Kurtzweil left for the USA. The community also needed an additional religious slaughterer besides reb Nahum Shochet. The community board met and decided to publicize the availability of a cantorial and slaughterer positions in the city of Jaslo. Furthermore the ad stipulated that whoever is qualified for both positions will have preference.

The community interviewed many candidates and decided to select reb Elimelech Shochet from Rudnik that was known as Elimelech Rudnik. He was asked to assume his positions in 1919. (It must be noted that his father Mendel from Rudnik was also religious slaughterer in Jaslo in the nineties of the previous century.

He was well liked by the community and his musical abilities soon became known in the city. He conducted the services and was an excellent cantor that remained within the traditional cantorial boundaries. He possessed a powerful tenor voice that was very lyrical. He conducted the service with authority and musical ability. He also composed several musical marches worthy of a student of Yossele Rosenblat (he was one of the first pupils of Rosenblatt's choir in the city of Munkacz) and created several melodic tunes for parts of the services.

He retained most of the choir except for the addition of two of his sons, Kalman and Meir. Both children had fine voices and enriched the choir. I still remember the solo performance of Kalman on the high holidays when he sang the prayer "Adam Yesodo" or the basis of man is dust... His father wrapped in his prayer shawl listened and continued the service begging for divine indulgence.

The cantor Elimelech also sang in the sukkah of the rabbi on the eve of Hashanah Rabba. He loved to sing "Melech al Haaretz" or ruler of the world... Still other prayers such as "Melech Rachman" or G-d that forgives... Who could resist listening to his cantorial rendition on the seventh day of Passover of the song "Pessah Amunim" that enthralled the audience.

[Page 254]

A special treat was listening to him every Saturday as he sang at the third meal ceremony in the small "Kahal Shtibel". As the Sabbath was leaving, he escorted it with beautiful melodies and special songs. He was familiar with scholarship and interjected in his discussions quotes from the scriptures or Hassidic Rabbis. He was particularly fond of telling stories about the Old Hassidic Rabbi of Dzikow where he once studied.

His sons received a very orthodox education at home and at the study center. With the outbreak of World War II, he left Jaslo with his sons and two daughters and wound up in Russia. He managed to survive and reached eventually Palestine.

[Page 255]

While singing the famous song "Yedid Nefesh" during the month of August, he was taken ill and on the sixth day of the Month of Av, 1949, he passed away. He left four daughters in Israel. The oldest daughter Bracha Katz was very active in the political movement of the "Hapoel Hamizrahi". She has been in Israel for 18 years. The three other daughters were, Chaya, Emalia and Sarah. He also had three sons, Kalman who had a jewelry store in Tel Aviv, Meir was a doctor with the medical association and Mendel settled down in Haifa. One of his son-in-laws was Tzvi David Zilber, the son of Naphtali Zilber from Jaslo, who is presently a teacher at the Nachlat Itzhak School near Tel Aviv. His wife Hadassah and two of his daughters Lea and Rachel perished in the shoa.

**Elimelech Tzukerman
slaughterer & cantor**

Shmuel Ciser

He was known by his nickname Shmul the milkman. He was a traditional man, devoted to his dairy work Morning and evening he traveled to the manor outside the city to collect the milk and then distribute it to his regular customers. He also produced butter, cheese and other dairy products at home. Lived all his life on Nowa Street, in a single story house. He had two sons and four daughters. His oldest son Moshe worked in the distillery and later left for Belgium. His second son Zelig was a painter. All his daughters were members of the Zionist movements.

Lib Citronenboim

The name Citronenboim is not a mere name in Jaslo but stands for a very influential family. The family opened the first bar in the city. Leib Citronenboim was born in Zmigrod to Mordechai Citronenboim. The former was the brother in law of Yaakov Pinhas Krisher. Leib was an old time resident of the city and a devoted Hassid. He read the torah for the worshippers in the study center from the first day of its inception to the last day of his existence. The bar was active seven days a week and it was frequently called the Sabbath bar for Jews used to come to drink a beer on the eve of Shabbath and in the afternoon of Saturday or holidays. The proprietor had a large index with all the names of the city residents. Each customer was thus recorded and tickets were inserted in the account for every beer that was consumed. The hosts were also treated to cooked chickpeas and nuts as an appetizer for the drinks. People sat and enjoyed the beer exchanging political views or opinions and discussed present day events or local politics. Frequently, there were heated debates that reached the street. The drinking bills were settled after Saturday.

[Page 256]

With his early death, his wife Liba Citronenboim assumed control of the business and conducted it with skill and ability. She was a simple and modest woman. They had three daughters and six sons. The sons were raised in the traditional religious atmosphere but were also involved in the general world. The oldest son Benyamin Citronenboim was a hard working honest man and lived all his life in Germany until the Nazis forced him to flee to Palestine in the early thirties. He settled in Petach Tikwah where he passed away recently. He left four sons and two daughters; almost all the children remained in Israel. Shmeril Citronenboim, the second son, lived in Krosno where he was very influential and active in the community, his in laws were the Freund brothers, his father in law was Simha Rotfeld that lived in England. His daughter is in Haifa and his son was in the USA. Yehoshua Citronenboim lived in Mainz, Germany since 1914. Motil Citronenboim lived in Gorlice where he was very active and a member of the community board. He left Poland for Palestine and settled in Jerusalem where he works for the Jewish Agency. He has two sons, one in France and the other one in the USA. Itzhak Citronenboim remained in Jaslo after his marriage and managed the pub. The last son, Awraham Citronenboim grew up with his grandmother but died at a very young age. His son Avi Wolf Citronenboim left for Vienna where his mother resided for many years.

One ambitious and intelligent daughter, Sarah Citronenboim married Shalom Weissberg who died shortly after the wedding. She remained a widow and resided in her parent's home with her son Israel that was called Israelik Citronenboim in honor of his father. The second daughter remained at home for she was slightly disturbed. The third daughter was married to Chaim Gutfreund, a well to do and a Hassidic follower.

Israel Citronenboim -Weissberg was an excellent student at the study center and had an excellent voice for reading the torah. His reading evoked deep felt emotions to those that followed the text.

[Page 257]

He was an avid follower of the Hassidic movement and spent a great deal of time in the rabbi's house. In spite of the fact that was extremely religious and an avid follower of the political line of the "Agudath Israel" movement, he was well read in the general non-religious literature and tended to take an interest in modern education although remained devoted to the extreme religious principles of Judaism. He married to Rozwadow where his father in law lived, reb Arieh Kuss, a well to do and respected member of the community. He began to indulge in commerce and began to follow the Hassidic court of the Rabbi of Sciucin.

With the outbreak of World War II we found him in Russia with his family. Following the war he reached Paris, France where he settled. Writing these lines, I am informed that he fell ill and all the medical efforts failed to save him. He passed away the last Saturday of Passover 1950 in France. His body was shipped to Israel where he was buried in Petah Tikwah. (The author was the only person from Jaslo to attend the burial). He left a wife and two daughters in France.

Yaakow Zeev Ciechanowski

Yankele was his nickname amongst the good students at the study center in Jaslo. He was the son in law of Benyamin Unger. He was modest and run from publicity. He was a fine and honest man. He devoted himself daily to the study of the torah in spite of the fact that he also worked in his father in law's store.

He was a very accommodating person and gave charity with a large hand. He was a friendly and engaging person, devoid of self-indulgence. His children received a very religious education and strict adherence to the commandments as he himself strictly observed all the legal precepts of Jewish law.

He assumed the management of the store with the passing of his father in law. He worked for several years and then suffered a heart attack in 1935 and passed away. He left a wife, two sons named Chanoch and Shmuel and two infant daughters.

[Page 258]
Yeshayahu Cylinder
He was the son in law of Hersh Weinstein from Zmigrod. Very religious person that lived his entire life along Karzimieza Street where he had a grocery store that also sold paints and chalk in bulk. In the thirties, he left Jaslo and settled in Vienna. His store passed to his son in law Yekutiel Korman.
He had three daughters and a son. They all received a general education. His son finished his medical studies and left for the USA. He is well known amongst the former Jews of Poland. Rumor has it that two of the daughters are also in the USA. One daughter survived the shoah to reach Israel where she lives in Tel Aviv with her husband Dr. B. Fliksin, medical administrator of the joint organization in Israel.

Simcha Bunem Tzimet
He was born in Zmigrod. He was a Levi. He settled in Jaslo in the seventies of the previous century. He was very pious and well respected. He dealt with wheat and somewhat later started to trade with furniture. He had four sons: Wolf, Leib, Zacharia and Moshe. They all received a traditional education from the early Hebrew teachers in the city. They were all known as very religious, strictly observant, and well to do merchant people. They all owned their homes in Jaslo and were the first Jews to do so. The only daughter in the family was married to Rabbi Stroich of Neumark. Two grandsons and two granddaughters of this rabbi reside in Israel, (The children of Rabbi M. Shtern of Bilitz). One of them married in Tel Aviv Dr, Micha Ben Ami, the son of the author Ch.M. Ben Ami. Another grandson is Rabbi of a Yeshiva in Brooklyn New York.

Wolf Tzimet
He was the oldest son of Simcha Bunem Tzimet. He dressed well, very sensitive and somewhat distinguished looking with the large beard on his face. He was very active in all community affairs of Jaslo. He actively participated in the building of the study center and later of the synagogue in Jaslo. He was elected to the community board as well as to the municipal council.
He lived almost his entire life in a home behind the municipal building. The house contained a large warehouse of timber that served his regular and steady customers. He was called Reb Wolf. He was a stickler in adhering to the commandments and observed the easy ones with the same devotion as the demanding ones. I remember that in 1921 or 1922 there was a shortage of etrogim (fruit used in the holiday of Sukkoth) and most of the people of the city could not obtain one. The well to do inhabitants managed to get etrogim for the Rabbi, the study center and the synagogue. My father was then the beadle at the study center and had possession of the etrog that was to be used at the study center. As usual, my father arose very early especially on the first day of the Sukkoth holiday to immerse himself in the mikvah prior to the blessing of the etrog. Outside it was bitter cold and a misty cloud obstructed visibility on the ground. He opened the door of the house and to his surprise there. Was somebody outside the entrance door. He was taken aback but soon recognized Simcha Tzimet. The latter told him that he wanted to be the first person to bless the etrog but had to wait until he heard the door open in order not to awaken the whole house.
On the anniversary day of the passing of his parents, he conducted the services. He did not have the voice but the worshippers followed his reading with respect. He was honored member in the community. On the High holidays and other festivals he was called to the torah and given the second "Aliyah" or the Levi portion. This tradition was observed to the last day of his life. He would usually go up to the bima and stand there while the priests would walk up to the podium to bless the congregation. He assumed a position of a go between the community and the priests.

[Page 259]

He lived to a long ripe old age of 90 years and left after him four very observant sons. (His only daughter died in childbirth and left an infant daughter that was raised at the house until she married a torah student from Bilitz). One of her sons, Moshe left Jaslo and lived in Switzerland while the younger son, Yossil, remained in Jaslo and studied until he married to Gorlice.

[Page 260]

Betzalel Tzimet

He was the oldest son of Wolf Tzimet. He was the son in law of Naphtali Salomon. Extremely religious and behaved like the most important of the Tzimets in town. He lived with his father and worked together the business of selling timber. He prayed at the study center and had a seat along the eastern wall. He had two sons named Bunem for his grandfather and Mandil. He also had two daughters and the oldest one married the son of the judicial head of Litowisk.

Meir Tzimet

He was erudite in Jewish scholarship. He was married to the daughter of Rabbi Benyamin Geller, the head of the judicial council of Bobraka. (He was a great rabbinical scholar and a member of the board of the Rabbinical Association of Rabbis of Poland). He opened a jewelry store. During World War I left Jaslo but then returned to the city. Later on he moved to the hamlet of Stryzow. He had several sons that received an academic education.

Lib Tzimet

The second son of Simcha Tzimet was well known in the city of Jaslo. He was tall and well proportioned and had a large beard that reached his neck and curled side curls that gave him the appearance of a great Rabbi. Below his eyebrows were two shining eyes that emitted soft looks and gave the impression of wisdom and sharpness. He spoke as tough ach word was measured and weighted. He believed in saving words and attached great importance to what he said. He loved to hear the expression; Leib Tzimet said or Leib Tzimet meant to say.

He was very conservative and his behavior was a bit strange resulting in difficulties with his friends from the past namely Mendel Meller. The two constantly fought bitterly and sometimes even cursed each other. Leibish or as he was called Leib slowly distanced himself public life and concentrated himself with his family and his affairs. He even abandoned international politics and merely devoted himself to his business. Here he excelled for he was a shrewd and clever businessman. He worked from sunrise to sunset in his store. He worked by himself; his sleeves were always rolled up and exposed his elbows. The fringes were always exposed and flew with the wind. He was always going and coming from the store to the warehouse or to the carts or vice versa. He frequently helped load the peasant carts in front of his house. They usually loaded various machines or barrels of all sorts. Frequently he helped the farmers unload their merchandise for his warehouse.

[Page 261]

He was one of biggest merchants in the city and had the largest selection of agricultural machinery ranging from harvesters to plows. You could also find there bags of cement, paint, barrels f tar, pails, metal wires, heaters and light projectors. He was very busy but never failed to attend morning or evening services. He was very careful to observe the minutest commandant with the implements. He was straight in his business and his word was sacred to him. For years he read the instructions to the shofar blower on Rosh Hashanah. He would pull the large prayer shawl over his head and enounce from the bima in his deep voice the instructions. I can still hear his voice when he prayed before the open holy arc, the evening minha service on Yom Kippur eve. The prayer was moving and full of emotional pathos that affected most of the worshippers at the study center.

He was close to the Rabbi of the city but was not Hassidicaly inclined still his name was placed on the community list and he was selected to the board of the community. He was also called or nicknamed the old man.

He attended several meetings of the communal board when he fell ill with a terminal disease. Doctors were called in but to no avail. He even raveled to Vienna to visit medical professors but the disease progressed and he passed away. He left two sons and five daughters. He insisted on being buried with his favorite psalm book that was well used. He stated that this was the only think that was really his from all his life work.

Three of his son-in laws lived in Jaslo. The oldest son in law lived in Grybow and the youngest named Meirtchik, a modern orthodox student, lived in Krakow. The third son-in-law was Yossef Pearlberg a quiet studious type that had a wholesale haberdashery and paper store. His fourth son in law was Moshe Kaufman related to the famous rabbinical Rubin family of Korczyna. He devoted himself to the study of the Talmud and dedicated daily his life to it. His sons were also raised in the same spirit of Hassidic thinking. He had a small store at the Bronglewicze house in the market square.

The fifth son in law was Hertzel Ashkenazi who devoted himself to the study of the scriptures. He was also well read in general. He dealt with promissory financial notes for which he obtained a rabbinical permit and also dealt with currency exchanges.

His youngest son Bunem Tzimet was a talented and spirited youngster but a bit strange in his daily behavior. He was a regular at the study center and was very active in the "Agudath Israel. "

[Page 262]

He also attended biblical lectures given by Yossif Frumowicz and literature lectures by Kiczkowski in spite of the fact that he was very orthodox in his outlook and very conservative in his political views. He was well versed in the Talmud and understood its pages. He also incorporated the knowledge he acquired from the lectures in is Talmudic discussions. He also read secretly material from the enlightened movement. He wore a short velvet hat, dressed in black but shaved his beard.

He was merely twenty and very busy with his father's business.

He also sold books on the side to make extra money. (The last Talmud books that I bought from Wilno for the study center were purchased through him). He married the granddaughter of Rabbi Steinberg of Brod. With his brother Yossil they conducted their father' business.

Yossil Tzimet

The oldest son of Leib Tzmet was a very pious man and distanced himself from the public eye. Communal affairs did not interest him and was very careful when speaking to people. He was very pleasant in general. He lived almost his entire life at the home of his father and worked in the family business. He attended regularly services and the study sessions at the "kahal shtibel".

Lately, prior to World War II, he began the opening services of the High Holidays. His wife Goldzi Tzimet, the daughter of the well to do owner, Kalman Reich, was very involved in the community. She was very active in social work and also collected monies for the needy and the social institutions.

[Page 263]

For many years she headed the Beith Yaakow school and frequently dealt with the wife and daughters of the rabbi.

Yakil Tzimet was their only son. He studied at the study center but lately began to study general academic materials that influenced his thinking. He still followed in his father's footsteps.

He was a serious follower of the local Mizrahi branch. He was a good public speaker and knew how to tackle public issues. He helped establish the Mizrahi public school in the city. He was also the treasurer for the school and dreamt to settle in Palestine. Unfortunately his dream vanished with the destruction of the Jewish community of Jaslo.

Zacharia Tzimet

A son of Simcha Bunem Tzimet. He was educated and well read. Sympathized with the Zionist movement that began to spread throughout the Jewish population. He was a good businessman but then left for Germany. One of his daughters is married to the Wolff family and they live in Tel Litwinsky. Their house is known for its warmth, tradition and hospitality.

Moshe Tzimet

One of the most important individuals in the Jewish community. He was a quiet man and very unobtrusive. Behaved in an aristocratic manner. He had a great deal of integrity and behaved in a like manner. He was very pious and well connected to the rabbinical world. He was a man of few words but very decisive and tactful.

His house was known for its warmth and charity. He raised his children in the very orthodox tradition. In the business world he was known as a fair and straight man. He had two large stores. One sold bulk and retail groceries and sweets in the market while the other store located along Iglena sold furniture.

In spite of his busy financial and commercial schedule, he always set aside time for his prayers in the synagogue where he also exchanged some words with other worshippers. With the destruction of the study center during World War I, he joined the Rabbi's study center and remained a member of this congregation until his last living day.

He shied away from public debates or political stands, he revolved around his family, educating his children and his commercial affairs. With age, he became seriously ill and the doctors could not save him. He died in 1924.

[Page 264]

His oldest son Hirsh Tzimet was an excellent student at the study center where he studied until he was married. He studied and delved into various aspects of Jewish knowledge. He rounded out his Jewish education and became a staunch supporter of the "Mizrahi" movement in Jaslo. Following his marriage he left Jaslo and settled in Przemysl where he opened a paper store that was very successful. After a few years he decided to fulfill his Zionist dream and sold his business and left Poland for Palestine. He settled in Jeda (today Ramat Ishai). He wanted to open a knitting workshop there. The venture did not materialize and he eventually settled in Jerusalem where he opened a large bookstore that served primarily the British mandate clerks since most of the books were in English. He lived along Julian Street but left the area following the war of independence. He settled in the center of the city of Jerusalem.

He lost his only son Aaron in the War of Independence. His soft-spoken son died on the 17th day of the month of Tishri 1949 (the second day of Hol Hamoed Sukkot). The late Aaron grew up in Jerusalem and was very popular amongst his friends. He loved the city where he received his religious and general education.

He was a good-looking man, courageous, and well respected by the numerous customers that he served in his father's store. He treated everybody with respect and insisted on the same treatment for himself. He was able to impose himself on those that tried to denigrate the Jew. The summer of 1948 affected him as all the other Jews in Jerusalem, namely they had to defend their newly established country, especially Jerusalem that was shelled almost daily... He participated in many engagements namely, the battle of Sheich Jarrach, the police academy training school, Yemin Moshe, Har Tzion, Ramat Rachel, Malcha and many other places. He was always in the forefront of the battle.

[Page 265]

Aaron Tzimet
Hero of the War of Independence

On Wednesday (the second day of Hol Hamoed Sukkot Tashat), 19th October 1948, he and his friends lead an attack on the Arab village of Beitar, South Jerusalem. He is mortally wounded but the smile is still on his lips as he uttered the fatherland is ours.

A fine lad, devoted to the family, close ties with friends, and devotion to the newly created state and to the words of G-d. All his dedication he draws from the Jewish historical sources that he studied with devotion and they gave him the necessary courage. (Loosely translated from the (eulogy that appeared and was written by A.A.Jerusalmi)

Moshe Tzimet also had two daughters that were deeply involved in the activities of the Bnot Agudath Israel or the women counter part of the Agudath Israel and headed the Beith Yaakov School for girls. The oldest daughter Faiga married Meir Illiowicz of Krosno who was a Talmudic student and concentrated on his studies, he avoided all public activities.

[Page 266]

He was a regular participant at the study center of the rabbi. He was a merchant in the store of his father in law in the market.

His second daughter Haya married Meir Moshel, the son of the well to do Mendel Moshel of Sanok, who was a student of the famous Rabbi Shapiro who was the judicial head of the rabbinical court of the same city. (He was the founder of the Yeshiva Chochmei Lublin, member of the Polish Parliament as a representative of the Agudat Israel, later headed the rabbinical office of Piotrikow and Lublin). He was a talented individual with an abundance of energy and enterprise. Always neatly dressed, a follower of the rabbi, and very active in the political party of the Agudah Israel. He was one of the younger leaders of the party and was involved in all the minute details of the movement.

He traveled to the opening of the Yeshiva Chochmei Lublin in order to partake in the festivities. When the head of the Yeshiva passed way, he eulogized him before a large audience in the synagogue. His words were impressive and left deep impressions on the participants. He became known as a good speaker, familiar with Judaic knowledge and a capable public figure in the community.

He was placed on the ticket of the community board and was elected member. His name was also placed as a candidate for municipal office on behalf of the merchants association. He defeated a relative, Betzalel Tzimet who also ran for office on another list.

He visited Palestine in 1935 with the opening games of the Maccabiah. He intended to stay in the country but things did not work out and he returned to Poland. He described to fiends the country, the life style and the people. According to his cousin, Hersh Tzimet, he was a bit disappointed but deep in his heart he hoped to return to Palestine but events will overtake his plan.

He had a nice income from his wholesale and retail haberdashery store within the place of his father in law in the market.

He had no sons. With the German onslaught on Poland he managed to reach Lemberg but decided to return to Jaslo and was one of the first German victims in the city. From the entire family, only a sister remained alive Rike, who married the student Awraham Yehoshua Heshil Liberman (Livni), the son of the Rabbi of Dobri. They had a jewelry store in Tel Aviv on Allenby Street.

[Page 267]

Leibish Tzimet

The second son of Moshe Tzimet was a religious student at the study center. He was a quiet and genial person. Following his marriage, he settled down in Jaslo to manage the furniture store that he received. He was also very active in social organizations namely the association of young unwed girls. This organization helped financially the girls to wed. He personally went with the musical band to the homes of the intended brides and grooms on Saturday evenings to ask for contributions for the association to help poor girls to wed. He was also active in the burial society and was one of its officers. He was also a member of the board of the synagogue on Florianska Street (Souveniover). He had five sons.

Awraham Tzimet

He was born in Zmigrod and settled in Jaslo. He was a wheat merchant and lived in his house on Kurlewskiego Street He was a simple Jew that followed the precepts of the Hassidic Rabbi of Rymanow. He had two daughters and three sons. His oldest daughter lived in Istrik. According to rumors, one of his sons lives in France.

Lipa Tzimet

He was also a wheat merchant like his brother. He was very active amongst the merchants of the city. Transactions were made in his name; his suggestions were circulated amongst the merchants... Lipa said... Lipa did... He was successful and bought a piece of land on which he built a three story house. The first large Jewish edifice to be built in Jaslo following Polish independence.

The Rabbi of Rymanow was invited to the opening of the house and with him came many of the Hassidic followers that were very happy to spend a Sabbath with their rabbi in the house of Lipa Tzimet. Amongst the guests was the well to do Hassid from Rzeszow, Asher Zilber. (He lives presently in Czernowic; he is about 90 years old). This Saturday provided many stories for the inhabitants of Jaslo.

He gave charity and supported many institutions. Suddenly, his commercial enterprise began to flounder and collapsed. He had three daughters that received a high school education. Two survived the war. One of them is the daughter in law of Shlomo Weingarten, they live in Paris.

[Page 268]

Moshe Mandil Tzimet

He was the son of Alter Levi Tzimet from Zmigrod. He was very religious, Hassidic in outlook but well read in Jewish knowledge. He owned a haberdashery store in Stillman's house that was located in the market. He did very well and eventually bought the house from Stillman's inheritors where he continued to live. He had several sons that were raised along the precepts of the Hassidic Rabbi of Bobowa. His oldest son Yaakov, known as Yankel, had a very pleasant voice and was an assistant in the choir of Avish Neuman during the High Holidays.

Benyamin Tzinger

He was a quiet person, always dressed formally, and wore a hard hat. He gave the impression of a high school teacher or writer in his mannerisms. He was a tailor that barely scrapped together an income to feed his family. He lived in the house of Goldstein most of his life.

Rabbi Yona Tzanger

He was the son in law of Elimelech Teller and Awraham Hersh Brenner. He served as Rabbi before his successor Rabbi Yehoshua Heshil Rubin assumed office. He was rabbi when there were a few Jews that concentrated in the suburb of Ulaszowice near Jaslo. Unfortunately, he became ill and passed away in the prime of his life.

Tzafat family

This family resided in Tarnowici for years. They were traditional people and were traders.

[Page 269]

Kof ק

Zalka Kanarik

He was a member of the inner court of the rabbi of Dukla and moved to Jaslo when the rabbi moved to the city. He was a very clever and wise man. He had black shiny eyes, a happy disposition and was content with life. He always had a smile on his face as though he laughed at the world, yet he was aware of its existence. He respected himself as a Jew, who was familiar with the laws, traditions and in addition to everything had an important position that not too many people reached.

Simche Kaczkowski

He was a modern person for the time. He was a barber, administered leeches and prescribed glasses. He also administered remedies and acted as a male nurse, thus the nickname "doctor." He was sued following medical complications as a result of a tooth extraction. He lived in the house of Hersh Shpringer on Nowa Street. He passed away prior to World War I.

Gustav Koczakowski

He was well known among the Jewish youth of Jaslo and those who never met him personally heard of him. At the age of two, he was sick and the disease blinded him for life. He was a very interesting person and very familiar with classical and modern literature, namely the songs of Schiller, Goethe, Heine, Kochanowsky, Mickewicz, Slowacki and he memorized the writings of Nietzche and Schopenhauer.

He knew by heart entire sections of Shakespeare and Bernard Shaw that he could recite instantly. He had great respect for the French writer Emile Zola and was an excellent historian who spoke Polish, German, French, English and Latin fluently.

He conducted an extensive correspondence and was a very capable accountant. He was familiar with the environment in spite of his blindness and was familiar with the local political scene and the situation of the Zionist movement in Jaslo. While a student at the school for the blind in Vienna, he familiarized himself with Zionism through the writings of Herzl and his revolutionary Jewish ideas.

[Page 270]

He had excellent hearing and was very knowledgeable in music. He played the piano, the violin, and recited and sang poetry according to the melody.

He was a very popular teacher and had many students. The youth of Jaslo, especially the religious youth, loved to chat with him. Young men and women who lacked writing fluency approached him secretly to write letters in Polish or German to their sweethearts or their families for them. He was very helpful and frequently wrote the letters in particular styles that benefitted he parties. The latter were pleased with his work and he helped them immensely.

Lately he lived in Mendel Meller's house on May 3rd Street. He had one son and two daughters who received an academic education. The son was the secretary of the community for a number of years.

With the outbreak of World War II, they left Jaslo for Lemberg, where the son died. The father reached Russia where he also died.

Adolph Kaczkowski, attorney

He was the brother of Gustav Kaczkowski, one of the best known attorneys in the city of Jaslo. He was an assimilated Jew and had a slight contempt for Jews, the Jewish community and the Zionist movement. He lived near the district court house and had three daughters.

Max Kugel

He was the owner of an elegant bar in the Steinhaus house in the market. In his youth, he worked for Bogusz Steinhaus as a waiter and later rented the place. The Polish intelligentsia and assimilated Jews met frequently at the bar. The inn sold non-kosher meats and was open on Shabbat and holidays. On the eve of Yom Kippur the owner rushed to the synagogue to pray the "minha" service and distributed charity. His children received an academic education.

Moshe Kodler

He was an enlightened progressive Jew and a member of the Zionist movement. He was an honest and moderate person.

[Page 271]

His voice was barely audible and he was a wholesaler. His sons were members of the Zionist movement and the family lived along May 3rd Street.

Tzwi Kolber

He was a progressive, honest and quiet person. He was a timber merchant and lived in his house on Iglena Street. He had two sons and a daughter who were members of the Zionist youth movements and helped their father.

The widow Koller

She settled in Jaslo in the 1920s when the "Beit Yaakov" school for girls opened. Her daughter was a teacher and guidance counselor at the school. She had one son who was a member of the Zionist movement and gave private Hebrew lessons.

Shulem Kunst

He was married to Wolf Eintziger's daughter and had a haberdashery store on May 3rd Street at the house of Mendel Meller. He was a refined man, at ease in dealing with people. He had a clear conscience and acted in good faith. He was a loyal member to the Mizrahi movement and joined the services at the Mizrahi synagogue. He was one of the co-founders of the Mizrahi School and kindergarten. He was a party follower and tried to implement the party line. He devoted most of the energies to the popularization of the party. He dreamt of leaving Jaslo for Palestine but the dream was not realized for he died

Betzalel Mordechai Kuflik
He was a G-d fearing Hassid and very charitable. He set aside hours to continue his religious studies.
He was born in Istrik to an old Hassidic family and settled in Jaslo following his marriage. He opened a grocery but took ill and soon passed away in the prime of life. He left a wife, three sons and a daughter. The grandfather, who continued to reside in Istrik, took the oldest son Awraham Yehoshua and the daughter Dworah to his house. The two younger children Yossef and Aaron remained with their mother in Jaslo. (Aaron contracted tuberculosis and passed away as a youngster.) Awraham left his grandfather when he grew older and so did Dworah, who settled in Germany.

[Page 272]
Awraham Yehoshua Kuflick
He continued his religious and general studies and is presently working for the Jewish community in Zurich, Switzerland. He visited Israel twice (one of his sons studies at the Hebron Yeshiva in Jerusalem and his daughter is married to an outstanding student at the same yeshiva). Dworah, her husband and two daughters live in Haifa. Yossef perished during the Shoa.

Moshe Kaufman
He was born in Korczyna and was married to Leib Tzimet's daughter. He was a poor and honest person who opened a small store that provided him with a living. He continued his religious studies daily.
His sons received a very religious education.

Hersh Korzennik
He was one of the first Jewish homeowners in the city. He was a Munkatcher Hassid and had a bakery along Nowa Street. One of his sons, Shmuel Zeinwil, was a tailor and followed the Hassidic pattern of life. He left for Vienna but was forced by the Germans to leave in 1939 and returned to Jaslo, whereupon the Poles arrested him under the pretext that he was an Austrian spy. He was sent to the famous political prison of Kartuz Bereza.

Zelig Korzennik
He was the second son of Hersh Korzenik and very religious, good natured and G-d fearing. He presented himself nicely and distributed charity. He was a regular member of the study group of "mishnayot" at the "shtibel" synagogue.
With the passing of his father, he continued the baking business until 1919. (During World War I his bakery was attacked several times by mobs demanding bread that was not available) He sold the bakery to the Mandel brothers and retired.
He had two sons and three daughters. One of his sons was Moshe who owned a clothing store in Rzeszow. The oldest daughter married M. Dar of Tarnow whose business flourished. He was also a partner in the famous clothing factory "Wurtzel and Dar" that was well known in Poland. Lately he acquired ownership of the rubber plant "Wudeta." The family had a son and a daughter who was deaf-mute.
The son and his family came once to visit the parents. The grandson played near a boiling tank of water, fell into it and died.

[Page 273]
Shlomo Korzennik
He was a modern person and following his marriage settled in Jaslo where he opened a clothing store in his father's house and later moved the business to the house of Doctor Willusz.

Yehiel Korzenik
He was an educated person and had modern views on life. He was a wealthy person in the community. He owned a house on Sokola Street and exported eggs to various countries. He had three daughters who received an academic education.

Yekutiel Zeew Korman
I met Yekutiel Zeew Korman daily for many years; he was one of the first worshippers to arrive at our daily service. He attended the daily lectures given by Chaim Wekselbaum until he passed away.
He was spiritually inclined and wrote articles dealing with religion. He was pleasant and cordial in his relations with other people. On arriving at the synagogue, he proceeded to his seat located along the northeast side, wrapped himself in his prayer shawl and began to pray with great devotion, pronouncing each word distinctly. When required he would gently pick himself up and leave with trepidation.
He was the Torah reader at the study center until he passed away in the harsh winter of 1928. He read correctly and stressed the accentuations. He began the services on the High Holidays. He lived almost all his life on Florianska Street where his wife ran the grocery store and the daughters assisted. He had four daughters and two sons. The oldest son Gershon reached Palestine after he left Germany in 1933. He was a modern person and opened a successful toy and curtain store.
The daughters married religious fellows and yeshiva students. The oldest married her cousin, the son of Mordechai Korman, who was a quiet, friendly store owner. The second daughter married the Hassid Israel Mai who acquired the store from Yeshayahu Cylinder and succeeded. The third daughter married Eliyahu Teichthal and the fourth, Miriam, finished the teacher seminary in Warsaw. She was the author of the journal "Bnot-Mizrahi" or Mizrahi girls. She left for Palestine where she married Shlomo Krisher.

[Page 274]
Awraham Korman
He was the second son of Yekutiel Korman. He was highly erudite in Torah knowledge. He was a student of the study center and in his youth was one of the founders of the Mizrahi youth branch in the city. He devoted himself to the movement and was a steady member of the congregation of the Mizrahi synagogue where he read the Torah.
He married the granddaughter of Yaakov Pinhas Krisher and opened a jewelry store on Kosciuszko Street. He left Jaslo with his family and reached Russia where he survived the war. He then reached Israel with his wife and daughter and they settled in Tel Aviv where they started a business.

Chaim Korn
He was the brother in law of Yaakov Freund of Ulaszowica. He was very influential and distinguished for his honesty and integrity. He was a Hassidic Jew and owned a hotel on Iglena Street. Later he opened one on Kosciuszko Street that he managed with his sons. Subsequently his son Benyamin and Chaim Korn managed the hotel until World War I.

Dawid Eliezer Korn

He was the son of Chaim Korn. He was a Hassid in soul and body and studied the Torah daily. He was also inclined to music and was one of the better musicians in town. He was one of the founders of the association "Haknassat Kala" that helped poor girls to wed. He devoted a great deal of time to the organization. He was one of the musicians of the choir that played for the benefit of the above organization. The choir included many capable musicians that placed it on a high musical level. The choir donated a great deal of time to other charitable organizations.

Shmuel Korn

He was a dairy man. He negotiated with farm owners and purchased their milk. He also sold cheese and butter that he himself produced. He was a simple person and was nicknamed Shmuel limb since he lost his hand in World War I. It was interesting to see how he put on the phylacteries using his lips instead of the hand that was missing.

[Page 275]

He lived on Korlowski Street and had four sons and two daughters. All the children belonged to the Zionist movement.

Mrs. Kornblit

She owned a kiosk in the bus square and had an employment agency for maids. She had an only son named Elisha who was a Bobower Hassid and devoted himself to Torah study.

Awraham Kornhauser

He was one of the oldest attorneys in town and his office was closed on Saturday and holidays, a rarity among Jewish attorneys in Jaslo. He was tall and aristocratic, looking similar to Dr. Herzl.

He was extremely devoted to the Zionist cause from its initial days. He fought on behalf of the movement and was elected several times to be a representative at the Zionist congresses.

[Page 276]

He was very active from his first day of arrival to Jaslo. His life dream was Palestine, the essence of his life, and he devoted to all his energies to it. He even closed his office to tend to party affairs when the need arose. Zionism was his ideal and everything was next on line. He of course had many enemies who opposed him and his ideas bitterly. As a member of the old Zionist guard and the head of the community council, he suggested that the community hire a modern Zionist rabbi for the city. The uproar that followed, cause a great deal of resentment amongst the very religious Jews.

He had a strange personality in his behavior. As a high school student in Tarnow he tended to lean to assimilation and became a non-religious person. He then read Leon Pinsker's "Auto-emancipation" and Herel's "The Jewish State". He read the books and accepted these ideas. He became a convinced and fanatical Zionist. He was a bachelor and as such did not have a prayer shawl. Later in life, he bought a fine silver lined prayer shawl. He wore it on Shabbaths, holidays and yizkor days when he attended the synagogue. Occasionally he was called to the Torah and he received honorable invitations to participate in the Simchat Torah celebrations at the synagogue.

Birthday party for Dr. Krohauser in Jaslo

His seventieth birthday was celebrated in the community center of Jaslo. Many famous and influential people participated in the celebration, many delegations from other areas came as well as a delegation from the Central Zionist office in Poland, the editor Dr. Berkelhamer of the Jewish Polish newspaper "Dzienik" or daily, from Krakow, the senator Bodek representing Lemberg, and Dr. Belech from Gorlice. He was presented with a scroll on which were inscribed all the well-wishers. The scroll was placed in a silver holder. The Germans killed him in the Shoah together with the Jewish community.

[Page 277]
E. Kornmehl
He was the son in law of Mordechai Karp and a doctor. He was the only Jewish doctor to work for the general governmental health insurance office in the city. He was well regarded and respected by his Jewish and non-Jewish patients. He escaped to Russia with his family prior to the German arrival. He survived the war years in Russia and returned to Poland following World War II where he settled in Wroclaw and began to practice. He suddenly died of a heart attack while still very active. His wife and only son left Poland and reached Israel three years ago. The son finished in Israel medical school and works at Hadassah Hospital in Jerusalem. Mrs. Kornmehl was highly respected in the community and especially in the Zionist movement of the city of Jaslo. She was very active in social work and helped the sick, orphans and needy people. She always had a smile on her face for the people that came to see her. She always listened attentively and tried to help solve the problem with sensitivity and finesse. Her confidence and self-assurance helped many of the needy. She was also very active in Russia on behalf of the Jewish refugees of Poland and helped in every possible way.

Dawid Hersh Kornfeld
He was a long time resident of the city and lived on Kazimierska Street. He exchanged currencies and died of old age with the outbreak of World War I. He had two sons and a daughter.

Wolf Kornfeld

He was a modern person and was Amar's business partner. They had several houses and rented flats. He received two houses from his father when the latter died. The properties belonged previously to Alexandrowicz and were located in the corner between Kazimierz and Nowa Streets. He played cards for hours at the "Krakowski Hotel" with other well to do people. Then he ran for office and was elected to the community board as a representative. Being the oldest member of the board, he became the head of the community council. His administration favored the very religious and the rabbi. He never personally took a stand but followed the line of least resistance as long as his tranquility was not disturbed.

He had a son and a daughter who received a high school and academic education. The son named Salo was very active in the Esperanto club in the city and following World War I settled in Paris. His daughter left Jaslo following her marriage.

[Page 278]

Bernard Kornfeld

He was the second son of Dawid Hersh Kornfeld and owned a bank on May 3rd Street. Business disappointed him and one day he closed the bank and disappeared. For days, nobody knew what happened to him. He reached Przemysl but was very depressed. He lost his senses and committed suicide at the hotel. He left a wife and a son who received a high school education.

Israel Meir Kornreich

He was one of the oldest inhabitants in Ulaszowica and one of the first to be elected to the community council. He sold spirit and beverages from his home. He was very traditional, nicely mannered and acted as an important man in town. Lately he devoted himself exclusively to his business. He was a brother in law of Itche Reich and related to Baruch Margolies and Aaron Freund.

Moshe Hersh Kornreich

He was the son of Israel Meir Kornreich and the son in law of Itche Reich. He was also involved in the spirit business. He then closed the business and opened a clothing store. This venture also failed and he started another business. He had one daughter.

P. Kurtz

He was a rich man and owned the movie house named "Sokol" and sold timber and coal. He tended to assimilation and distanced himself from Jewish affairs. He had two sons and two daughters.

[Page 279]

Yossef Kurtzweil

He replaced Cantor Turbowski in Jaslo in 1915. He was from Eastern Galicia and hired as chief cantor. He had a pleasant tenor voice. He prayed with feeling and emotion. The excellent choir of ten helpers supported the cantor. Many people came just to hear him conduct services. His choir consisted of three tenors: Moshe Nussbaum, Betzalel Lipczer and Leibish Bleiman. Four sopranos: the author of the book, Mendel Shindler (now in Paris), Simche Rothfeld now in England) and Moshe Goldschmidt (now in Tel Aviv), Moshe Schecht (now in Haifa). Dawid Weitz, Awraham Itche Apfel were altos and Berish Brun was bass.

He lived all his life in Hershel Shpringer's house. His flat was small and consisted of two small, dark, damp rooms. He had two daughters and one son named Berish.

He was by nature a quiet and satisfied person and. The measly salary that he received from the community for his cantorial services barely covered his living expenses in spite of the fact that everybody was pleased with his performance. After three years of service, he left Jaslo for Germany and then for the USA.

Eliezer Kiehl

He was one of the few natives of the city of Jaslo. He was a merchant and imported flour. He was very religious person and was the beadle of the study center following Yoel Bodner's resignation. He lived on Iglena Street where his father also resided. The latter was also an importer of flour in his younger days. He had two sons and several daughters who received a traditional education. His oldest son Beril was a student of the study center. He was skinny, tall but had fists of iron. All the boys feared these fists. Thus, it came as a great surprise when the medical army doctor rejected him for military service by calling him a skinny runt. The girls of the family joined the Mizrahi youth movement.

[Page 280]
Moshe Kilig

He was one of the oldest cohanim in the city. He provided dairy items to the people of Jaslo but later opened a kiosk where he sold candies and seltzer. The kiosk was in the main square of the city.
He was a modest Hassid and prayed at the rabbi's synagogue. He had two sons and one daughter who became a widow early in life. Her husband left her with a small baby who grew up with Alter Kilig.

Alter Kilig

He was the oldest son of Moshe Kilig and a merchant on Czickiego Street opposite the municipal high school. He was very religious, withdrawn, and kept his distance from people. He adopted his sister's daughter and maintained her until she was married to Shlomo Epstein who later became a fine Talmudic scholar. The uncle maintained the young couple for years.

Avigdor Kilig

He was the second son of Moshe Kilig and the exact opposite of his brother. He was involved in the community and was very energetic. He was a student of the study center and continued his studies after World War I. He spoke fluent Polish and German that resulted in his editing the correspondence between Jewish institutions and the Polish authorities. He married a daughter of the San family who owned the "Grand" hotel in the city. He dressed traditionally in the Hassidic manner; shtreimel and silk clothing on Saturdays and holidays. He traveled to rabbis and was well liked. He stood for elections and won a seat on behalf of his Mizrahi movement. He dreamt of settling in Palestine one day but the dream never materialized due to Hitler. He shared the fate of the Jewish community of Jaslo.

Leibsh Kinstler

He was a native of Zmigrod and very quiet. He was traditional and prayed at the study center. He was a grain merchant and had one daughter who was married to Shmuel Zilpan of Siniawa.

Mendel Kinstler

He was a brother of Leibish Kinstler. He was a modern person who owned a grocery
[Page 281]
on Koeciuszko Street. He had five daughters and three sons. Some of the children received a high school education. His oldest son Kalman is presently in Melbourne, Australia. The second son Awraham resided in Rome and then moved to Australia. The third son Leibish perished in the Shoa. The oldest daughter was married to the engineer Yaakow Grubtuch, the second son in law was the son of Dawid Hellman. The third son in law was doctor Shomer who worked at Niglowic. The youngest daughter was married to Doctor Itzhak Bezner, a grandson of the

famous donor Itzhak Yehuda Rubel. Itzhak Bezner became a high official of the Israeli treasury (he was killed in a plane crash flying to Holland).According to rumors the oldest daughter tried to bribe an official of the ghetto by offering him 50,000 zlotys in gold pieces to enable her to escape the place but it came to nothing.

Yehoshua Kippel

He was the son in law of Wolf Eintziger and strictly observed the commandments. He prayed regularly at the synagogue and was a member of the "Hevra Kadisha" in the city. He lived on Karmelicka Street and had a store. He had two sons and several daughters.

Moshe Kirsh

He lived for many years in the village of Kobelow. He was very religious and a grain merchant. He also dealt with other agricultural produce. He later bought a flourmill in Pilzno and made a nice living.

He had two sons who left for Germany. Feiwil was the oldest who studied and acquired a general education. He left Germany and managed to reach Palestine where he settled in Tel Aviv and opened a clothing store for women. The second son Chaim lives in Rishon Lezion.

Yaakow Kalb

He was an influential figure at the "Hevra Kadisha" in the city. He was extremely pious and prayed at the study center of the rabbi. He was one of the oldest workers at the distillery of Itzhak Yehuda Ruvbel in Siowniow. He earned a nice salary and had two sons and two daughters. The oldest daughter married Yehoshua Grinfeld from Dukla who was a Bobower Hassid. He had a haberdashery and sold sewing articles. The second daughter married Hertz Shlaf who was also a Bobower Hassid but a bit more moderate than his brother in law. He read newspapers, books and was familiar with the surroundings. Lately he left Jaslo.

[Page 282]

Leibish Kalb

He was the oldest son of Yaakow Kalb and studied at the study center. He also read a great deal and tended to associate with people who followed the Zionist path. He married to Przedmiescze where he opened a grocery. He had three sons and one of them left his religious studies and worked at a dentist's office.

Zishe Kalb

He was the second d son of Yaakow Kalb and was a student at the study center where he devoted himself to the study of the Torah. He tended to Hassidism and following his marriage, he started a business. Later on he opened a store on May 3rd Street where he sold wool, silk and stylish materials. He succeeded in business and attracted a large fashionable clientele. The business did not detract from his religious observance, on the contrary, his attraction to the Bobower Hassidut increased. His only son followed the father's example. Zishe Kalb continued to propagate the ideas of Bobow. He was helped in this endeavor by Pini Shtrum and Abish Neuman. They made nice inroads among the very religious youth of Jaslo. He also attended the daily Talmud lectures. He lived on Sokola Street in a house that he bought in the twenties.

Zalman Kalb

He was an honest and fair person. He was unassuming and an early riser to attend services. He was the first among the clothing merchants at the synagogue. Lately he joined the Dukler Hassidim and became closely associated with the court of the rabbi and prayed at his study center.

(His wife was an Altman, one of the first Jewish families to settle in Jaslo.) He lived all his life in the house of Mendel Gross and had one son named Yossef and five daughters. Three of the daughters made aliyah to Palestine as pioneers and the oldest lived at Kibbutz Yagur in the early twenties. The second daughter lives in Haifa and the third one lives in one of the settlements. According to rumors, the son lives in Belgium.

[Page 283]
Moshe Kalb
He was the son in law of Zelig Miller and frequently led the mishnayot sessions at the "Kahal Shtibel" or small synagogue and read the Torah at the big study center until he passed away.
He kept away from public honors and shied away from publicity. He was a merchant.
He lived at the house of Olbertowicz next to the synagogue and had four sons and three daughters who received a general education; the youngest son was named Tanhum. Following his death, the family left Jaslo and headed for the USA where some of his sons already resided. One of these sons was Motil who owned a factory. Another son resided in Katowice until the out break of World War II.

Berish Klausner
He was an ordinary Jew who kept his tradition. He sold furniture and lived on Siowniowi Street. His sons left Jaslo for the USA prior to World War I. He raised his grandson who passed away. He then left for the USA.

The Klausner family
With the great battles in and around Gorlice in World War I, the family left the area and settled in Jaslo. The father passed away in Gorlice and left a wife with several children. The family settled in Jaslo but later left for Germany with Polish independence. Part of the family reached the USA with the rise of the Nazis in Germany. Only one son named Moshe Klausner reached Palestine in 1934 and settled in Tel Aviv. He was a very religious young man and accepted his lot. He always had a pleasant smile and struggled to keep his family going. In the winter of 1950, he became ill. The Streets of Tel Aviv were covered with snow, it was bitter cold, the skies were cloudy, a rare site for Tel Aviv when Moshe Klausner was taken to Hadassah Hospital where he passed away. He was merely 46 years of age and left a wife and two small children. May his memory be blessed.

[Page 284]
Israel Kalter
He was the brother in law Moshe Zilberstein and a Talmudic scholar. He was a merchant and left Jaslo for Germany prior to World War I.

Yehoshua Klein
He was an enlightened person and followed the recent modern trends. He was well read and a timber merchant. He settled in Jaslo following World War I and lived in Mendel Meller's house. His daughter made aliyah to Palestine in the thirties.
Ozer Klein He was a brother of Yehoshua Klein and was well read. He was also a timber merchant and settled in Jaslo following World War I. One of his of his sons reached Israel and settled in Holon.

Peretz Kleinberg
He settled in Jalso following the battles around Gorlice in 1914. He was a Hassid and familiar with the torah. He was a steady member of the study center of the rabbi. At first he sold coal and then switched to kitchenware. Lately he also represented several sock firms from Lodz.
He had two sons named Baruch and Kalman and two daughters. The oldest daughter was Riwka and the other one was Pesia. They received a traditional religious education as was the custom amongst very religious families. He lived at Wil's place and then at the Targowica.

Feiwil Klinman

He was born in Sandz and was the son in law of Elimelech Teller. He was very religious, rich and respected. He owned a house in the market square. He previously owned a house at the bottom of Korlowski Street. He was a wholesaler of grocery items.

Every year he walked to the Kol Nidrei service on the eve of Yom Kippur wrapped in his kittel- or white robe and prayer shawl. He also carried a "machzor" or holiday prayer book and a white pillow since he remained the entire night at the synagogue reciting psalms. He had four sons named: Hersh the oldest, Chaim, Monie and Baruch. They all received a religious education and all studied at study center in their youth. They were all quiet, well-behaved people who were business persons.

[Page 285]

Monie was very religious and devoted himself in his youth to mystical books together with his neighbor Eliezer Hauer. His two sons in law were Yoel Margolies and Shmeril Shertz.

Reuven Klinman

He was the son in law of Yudel Bodner and a Talmudic scholar. He devoted time to the study of the Torah even after his marriage. His wife Feige was as an excellent merchant at her father's store until she married. He was a sugar and flour importer and lived on Kosciuszko Street.

Nathanael L. Klinman

(See Israel Wilner)

Hersh Keller

He was a quiet man and dressed modern. He wore a bowler and gave the impression of some modern German rabbi. He was a tailor and barely made a living. He was supported by his sons and lived in a rundown flat on Sokola Street.

Zelig Keller

He was a smart fellow and known for his speaking abilities and wisecracks in his younger days. He used to be a member of the Poalei Tzion and following his return from Russian captivity became known as a radical of the left. He was a tailor and for a while operated the kiosk next to the distillery.

Shmuel Knobloch

He was from the hamlet of Rymanow and settled in Jaslo following Polish independence. He was well mannered, respected for his appearance and his white beard gave him additional stature.

He made a nice living from his general store and his skin business. He had four sons who received a traditional religious education and tended to the Mizrahi movement. They were Aaron, Moshe, Israel Itzha, and Dawid. One of his daughters was married to a Talmudic scholar from Glogow who was a distinguished student of the Rabbi Itzhak of Shalkish, author of the book "Beith Itzhak." Rumors have it that the youngest son Dawid survived the war and is presently in Melbourne, Australia.

[Page 286]
Dawid Kannengisser

He was the son in law of Pearl Rapaport and a Hassidic Jew. He worked with his father in law who became ill and passed away at a very young age.

Moshe Kanner

The Kanner family was known throughout Western Galicia as a rich and large family. He was a Torah student and enlightened. He conducted himself as a Hassid and lived in Mani Eintziger's house on Nowa Street. He discounted checks, dealt in currency exchanges and granted short-term loans.

There was once a dispute between him and Yossef Meller about 500 Austrian reinish. Both came to the religious court presided over by the rabbi. Yossef Meller promised to swear before a Torah that he was telling the truth. The date for the swearing was set and it was to take place at the great synagogue. Large candles lit the synagogue and a large crowd appeared. The shamas brought a black shrew from the cemetery and Yossef Meller dressed in a white kittel was about to take the oath. Suddenly, Eliezer Blum shouted and screamed against the whole procedure. He was supported by many members of the community. They all protested the ordeal that Yossef Meller faced. He was a man of charity, good deeds, helped poor people in the city and an honest person. They stated that the treatment was unfair. Negotiations and discussions began to alleviate the procedure and finally Yossef Meller was excused from the oath. With the outbreak of World War I, the Kanner family left the city and settled in Krakow.

P. Kaplan

He was from Szidlowce, Poland and settled lately in Jaslo. He was a shoemaker and opened a workshop at Eliezer Rosner's place in the market.

Dawid Krebs

He was a traditional Hassidic Jew and a baker. His private and family name were unknown in the city. Only his wife was known as Roda the baker. He lived all his life in his house opposite the great synagogue. In his late years, he became blind and Yossef Menashe used to walk him to and from the synagogue.

[Page 287]

Moshe Krebs

He was originally from Zmigrod and settled in the twenties in Jaslo. He lived all his life in Goldstein's house. He tended to follow the Mizrahi movement's ideology and was a grain merchant.

Itzhak Leib Krupki

He kept his religious tradition. He was quiet, modest and sold fruits. He lived all his life in the market. He had several sons who were members of the Zionist youth movement. Two of sons made aliyah and one settled in Tel Aviv and one lives in Tzfat.

Chaim Kriger

He was a religious Jew close to Hassidut. He was a shipper of goods and had several sons and daughters. He lived in a wooden barrack along Kosciuszko Street. One of his sons who returned from Russian captivity in World War I, left for Vienna and eventually reached Canada.

Dawid Krizwirt

He was one of the old Talmudic scholars in the city. His integrity and rational pleasant manner of speaking made a nice impression on people. He was a timber merchant and passed away of old age during World War I.

Betzalel Krizwirt

He was the son of Dawid Krizwirt and a Hassidic Jew. He gave a very religious education to his four sons who studied at the study center. He was a close friend of Rabbi Mandil and was a regular member of the service at the study center of the rabbi. He was elected to the community board on the very religious ticket. He served at this post until the outbreak of World War II. He was a timber merchant and lived on Florianska Street

[Page 288]
Bril Krizwirt

He was the youngest son of Dawid Krizwirt and very pious. Following his marriage, he resided in Jaslo, exchanged foreign currency, and discounted financial notes. He made a nice living.

Yaakow Pinhas Krisher

The Jaslo Jewish community was relatively a young community, a mere 70 years of existence. Still some families managed to extend their influence and wealth over the entire community. One such large family was the Krisher family that always appeared on the community rosters whether politically, socially or financially. The father of the family was Yaakow Pinhas Krisher who was born in Sandz and married the daughter of Mordechai Citronenbaum in Zmigrod. He was also the brother in law of Leib Citronenbaum who owned a pub in Jaslo.
Sometime between 1880 and 1881, a few years after he married, Yaakow Pinhas Krisher left Zmigrod and arrived at Jaslo where he opened a shoe store and a haberdashery in the center of the city.
He was an excellent entrepreneur and developed his plans with tenacity. He was a sharp businessperson and was one of those who built the great study center, the ritual bathhouse and was elected to be the beadle of the study center for years to come. As one of the well to do property owners of the city, he had an honorary seat at the study center.
With the outbreak of World War I, he fell ill and passed away in 1915. He left a second wife (his first wife died young), six sons and two daughters. Five sons remained in Jaslo. The sixth, Moshe Krisher, married to Stryj in Eastern Galicia. His first son in law was Ben Tzion Maisels, a descendant of a famous family and well read. He left for Leiptzig, Germany. His daughter was married Awraham Korman who was the son of the scribe Yekutiel Zeew Korman of Jaslo. The couple lives in Tel Aviv. His second son in law was Yehoshua Citronenbaum the son of Leib Citronenbaum. The couple left Jaslo for Germany prior to World War I and remained there for many years. From his second wife he had two sons named Yossil and Benyamin who left Jaslo with Polish Independence. They headed for Germany where they remained until the Nazis took power.
[Page 289]
They then left for the USA. He also had a daughter who married Pinhas Zeiden from Rzeszow.

Chaim Krisher

He was the son of Yaakow Pinhas Krisher and was well read. He was moderated in his opinions and in outlook. In his youth, he studied at study center and was one of the first students there. He was a good student and wore a "Kolpack" or Hassidic hat on Saturdays and holidays. Following his marriage, he opened a haberdashery and a shoe store on Kazimierz Street and then on Kosciuszko Street that was called by the Jews the railway street.
He was attracted to community work in his early youth and continued with it throughout life. He was active in most community institutions of the Jaslo Jewish community. He devoted a great deal of time to these activities. He was vice chairperson of the community board,

chairperson of the "Hevrah Kadishe," the beadle at the great synagogue and a member of the "Talmud Torah" board. As beadle of the great synagogue he placed the synagogue at the disposal of the Zionists where they held assemblies and large meetings. He introduced Dr. Thon, the famous Zionist leader, to the public in Jaslo by enabling him to speak at the great synagogue.

He had four sons and a daughter. The oldest son Hersh Krisher followed his father's example and soon began to be active in the Zionist movement. He became chairperson of the local Zionist committee, member of the Yeshuron board, and sold shekalim prior to Zionist conventions. He married to Ziwec where he opened a haberdashery. With the outbreak of World War II, he reached Russia where he survived. He then arrived in Israel and settled in Jaffa where he holds an important governmental post.

Shlomo Krisher

He was was the second son of Yaakow Pinhas Krisher and was a student at the study center. He then studied at the "Tachkomeni" Seminar in Warsaw. He was very active in the Mizrahi youth movement and a member of the Keren Kayemet and Keren Hayesod boards in Jaslo. He also sold shekalim prior to Zionist conventions and frequently had to defend himself against political opponents. Later he was elected chairman of the Young Mizrahi branch in the city. He made aliyah and a large party was given in his honor. He left Jaslo in 1933 as one of the first Mizrahi pioneers with the daughter of

Yekutiel Korman. She finished a seminar for kindergarten teachers in Warsaw. She was a very influential and active member of the daughters of the Mizrahi movement. They had made a promise to start their family life in the Holy Land. Indeed, they were married in Tel Aviv and have a curtain and upholstery store in this city

[Page 290]
Yossef Krisher

He was the fourth son of Yaakow Pinhas Krisher and reached Israel following World War II. He spent the war years in Russia. He settled in Ramat Itzhak and worked as an electrician. The third son of Krisher, Itzhak, is in the USA and the daughter perished in the Shoa.

Yehoshua Krisher

He had a haberdashery on Kosciuszko Street and prior to World War I, on the eve of the war his house that contained the store burned to the ground. On returning to Jaslo following the war, he reopened his store in the market square where Moldauer and Shedel, descendants of the Winfeld family used to have their store. He also imported sugar. He was a very social person and had a nice approach to people.

As a person of influence and wealth, he had influence with the various local authorities and used the influence on behalf of Jewish prisoners who needed help.

He had five sons and two daughters. His oldest son Benyamin was an excellent businessperson and very active on behalf of the Zionist youth movement and later on behalf of the Zionist labor movement.

During the thirties he left Jaslo for Rzeszow. His second son Motik was a student at the study center and later studied at the "Tachkomeni" seminar in Warsaw. He was a member of the Young Mizrahi branch in the city and in the twenties left Jaslo for Belgium where he continued his studies. He eventually reached the USA.

His third son Ephraim Fishel left for Palestine as a pioneer about twenty years ago and became a member of a kibbutz in Israel. He later settled in Haifa and works as a clerk. His daughter survived in Russia and reached Palestine where she settled in the area of Haifa.

Yoel Krisher

His business was known in the city as "Zrudlo Taniuszici" on Kosciusko Street. He had a haberdashery and a toy store. He was a religious person but tended to the Zionist movement. He expressed his opinions on different city matters but generally distanced himself from involvements.

[Page 291]

He had five sons, three daughters. All children were members of the Zionist youth movement, and some received an academic education. Two of his sons and a daughter are in Israel and live in Haifa. One of them, Shmuel, is an engineering architect that made aliyah in 1933

Elimelech Krisher

He was also the owner of a haberdashery store that also sold fashionable items and hats. His store was located along May 3rd Street and the corner of Kosciuszko Street. He attracted a wealthy clientele. He was very successful and built a three-story house on Asnika Street.

He was a typical person with a modern outlook on life but was very conservative. He met cultured people and devoted Zionists but Zionism did not affect him. He loved to show off and sought honors. He became the beadle of the rabbi's study center. He was a Hassidic Jew and soon became involved in the planning and executing the various Shabbath, holiday and other special days dinners on behalf of the rabbi. He was in charge of distributing the beer at the parties and loved the honor.

He decided who gets the first and last beer. He served in this capacity for many years

Shabbath morning he would wear his shtreimel and Hassidic outfit, but for the afternoon services he would wear modern clothes. He was elected to the community board on the ticket that represented the rabbi and was a member of the council until the outbreak of World War II.

He had two sons and a daughter. His son Fishel was a student at the study center in his youth. He devoted himself to Torah study and became very religious and pious. He was a good student and continued his studies in Warsaw where he finished the rabbinical seminar. He was ordained as rabbi in the capital and began to officiate as rabbi.

Itchele Krisher

He returned in the twenties and settled in Jaslo. He opened a cleaning concession store that chemically cleaned clothing. The factory was in Krakow. The business was a success in the first years.

[Page 292]

He was a very pious Jew and prayed at the big study center. Once he was about to lead the services when the beadle dismissed him and sent somebody else to conduct the services. He was furious and felt insulted. There was no explanation for the insult. Itchele Krisher approached the beadle and slapped him twice for the insult he caused him. The action was seen and heard by everybody in the study center and eventually went to court.

Benyamin Kramer

He was a member of the intelligentsia and one of the most influential people in the city. He was one of the first dedicated Zionists when the movement began to grow and expand. He was a close friend of Dr. Kornhauser and supported nicely all charitable institutions in the city. When the various religious ornaments disappeared from the synagogue during World War I, he volunteered to replace them with pure silver ones.

He lived in his house on Kazimierz Street and was a wholesale flour and sugar importer. He also dealt with gas and was a partner in a broom factory. His two sons and daughter used to ride their horses as though they were princes. Of course, they rode for the fun and sport. They all received an academic education in Vienna. With the outbreak of the war he reached Lemberg where he became ill and died. His son Henoch died in Samarkand, Russia. His second son Samek was killed in the ghetto uprising in Warsaw. The daughter managed to survive and lives in Europe.

Moshe Krantz

He was a short, heavyset person. He was a shoemaker and nicknamed Moshele the"
shoemaker." He barely made a living while working with his sons, who were all shoemakers.
He lived all his life on Korlowski Street opposite the girls' school.

Awraham Krantz

He was the oldest son of Moshe Krantz and a shoemaker. He barely made a living and became
ill at a relatively young age. He passed away and left a sick wife and a child who lived opposite
the synagogue.

[Page 293]
Dawid Karp

He was the son in law of Moshe Margulies and very pious. He was very involved in the
community and was well built and tall. He was very witty, sharp and prayed at the study center
of the rabbi and was a close supporter of Rabbi Mandil.

He distributed merchandise from Krakow, Rzeszow and from various wholesalers according to
previously placed retail orders. He distributed the merchandise in the city and vicinity. He had
an annual train pass that was needed in his business. He lived all his life on Iglena Street and
had two sons and one of them died as a youngster due to heart problems.

Mordechai Karp

He was the son in law of the famous benefactor Yehuda Rubel and the bright star that dazzled
for many years in the city. As a youngster in Ulanow near Rudnik, he dressed according to the
Hassidic manner. He wore a kolpack on Saturdays and holidays. He was a student at the study
center and dedicated himself to Talmudic studies. He was also a very sensitive person and gave
extensive charity, sometimes beyond his means.

It is said of him that he had large debts due to donations to various charitable institutions and
could not settle the accounts. He threatened his father that he will not marry unless all his debts
are settled. Of course, his father settled the debts and his son married.

He was very sharp and enlightened person, his ideas were accepted by the public; Jewish and
non-Jewish. He was a municipal councilor and a member of the community board for many
years. He was one of the finest personalities in the city. Until 1914, he dressed in the Hassidic
manner, namely silk clothing and a large shtreimel. His house was open to all needy and
hungry in the city. Here they received food, clothing and even money.

[Page 294]
He raised an orphan at his home who later left for Palestine where he settled in one of the
kibbutzim He was one of the wealthiest people in the city and lived in a big house on
Kazimierz Street. He was a timber and egg merchant who also exported to distant countries.
He was also a partner in the spirit distillery in Suwionow.

The signs of spring were in the air, the sun was shining and suddenly darkness struck on
Passover of 1926. He passed away instantly at the seder night of Passover. The news shocked
the entire Jewish community. He was buried the next day and the Jewish population
participated en masse at the funeral that also included municipal officials. Members of the
police force carried the coffin to the cemetery He left a wife and four sons and two daughters.
All finished academic studies and received diplomas. They were all active in the Zionist youth
movements and were the founders and leaders of the "Hashomer" movement.

The oldest son Yossef was doctor of law and economics. He is presently in London where he
represented the Polish government there. He toured Israel and he hopes to settle there.

Lonek (today Arieh Amitai after he changed his name) was the second son of Mordechai Karp
who left for Palestine in the twenties as a pioneer. Presently he is an engineer and works for the

Ministry of Labor (the public works section). He married Tamar, the daughter of the author Tzwi Kerel of Lemberg (now in Tel Aviv). She is a teacher at a girls' school in Jerusalem.

The third son Yehiel died during World War II and the fourth son Moshe or Mundek finished law studies and became an attorney. He survived in Russia and reached Israel where he settled in Jerusalem and works as an attorney for the municipality. His oldest daughter married Dr. E. Kornmehl. She reached Israel with her son and lives in Jerusalem.

[Page 295]

Resh ר

"To eternalize the heart pains…"

Chaim Rapaport

My sufferings are boundless for my saintly father and mother who died a cruel death at the hands of the Germans in the forties.

Chaim Rapaport

[Page 296]

I am not able to do justice to my ancestry but I must memorialize them so that my children will have a record of my father and his ideals. He dedicated himself to his faith and demanded nothing in return. He served his religion in the purest and noblest sense of the word. I must stress his dedication to the education of his children and those of his friends in the traditional Orthodox ways.

For 28 years, I resided in Jaslo and never heard him complain and there were terrible events, namely; storms, rains and blizzards. Regardless of these occurrences, my father rose early in the morning and awakened us to proceed to the study center to study prior to the beginning of services. Following the services, we studied the Bible and the Talmud. He was a very talented and scholarly teacher known in the community. (He refused the post of rabbi following his marriage).

The commandment "and you shall teach your children" he implemented to the fullest. No other parent did so much for his children in the mornings and evenings as my father. Our sages say (Brachot 17), "What benefits do women derive from the Torah since they are exempt from studying it? Their reward is granted by the fact that they prepare everything so that their husbands can study at the study center."

My late mother was an excellent housekeeper and provider. She worried about her husband and did everything to enable him to devote himself to broaden his Torah knowledge and that of their children. Both struggled to provide their children with regular and spiritual food so that they would continue in the path of their ancestry.

I must also stress his devotion to Zion and his homesickness for the Holy Land. The Palestine atmosphere was always present at home and influenced our thinking. Thus, our decision to settle in Israel.

[Page 297]

My father tried to impress the religious and extreme religious Jews with the importance of reviving of the Holy Land. He spoke and popularized the idea that frequently led to unpleasant confrontations with bitter opponents of the concept. Each month he sent his contribution to the "Yishuw Eretz Israel" fund or Yishuv fund that headed Chaim from Drohobicz.

He was in contact with the Palestinian office in Jaffa prior to World War I. His dream and aspiration was to visit the Holy Land, especially the Temple area in Jerusalem. Unfortunately, the Germans prevented him from realizing his aspirations for they killed him on entering the city of Jaslo.

My brother Shmuel escaped the Germans clutches and reached Palestine where he settled in Tel Aviv. Itzhak, my younger brother graduated from an English University. He is now chief rabbi of Melbourne, Australia.

Yuta Rapaport

Issachar Dow Rapaport

Yehuda Rapaport

My two younger brothers; Issachar Dow and Yehuda Rapaport, were students at the study center when the Germans killed them in the Shoa.

[Page 298]

My sister Riwka, her husband Elyahu and their daughters Hanna and Sarah lived in the hamlet of Lipiani in Czechoslovakia. The Germans killed them during the Shoa.

Riwka Rapaport, her husband and children

My sister Rachel left for Palestine in 1936 and married Dow Weinstein in Tel Aviv.

My father settled in Jaslo in 1906. He was born in the hamlet of Rudnik, Galicia. His father was the great Rabbi Issachar Dow of Radusic. (He spent a great deal of time near the great Hassidic rabbi of Sandz). His grandfather was Rabbi Itzhak, head of the judicial council of Radusic. The father of Rabbi Itzhak was Rabbi Eliezer who was the head of the judicial council in Siedlowce. He was very religious and pious. It was said about him that he was one of the 36 just people in the world. His father was Rabbi Dawid, a grandson of the author "Panim Meirot," or the shining face, written by Rabbi Meir from Eisensdadt who was the nephew of Rabbi Shabtai Hacohen.

Rabbi Issachar Ber of Radusic was the son of Rabbi Itzhak and Miriam. He served as an attendant to the famous Rabbi Ber of Mezricz. The latter rabbi said that he prayed in the name of the 120 students that he taught. (He died on the 13th day of the month of Sivan, 1843.)

[Page 299]

My father had two sisters; Nehama and Etil who lived in Lodz and two brothers; Yaakow Kalman Finkler, who also lived in Lodz, and the younger brother was Rabbi Itzhak Finkler-Weingarten who was rabbi of Siedlice.

My father's mother was named Hannah and she was the daughter of the well known Hassid Shmuel Halevi Weingarten of Rudnik (He supported my grandfather for 25 years until he was appointed rabbi of Lodz).He was the son of Rabbi Kolonimus Halewi, one of the important Hassidim of Rabbi Naphtali of Ropczyce. Grandmother's mother was the daughter of Rabbi Yaakow, the son of Rabbi Dan Mordechai, the head of the judicial council of Lejansk following the death of the author of "Noam Elimelech" or words of Elimelech.

My mother was born in Korczyna to a Hassid named Gad Asher Gutwein. He was known for charity and was the treasurer of the charity fund "Kollel Jerusalem" or Jerusalem study group. On Yom Kippur in 1935, at the end of the prayers, he stood on the bima, stretched out his hands to the table, and passed away. His father Yaakow Itzhak was a scholar of the Babylonian and Jerusalem Talmud. He passed away in 1924. He was the son of the rabbi of Stryzow.

My maternal grandmother Sarah was the daughter of the Hassid Moshe Nathan whom hoodlums killed while on a business trip to Hungary. She was a very religious and pious woman who died in 1885. (See section dealing with Moshe Nathan Gutwein.) She was descendant of Rabbi Ekliezer–Lipa, the father of the saintly Rabbis Elimelech of Lejansk and Zushe of Honipoli. My mother had two brothers; Moshe Nathan and Yehuda. He also had two sisters Leah and Etil. (The first one married Rabbi Eliezer –Lipa Fessel and the second one married Shimon Zeew Rothenberg)

My eyes shed tears as I remember the entire family that was killed and among them my son in law Rabbi Yehiel Tzwi Beer, the judicial head of the hamlet of Huskow

(the birthplace of Rabbi Lewi Itzhak of Berditchew). A follower of Issachar Dow of Litobisk; the rabbi of Nitra in Czeckoslavakia was the father of the rabbis of Makow and Maszina. He was a saintly person and refused to accept the position of a rabbi in a big city stating that his position as head of a small yeshiva gave him time to study.

[Page 300]

The mother in law, Yuta Rachel, was a pious and charitable person. She was the daughter of Rabbi Yaakow Shuem Hertzig, judicial head of Niznikowic, the son of the head of the judicial council Rabbi Wolwish of Ulanow. The latter had one son named Dawid who assumed his father's position. He had four daughters named Tziporah, Sarah, Neche and Yochewed who married to students of the Torah.

My father in law the rabbi had three sons. The oldest was Wolwish, the second one was Mordechai Dawid and the third one was Naphtali. All of them were Torah students familiar with the Bible and Talmud and G-d fearing. He also had four gentle daughters; Riwka, Pesia, Batshewa, and Haya. The German and their supporters killed all of them during World War II (1939-1945). May their deaths be avenged.

> **The deer in the Mountains of Jerusalem Memorial**
> In memory of our beloved Yehiel Tzwi (Hershele), the son of Rabbi Dawid and Hantche Weinstock of Vienna, who were killed by the Germans during the Shoa). He was a student of the Hebron Yeshiva and the Hebrew University. He sacrificed himself in order to defend the Hadassah Hospital and Hebrew University convoy that was attacked on the way to Mount Scopus in April of 1948.
> May he rest among the heroes of Israel!

Yossef Rapaport

He was one of the old cohanim in the city. He was well mannered and a scholar. He was a Hassid with a silver beard that covered his face and reached his shoulders. He lived on Korlewski Street, had a grocery, and sold grains. With the outbreak of World War I, he was sick and shortly thereafter passed away. He left a wife, a son Chaim Yudel and a daughter Etil. The widow Pearl moved to the house of Eliash where she opened a wholesale store. Her son was a student of the study center and following his marriage moved to Tarnow. Pearl became ill, underwent surgery but the surgery failed and she died. Her daughter took over her business. She married Dawid Kannengisser who soon became ill and died. He left her with an infant daughter. She later remarried Yossef Pfepper. (See above.)

[Page 301]

A. Rapoport

He was a quiet, reserved and kept tradition. He owned a jewelry store on Kosciuszko Street and did engravings and fixed watches. He died as an old man with the outbreak of World War I.

P. Rapoport

He was the son in law of Eli Hess. He was a religious person and a loyal member of the Mizrahi movement and one of the founders of the Mizrahi School. He was a timber merchant and lived on Florianska Street.

Eliezer Raab

He was the owner of an inn on Cieckiego Street on the way to the railroad. He was a quiet and well-mannered person who kept to himself. He observed the commandments and prayed at the study center of the rabbi.

He donated a sefer Torah to the synagogue prior to World War I. A huge crowd escorted him and the Torah to the study center. The procession was proceeded by a band of the "Haknassat Kala" organization and all along the road, torches and firecrackers lit the way.

He died as an old man following a disease. He left a wife, four sons and three daughters. His oldest daughter married Shmuel Seinwil. One of his sons, named Kalman, was a clerk of the "Ludowy Bank" who escaped to Jaslo with the outbreak of the war with the donated Torah in his hands. He reached Lemberg but had to hide the Torah. He is now in the USA. The oldest son lived in Lemberg.

Leibish, the second son, was married to the daughter of Shlomo Geminder and owned a printing press in Tarnow. The youngest son, Yehoshua, left for Palestine and settled in Haifa.

Pinhas Raab

(See Mandil Miller)

Beril Rabi

He was a merchant. With the outbreak of World War I, he left for Hungary and remained there a considerable period. He was a religious and prayed at the
the study center. He lived on Nowa Street and was a businessperson. He left Jaslo in the thirties. He had three daughters and a son. One of his daughters left for Palestine where she settled in Yazur. His wife and a son live in the USA.

[Page 302]
Itzhak Yehuda Rubel

On top of the "Talmud Torah" building, that was the highest building in the city, there was a black marble sign with the following inscription:

> "The   Jaslo   Talmud   Torah
> In honor of Itzhak Yehuda Rubel".

The place was scheduled to be a "kloiz" or a synagogue, but with the completion of the main synagogue, the plan for the building was changed. He was highly respected and always referred to as Itche-juda Rubel with reverence. The people took pride in his residing in Jaslo. He invited a special scribe to write a sefer Torah in his behalf that he donated to the synagogue. He also commissioned a curtain for the Holy Ark studded with precious stones.

He was very rich and owned a great deal of real estate, including forests, a large estate, a vodka distillery in Siowniow, and owned a brick and tile factory. He was estimated to be worth about a million rheinish in gold. His house was open to everybody. He distributed charity to the poor and to the social institutions in the city and enjoyed the act of giving.

He sympathized with the Hassidic world and was supposedly a follower of the rabbi of Sieniawa. He sent contributions to many Hassidic rabbis and their grandsons. He was well acquainted with the rabbinical world. Every winter, he sent wood and potatoes to the synagogues of Jaslo. He employed Jewish workers in his enterprises and paid them well. He was especially fond of his Hassidic manager, Baruch Leib Shtams from Gorlice. The latter erected a small synagogue and built a mikve on the estate of Itzhak Yehuda Rubel.

[Page 303]

Yekil Kalb was also one of the old time workers at the plant. He treated his employees with respect and they treated him with reverence.

He was well liked and influential in the city but never abused his power. He led a full life and died of old age. Municipal and district officials participated in his funeral as did the entire community.

The local rabbi eulogized him and Shlomo Schmidt eulogized him on behalf of the Talmud Torah institution and the student body. The eulogy was moving and some people shed tears.

He left three daughters and four sons who were all businesspersons and well known in the community. They continued to observe tradition but were more modern and adhered to Zionism. Their children however already attended academic institutions.

His three son in laws were: Awraham Goldman, related to the lawyer Yaakow Hertzig, the second one was the erudite benefactor Moti Karp and the third one was scholarly Shlomo Bazner, a descendant of a famous East Galician Jewish family. (The Bazner family resided on a large estate for many years.

Dr. Itzhak Bazner

[Page 304]

They lived like princes in Baborkuwka, district of Skala, and produced many community leaders, artists and rabbis.) He died relatively young and the family resided in Czortkow. He left a wife, two daughters and one son, who graduated from the University of Krakow with the diploma of doctor of law and economics. Dr. Itzhak Bazner was a very high official at the Israeli treasury and was killed in a plane accident while flying from Rome to Holland on March 22, 1952.

The accident occurred near Frankfurt, Germany, where he was to negotiate German reparations agreements for Shoah survivors. They flew his body to Israel where he was buried on April 1, 1952

His son Nehemia left Jaslo following his marriage and settled in Rzeszow but later returned to Jaslo. His daughter lived in Tel Aviv and the second son Leibish lived all his life in Rzeszow.

Elhanan Rubel

He was a very successful businessperson and built a beautiful house on Kosciuszko Street opposite the "Oszcidonosci Ban." This was the most beautiful and modern house in the city.

Reuben Rubel

He was the youngest sons of the family. He was a forest merchant and had a nice house on May 3rd Street corner of Asnika Street. (One of his sons reached Israel and works for "Hamashbir" organization in Tel Aviv.) He prayed at the great synagogue along the eastern wall. He was one of the important people in the city. His sons were members of the Zionist youth movements in the city and members of the sport club

"Maccabi" His wife was active in social institutions and "Wizo". They fled to Kolomaya with the outbreak of World War II where he passed away. His son Lonek was killed in Sambor and the oldest son Feiwil (Fridek) survived the war and lives in Katowice. One son named Itzhak (Eisik) reached the USA.

Rosenbush

He was one of the attorneys in the city. He distanced himself from Jewish life and was an assimilated Jew. He lived on May 3rd Street and had a son and a daughter.

[Page 305]
L. Rosenblit

He was one of the leading officials at the oil refinery in Niglowic. He reached Lutzk with the outbreak of the war and lost his mind.

Uziel Rosenwasser

He was one of the Gorlice refugees who settled in Jaslo during World War I. He was a quiet Hassidic person, studied the Talmud daily and prayed at the study center of the rabbi. He lived almost his entire life on Korlowski Street and was a merchant.

His oldest son Moshe studied at the study center and left Jaslo following his marriage.

He had a stand in the market and sold general items.

One of his daughters, Czarna, married Yaakow Trenczer of Krosno. He was very religious and familiar with religious literature. He was a tailor and they lived in Jaslo.

Chaim Rosenfeld

He was a modern man in the spirit of the time. He was a businessperson, prayed at the Yad Charutzim synagogue, and later became president of the association.

He lived in the Eliash house where he had a furniture store. He had three sons and one daughter who received a high school education. The second son, Itzhak, graduated as a lawyer and opened an office. They were members of the Zionist organizations and played soccer for the local Maccabi club

According to rumors, Chaim Rosenfeld and his son Awraham (Romek) reached Israel. Awraham's wife is the daughter of Tzwi Bergman of Targowice. They live in one of the new suburbs of Kfar Saba. Chaim Rosenfeld's wife died following a disease in the month of Shwat in 1942 in Samarkand.

The Germans killed Itzhak and Leah in Dubno and Dawid in Lemberg.

Eliezer Rosner

He was an old timer in the city and the son of Mordechai Rozner. He was a grocery wholesaler in his house that was located in the market near the municipality. Most of his customers were farmers from the area and referred

to his place as "Rozner under the clock" or "under the clock" since there was a big city clock hanging from the municipal building. His house was small in comparison to the city building and it gave the impression of a tiny addition.

[Page 306]
Yehiel Rosner

He was the second son of Mordechai Rosner and called Itchal Rozner. He owned an inn in the market. Naphtali Walfeld previously owned the place. He was a serious minded individual and had a large house where a dozen people met for years on Saturdays and holidays to conduct services.

He had two sons and the younger one was Yehoshua who worked for a while at the municipal concrete plant to learn for use in Palestine. He did not succeed and abandoned the Palestine interest.

Chaim Rosner

He was the older son of Yehiel Rosner and studied at the study center. He was a quiet and honest person. He helped the father in the inn.

Moshe Rosner

He was the son in law of Shriar, the owner of the factory "Shreier and Gartenberg" and the oil refinery that employed a thousand workers in Niglowic.

He was very involved in Jewish life, as opposed to some of the well to do families that distanced themselves from Jewish life. He was an educated individual and in his youth even studied Talmud. He gave charity to institutions and individuals.

Each month he personally advised his accountant to send checks to revered rabbis and urged them to use it for charity and to pray for his health.

[Page 307]
With old age his memory began to lapse and he took on Mordechai Dawid Adler to walk with him and escort him on his errands. His mind deteriorated and Mordechai Adler became his watchdog and his memory disk. Indeed, Mordechai Adler tended to him and became his eyes and mouthpiece. Daily they walked about the municipal park near his house. It was not a pleasant picture in spite of the gold-framed glasses.

He wrapped himself in his big Turkish tallit as he headed for synagogue each Saturday and holiday. He prayed with devotion. He had one son who was an attorney and a daughter

Leibish Roth

He was always the first to morning and evening services. On occasion when I reached the study center in the middle of the day, he was also there studying the Talmud.

I remember him sitting on the bench before the bima facing the holy ark. Thus he sat for years with his yarmulke on top of his head, his red creased forehead and below his eyebrows were two burning eyes and from his mouth emerged the studying tune which is used in studying the Talmud. The voice was barely audible but it was there and to this day the tune still rings in my ear. On the table next to the Talmud was his red kerchief and two snuff boxes. He was talking to himself as though explaining to friend difficult passages of the Talmud. He was accustomed to study difficult and not popular Talmudic texts - "Hazerot," "Eruvin," "Zvachin," " Minhot," "Meila," " Kritot," etc. His beard reached his chest and was known in the city. The mind continued to indulge in theoretical arguments of the Talmud, completely detached from this world.

He was one of the few surviving Gorlitzer Hassidim and was very involved in the "Hevre Kadisha." He was a friend of the rabbi and prayed in his study center.

He had two sons and several daughters. Yudel, his second son, left for the USA with the creation of the Polish State and was very successful.

Meir Hillel Roth

He was born in Brzeszow and settled in Jaslo around 1908. He opened a grocery on the road to Niglowic. He was a Sadigorer Hassid, knowledgeable, well-read, pleasant conversationalist who interlaced sayings of the sages in his discussions.

He was called to the Austrian Army in 1914 and his family left for Vienna, where they remained for some time and then left for the USA in 1920. He had two sons and three daughters. They received a very religious education and are presently religious.

He was influenced by the idea of Zion and realized his dream when he settled in Jerusalem in the fifties and opened a zipper factory. He purchased a nice home in the German Colony. He is very happy to have fulfilled his dream of living in the Holy City. He is known in the area and was elected to the Katamon community council

Meir Berish Rothfeld

He was a super scholar in the city and one of the few remaining Alsker Hassidim. The community appointed ritual slaughterer after Zelig Miller. As an old time Hassid immersed in the study of the Torah and feared G-d. The community approved his saintly behavior and appreciated it.

He lived all his life near the study center in a small flat where he managed to broaden his knowledge of the Torah. Prior to the outbreak of World War I, he suddenly fell ill and accepted his pains with fortitude. Still the disease progressed; he traveled to Krakow to consult doctors, surgery was performed but to no avail.

The son in law of Sh. Shnirer (the brother of Sarah Shnirer from Krakow) acted as the ritual slaughterer during World War I in Jaslo.

[Page 309]
Herzl Rothfeld

He was the son of Meir Berish Rothfeld and was the son in law of Nahum the slaughterer. He was deeply involved in religious studies and used to say, "These are the words of G-d but the individual has to choose." Of course, not everybody can choose or select". He devoted himself to "Seder Moed" and "Brachot," two particular sections of the Talmud.

He studied daily these tractates with Mendil Shpiler who was a slow learner but ambitious. He showed great patience with the slow learner and explained to him the intricacies of the text.

He was a partner in the soda factory and lived on Nowa Street. He had three daughters, one of whom was a teacher at the "Beit Yaakow School" for girls. His son Simcha was a religious student and lives in England.

Tertel Rotter

He was an old resident of the city and owned a flourmill on the way to Zmigrod. He was a clever and generous man. He had three sons, Zushe, Moshe, and Mendil Rotter. All received an education, were members of the Zionist movements, and resided in Jaslo where they conducted business. His daughter was married to Chaim Shlomo Blut. (See above)

Shmuel Mendil Ross

He was an elementary teacher in Jaslo. He was an honest and G-d fearing person. He prayed with a great deal of conviction and devoted time to the poor people in the city. He had several sons raised strictly in accordance with the Torah. One of his sons was Yaakow and the other was Feiwil. His daughter married Rabbi Yehoshua Horowitz of Frysztak. He was a student of the Talmud and they lived on Schajnochy Street next to the Talmud Torah.

With Polish independence, he left for the USA for the second time. His family remained in Jaslo and was involved in business. The entire family eventually left for the USA.

[Page 310]

Yona Ritner

He barely made a living fixing brooms and brushes. He was religious and kept to his faith. He prayed at the study center of the rabbi. He had several sons, one of whom drowned as a sailor during World War II. One son survived and settled in Yehudia in Israel

Itzhak Reich

He was called Itche Reich and he was a grocery wholesaler on Kazimeirz Street. He also had a salt monopoly for dozens of years. He was from Hungary and presented a nice picture with his large beard that covered his face. He was one of the old timers at the study center services.

He managed his house in the traditional religious manner. He had four daughters and five sons - Nathan, Mendil, Shlomo, Yehoshua and Hersh. They studied at the study center and helped their father in his business. The sons were quiet, well-mannered people. One of them lived in Kaszoi, the second one in Sandz; two lived in Krakow and Reshow and the youngest lived in Jaslo. One of his sons in law lived in Tarnow and was a member of the Mizrahi movement. His third son in law was Burkosz and two of his sons, Yehoshua and Hershel, survived the war and are in the USA. Another son of Itche Reich lives in Israel

Zeew Reich

He was the youngest son in law of Itche Reich and he comes from Sanok. He was student of the Talmud and familiar with religious books. He opened a shoe store in Yossef Menasge's house and did very well.

Moshe Reich

(See Yerucham Frei)

Reichman, attorney

He lived in the house of Mendel Meller on May 3rd Street. He was not involved in public life. He devoted himself to his legal work.

Dawid Ring

He was a quiet person and worked as a watchmaker first in the house of Shmuel Lehr and then on Florianska Street. He had one son and a daughter. The son reached Israel and settled in one of the settlements.

Abish Rinhald

He was one of the first Hassidim and had a very distinct face. He was honest and well raised. He descended from a well-established family in Tarnow that included many rabbis and religious scholars.

He owned a haberdashery and sold dress supplies. He lived almost his entire life on Korlowski Street. He prayed at the study center of Rabbi Mandil and later at the great synagogue. His oldest son, Itzhak, was a student of the study center and settled in Sandz following his marriage His second son, Simcha Ber, was also a student of the study center. He broadened his horizons and left for the USA with the creation of the Polish state.

Mordechai Dawid Riss

He lived all his life in Dembowce and conducted business. He was spiritually inclined and familiar with religious literature. He followed Hassidism and was a fine host. He had a mikve and a small synagogue in his house where the Jews from the vicinity prayed on Saturdays and holidays.

He had six sons and two daughters who received a very religious education. They were all fine and gentle children. One of his sons, Feiwil, the son in law of Shulem Topoliner, left Jaslo for Palestine in 1933-1934 and settled in Haifa. He became ill and passed away in 1961 after a great deal of suffering. One of his sons, Simcha, lives in the USA.

Naphtali Riss

He was the son in law of Moshe Werner and educated. He was very strict in his observance. He had a grocery in Jaslo until 1913 and then left for Germany.

He reached Palestine in 1936 and settled in Tel Aviv where he conducted business. He suddenly took ill and passed away in 1962.

[Page 312]

Itzhak Randal

He was an old timer in the city and a very pleasant person. He was a grain merchant His son Yaakow was well read and expressed his opinion on every subject. He loved to joke and clown about with people. He was also a grain merchant. The family left Jaslo for Pilzno with the outbreak of World War I.

Awraham Ressler

He was one of the first Hebrew teachers at the Targowica. He was a dedicated and faithful Hebrew teacher who taught generation after generation of Jews in the city.

He conducted the Mussaf services on the High Holidays at the Yad Charutzim synagogue. He had three sons, Chaim Mendel, Zeew and Yehiel, and two daughters. He had a long and productive life and lived in the same wooden barrack in the Targowice. He died about the time of the creation of the Polish state.

P. Ressler

He was the second husband of the widow Miriam Weber and he stems from Hungary. He was an extremely well mannered person and loved music and song. He was a tailor and lived on Korlowski Street.

Eliezer Raah

He was an enlightened and tall individual. He had a yellow beard that covered his face friends and acquaintances liked him. His simplicity was contagious. Familiar with music, he conducted services on Saturdays and holidays. He also conducted the Mussaf services in Dembowce for many years.

He had a haberdashery and a teacher at the Talmud Torah. His wife and the sons managed the business. One of his sons, Srulik, died from tuberculosis in spite of the medical efforts to save him. He lived all his life with his father in law, Abish Rinhald, on Korlowsky Street.

[Page 313]

Shin ש

A. Shadel

Shadel and Moldauer were sons in law of Leibish Wilfeld and they inherited the business in the market place when the latter died. Shadel had a serious road injury and died as a result. City people barely knew Shadel.

A. Shedlisker

He settled in Jaslo during World War I. He was a quiet person minding his own business. He polished copperware and was the local locksmith. He made a nice income and lived in a cellar apartment in the corner of the market opposite the church. His son finished medical school and lives in Paris, France.

Shimon Shoder

He was a community leader and well known in the city. He was the son in law of Benyamin Kramer and was involved in many municipal institutions. He was elected to the community board on the ticket of the artisans. He was a devoted member of the fire brigade and other institutions.

Spiritually he was inclined to assimilation and was shocked when Zionist intellectuals began to distance themselves from him. He had a son and a daughter who finished high school and continued their education. His second wife was a Shpringer who opened a large beauty salon where some Jewish girls worked.

Moshe Shochet

He is a descendant of a famous Jewish family in Lemberg. He moved to Jaslo about 1900 and worked as an engineer with the railroad. He was an enlightened person and kept to himself. In 1913, he built a three-story house along May 3rd Street. He became ill during the twenties that resulted in a paralysis. The disease lasted until he died in 1927. He left a wife, four sons (his daughter died as a youngster in Vienna during World War I).

[Page 314]

All his children received a higher education but left studies and helped the mother run the large printing plant of labels. The business started as a small shop and grew to be a very impressive plant in Poland.

The wife of Moshe Shochet was an intelligent woman but had no printing experience. She acquired the knowledge gradually and kept expanding the place by the day. She was the dominant personality of the enterprise that employed about 150 workers. She was involved in social and Zionist work in spite of devoting all her energies to the printing plant. She developed commercial ties with Palestine fifty years ago as part of her devotion to Zion. Everything about the Holy Land was dear to her.

She fulfilled her dream of settling in Palestine where she arrived in the thirties with two sons. Naphtali arrived first followed by Riszek. In Tel Aviv, the family started a big printing business where only people from Jaslo worked.

Two years ago, her oldest son Ludwig and his wife arrived in Israel after a long and tortuous trip. The wife was the daughter of Tzwi Baumring. She was formerly married to Leopold Shochet, a brother of Ludwig. The couple reached Russia prior to World War II where Leopold died relatively young. Ludwig's son also recently reached Israel. The family lives on Pines Street in Tel Aviv.

Asher Yeshayahu Shwimmer

He was a quiet, well-mannered and soft-spoken individual. He was one of the old Rymanower Hassidim who patiently explained his concepts to listeners. He was the son in law of Mordechai Rosner who was the father of Eliezer and Yehiel Rosner of Jaslo. He owned an inn on Kazimierz Street in the house of Kornfeld. He died as an elderly person in the twenties.

He had several daughters and four sons who were gentle and well mannered. One of the sons was Pinhas who took part in the formation of the militia to defend Jews against the pogroms that took place following Polish independence. He married the daughter of Manas Hertz. His young son Feiwil kept the inn going for many years. The oldest son left Jaslo after his marriage.

One daughter left for Palestine and settled in Bnei Brak.

[Page 315]
Mordechai Dawid Shwinger

He was a quiet person and was a furrier. He also sold hats and bowlers that brought him a nice income. He was the son in law of Shmuel Lehr and lived in his house all his life. He became ill and died of exhaustion. He left a wife, two sons and three daughters.

Ephraim and Henech Shwinger

They were the sons of Mordechai Dawid Shwinger. Both were ambitious and enterprising. They also sold hats at the house of Dr. Willusz in the market square. They were also furriers and prepared winter leather coats.

Ephraim married the daughter of Nathan Siegfried and they reached Russia with the outbreak of World War II. They survived the war, reached Austria, and then came to Israel where they stayed for a short period.

Abba Shulew

He was a real estate man. He was intelligent and well read. He settled in the twenties in Koblow. He was a very religious Jew and came to pray in the great synagogue every Saturday and holiday. Here he also engaged in small talk with the city people. His daughter recently left Poland and came to Israel where she settled in Tel Aviv.

Reuven Shuman

He was a modest, honest and traditional Jew. He lived all his life in Przedmiescze where he had a grocery. He died relatively young and left a wife, two sons and three daughters. With the creation of the Polish state, the family left for the USA.

Chaim Shuman

He was the brother of Leib Shuman and settled in Jaslo following World War I. He was a good-natured Hassid, well acquainted with religious literature. He also had his feet on
[Page 316]
the ground. He was a regular worshipper at the great synagogue and was a timber merchant. He lived on Sokolow Street.

He had a number of sons and the oldest one was a scholarly student and a member of the mizrahi movement. He left Jaslo in the twenties and settled in Metz, France. The youngest son Dawid finished the teacher seminary named "Poznanski" in Warsaw and left Jaslo for Palestine in the thirties. He married the daughter of H. Mishuri, principal of the "Bilu" school in Tel Aviv. She is a teacher in Rehovot.

Shumer, Dr.

He was the son in law of Mendel Kinstler. He was a high official at the oil refinery in Niglowic (See above)

Simon, Shor Dr.

He was a doctor with the railway system in Jaslo and vicinity. He did not mingle with Jews and lived on Cickiego Street at the corner of May 3rd Street, opposite the municipal park.

He had one son who was spectacularly handsome. He was also an excellent student and wanted to study Hebrew. In this connection, I will describe an incident that took place. When I was about 15 or 16 I gave Hebrew lessons to youngsters. Among the students was the son of Doctor Shor… Following a few lessons, the students picked up a few words and one of the students knew the meaning of the word

"Shor," namely ox in German and Yiddish. The connotation of the word assumed a negative implication. The students kidded the young student and he took it seriously. When I returned to the lessons, I tried to explain to the offended student that the name is not derived from ox but rather from the Hebrew word "meshorer" or poet or from the word "shira" or singing. I also brought some examples, namely the famous cantor from Lemberg was also called Baruch Shor and the famous professor at the royal conservatory in Moscow was also called Dawid Shor. My naïve explanations did the job and the student felt better. (During the German occupation, the student became a teacher in the ghetto school of Jaslo.)

[Page 317]
Dawid Shwartzman

He was a serious and moderate person. He was the son in law of Zelig Beam and familiar with religious books. He dressed impeccably in the style of religious scholars. He was a merchant for years and then opened a laundry detergent factory with Hertzel Rothfeld. He lived in Elimelech Goldstein's house his entire life until he became sick. He never recovered and passed away at a relative young age. He left a wife and two sons, one was a clerk and the other one was a merchant.

Tzwi Shtoyar

Morning and evening Hershel Shtoyar walked slowly from his home at the far end of Koscziusko Street to the synagogue to pray with the congregation. He was short, skinny and tried not to draw attention. He had a pleasant disposition and was content with his lot. He started out as a timber merchant and later became a manager for various flourmills namely Baumring, Werouter, Goldflus-Wistrich. He eventually made aliyah.

He had four sons who received a high school education and the father was very proud of their achievements. They attended the Polish high school. The Balfour Declaration influenced them and immersed them in Zionist activities. They were the first to join the pioneer movement of the "Halutz" organization and contributed greatly to the activities of the movement in Jaslo.

One day in 1920 a rumor circulated throughout the city that Zeew Shtoyar stopped his studies. He decided to leave for Palestine. The people did not believe their ears; they could not understand the situation. There was only one person who did this before him, namely Berish Meller. The decision became the topic of the day for a long period in Jaslo.

Shortly thereafter, the second son, Yehezkel, also stopped his studies and left for Palestine. He is presently in a kibbutz. The Jewish population in the city began to take notice of the fact that the word Zion assumed practical meaning. It began to attract youngsters to the cause who were willing to face all difficulties in the task of rebuilding Zion. This was no longer some mystical word concept but pragmatic reality. Zion's sleeping days were finished, a generation of builders appeared.

[Page 318]

Israel and Itzhak Shtoyar also left for Palestine. The parents remained in Jaslo but they too received an invitation to settle in Palestine.

The parents are now in their eighties, promenading in Tel Aviv and seeing their children and grandchildren. They are reaping the harvest that their sons invested in the land. They are breathing the free air of Israel.

Aaron Shtorch

He was one of the refuges from Gorlice during World War I who settled in Jaslo. He was very religious and prayed at the study center of Rabbi Mandil. He exchanged monies and was a member of the exchange at the corner of Kosciuszko Street. His father also sat there. He died in the twenties.

Yaakow Storch

He was the son in law of Moshe Nathan Gutwein and a native of Gorlice. He was a torah student and familiar with Jewish law and its finer points. He was a Bobower Hassid and a very religious person. He opened a store in Moshe Shpringer's house in the market.

He prayed at the study center of Rabbi Mandil as did his father in law. In the last community elections, he gained a seat on the community board on the Bobower ticket. He defended their interests until the outbreak of World War II. He lived on Florianska Street. His wife Esther gave birth to twins and later she gave birth to another child. The entire family perished in the Shoah.

Beril Stillman

He was one of the first Jewish settlers in Jaslo. He was a merchant and in his spare time was active in the community. He was very busy negotiating the purchase of land from a local feudal lord on Siuwniow Street. The land will be used as a cemetery for the Jaslo Jewish community. He passed away and left many sons and daughters who resided in Jaslo

Shmuel Stillman

He was the son of Beril Shtillman and had several houses in the city. He also
[Page 319]
Imported flour and had a grocery wholesale business until 1914. He owned a house in the market that was later sold to Moshe Mendel Tzimet.

His son Leibish finished law school and settled in Rozwadow where he opened an office. His daughter married to Lemberg.

Wolf Stillman

He was the second son of Beril Shtillman and had a grocery wholesale and retail business until lately. He had a house on Kosciuszko Street. He had four daughters and two sons. One daughter left for the USA, and another one married the son of Eliezer Wolker. The latter couple left for Palestine and settled in Jerusalem. The husband worked at the Dea Sea plant until he became ill. The cancer resulted in his death.

His son Moshe Shtillman was one of the founders of the "Yeshuron club" and was very active in the distribution of the blue boxes for collecting money for Zionist causes. He lived in Bochnia, was one of the wealthy people and owned a flourmill, brick factory and fishponds. He survived the war and reached Israel where he settled in Jaffa. His second son Leibish died in the Shoah.

H. Stein attorney

He was an attorney and active in the community. He was a Zionist and defended these interests. He had personal charm and radiated warmth prior to speaking to people and convincing them of the necessity of Zionism. He headed the Zionist movement and helped to expand it. He was the first to allocate communal funds to the Keren Kayemet and Keren Hayesod drives. His son and daughter received an academic education.

He managed to reach London with his family prior to the German conquest of the city.

Attorney H. Stein

[Page 320]

Tzwi Elimelech Stein

He was the son in law of Hershel Weinstein from Zmigrod. He was good-natured, tall and had a kind face. He was a cattle merchant and exported meat and animals to Vienna. He escaped the Germans and lives in the USA

Hersh Shteinbrecher

He was a religious and friendly person. He was a good natured and honest individual who was active in the local "Hevrah Kadishe" society. He had one of the first butcher stores in the city.

Following his death, his wife and her two sons continued the business. She gave extensive charity to the needy and even treated them to meals and provided them with some cash.

Chaim Steinhaus

He was from Zmigrod and a very energetic businessman who took commercial risks. The gentiles respected him for his determined steps. He was the first Jew to open a business in Jaslo. He received a special permit from the Austrian Emperor that enabled him to settle and open a store in the city. Other Jews followed him and this led to the creation of a Jewish community in Jaslo. Jews began to leave the old enclave of Ulaszowice for Jaslo proper.

The old timers stated that Chaim Steinhaus wore a shtreimel on Saturday and holidays and kept Jewish tradition in his youth. His many contacts with non-Jews and his very liberal home atmosphere led to the weakening of his religious customs. He was the first Jew to send his sons to the Polish high school and exposed them to very modern trends. He left most of his estate to his sons.

Itzhak (Ignaci) Steinhaus, attorney

He was the oldest son of Chaim Steinhaus and had the largest legal office in the city. He was a rich man and owned tens of houses. He was completely detached from Jewish life, much assimilated, abandoned completely Jewish traditions. This extreme, assimilated Jew presented himself for parliamentary election in 1903 for the seat of the district of Belz, a stronghold of Belzer Hassidut. He had the support of the great Belzer Rabbi and was elected to the imperial Reichsrat of Vienna. (He was one of the armed defenders of the city during the wave of pogroms in 1898.)

[Page 321]

He had two sons and a daughter who received a higher education. The son Wladislaw fell as an officer in the Polish legion in 1916. One of the daughters married a non-Jew by the name of Chwistuk who liked Jews and later became one of the righteous gentiles. He was a professor at the University of Krakow. Doctor Itzhak Steinhaus left Jaslo with the creation of the Polish State.

Baruch (Bogoslaw) Steinhaus

He was the second son of Chaim Steiinhaus and nicknamed Bogusz. He remained in Jaslo until he passed away. He also distanced himself from Jewish life and refused to have contact with Jews. The old timers still remember him refusing to attend services when they needed a tenth person for the service quorum. (He was thirteen years old but refused to attend services.)

He was extremely rich and managed the commercial bank on May 3rd Street. He obtained the title of royal adviser and participated in many municipal institutions. He opened a bar in his house in the market where the the Christian intelligentsia met (the place was later bought by Max Koegel).

He had three daughters and a son, Hugo, who was a professor of mathematics at the Technical School in Lemberg; presently he lives in Wroclaw (Breslau) and is rector of the university. He is known as a great mathematician in the world and his method of solving problems is known as the "Steinhaus Method."

He passed away in the twenties and was buried in the Jewish cemetery. The casket was transported in a black hearse in the Christian manner but the crosses were removed and many Christians participated at the funeral.

Yossef Shteiner

With the establishment of the Polish State and the pogroms, he left his hamlet of Jedlice and settled in Jaslo. He was known as Yossil Jedliczer. He was a quiet and observant Jew who prayed at the study center of the Rabbi and lately became a Dukler Hassid.

He was a merchant who also had a kiosk next to the great synagogue on Schajnochy Street. He had several sons and daughters who helped him in the business. All children received a traditional education. One of the daughters settled in one of the settlements. His son Tzadok lives in the USA.

[Page 322]

Awraham Mordechai Shtayer

He was the son in law of Yaakow Freud and was a religious scholar. He was a Hassid who was well mannered and a pleasant conversationalist. He made a living as an agent and shipper of ordered merchandise from Krakow for local retailers. He lived next to the post office. With the establishment of the Polish State, he left Jaslo for the USA. Several years later, the entire family joined him.

Shteller family

The family lived in Jaslo until the end of World War I and then left for the USA.

Baruch Leib Shtams

He was the head accountant of the spirit distillery that Itche Jyda Rubel owned in Siowniow. Eventually he became the most trusted employee of the owner and actually managed the enterprise.

He was born in Rudnik and was an old Gorlitzer Hassid. He was a scholar and frequently took an individual stand. He was an honest, devoted and deeply religious person as befits the early Hassidim. He frequently conducted services and dealt extensively in Jewish mysticism namely the books of "Kabbalah," "Zohar" and

"Sifrei Yeraim". He also did not neglect his study of the Talmud and fasted every Monday and Thursday.

He was instrumental in building a mikve and a small synagogue in the fields of Siowniow next to the estate of Rubel. On work breaks, he would enter the synagogue to study his Talmud and commentaries. This was his aim in life.

[Page 323]

His wife Hadas was also a saintly woman who gave a great deal of charity and helped the poor and indigenous people. She secretly helped many a needy persons and is entitled to all the compliments that she earned.

With age he became ill, cleansed himself, and passed away. He left two sons and two daughters who resided outside of Poland.

Following his death, his wife left for Palestine. Her oldest son Anshil moved from Jaslo to Jerusalem prior to World War I. He was a Hassid and G-d fearing man like his father. He was a kind person and was the rabbinical messenger all his life. He passed away recently and is buried in Tzefat (Hershel Shtams that was raised in the house of Baruch Leib Shtams was the son of Anshil Shtams).

His second son was Shulem Shtams who was a quiet and studious type. He was at peace with himself. He was happy with his lot and concentrated on performing good deeds. He left Jaslo for Germany in his youth and later reached Palestine where he settled in Tel Aviv.

Pinhas Shtrum

We can safely say that he was the brain of the Bobower Hassidim in Jaslo as Abish Neuman was the heart of this Hassidut. He initiated, planned and executed ideas. He was the son in law of Yehoshua Ganger

He met daily with Pinhas Shtrum in the store or in the street and discussed for hours Hassidut and how to increase the following of the Bobower Hassidut in Jaslo. One must admit that they did an excellent job, for the membership of the Bobower Hassidim kept growing especially among the youth.

The large, young following was in need for a place to meet and study. The obvious place was a yeshiva. Yehezkel Dawid Shlaf offered a piece of land on Wisoka Street and the yeshiva began to take shape.

He was an educated person and was involved with people. He did not limit himself to religious people but kept in contact with all kinds of individuals. He wore a shtreimel and silk clothing on Shabbath and holidays and on regular days wore modern

[Page 324]

clothing. He wore sport jackets and outer jackets and dressed in the European manner.

He made a nice living from his silk weaving shop and the latest fashionable wool colors, carpets, and furs. His place was in the market, and he sold the finest quality products. However, his soul was not in the business but in Hassidut and to it he devoted his loyalty. The business suffered but he was happy. He gave charity and contributed heavily to the yeshiva of Bobow.

He, his wife Bronia, a son and a daughter left Jaslo with the outbreak of World War II. He reached Russia and survived the war. Eventually he arrived in Israel and opened a perfume business on Allenby Street in Tel Aviv.

Awner Shtern

He was head accountant and purchasing agent for the oil refinery in Niglowic. He was a wise and witty man. He managed to escape with his wife from the Germans and after a great deal of suffering reached Israel where he holds a high position in the government.

Menashe Shtern

He was a very religious, modest, cool tempered and sick person. He was a glazier until he became sick and later passed away. He left a wife, two daughters and five sons who received a traditional Jewish education. One of his sons, Shimon, was a member of the study center and an excellent Talmudic student. They were all Dukler Hassidim and lived on the road to Przedmiescze. They had a haberdashery for many years on Kazimierz Street.

Shimon Shtern

He was one of the old residents of the city and lived all his life in the small wooden barrack on top of the hill next to the cemetery on the way to Siowniow. He was the first undertaker of the Jewish community of Jaslo and in the summer you could not
miss him if you headed in this direction. He sat on a bench, leaned on his cane and tanned himself in the sun.

[Page 325]
Yossel Stern

One of the sons of Shimon Stern was religious. He was a shipper of goods and successful. His daughter managed to save herself during World War II and reached Israel where she settled in Nachlat Itzhak.

Menashe Shilat

He was nicknamed "the small Menashele" due to his small statue. Physically he was small but in spirit, he was tall and energetic. His pigeon eyes were soft and gentle.
He was always among the first ten congregants to arrive for services at the study center. He headed to his seat located along the northwest wall, wrapped himself in a big talith and prayed with great devotion.
On the High Holidays, he started the services, a traditional gesture bestowed on him until World War II. He was from Dembice and settled in Korczyna following his marriage. This small hamlet was a center of piety and Hassidut.
He was a kindhearted person who contented himself with little and served loyally the forest and timber merchants who provided his livelihood. He had six sons and two daughters. Two of the sons; the oldest Awraham left for the USA prior to World War I and the youngest Yehezkel left with the creation of the Polish state. The third son Yossil was a Talmudic student and lived in Rzeszow. Three children lived in Jaslo.

Reuven Shilat

He was the son son of Menashe Shilat and scholarly. He was a gentle and moderate person who married Towa, the oldest daughter of Reuven Yossef Neiwirth of Korczyna. He worked for the timber and forest merchants and prayed at the great study center. He distanced himself from publicity and led a quiet and simple life. He lived in the house of Amer and Kornfeld on Kazimierz Street.
He had four sons and three daughters who received a very religious and Zionist education. The oldest son Meir was a student at the study center where he seriously studied the torah. He was a very good student, gave private lessons, and later became a clerk in the wood companies. He was very active in the youth wing of the mizrahi movement, later he was the secretary of the group and the secretary of the local Keren Kayemet l'Israel or K.K.L. branch until he left for Palestine. He left in 1933 and married Tziporah, the daughter of Elimelech Freund. She was

very active in the women's branch of the mizrahi movement. They settled in Jerusalem where they lived until the first truce during the independence war. Because of his shipping work, he moved to Tel Aviv.

[Page 326]

The second son finished the seminary for teachers named "Poznanski" in Warsaw and received the post of religious teacher in the public school of Jaslo. He was the son in law of Nathan Franzblau. He was appointed as the official translator for Hebrew and Yiddish by the Polish government in 1934 to the district court of appeals of Krakow. He was active among the Jewish youth and encouraged them to study Jewish subjects. He continued his teaching career even during the ghetto days of World War II.

The third son was Israel who left for Palestine in the thirties. He was a member of the Jewish underground in Palestine and hunted by the British authorities. He is presently manager of the "Hadassah Hospital" in Beer Sheba.

The fourth son was Hershele who was devoted to the study of the torah and to the hassidut of Bobow. The daughters were named Bluma, Rachel, and Pearl who belonged to the "Halutz" movement and perished in the Shoah.

Moshe Shilat

He had two daughters, Roda and Rachel. He was an understanding and knowledgeable individual. He was interested in the world, politics, municipal affairs and expressed his opinions intelligently. He was a loyal member of the Mizrahi movement. He was a disabled soldier from World War I and walked on crutches, but did

[Page 327]

not miss the daily services. He also tended to his mother and father. He lived on his military pension that he received from the government.

Alter Shilat

He hardly spoke and considered speech a wasteful and sinful activity. In his youth he was a devoted student of religious materials and later in life continued to set aside time for his daily lessons in Talmudic studies. Following his marriage he returned to Jaslo and received a job at the distillery of Rubel in Siowniow and his wife Miriam was a midwife. They had two daughters, Yochewed and Ravchel.

With the outbreak of World War II, he left Jaslo by himself and survived the war. He reached Israel and settled in Tel Aviv.

Michael Shingel

He was the son of Moshe Yehuda Shingel and owned an estate with a liquor license in Siedliska near Moszczenica. He was a tall man with an impressive face and a determined walk of authority. He had two daughters who acquired a higher education and one of them settled in Tel Aviv,

Members of the family live in the USA where they altered the name to Langal. His sister was married to the son of Zeew Bernsdadter of Jaslo and one brother, Yerachmiel, fell in 1916 during World War I.

Naphtali Shindelheim

He was for years the only tobacco merchant in town. His store also carried Hebrew and Yiddish papers which was rare in those days for the number of Hebrew readers was miniscule, He also sold lottery tickets and his store was an attraction for ticket holders and passers by, people who looked at the weekly winning names displayed on the board. He and his family left for the USA with the creation of the Polish state.

Dawid Shindler

He was an honest and G-d fearing Hassid who attended the early and late services with punctuality. He produced candles and wax and lived on Schajnochy Street. He
was one of the first beadles to be elected following the restoration of the study center that was destroyed during World War I by the Russians.

[Page 328]

He lived in Germany and settled in the thirties in Palestine but could not adjust to the country and returned to Germany. His stay was short lived and after two years he returned to Palestine with some members of the family. He left his son Yehezkel in Germany where he perished in the Shoah.

Yehezkel distinguished himself as a youngster in his studies. He was a good student and absorbed the passages of the Talmud with relative ease. He was an honest Hassid and even in Frankfurt, set aside hours to continue his studies. He gave lectures, devoted time to charity and was active in social communal affairs. His father brought the sefer torah that he wrote to Israel. His oldest son, Mendel, left Germany. Presently he resides in Paris where he is a merchant. He visited Israel in 1950.

Four daughters live in Israel; one of them lives in Kfar Hassidim and the others in Tel Aviv. Dawid Shindler continues his habit of getting up at midnight and heading to the synagogue where he thanks the lord for everything.

Michael Shifs

He was an observant and quiet person who lived at the Targowica prior to World War I. He had a nice income from his shoe repair shop where tens of shoemakers worked. He later moved to Nowa Street and eventually bought the building and added additions and improvements.

Lately he also opened a shoe store in the market square in Moshe Mendel Tzimet's house with the assistance of his sons. He had five sons and four daughters, some of whom did not live in Jaslo.

Shalom Shikler

He was the son in law of Shlomo Unger. He was an educated and well-mannered person. (See Benyamin Unger)

[Page 329]

Awraham Schecht

He was an educated and literary man who had a clear and noble spirit. He was a Czortkower Hassid and a member of the Mizrahi movement. His house was a reception center for visiting members of the party to Jaslo. He was moderate, modest, and gifted with his hands. He was a watchmaker who learned the trade by observation without formal training.

Prior to World War I, he sold musical instruments in the market square and later moved to Elimelech Goldstein's house. He had a few sons and daughters who received a traditional education. One of his sons, Moshe, left for Palestine as a pioneer in the thirties. He settled in Haifa and his sister settled in kibbutz Dan. The oldest son of the family, Elimelech, lived in Krakow.

Itzhak Yaakow Schechter

He was born in Ryglice near Tarnow. He was the brother of Awraham "Mocher Sfarim" or bookseller. He came annually to Jaslo and sold religious books, prayer shawls, and religious items that he sold at the study center. He was the son in law of Elimelech Goldstein, lived for many years in his house, and was a merchant.

He was a very religious Jew and observed the commandments in the strictest sense of the word. He was satisfied with his lot in life.

He had three sons and six daughters. His youngest son Zeew was amongst the first Zionists in town and left for Palestine in the twenties. He worked on road construction sites in Palestine. Presently he is a section manager in the "Shalev" company and lives in Tel Aviv.

His oldest son, Chaim, his youngest brother and sister live in London. One daughter lives in the USA.

Ephraim Schechner

He settled in Jaslo at the end of World War I. He was a very religious Jew and raised his children in the same spirit. He was a tailor and sold ready to wear clothing. He lived on the hill behind the municipal building.

[Page 330]

Asher Shlissel

He was a religious Jew who prayed at the study center of the rabbi. He settled in Jaslo in the thirties and opened a store where he sold wrapping paper and paper bags. The store was located on Kazimierz Street.

Shliffer family

The family settled in Jaslo in the twenties and lived on Florianska Street.

Aaron Shlanger

He was the son in law of Tzwi Bergman and lived at the Targowice. He worked and his wife was a known seamstress and the family had a nice income

Yehezkel Dawid Hacohen Shlapf

His home was one of the nicest spiritual places in Jaslo. His home was a symbol of fine living mixed with a love of torah and respect for religion. We can describe his place as a traditional Jewish home in Jaslo.

He observed all the rules of interpersonal relationships to the highest degree and carried out all the commandments to the end degree. He did this in the spirit of brotherly love. Charitable and social work was an essential part of the existence of the family that considered and believed that every individual was in the image of G-d.

He was very religious and observed strictly the laws. He was a regular member of the study center of Rabbi Mandil and attended his services. He leaned to Hassidism and raised his son in the same spirit. He and his wife, Hannah had seven sons. The oldest was Israel Moshe, then Naphtali Hertz, Awraham, Chaim, Mordechai, Nahum and Gedalia Yossef. He sent his oldest son to the Yeshiva in Bobow prior to World War I. He

established the family tradition of sending the boys to this yeshiva and they all became Bobower Hassidim with convictions.

[Page 331]

The commercial and industrial opportunities widened in Poland especially in Lodz and Warsaw with the creation of the Polish State. The Shlapf family was an enterprising family and saw new opportunities. They established contacts with some of the producers of haberdashery items in the above-mentioned cities. They also established contact with the large drug and cosmetics industries in the USA and France. Their wholesale business expanded rapidly and they provided the retailers in Jaslo with many of their goods.

They traveled and visited many places and met many people but did not alter their traditional behavior. They had beards and side curles, dressed in the traditional religious garb with black velvet hats. They all continued their studies at the yeshiva of Bobow or Ushpizin and the study center of Jaslo,

The sixth son, Nahum, was the most brilliant and devoted Talmudic student. He was bright and had a fast grasp of difficult problems. He studied with the Rabbi of Labowa, and Krosno, he became known as a Talmudic scholar. He was ordained as Rabbi and received a position.

Israel Moshe married a woman of Ushpizin and settled there. Naphtali Hertz married the daughter of Yekil Kalb of Jaslo. They resided in Jaslo but later left the city. Awraham married a woman from Tarnow. They lived for a while in Jaslo but then left the city. The fourth son Chaim married the daughter of Reuven Peretz Kaufman who was the ritual slaughterer of Neimark and later Krosno. He was the brother in law of Yossil Rosenblat. His wife died after three years of marriage while giving birth to a child in Krakow. The baby girl Riwka survived.

Chaim was the driving force of the family business lately and was involved in community affairs. He was the assistant secretary of the community board and

[Page 332]

treasurer of the community. He held these positions until the outbreak of World War II. He was also the assistant manager of "Bank Ludowy," the manager of the needy revolving fund association and distributed funds to the needy without publicity.

Mordechai remained in Jaslo following his marriage and purchased the tobacco store from the gentile Jaklinski who was a disabled soldier and had an exclusive monopoly on the sale of tobacco in the city.

Nahum married the daughter of the Rabbi of Bukowsk and remained in Jaslo. They had one son named Gdalia Yossef.

The home of Yehezkel Dawid Hacohen Shlapf was an open and warm house; the family welcomed guests and visitors and contributed handsomely to many institutions. He donated in the thirties a plot to build a yeshiva on Wisoka Street. The family received tremendous publicity when it invited the saintly rabbi of Bobow to open the yeshiva. He accepted the invitation to stay in Jaslo for Shabbath. The Rabbi, Tzwi Halbershtam, or the Bobower Rabbi arrived in Jaslo with hundreds of followers. They all wanted to be near him and a large reception was planned.

Pinhas Shtrum was one of the initiators to invite the Rabbi and he took a special taxi to Tarnow to await the arrival of the Rabbi and escort him to Jaslo. The rabbi arrived in the evening to Jaslo escorted by his two sons.

There was a big reception plan that included the erection of an entrance gate decorated with greens, shrubbery and several Holy Scripture quotations. A musical band was ordered and several yeshiva students planned to ride "Cossack" style on horses with banners proclaiming Bobower cadets. Torches and firecrackers were planned as well as a large delegation of elderly Jews carrying torahs to receive the Rabbi. At the last moment the plan was cancelled for fear of anti-Semitic provocations. No one wanted to assume responsibility for a Polish act against Jews, be it stoning or bombing. The Jaslo Hassidim of Bobow decided to cancel all the plans and to receive the Rabbi warmly by the large crowd of onlookers. The crowd received him with a spontaneous "Shulem Aleichem."

The Rabbi attended the Shabbath service at the great synagogue and conducted the mussaf service. Tables were set at the study center. The family Shlapf received all the publicity and their fame reached a zenith in the community.

[Page 333]

I will presently sketch from memory some fine characteristics of the personality of the great and noble Rabbi of Bobow. He represented the highest and most elevated level of piety (he was shot in Lemberg by sinful murderers, may G-d avenge his death).

The Bobower Hassidut grew rapidly between the end of World War I and the late thirties. This movement grew throughout Western Galicia and had thousands of followers who cherished the sight of the Bobower Rabbi and tried to get as a close as possible to the saintly figure. His followers accepted unquestionably all his expressions and sayings.

The Bobower tunes even penetrated other Hassidic courts. Music played an important role in the expanding Bobower Hassidic movement that even reached non-Hassidic Jews. This movement also seriously affected Jaslo although the city did not have a large Hassidic following prior to the appearance of the Bobower campaign. The religious and some non-religious youth flocked to the Hassidic movement. What wonderful magnetic forces were present in the personality of the Rabbi who managed to attract all these youngsters to his camp. The rabbi was able to ascertain situations, understand and inspire leadership. Thus, he concentrated on the young generation that represented the future. The young generation felt close to the Rabbi and flocked to his court. The place became crowded and frequently they had to accommodate the visitors in the Rabbi's private home. Many young people left their homes and families to be in close proximity to the saintly rabbi.

The admirers of the Rabbi and some people who had no connection to Hassidut were impressed by his great musical ability to compose Hassidic musical arrangements and tunes for the meal time songs of Shabbath and holidays. The tunes had a beat of their own and a deep religious meaning, namely "Brich Shmayu," "Rebon Olam,"

"Lecha Dodi," "El Adon." How refreshing was the melodic rendition of "Shir Lemaalot Essa Einai el haharim," "Shmona Esrei" of Shabbath, "Melech Kol Haolam Kulo," how much piety was devoted to these passages through the musical tunes. A special effect and deep devotion to the faith was in the Bobower tunes. The young Bobower Hassidim carried these tunes throughout Western Galicia where the local people began to hum them. Thousands of followers adhered to this

rapidly expanding Hassidic movement. Soon the movement had branches throughout Galicia.

The head of the Jaslo Bobower branch was the Shlapf family, Abish Neuman and Pinhas Shtrum. There were some external differences among the members but they were devoted to the faith and were ready to sacrifice themselves for this belief.

Yehezkel Dawid Shlapf lived to a ripe old age when he became ill and passed away prior to World War II. A large crowd attended the funeral. Only two of his sons managed to survive, Chaim and Nahum, who returned from Russia and left for England where they settled in London.

[Page 334]
Shlomo Schmidt
He was a teacher and had a broad education. He was very influential in spiritual matters in the community. He was very active in community affairs and in the Zionist movement. He was a teacher until 1914 at the local Talmud torah where he taught according to a new system that was successful.

With the outbreak of the war, he left teaching and became a businessperson. He had good connections with some manufacturers of Lodz and became one of the main suppliers of haberdashery. The small city storeowners and merchants from the nearby hamlets and villages were his customers. His business venture expanded with each year. His sons Moshe and Chaim assisted him in the business. He purchased the house where he lived from the gentile owner. For years, he lectured every Shabbath afternoon at the great synagogue. The participants enjoyed his lectures where he explained difficult passages with simplicity and understanding.

His reputation as a merchant grew with time among the city merchants for he was restrained and had a calm approach to things. As an old member of the Mizrahi movement, he was placed on the ticket of this party for the upcoming elections to the community. He won a seat and headed the Mizrahi faction within the community board.

[Page 335]

In his spare time, he read many classical and modern books dealing with inquiry, philosophy, and science. He was one of the few People who read daily the Hebrew press in Jaslo and was familiar with the language.

He sat one day in the Rabbi's study center, and browsed at a "Humash" or bible with commentaries by Moshe Mendelson (leader of the enlightenment, translator). One of the busybodies noticed the book and immediately called his friends and explained the "sin" of Shlomo Shmidt. Hotheaded youngsters saw an opportunity to act out their passive life and joined the extremists in their shouts that the place was sinful. They tore the humash from his hands and burned it in the yard of the study center. He never returned to the study center of the rabbi and attended regularly the synagogue of the Mizrahi movement whose ideology he supported. He vehemently defended his position against all the attacks by anti-Zionist elements. His three sons, Moshe, Chaim and Yaakow devoted themselves to the Zionist movement and showed interest in leaving for Palestine but the dreams were never realized. One daughter survived the war and settled in one of the settlements in Israel.

I. Shmidling

He was an enlightened person with far reaching ideas that preceded his time. He was a well-known merchant in town who owned an undergarment factory on the road to Zilkow. He was a wealthy person and a member of the Zionist movement in Jaslo. He had one son.

Matityahu Shamir

He was an educated Talmud student and familiar with religious books. He was one of the early Mizrahi Zionists in the city. He sold ready to wear clothing and lived in the market. About 1923/1924, he left Jaslo for Belgium.

Shenborn, Doctor

He was an attorney and the son in law of Ignaci Steinhaus and had an office on Kosciuszko Street. He was extremely assimilated and distanced himself from any contact with Jews.

[Page 336]
Yaakow Meir Shenberg

His family was known in Bedzin. He was the son in law of Moshe Faust and familiar with the environment. He had a general education and was a member of the Zionist movement. He dealt with timber all his life. He and his family managed to reach Russia prior to the arrival of the Germans. They survived the war years in the Soviet Union and returned to Wroclaw (Breslau) Poland where they settled.

On the last day of Pessah, his wife went to the synagogue to recite the prayers for the dead and entered the women's gallery at the top of the stairs. Suddenly a small fire started and all the women rushed to the stairs leading downstairs. The railing gave way due to the pressure and panic started; many women fell to their death including his wife. The event shocked the entire Jewish community, which grieved the tragic event. Most Jewish inhabitants participated in the funeral where the rabbi delivered a moving eulogy for the victims of the synagogue.

Lately he reached Israel with his son who finished medical school. He works for the "Beilinson" Hospital near Petach Tikvah and lives in Ramat Gan.

A. Sheingut

He was the second son in law of Moshe Nathan Gutwein. He was a religious student and knew his Talmudic studies. (See Moshe Natan Gutwein).

P. Shendorf

He was the third son in law of Moshe Natan Gutwein.
(See Moshe Nathan Gutwein.)

Shulem Shneider

He was a Tchortkower Hassid, very smart and well acquainted with the real world. He loved to jest on his uncle's account and told Hassidic stories. He was a clerk in a timber store.
He was stationed in Przemysl during World War I. He remained in the city after his discharge. His son was a great scholar and was ordained as a rabbi at a young age by a group of famous rabbis.

[Page 337]
P. Shnep

He was one of the clerks at the oil refinery in Niglowic. He lived there and his son finished law school and opened an office in Jaslo.

P. Shenkopf

He was the son in law of Lipcze Werner. He was an engineer and lived all his life in Przedmiescze.

Pinhas Shafet

He was an enlightened individual who owned a pub near the railway. He had three sons and three daughters.

Yehezkel Shpiler

He was a butcher and earned his wages honestly with integrity. He delivered meat orders to the homes since he did not have a store. He was pleased with his lot. He died rather young and left a wife and four sons who continued the business.
One of his sons, Mendel, became pious and adhered to the "Belzer Hassidim." He left for Krakow where he sat at the Belzer synagogue and studied for many years. He returned to Jaslo and was extremely religious. He devoted himself to the mikveh and prayed with great intensity and determination. He grew a beard and long side curls. He dressed in silk clothing, sat, and studied the Talmud at the study center.
One of the sons learned sewing, one was a clerk in a commercial house and the oldest, Zishe, was a cattle merchant.

Dawid Tzwi Shpirer

He was one of the first butchers to open a store in Jaslo. He observed the laws and was a warm hearted Jew. He had three sons who were also butchers. The oldest son, Zelig, was the son in law of Shmuel Zinwil Korzenik of Jaslo.

Reuven Shpirer

He was the second son of Dawid Tzwi Shpirer who had a butcher stand in the market. He was very religious and gave charity. He was honest and fair and lived at the top of the hill behind the municipality. He died and left a wife, four sons and three daughters.

[Page 338]
One of his sons, Menie, was the leading soccer player for Maccabi as a goalie. The second son was the son in law of Yaakow Hershfeld. The third son, Dawid Tzwi,

received a high school education and left for Palestine as a pioneer. He lives in Tel Aviv. The fourth son of Reuven Shpirer, Ephraim, lives in the USA. One daughter left for Palestine as a pioneer and lives at the kibbutz Merchavia. Recently another slaughter and her husband came to Israel. The third daughter died in the Shoah.

Shmuel Shulem Shpirer

He was the third son of Dawid Tzwi Shpirer and had a butcher store in the market. He was a quiet and well-mannered person. He had seven sons who followed the business world and two daughters. Two sons survived; one son, Zelig, lives in Bromberg and the other son, Yossef, came to Israel following the war and settled in the Hatikvah section of Tel Aviv.

Alfred Shpirer, Doctor

He settled in Jaslo in the twenties and opened an office in the market but later moved to the street where all the lawyers had their offices. He won a seat in the thirties to head the community board and remained at this post for one term. He did not belong to a political party but leaned to Zionism. His opinions were acceptable in the community.

A.Sheffel

He was the son in law of Brochil Hayos, the husband of Tziporah. Following his marriage he opened a large kiosk stand near the distillery where he sold soda, fruits and sweets. He later moved to the house of Moshe Mende Tzimet in the market. He made a nice living.

Israel Shefetz

He was one of the first members of the enlightened movement in the city. He was the son in law of Elimelech Teller. He was familiar with local politics and local problems. He was outspoken and expressed his views regardless of the consequences. He lived lately on Kazimierz Street, had a haberdashery and sold stylish items. He had five daughters and one son, Awraham, who lived in Warsaw; his daughter was a
nurse at the Hadassah hospital. One of the daughters left as a pioneer for Palestine and lives in Ramat Itzhak.

[Page 339]

Menashe Sherber

He was one of the first residents of Ulaszowice, He was an enlightened person in those days. He made a nice living from the inn that had a large garden where parties and meetings took place. He had two sons and two daughters. He left for the USA with his family prior to World War I. One of his sons was active in the Jaslo landesmanshaft in the USA.

P. Shperber

He was a quiet person. He lived on Korlowski Street and was a tailor.

Hirsh Shpringer

He was an old, active Zionist leader. He was also active in the Yad Charutzim association. He lived in a small wooden house on Nowa Street, had a small grocery, and was a partner in the soda factory in the city.

He started out as a copper grinder in his youth but then became a merchant. He was nicknamed "flat nose" because his nose was not visible. One merely saw the nostrils.

He was an early Zionist and very devoted to the cause; he frequently left the business to attend to party functions. He was very active prior to elections and saw but one place for Jews-Israel. He adored Herzl and considered him an angel sent from heaven to solve the Jewish problem in the world. His words came directly from the heart and influenced many people.

His daughter, Rachel, left for Palestine as a pioneer in the twenties but had to return due to an illness. He had several sons - Chaim, Yehiel, Berl, Shmuel. Two or three of them died as adults. In spite of his grief, he continued to lead an active life and won a

[Page 340]

seat on the community board as a representative of the Yad Charutzim association. He was a member of the board for many years.

Yehiel Shpringer

He was the brother of Hirsh Shpringer and his brother in law. He worked as a copper polisher and later opened a grocery on Florianska Street. He was also a partner in the soda factory. He was a quiet individual, member of the Zionist movement and one of the larger contributors to the Keren Kayemet L'Israel fund. He had five sons who were very active in sports and played for the maccabi soccer team. One of his sons arrived recently in Israel and settled in an area near Kfar Saba. Two of his sons remained in Russia.

Moshe Shpringer

He was a very wealthy individual and owned a store for merchandise in his house in the market. Lately he liquidated the business and dealt in money exchanges and renting his apartments. His sons received a higher education and one of them was a licensed pharmacist.

Elezer Shpringer

He was the only who worked for the post office as a letter carrier for thirty years. He wore the uniform of the postal services. He was traditional and was one of the founders of the "Hachnassat ala" association in the city. His son graduated as a dentist and was a member of the Polish soccer club "Czarna." He married a gentile servant that upset the parents to no end.

Leib Shperling

He was a very religious Jew whose beard reached his chest. He worked for a living and then opened a dairy store on Florianska Street. He also opened a clothing store with Shmuel Weinberger but the latter left for America and the store remained in his hands.

He prayed at the study center and was a follower of the Rabbi of Dukla. He had three daughters and a son. The oldest daughter left Jaslo and lives in Paris. The son survived the war and reached Israel.

[Page 341]

Martzel Shriar

He was a partner in the company of "Gertenberg and Shriar." He lived all his life in Vienna where he died.

Mendil Sharmar

He was a traditional Jewish merchant. He lived in the hamlet of Borzic near Jaslo.

Shmuel Sharmar

He came from Koloszyc and settled in Jaslo in the twenties. He opened a clothing store in Zalman's house on Florianska Street.

Shmeril Shertz

He was a religious individual with a great deal of Talmudic knowledge. He was a Hassid of Sadigora and gave lectures at their synagogue. He was the son in law of Feiwil Klinsman and opened in his house a retail shoe store. He later became a successful shoe wholesaler and spoke of settling in Palestine but the dream never materialized. He was an excellent traditional service leader and was a warm and sensitive individual.

Tav ת

Ephraim Teumim

He came from the village of Wilkocz and was a descendant of distinguished rabbinical families. He married into a wealthy family of Wolkowicz. Following his marriage he lived with his father in law and became a manager of his many commercial and financial enterprises, namely forests, liquor, and banking. He later became independent and managed his own businesses.

His father was Rabbi Naphtali Hertz Teumim, judicial judge in Wilkowicz and the author of the book "Shaar Naphtali" or gate of Naphtali. He was a descendant of Rabbi Moshe Teumim of Horodenko who was the son of the sister of the great Talmudic scholar Yaakow of Lissa who authored the following books "Havaat Daat", "Netivot" and others...

[Page 342]

The Teumim family claimed some relationship to the royal line of King Dawid.

His in law was Tzwi Elimelech Teitelbaum of Koloszyc who was a rich person and related to the famous Teitelbaum family.

With the outbreak of World War I, he left Wilkowicz with his wife, two daughters and son Elimelech. He found relative safety in a place far from the battlefront. He returned to his community following the end of the war and found his house burned to the ground, his property destroyed and his financial assets depleted due to the galloping inflation in Poland following the war.

Depressed and hopeless he decided to move to Jaslo where he rented a small room for the entire family. His mental situation did not improve with the city's hardships. He was alone without friends in this modern city. He accepted his fate with resignation but hope. His faith was not shaken.

On reaching Jaslo he established the mishnayot group that met between the minha and maariv services at the "shtibel synagogue" next to the main synagogue and also tried to attract followers. Jaslo was not familiar with him and the population was not inclined to support Hassidic descendants or rabbis. He was no longer able to start a business and had little income to sustain his family. His mental condition deteriorated with time and affected his entire outlook in spite of the fact that he continued his saintly life pattern. He accepted his lot with grace and did everything in his power to keep his faith intact.

He became ill, bed ridden and again accepted his lot. His face was pale and one saw merely the two shining eyes and the lips that turned skyway as if he was talking to the almighty and explaining to him his record of deeds on the ground. He accepted the suffering as the prelude to entering heaven.

[Page 343]

He passed away and left a wife, two daughters and a son Elimelech. The son matured and began to provide for the family. Elimelech was a smart and enterprising young man who assumed the family responsibility. He obtained a position with the help of friends as a salesperson for the insurance company "Phoenix." He soon established himself as an excellent and trustworthy sales representative. His financial situation improved and he saw that his two sisters were married. The oldest one settled in Krakow where her economic position was pleasant. The younger one married Benyamin Teitelbaum who opened a shoe store.

The older sister was Malka who married Moshe Dim and they had a daughter Sara (Sala). They all perished in the Shoah.

In writing these lines, I am informed that Elimelech survived the war and lives in the USA.

One of the influential groups in the city was the mishnayot group established by Rabbi Ephraim Teumim. It grew and attracted many new members, namely Nahum Shochet and Chaim Rapaport.

Many people signed up as founding members of the group that had special by-laws and membership dues. The group accepted special contributions for the the various charity groups and anonymous grants to people in need. When a member of the group died, the association recited prayers for the entire year for the departed. Members belonged to a special squad whose responsibility it was to keep records and post the name of the deceased on the special board at the study center. On the memorial day of the deceased, the members of the association met as a whole and studied mishnayot and then recited the kaddish on behalf of the departed member and a prayer to the almighty to accept the deceased.

This family resided in Tarnowici for years. They were traditional people and were traders.

[Page 344]

[empty]

[Page 345]

The rolled parchments
(Referring to holy scrolls)
End and Finality
Tartzat-Tashab
1939-1942

[Page 346]
[empty]

Chapter 30

[Page 347]

September 1, 1939

A thick cloud hung over the city
Hidden were the morning stars
Friday morning
The people were still asleep.

Somewhere in the distance, a child was crying.

At the end of the street, one noticed a Jew heading to the synagogue to pray where another Jew was sitting next to the holy arc and reciting psalms audible to our ears:
"Listen to my prayers dear G-d, and protect me from my enemies...My bones are burned as a hearth and my heart is smitten like grass....
Who will provide me wings so that I may fly like a pigeon ..."
In the northeast corner of the synagogue stands a young student who concentrates on the Talmud that is in front of him. His pale face sees but the page and his hands are stretched over the Talmud that he studies daily...
Alongside the western wall of the synagogue stands a young student hunched over the Talmud, his forehead creased, his mind trying to resolve a difficult page of commentaries.
At the "Kahal Shtibel synagogue" that is part of the main synagogue the worshippers are already wrapping themselves in their prayer shawls.
The early morning rises.
The coach returns from the railway station and you can hear the thundering hoofs of the horses on the cobblestones.
In one of the yards, we hear the door opening with a cringing noise.
The stands are being assembled for the market day of Friday.
It is five o'clock in the morning...
Suddenly... the sound of flying engines in the skies... Noisy explosions in the distance.

[Page 348]

Near the hamlets of Modrowka and Niglowic, the first bombs are falling, according to the residents of Jaslo. The people awakened and jumped out of their beds. The residents hear loud noises in the streets, total chaos.

– Our planes...Maneuvers...!
The injured are begging for help... there are dead people.
– Enemy planes?
– German planes...!
– "Cursed are the Huns!"

– The spillers of human blood and blood will be spilled!
– Hopeless and mad...
– Senseless despair...
The German attack on Poland is beyond comprehension. From this Friday, the people of the city no longer comprehend what is happening except that the market does not open. There are no sellers and no customers...
Who remembers that it is the eve of Shabbath?
Who has the head to prepare for the Shabbath?
– The Germans have invaded...”
Who could have foreseen what this meant....
Orders followed orders, commands...dictates...
Listen! Stand here!
“No promenading! No meetings in the street!
Report to the office!
No lights at night, darkness... total darkness
The sun tended to set, a shadow chases a shadow, the soul trembles and the heart beats rapidly.
“Toward Shabbath let's...
The holy tears ...let's receive the Shabbath....
The face of the Shabbath...
Darkness and misty

[Page 349]
The Germans bomb and conquer...
“Preserve and remember”....
The first of September 1939

* * * *

Saturday morning, September 2nd, 1939, following a day of total uncertainty, a night of panic that seized everybody in the city, the big exodus began. According to the authorities, the men were to leave the city first...

Transportation costs jumped beyond expectation. The rental of cars, horse drawn carts or trucks became a very expensive item if available. Some trains operated others did not, the big railway stations became packed with people fleeing the countryside. The fear of Germans was on everybody's face.

Panic and chaos everywhere...

Many people still resisted the idea of leaving their home for various reasons... They remained at home and did not join the stream of refugees... Where? Who knows...!

The early dawn of Sunday, September 3, 1939, the Germans are still attacking and advancing on all fronts, cities fall at a very rapid rate.

Hysterical people are screaming...defeat and panic...the helpless Polish government has no solution, it abandons the capital of Warsaw where isolated and surrounded army units continue to fight a hopeless battle, there are no supplies, orders and counters orders are issued, the front line is disrupted, surrender and withdrawal is the order of the day.

Another day and another day pass.

The municipal authorities have left the city.

The refugees block the crowded roads. They are heading to Eastern Galicia, namely Brez'on, Lemberg, Stanislawow, Stryj, Sambor, Przemysl and Kolomaya.

Along the roads, bands of Ukrainians who rob them and sometimes kill them attack them. Overhead the German bombers drop their bombs everywhere. Is it possible to believe that the Polish Army that was defeated by the German onslaught at the initial stage of the battle will now establish a strong defensive line in the Eastern part of the country?

[Page 350]

The German planes continue to play havoc with the refugees along the roads who are trying to find shelter in distant places...

Refugees returned from the road since, for various reasons they could not continue their journey.

(The Warsaw radio announced that the president of Poland, the ministers and the government have left the country. The roads of Poland are crowded with a stream of refugees, wounded, dying and dead people.)

The country is in turmoil, the escapees and refugees accuse everybody, rumors spread to the effect that the "fifth column agents" are everywhere spreading disinformation and misinformation among the population.

Some of the people accept these stories.

Thursday evening, the city is a ghost town; the Jews already know what awaits them... The fear of tomorrow is present everywhere...

Grief and despair... The Germans entered Zmigrod.

Ha, what words...

* * * *

The Germans entered Jaslo on Friday, September 8th, 1939. At their head was one of most beastly beings named Luzkar, who was a doctor of sorts. On beginning his administration, he immediately showed his true colors and ordered that the Jews pay a fine of 40,000 gold pieces within the hour.

This behavior would continue throughout Jewish existence in Jaslo. Jews feared to appear in the streets and that resulted in the decline of commerce. The city food supplies started to vanish. The need for daily essentials became worse with each day. The people crawled so as not to be seen, and remained at home as shadows... The slightest knock on the door sent the people into panic and despair. Many fell to the ground and did not get up...

[Page 351]

The first morning of "slichot" (days prior to Rosh Hashana)

Ideas swirl through the mind to go services or to stay home...

Outside it is misty and eerie, here and there one sees a shining star , dogs are barking, ... The sidewalks resound from the heavy boots worn by the SS and I feel fear;

– The soul says go to services, the legs hesitate...

The gates of the synagogue are closed; I am not going to services.

* * * *

September 14th, 1939

Rosh Hashana– will they blow the shofar?

– Who will recite the holy prayer of "Netana Tokef"... for "He is fearful and threatening"...– ... "And who will perish in water..."

The Germans tried to torch the synagogue but at the last moment, they extinguished the fire.

A few individuals ventured into the street to see... to hear...

... The eve of Yom Kippur, everybody is at home behind locked doors, shedding tears onto the open prayer books... the sun is setting...

– The sky is red...From the windows of the synagogue fire balls emerge and ignite everything within reach– the unholy Germans torched the synagogue!

Some Jews risk their lives and enter the burning synagogue to try to save the torah scrolls. Feigale, the daughter of Chaim Dawid Nussbaum, is running to get the fire brigade but the Germans stop her. Through the windows, we see the burning synagogue but are helpless and fearful to react...With desperate bitterness, we keep quiet... The windows exploded one by one and the roof collapsed. The women's upper section crashed and the holy arc with the torahs is burning.

"And he will burn the house of G-d"

The synagogue that was one of the most beautiful synagogues in Poland (see page 44) has turned to ashes and debris.

The next day, the Gestapo took about 200 Jews to the market square where they waited for hours. Finally, they released most of the Jews except for 80 who were imprisoned.

[Page 352]

They were tired and exhausted from fasting for it was Yom Kippur. The Germans insulted and mocked them- - what a day of atonement. Locked behind bars they recited the prayers that they knew by heart: "and all the evil will disappear as the smoke in the wind"

A few days later, they released the imprisoned Jews.

On the eve of Yom Kippur the synagogue, was torched and blown apart. Gone was the crown of the Jewish community. The rest of the building will disappear and only the foundations will remain. With this destruction, the Jewish populated streets lost their soul. The voice of the torah was no longer heard, the synagogues were empty.

(Mr. Hochauser, one of the survivors of the ghetto of Jaslo told this to me. He was from Krynica but used to pray occasionally at our home in the ghetto in Jaslo where secret services were held... the heart was no longer in the prayers although the soul still flowered...) Deadly penetrating winds were stirred, and our defensive actions were disappointing and we felt hopeless but we still thought that things would improve with time.

The marketplace where about 200 Jews stood for several hours

* * * *

The Russians stabbed us in the back, they invaded Poland and reached Lemberg, Przemysl, Sanok and reached the river San (during the second half of September 1939).

All plans developed by the Polish Army to establish a strong defensive line in Eastern Poland and possibly lead to an attack on the German forces collapsed.

[Page 353]

(The Polish defenders of Warsaw held out until about September 20th, 1939 when the city was practically totally destroyed)

Poland has surrendered...

* * * *

Tens of people smuggled themselves out of the city at night in the hope of reaching the new Russian border across the river San. There most of them were picked by the N.K.V.D. or Soviet secret police. Some managed to return to Jaslo

Soon eyewitnesses described horrible events that took place along the roads, namely Jews were killed: Mendel Bodner, Moshe Meir Freund, A. Shuman, near the hamlet of Istrik. Chaim and Elimelech Krisher, Moshe Hersh Kornreich, Sh. Zommer, Leibish Waks and his daughter near the city of Sambor. The angel of death continued his harvest (the most dastardly act was the killing of a Jewish boy who had in his pocket some sort of caricature).

Jews with beards and side curls had to shave them in order not to attract attention. They frequently wrapped their faces in large kerchiefs to avoid showing that they shaved.... (Told by survivors)

The elderly Mendel Meller who went out for fresh air was forced to wrap his face and, as usual, joked about it, saying that he has a toothache....!

* * * *

The regular Polish schools opened in August of 1940 but Jews did not attend them. The Jewish children had no school until Chaim Shield came along with the idea of opening a Jewish school in the ghetto.

The management of the school that was established was under strict German supervision. It managed to establish a good schools program (History, Bible, and Talmud). Children until the age of 15 years attended the school in spite of German objections. The latter insisted that the age should be limited to 12 years since older children could work.

[Page 354]

To save the older children from hard physical labor, the school registered them as 12 year olds. The children received report cards with the permission of the German supervisors at the regular school intervals. Purim and Hanukkah parties were organized to cheer up the participants. Some of the parents attended these parties and they sung national songs. The children's choir sung the songs with the bright Hanukkah lights behind them. Hope and Faith were implanted in the children and the wonderful stories of the great miracles impressed the students.

We must remember and praise Yosef Frumowicz who devoted himself completely to the school project (he was shot during the roundup at the assembly point in the yard of the church). We must also mention the other devoted people namely Sarah Diller (managed to escape from the Gestapo), Ehrenfreund, Brudder, Shield and Doctor Shorr.

* * * *

In one of the days of 1940, the Russian occupying army surrounded and arrested all Jews in Lemberg and other cities under its occupation who refused to surrender their Polish citizenship in lieu of Russian citizenship. Within a few hours, thousands of Jews were told to pack their things, were escorted to awaiting trains, and transported to unknown destinations. Some of the Jews were from Jaslo and they did not have the slightest chance to call or write to the families. The trains roared across Russia with thousands of frightened and scared former Polish citizens. They traveled for days and weeks in sealed railway cars until they reached unknown destinations.

At first, most Jews considered this a disaster for they were in the depths of Russia and it seemed to them that they would die in the forsaken places. (Indeed, many people died of starvation, disease and even loneliness). But due to the intervention of Polish personalities (like General Anders and Wanda Waszilewska), their lot improved. They were able to join the Polish Army and participated in the liberation of Europe from the Germans. All of these soldiers remained in Europe and many of them left for Israel, some of them went to the States and some remained in Poland and Russia.

* * * *

The ghetto of Jaslo was established after March 15th, 1941 and included the following streets: Widok, (named for the view of the synagogue), Wisoka, Targowica, Korlewski and Schajnochy. All Jews had 48 hours to leave their residences and move into the ghetto.

The Germans brought about 6,000 Jews from Lodz and dumped them at the Jaslo railway station. Dangers lurked everywhere, the ghetto was extremely overcrowded. My father picked up 20 Jews from the railway depot and brought them home.

[Page 355]

He (my father) continued to awake each day at about two or three in the morning to visit bakeries and collect some bread for the poor people.

Korlowskigo Street
(A street of the ghetto)

Until June 22nd 1941, I received letters from home through Czechoslovakia where my sister lived and through occupied Eastern Galicia from my son in law who was killed in the shoa, then everything stopped.

The limping Gintz, an inhuman creature that only Satan could create soon replaced Luzkar as the head of the police.

[Page 356]

He also carried the title doctor. His cruel orders knew no satisfaction. The diabolical dictates changed from hour to hour. He started the policy of mass shootings and arrests. People would disappear and nobody knew what happened. The apartments were confiscated. The inhabitants of these flats and stores had to move to the ghetto.

The cruel order of banishing the Jewish inhabitants to the ghetto, the daily shootings and other cruelties weakened the Jewish population. Their numbers declined and so did their spirit. The faces of the ghetto inhabitants told us everything. Children left their homes and babies were taken from their mothers and killed.

Where are the skulls and the blood of the killed, do the deep field swamps of Warzica, Jarniowka and Sibenia contain them?

Where was the old man Lipcze Werner killed and where is his grave?

Where was the attorney A. Menashe led in the forest of Koblow, tortured, and killed?

Where are the people who were killed daily?

One morning the Gestapo arrested 50 people and took them to the cemetery. They tortured and shot them.

With the arrival of Gintz also arrived another sadistic officer named Raushwitz who headed the Gestapo in Jaslo. His appearance made the inmates tremble with fear for his cruelties. He killed people for his pleasure.

One day he had an idea to celebrate his wedding. He ordered the Judenrat to assemble all Jewish artisans and merchants at the house of A. Goldstein. On reaching the place, they were told to bring whatever merchandise they had in their possession. The artisans were told that that the orders must be executed to the total satisfaction of the devouring wolf. The bloodthirsty Raushwitz who was about to be married ordered all the Jewish women to bring him jewelry and insisted on a Jewish band headed by D. Bernstein that would be playing Jewish melodies for the Gestapo butchers.

Leibish and Maltczi Piar
(They died at the death camp of Theresenstadt)

(See page 234)

(Maltczi, nicknamed the mother of the city, also died at Theresenstadt)

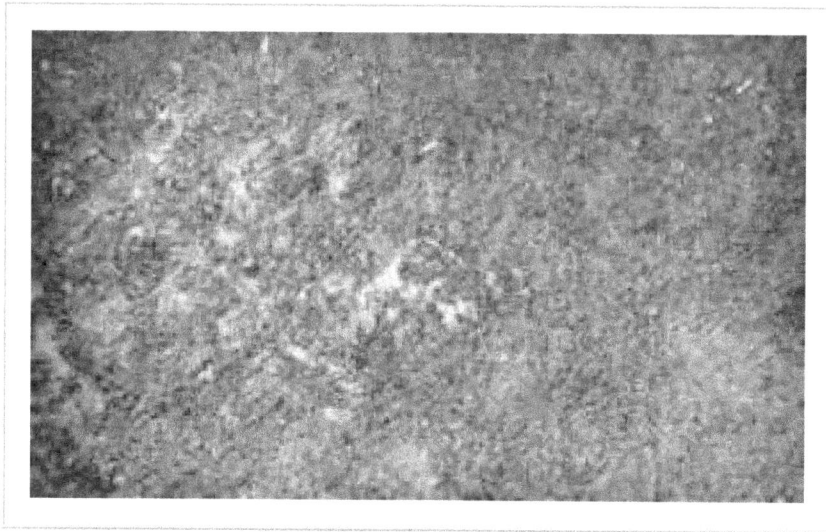

**The cemetery of Jaslo
(the Germans pulled out the tombstones
and used them to pave the streets)**

[Page 357]

Several weeks passed and a new order to the Judenrat. One hundred Jews must present themselves for various work details. The Gestapo immediately detained them and trucked them under military escort to the labor camp of Pustkow near Tarnow. Thousands of Jews worked there and died there from starvation and hard work.

Gintz closed the ghetto completely and ordered a fence around the ghetto. Anyone caught outside the area was to be shot. Dr. Tzucker tended to a sick patient; he and wife were shot at the cemetery, he for so-called communist activities. (The son of Shmulowicz was caught and his wife begged for mercy. They were both shot on the spot, according to a letter from Professor Pirak from Jaslo)

During the forties, an article appeared in the newspaper "Haaretz" that is published in Tel Aviv and under the headline "One of the stages of Hell " (London 17 ST"a, RADIO)

"Polish sources inform us that a ghetto for Jews was created in Jaslo, southern Poland that bears no resemblance to anything that we have seen so far. . .Thousands of Jews are locked in small cubicles near the entrance to the jail. The living conditions are the worst; these people have not been fed for days. They live on scraps of food from the non-Jewish prisoners. In the first few weeks, many of the Jews died, a fifth of the Jews died of starvation, tortures and exhaustion.

In the ghetto, the people are getting weak and protecting their life that is in constant danger. One day the Jews had to surrender all their furs for the German soldiers on the eastern front. This order was not terribly successful for many Jews sold their furs before the order to the farmers in exchange for food and milk for their babies. Some preferred to destroy the furs. The campaign was

not terribly successful. The implementation of the order resulted in the death of a few Jews. The local Gestapo officials took the good furs for their female companions who wore them in public.

[Page 358]

The people barely recovered from the last campaign when rumors began to circulate that there were too many Jews in the ghetto of Jaslo. The order soon came from Gintz and 150 Jews were sent under S.S. guard to Frysztak and then to Warzice where ditches were prepared in advance by Jewish workers from Jaslo. All 150 were ordered to disrobe including Mendel Meller who was wrapped in his talith and shot.

The next day Jewish girls were sent to collect the clothing and to check them for hidden jewels.

I will mention here Dorothea Fliskin (the daughter of Yeshayahu Cylinder, the wife of Dr. Fliskin, the head of the Malben medical organization in Israel) for her courageous fight against the Germans. Her brave acts in the resistance in various areas of Poland need a full page where her anti-German exploits can be fully described.

The constant heavy bombardments of German cities and the rapid allied advances enraged the German killers. They increased the tempo of killing Jews. Gintz turned to one of the local rabbis who was related to the Rothschild family. He insisted that the rabbi call his relative and insist that he use his influence to stop the war or he would be shot. (There is another version to the effect that Gintz arrived in Zmigrod and asked a local rabbi to intervene with Rothschild...)

We must not forget that during this difficult period there were also certain weak characters in our community who were willing to exploit the situation for their personal gain and cooperated with the enemy. They tried to please the Germans and lick their boots in the hope of saving themselves. They robbed from their oppressed brothers; they blackmailed them and executed all orders given by their masters. They are well known and should be excluded from the community of mankind.

[Page 359]

* * * *

On Tuesday, August 18th 1942 (five days in Elul, Tashab), the final action of rounding up the Jews took place. About 800 Jews including women and children were ordered to assemble at the Targowica. They had to limit their luggage to 10 kilos and leave the rest at the place of residence.

The tears and anxieties of the departed can't be described. They were looking to the skies for a possible miracle that might change the situation ...

"Christian Kaleshtur" at the height of Florianska Street near Siowniow

The Jews had to line up and march to their death four abreast. They were led through the city streets under SS armed guards to the "Christian Kaleshtur" at the height of Florianska Street near Siowniow. There they spent the night in tears, worried and hopeless. In the morning, they marched them to the railway station where a train awaited them. The cars were loaded with brutality befitting the SS and the train rolled to the death camp of Belzec where they were gassed and their bones burned in the crematories. There their saintly souls left them and their remnants joined the thousands of other saintly Jews killed between the years 1940-1942.

The German murderers left a few young Jews in Jaslo to clean up the ghetto where the Jews lived for approximately a year and a half. Some of the Jewish workers also built a swimming pool on the outskirts of the city. They too wound up at the death camp of Przemysl and their destiny was similar to the other saints.

Few Jews managed to survive the war. They escaped the ghetto at night, were in constant danger, and were on the run. They had to leave the city and find hiding places. With the last round up of Jews, they shot I. Goldstein. The ghetto was now empty, the Jewish voices disappeared forever.

In the month of January (Shvat, Tashah), 1945, the Russian Army moved rapidly against the German forces and approached the city of Jaslo. A battle ensued that lasted some time until the city was liberated. There was great destruction and liberation

The Jewish history of Jaslo that lasted for about 70 years could only be remembered through the Jewish tombstones that adorned the paved streets of the city.

[Page 361]

Addendum
P1
Thank You and Bless You

Mrs Riwka Otenheimer (Ulman), Tel Aviv	for the colorful book bindings
Mr. Emil Yerachmiel, z"l, Vienna	for the paper donation for the book
Tzwi Tzimet, Jerusalem	for the copy printing edition
Sh.Z. Rachmil, Tel Aviv	for the contribution toward the book
Chaim and Nachum Schlapf, London	for the contribution toward the book
Pinhas Shtrum, Tel Aviv	for contributing to the binding costs

And to all former residents of Jaslo who helped in publishing the book

A. Harmoni	for constructive suggestions
M. Moher	for advising in the layout of the book.

P2

The author,
Moshe Nathan Even Chaim (Rapaport)
This family resided in Tarnowici for years.
They were traditional people and were traders.

Last name	First name	Maiden name	Birth date	Birth place	Residence	Trade or remarks	Father	Mother	Gen.	Groom	Disposition

List of Jews of Jaslo Prior and During World War II

Prepared by William Leibner

Source*

TJ - Rapaport - "A History of the Jews of Jaslo"

Last name	First name	Maiden name	Birth date	Birth place	Residence	Trade or remarks	Father	Mother	Gen.	Groom	Disposition
ADLER	Betzalel			Jaslo	Jaslo	bathouse attendant			M		
ADLER		Goldstein							F	Betzalel	
ADLER	Mordechai Dawid			Jaslo	Jaslo	salesman	Betzalel		M		
ADLER	P.			Jaslo	Jaslo				M		
ADLER		Goldstein		Jaslo	Jaslo				F	P.	
ADLER	Henoch Chenech				Jaslo				M		
ADLER		Miller			Jaslo		Moshe	Mihket	F	Henoch Chanich	
AMENT	Meir			Kolczyce	Jaslo				M		
AMENT	Shmuel			Jaslo	Jaslo		Meir		M		
AMENT	Moshe			Jaslo	Jaslo	grocery	Meir		M		
ALEXANDROWICZ	Yaakow			Jaslo	Jaslo	distillery			M		
ALTHOLTZ	P			Jaslo	Jaslo				M		
ALTMAN	Yehoshua			Jaslo	Jaslo				M		
ALTMAN	Berish			Jaslo		wood merchant	Yehoshua		M		
ALTMAN	Shlomo			Jaslo	Vienna		Berish		M		
ALTMAN	Yossil			Jaslo	Jaslo	grocery	Yehoshua		M		
ALTMAN	Yehoshua			Jaslo	Jaslo		Yossil		M		
ALTMAN	Meir			Jaslo	Jaslo	maccabi	Yossil		M		
ALTMAN	Abba				Jaslo	eggs	Yehoshua		M		
ALTMAN	Blumcze				Jaslo		Yehoshua		F		
ALTMAN	Chaim			Jaslo	Jaslo	eggs		Blumcze	M		
ALTMAN	Hersh			Jaslo	Jaslo	grocery		Blumcze	M		
ANISFELD	Mordechai			Krakow	Jaslo				M		
ANISFELD		Tzucker		Jaslo	Jaslo		Alter		F	Mordechai	
ANISFELD	Yonathan								M		survived
ANISFELD		Elias					Shlomo		F	Yonathan	survived
ANTNER	Dawid	Stolar				carpenter			M		
APFEL	Yehoshua				Jaslo				M		survived
APFEL	Nahum			Madin	Jaslo	cantor			M		
APFEL	Eliyahu			Jaslo	Pilzno		Nahum		M		
APFEL	Kalman			Jaslo	Przemysl		Nahum		M		
APFEL	Yehoshua				Jaslo	finances	Nahum		M		survived
APFEL	Awraham Itz.			Jaslo	Jaslo	choir	Nahum		M		

List of Jews of Jaslo Prior and During World War II

Last name	First name	Maiden name	Birth date	Birth place	Residence	Trade or remarks	Father	Mother	Gen.	Groom	Disposition
APFEL	Shragai Feiv			Jaslo	Germany	brother	Nahum		M		
APFEL	Yudel Meir	Horowitz		Jaslo	Vienna	paper			M		
APFEL		Freund		Jaslo			Yaakow		F	Yudel Meir	
APFEL	P			Pocholenko	Jaslo				M		
ARMAN	Akiva	Podzamci		Podzamci	Jaslo	farmer			M		
ASHKENAZI	Hertzel			Jaslo	Jaslo				M		
ASHKENAZI		Tzimet		Jaslo	Jaslo		Leib		F	Hertzel	
AUSTRO	Eliezer	Halevi		Szandiezow		wheat			M		Palestine
AUSTRO	Israel						Eliezer		M		
AUSTRO	Moshe						Eliezer		M		
BALDENGRIN	Shlomo			Jaslo	Jaslo	butcher			M		
BALZAM	Moshe			Jaslo	Jaslo	attendant			M		
BALZAM		Meller				widow			F	Moshe	
BARUCH	Chaim			Wisnic	Wisnic	rabbi			M	Dinah	
BATMAN	Meir								M		
BATMAN		Meller		Jaslo	Jaslo		Mendel		F	Meir	
BAUM	Nathan			Jaslo	Jaslo				M		drowned
BAUM	Zeelig			Jaslo	Jaslo	building materials	Nathan		M		
BAUM	Nathan			Jaslo	Jaslo		Zeelig		M		survived
BAUMRING	Tzwi Hersh			Jaslo	Jaslo	grocery			M		
BAUMRING	Yaakow			Jaslo	krosno	doctor	Tzwi Hersh		M		
BAUMRING	Leibish			Jaslo	Jaslo	flour mill	Tzwi Hersh		M		
BAUMRING	Itzhak			Jaslo	Jaslo	dentist	Tzwi Hersh		M		survived
BAZNER	Itzhak			Jaslo	Jaslo	doctor			M		survived
BAZNER		Kinstler		Jaslo	Jaslo		Mendil		F	Itzhak	survived
BAZNER	Shlomo Zal			Jaslo	Jaslo	doctor			M		
BAZNER		Rubel		Jaslo	Jaslo		Itzhak Yeh		F	Shlomo Zal	
BECK	Yoel Men			T	Jaslo	timber			M		
BECK	Dawid			Jaslo	Jaslo	timber	Yoel Men		M		
BECK	Moshe			Jaslo	Jaslo	timber	Dawid		M		
BECK	Herman			Jaslo	Jaslo		Dawid		M		USA
BECK	Motel			Jaslo	Jaslo	construction	Yoel Men		M		survived
BECK	Mendel			Jaslo	Warsaw	lawyer	Motel		M		
BECK	Itka			Jaslo	Jaslo		Motel		M		shoa
BECK				Jaslo	Jaslo		Motel		M		killed
BECK	Zeelig			Jaslo	Jaslo		Motel		M		survived
BECK	Romek			Jaslo	Jaslo		Motel		M		survived
BELZER	Israel Eliy			Jaslo	Jaslo	skins			M		died
BELZER	Shachne			Jaslo	Jaslo		Israel Eliy		M		survived
BELZER	Feivil			Jaslo	Jaslo		Israel Eliy		M		
BENET	Tzwi				Jaslo	glazier			M		
BERGER	Shlomo			Koblow		wood merchant			M		

Last name	First name	Maiden name	Birth date	Birth place	Residence	Trade or remarks	Father	Mother	Gen.	Groom	Disposition
BERGER	Dawid			Jaslo	Jaslo		Shlomo		M		survived
BERGER	Mendel			Jaslo	Jaslo		Shlomo		M		survived
BERGER	Hersh Yaak			Koblow	Jaslo	brother	Shlomo		M		USA
BERGER	Meir			Jaslo	Jaslo	liquor license			M		
BERGER		Dam		Jaslo	Jaslo		Moshe		F	Meir	
BERGER	Dawid			Jaslo	Jaslo	chocolate			M		
BERGER	Berta	Haber		Jaslo	Jaslo		Israel	Sabina	F	Dawid	
BERGMAN	Feiga		1921	Zmigrod	Jaslo				F		
BERGMAN	Chaskel		1923	Zmigrod	Jaslo				M		
BERGMAN	Tzwi			Gorlice	Jaslo	wax			M		
BERKOWICZ	Yossef			Jaslo	Jaslo	barber			M		died
BERKOWICZ		Bruder		Jaslo	Jaslo				F		
BERNSTEIN	Dawid			Jaslo	Jaslo	music			M		
BERNSTEIN	Hanoch			Jaslo	Krakow		Dawid		M		
BEZNER	Shlomo				Jaslo				M		
BEZNER	Itzhak				Jaslo	doctor			M		
BIALYWLOSS	Alter Shu	cohen			Jaslo				M		
BIALYWLOSS	Mrs				Jaslo				F	Alter Shu	
BIALYWLOSS	Heinech			Jaslo	Jaslo		Alter Shu	Mrs	M		
BIAR	Shlomo			Jaslo	Jaslo	haberdashery			M		
BIAR		Brick		Jaslo	Jaslo		Ephraim		F	Shlomo	
BIAR	Shulem			Jaslo	Jaslo		Shlomo		M		Palestine
BIAR	Yaakow			Jaslo	Jaslo		Shlomo		M		shoa
BIDER	Eliezer			Gorlic	Jaslo	teacher			M		
BIDER	Uri			Jaslo	Jaslo		Eliezer		M		killed
BIDER	Shmuel			Jaslo	Jaslo		Eliezer		M		
BIKOWER	Elimelech			Bikowa	Jaslo	farmer			M		
BILT	Shmuel				Jaslo	talmudist			M		
BILT		Engel		Jaslo	Jaslo				F	Shmuel	
BINDER	Itzhak			Jaslo	Jaslo	vinager			M		
BINDIGGER	Hersh			Jaslo	Jaslo	yeast			M		
BINDIGGER	Sheindil	Handel		Jaslo	Jaslo				F	Hersh	
BINDIGGER	Ezriel			Jaslo	Jaslo		Hersh	Sheindil	M		survived
BINDIGGER	Zinwil			Jaslo	Jaslo		Hersh	Sheindil	M		
BINDIGGER	Shosha	Shtern					Menashe		F	Zinwil	
BLANK	Aaron			Dembowce					M		
BLANK	Yossef						Aaron		M		survived
BLEIMAN	Benyamin			Jaslo	Jaslo				M		
BLEIMAN	Leibish			Jaslo	Jaslo	tenor	Benyamin		M		
BLEIMAN	Michael			Jaslo	Jaslo		Benyamin		M		
BLIMAN					Jaslo	choir			M		
BLONDER	Feivel					kiosk			M		
BLUM	Eliezer			Jaslo	Jaslo	clothing			M		

List of Jews of Jaslo Prior and During World War II

Last name	First name	Maiden name	Birth date	Birth place	Residence	Trade or remarks	Father	Mother	Gen.	Groom	Disposition
BLUM	Lea	Miller		Jaslo	Jaslo		Zeelig		F	Eliezer	
BLUM	Israel Moshe			Jaslo	Jaslo	haberdashery	Eliezer		M		
BLUM	Eliezer	der blinder		Jaslo	Jaslo	etroggim			M		
BLUM	Sheindil			Jaslo	Jaslo				F	Eliezer	
BLUM	Yermiyahu			Jaslo	Jaslo	watchmaker			M		
BLUM	P.					pharmacist			M		
BLUMENTAL	Adam			Jaslo	Jaslo	engineer			M		survived
BLUT	Chaim Shlo			Pezalcew	Jaslo				M		
BLUT	Regina			Jaslo	Jaslo		Chaim Shlo	Hinda	F		
BODNER	Yudel			Jaslo	Jaslo	yeast			M		
BODNER	Mendel			Jaslo	Jaslo	wheat import	Yudel		M		
BODNER		Kliman		Jaslo					F	Mendel	
BODNER	Baruch			Jaslo	Jaslo		Yudel		M		survived
BODNER	Leibish			Siwniow		farmer			M		
BRAND	Shlomo	Kliner		Jaslo	Jaslo	books			M		
BRAND	Ita Naomi			Jaslo	Jaslo				F	Shlomo	
BRANSDORFER	Eliezer				Jaslo	slaughterer			M		
BRANSDORFER		Ganger		Jaslo	Jaslo				F	Eliezer	
BRASSMAN	Yehoshua			Jarniowka		farmer			M		
BRASSMAN	Awraham Itz.			Jarniowka			Yehoshua		M		USA
BRASSMAN	Itzhak			Jarniowka			Yehoshua		M		USA
BRASTADTER	Wolf			Jaslo	Jaslo	knitting			M		
BRENNER	Awraham H			Dembice	Jaslo				M		
BRENNER		Tzanger		Jaslo	Jaslo		Yona		F	Awraham H	
BRENNER	Yona			Jaslo	Belgium		Awraham H		M		
BRENNER	Eliezer		1883	Pezalcew	Jaslo				M		
BRENNER		Elias		Jaslo	Jaslo		Dawid		F	Eliezer	
BRENNER	Mendel			Jaslo	Krosno	attorney			M		
BRENNER	Abish			Jaslo					M		survived
BRICK	Ephraim				Jaslo		Ephraim		M		
BRICK	Michael			Jaslo	Jaslo	butcher			M		
BRICK	Livik			Jaslo	Jaslo		Michael		M		survived
BRICK	Idelia			Jaslo	Jaslo		Michael		F		
BRON	Berish			Nowy Sacz	Jaslo	bass cantor			M		
BRON	Yaakow			Nowy Sacz			Berish		M		
BRON	Mandil			Jaslo		Rabbi			M		
BRON		Rubin		Jaslo			Awraham Yeh		F	Mandil	
BRON	Yona			Jaslo	Jaslo	Rabbi	Mandil		M		
BRUDER	Zishe			Jaslo	Jaslo				M		
BRUDER	Yaakow			Jaslo	Jaslo	brother			M		

Last name	First name	Maiden name	Birth date	Birth place	Reside nce	Trade or remarks	Father	Mother	Gen.	Groom	Disposition
BRUDER	Michael			Jaslo	Dantzig		Yaakow		M		
BRUDER						dentist	Yaakow		M		
BRUDER	Halka						Yaakow		F		survived
BUCH	Shmuel			Kolaczyce	Jaslo	candies			M		
BUCH		Margolies					Moshe		F	Shmuel	
BUCH	Naphtali						Shmuel		M		
BUCHSBAUM	widow				Jaslo				F		
CEZAR	Shmuel				Jaslo	dairy			M		
CEZAR	Moshe			Jaslo	Belgium	distillery	Shmuel		M		
CEZAR	Zelig			Jaslo	Jaslo	painter	Shmuel		M		
CHAYIOS	Baruch			Jaslo	Jaslo	teacher			M		
CHAYIOS	Tziporah			Jaslo			Baruch		F		
CIECHANOWSKI	Yaakow	Yankel		Jaslo	Jaslo	talmudist			M		
CIECHANOWSKI		Unger			Jaslo				F	Yaakow	
CIECHANOWSKI	Chanoch						Yaakow		M		
CIECHANOWSKI	Shmuel						Yaakow		M		
CITRONENBAUM	Motil			Zmigrod	Jaslo				M		
CITRONENBAUM	Leib			Zmigrod	Jaslo	barber	Motil		M		died
CITRONENBAUM	Liba			Jaslo	Jaslo				F	Leib	
CITRONENBAUM	Benyamin			Jaslo	Germany		Leib	Liba	M		survived
CITRONENBAUM	Shmeril			Jaslo	Krosno		Leib	Liba	M		
CITRONENBAUM	Yehoshua			Jaslo	Mainz		Leib	Liba	M		
CITRONENBAUM		Krisher		Jaslo	Jaslo		Yaakow Pin		F	Yehoshua	
CITRONENBAUM	Motil			Jaslo	Gorlice		Leib	Liba	M		
CITRONENBAUM	Itzhak			Jaslo	Jaslo		Leib	Liba	M		
CITRONENBAUM	Awraham			Jaslo	Jaslo		Leib	Liba	M		died
CITRONENBAUM	Awi Wolf			Jaslo	Vienna		Awraham		M		
CYLINDER	Yehoshua				Vienna				M		
CYLINDER		Weinstein		Zmigrod	Vienna		Hersh		F	Yehoshua	
DAM	Moshe			Jaslo	Jaslo	butcher			M		died
DAM	Nathan			Jaslo	Jaslo		Moshe		M		
DAM	Awraham			Jaslo	Jaslo		Moshe		M		
DAMASK	Zeew			Jaslo	Jaslo	soap			M		
DAMASK		Amer		Jaslo	Jaslo		Awraham		F	Zeew	
DAN	Eliezer			Jaslo	Jaslo				M		
DAR	Shmuel				Jaslo	baker			M		
DENNER	Dawid			Jaslo	Jaslo	butcher			M		
DENNER	Benyamin				Jaslo		Dawid		M		
DENNER		Golds		Jaslo	Jaslo		Tzwi Hersh		F	Benyamin	
DILLER	Abraham			Jaslo	Jaslo	principal			M		
DILLER	Chaim			Jaslo	Jaslo	rabbi			M		died
DILLER	Israel			Jaslo	Jaslo		Chaim		M		survived
DINTENFASS	Eisik				Jaslo	grocery			M		

List of Jews of Jaslo Prior and During World War II

Last name	First name	Maiden name	Birth date	Birth place	Residence	Trade or remarks	Father	Mother	Gen.	Groom	Disposition
DOMB	Dawid	Edmond		Rymanow	Jaslo	bookeeper			M		
DOMB	P.					tinsmith	brother	of Daw	M		
DORSHT	Michael								M		
DORSHT		Altman					Berish		F	Michael	
DRENGER	Mordechai				Jaslo	education			M		
DRENGER	Elchanan			Jaslo	Jaslo		Mordechai		M		survived
DRENGER	Yaakow			Jaslo	Jaslo		Mordechai		M		survived
DRENGER	Menashe			Jaslo	Jaslo		Mordechai		M		died
DULBERG	Riwka			Jaslo	Jaslo				F		Palestine
DYM	Moshe			Jaslo	Jaslo				M		
DYM	Malka	Teumim		Jaslo	Jaslo		Ephraim		F	Moshe	
DYM	Sara			Jaslo	Jaslo		Moshe	Malka	F		
EDER	Moshe			Jaslo	Jaslo	education			M		
EDER		Thaler		Jaslo	Jaslo		Mordechai D		F	Moshe	
EDER	Nachman			Jaslo	Jaslo		Moshe		M		
EDER	Hersh			Jaslo	Jaslo				M		
EDER		Freund		Jaslo	Jaslo		Yaakow		F	Hersh	
EHERENFREUND	Yaakow			Jaslo	Jaslo				M		
EHERENFREUND		Kornreich		Jaslo	Jaslo		Meir		F	Yaakow	
EHRLICH	Shmuel Wol			Jaslo	Jaslo	glazier			M		died
EHRLICH	Leibish			Jaslo	Jaslo		Shmuel Wol		M		Palestine
EHRLICH	Naphtali			Jaslo	Jaslo		Shmuel Wol		M		
EHRLICH	Mendel			Jaslo	Jaslo		Shmuel Wol		M		died
EHRLICH	Rala			Jaslo	Jaslo		Shmuel Wol		F		
EHRLICH	Rachel			Jaslo	Jaslo		Shmuel Wol		F		
EHRLICH	Roza			Jaslo	Jaslo		Shmuel Wol		F		
EHRLICH	Neche			Jaslo	Jaslo		Shmuel Wol		F		Palestine
EHRLICH	Zlata			Jaslo	Jaslo		Shmuel Wol		F		
EICHHORN	Eliezer			Jaslo	Jaslo				M		shoa
EICHHORN	Hancze	Piar		Jaslo	Jaslo		Leibish		F	Eliezer	shoa
EICHLER	Itzhak			Jaslo	Jaslo	butcher			M		died
EINHORN	Moshe			Jaslo		yeast			M		
EINHORN	Awraham					porcelain			M		
EINHORN	Motel			Jaslo			Moshe		M		
EINTZIGER	Moshe			Jaslo	Jaslo				M		
EINTZIGER	Zeev Wolf			Jaslo	Jaslo	builder	Moshe		M		
EINTZIGER	Pinhas			Jaslo	Brzeszow	crystal	Zeev Wolf		M		shoa
EINTZIGER		Berger		Jaslo	Brzeszow		Shlomo		F	Pinhas	
EINTZIGER	Yaakow Nat	Or		Jaslo	Jaslo	technician	Pinhas		M		survived
EINTZIGER	Moshe			Jaslo	Jaslo	lawyer	Pinhas		M		survived
EINTZIGER	Yossef			Jaslo	Jaslo		Pinhas		M		survived
EINTZIGER	Esther			Jaslo	Jaslo		Yossef		F		

Last name	First name	Maiden name	Birth date	Birth place	Residence	Trade or remarks	Father	Mother	Gen.	Groom	Disposition
EINTZIGER	Zeev	Wilik		Sandz	Jaslo				M		survived
EINTZIGER		Berger		Jaslo	Jaslo		Shlomo		F	Zeev	survived
EINTZIGER	Menachem	Man		Jaslo	Jaslo	gabbai	Moshe		M		
EINTZIGER	Pessah			Jaslo	Jaslo	hotel	Moshe		M		
EISENBERG	Yaakow			Jaslo	Jaslo				M		
EISENBERG	Alter Chai			Jaslo	Germany		Yaakow		M		
EISENBERG		Zilbershtein					Moshe		F	Alter Chai	
EISENBERG	Chaim			Jaslo	Jaslo	skins			M		
EISENBERG		Baldengruen		Jaslo					F	Chaim	
EISENBERG	Reuven				Zmigroddayan				M		
ELIAS	David				Jaslo	property			M		
ELIAS	Leibish			Jaslo	Orzemysl	timber	David		M		
ELIAS	Shlomo			Jaslo	Jaslo	timber	David		M		
ELIAS	Abish			Jaslo	Jaslo	seltzer	David		M		
ELIAS	Moniek			Jaslo	Jaslo	soccer	David		M		survived
ELIAS	family			Przedmiscza							
ELLIOWICZ	Meir				Jaslo				M		
ELLIOWICZ	Faiga	Tzimet					Moshe		F	Meir	
EMER	Leibish				Jaslo	merchant			M		
EMER	Awraham				Jaslo		brother	of	M	Leibish	
ENGEL	Yehiel			Zmigrod	Jaslo	yeast			M		
ENGEL	Moshe				Jaslo		Yehiel		M		
ENGEL	Ozer				Jaslo		Yehiel		M		
ENGEL	Mordechai			Zmigrod	Jaslo	wheat			M		
ENGEL	Yehoshua			Zmigrod	Jaslo		Mordechai		M		survived
ENGLANDER	Chaim	cohen		Jaslo	Tarnow	hotel	Israel A.		M		
ENGLANDER		Solomon		Jaslo	Jaslo		Naphtali Sh		F	Chaim	
ENGLARD	Awrahm	cohen		Rymanow	Jaslo	wines			M		
ENGLARD	Rishka			Jaslo	Jaslo		Awraham		F		Palestine
FABIAN	Tuvia				Jaslo				M		died
FASS	Moshe			Jaslo	Jaslo	messenger			M		
FASS	A				Jaslo	barber			M		
FAUST	Naphtali			Jaslo	Jaslo				M		
FEBER	Chaim			Jaslo	Jaslo				M		
FEBER		Eintziger		Jaslo	Jaslo		Wolf		M	Chaim	
FEINCHEL	Moshe			Jaslo	Jaslo	haulage			M		
FEINCHEL	Yehezkel			Jaslo	Jaslo		Moshe		M		
FEINCHEL		Wekselbaum					Chaim		F	Yehezkel	
FEINCHEL	Yossef			Jaslo	Jaslo	paper			M		
FELDBRAND	Meir			Jaslo	Jaslo	skins			M		

List of Jews of Jaslo Prior and During World War II

Last name	First name	Maiden name	Birth date	Birth place	Residence	Trade or remarks	Father	Mother	Gen.	Groom	Disposition
FELDBRAND	Yossef			Jaslo	Jaslo	haberdashery			M		
FELDBRAND	Yekil			Jaslo	Jaslo	haberdashery			M		
FELLER	Awraham			Osiek	Jaslo	sardines			M		
FINDER	Eliezer			Jaslo	Jaslo	expeditor			M		
FINDLING	Awraham			Zilkow		farmer			M		shoa
FINDLING	Itzhak			Gorlice	Jaslo	socks			M		
FINK	P				Jaslo				M		
FISH	Ephraim			Jaslo	Jaslo	bakeries			M		
FISH	Shmuel			Hiclowka					M		killed
FISHBEIN	A.			Jaslo	Jaslo	binder			M		died
FLICK	Chaim			Koblow		real estate			M		
FORSHER	Yossef			Bobowa	Jaslo	shoe polish			M		
FORSHER		San		Jaslo	Jaslo		Mordechai		F		
FORSHTEHER	P				Jaslo	shoemaker			M		
FRANKEL	Shulem			Jaslo	Jaslo	tabacco			M		
FRANKEL	Yehoshua			Jaslo	Jaslo		Shulem		M		
FRANZBLAU	Wolf				Jaslo	haberdashery			M		died
FRANZBLAU	Yaakow			Jaslo	Germany		Wolf		M		
FRANZBLAU	Nathan			Jaslo			Wolf		M		
FRANZBLAU									M		died
FRANZBLAU	Itzhak			Jaslo	Jaslo	tailor			M		
FRANZBLAU	Israel			Jaslo	Jaslo				M		
FREI	Yerucham				Jaslo	bookeeper			M		
FREI	Shewach			Jaslo	Jaslo		Yerucham		M		
FREIFELD	Moshe Meir			Jaslo	Jaslo				M		
FREIFELD		Weil		Jaslo	Jaslo		Yaakow		F	Moshe Meir	
FREUND	Elmelech			Jaslo	Jaslo				M		shoa
FREUND	Bat Sheva			Jaslo	Jaslo		Elmelech		F		shoa
FREUND	Riwka			Jaslo	Jaslo		Elmelech		F		
FREUND	Ben Tzion			Jaslo	Jaslo	shoes	brother	of	M	Elimelech	
FREUND	Yaakow	Gorlice		Ulaszowice	Jaslo	innkeeper			M		survived
FREUND	Itzhak			Jaslo	Jaslo		Yaakow		M		
FREUND	Dawid			Jaslo	Jaslo		Yaakow		M		
FREUND	Israel			Gorlice	Jaslo				M		
FREUND		Freund		Jaslo	Jaslo		Yaakow		F	Israel	
FREUND	Israel			Jaslo	Jaslo				M		
FREUND		Getzler		Jaslo	Jaslo		Mordechai		F	Israel	
FREUND	Moshe Meir						Israel		M		
FRIEDMAN	Chaim Lipa				Jaslo	timber			M		
FRIEDMAN	Moshe			Jaslo	Jaslo				M		
FRIEDMAN	Yossef			Jaslo	Jaslo	grains			M		
FRIEDMAN	H.				Jaslo				M		

Last name	First name	Maiden name	Birth date	Birth place	Residence	Trade or remarks	Father	Mother	Gen.	Groom	Disposition
FRIEDMAN		Feinchel		Jaslo	Jaslo		Moshe		F	H.	
FRIEDRICH	Dawid			Gorlice	Jaslo				M		
FRIEDRICH				Jaslo	Jaslo		Dawid		M		
FRIEDRICH		Freund		Jaslo	Jaslo		Ben Tzion		F		
FRISH	Zinwel			Jaslo	Jaslo	crystal			M		
FRISH		Hollander		Jaslo	Jaslo		Abba		F	Zinwel	
FRIZNER	Lipa				Jaslo	hats			M		
FRUMOWICZ	Yossef				Jaslo	teacher			M		
FRUMOWICZ		Meller		Jaslo	Jaslo		Mendel		F	Yossef	survived
FRUMOWICZ	Naomi			Jaslo	Jaslo		Yossef		F		survived
FUHRER	Chaim			Jaslo	Jaslo				M		survived
FUHRER		Freund					Yaakow		F		killed
FURMAN	Dawid			Jaslo	Jaslo	umbrellas			M		died

Last name	First name	Maiden name	Birth date	Birth place	Residence	Trade or remarks	Father	Mother	Gen.	Groom	Disposition
GANGER	Baruch			Bobowa					M		
GANGER	Yehoshua			Jaslo	Jaslo		Baruch		M		USA
GANGER	Yossef			Jaslo	Jaslo		Yossef		M		
GANGER	Yehezkel			Jaslo	Jaslo		Yossef		M		
GANZ	Aaron Dawid			Jaslo	Jaslo	fish merchant			M		
GANZ	Naphtali			Jaslo	Jaslo	painter	Aaron Dawid		M		
GANZ	Israel			Jaslo	Jaslo		Aaron Dawid		M		
GANZ	Ita			Jaslo	Jaslo				F		
GELLER	Yehoshua			Jaslo	Jaslo	accountant			M		
GELLER	Tadzia			Jaslo	Jaslo		Yehoshua		F		died
GELT	Awraham			Jaroslaw	Jaslo				M		
GELT		Freund		Jaslo	Jaslo		Yaakow		F	Awraham	
GEMINDER	Shlomo			Jaslo	Jaslo				M		survived
GEMINDER	Arie			Jaslo	Jaslo		Shlomo		M		survived
GERBER	Dawid				Jaslo	baker			M		
GERNIK	family			Pszedmisce	Vienna						
GERTENBERG	Ignac			Jaslo	Jaslo	refinery			M		died
GETZLER	Mordechai			Zmigrod	Jaslo				M		
GETZLER	Dawid			Jaslo	Tarnow	herring	Mordechai		M		
GETZLER	Rima			Jaslo	Jaslo				F		
GETZLER	Yehoshua			Jaslo	Lemberg		Mordechai		M		
GETZLER	Wolf			Jaslo	Tarnow	paper	Mordechai		M		
GETZLER	Yossef			Jaslo	Jaslo				M		
GETZLER	Moshe Meir			Jaslo	Jaslo	talmudic lecturer	Mordechai		M		
GETZLER	Moshe Meir			Zmigrod	Jaslo	chocolate			M		died
GEWIRTZ	Nathan			Jaslo	Jaslo	teacher			M		USA
GINTZIG	Wolf			Gorlice	Jaslo				M		

List of Jews of Jaslo Prior and During World War II

Last name	First name	Maiden name	Birth date	Birth place	Residence	Trade or remarks	Father	Mother	Gen.	Groom	Disposition
GISSER	P.				Jaslo				M		died
GISSER	Eliezer			Jaslo	Jaslo				M		
GISSER				Jaslo	Jaslo				F	Eliezer	
GLAZMAN	Leibish			Jaslo	Jaslo	carpenter			M		
GLAZMAN	I			Jaslo	Jaslo				M		
GLEZER	Shimshon					teacher					
GLICHER	P.			Korczyna							
GLICHER		Stilman				widow	Shmuel		F	P.	
GOLD	Asher	Shames		Jaslo	Jaslo				M		
GOLDBLAT	Leibish				Jaslo				M		
GOLDBLAT		Brick		Jaslo	Jaslo		Ephraim		F	Chaim	
GOLDBLAT	Chaim			Siowniow					M		
GOLDFADEN	Itzhak Me			Jaslo	Jaslo				M		
GOLDFADEN	Nachman			Jaslo	Jaslo		Itzhak Me		M		survived
GOLDFINGER	Itzhak			Jaslo	Jaslo				M		USA
GOLDFINGER		Miller		Jaslo	Jaslo		Zelig		F	Itzhak	USA
GOLDFLUSS	Michael			Jaslo	Jaslo	flour mill			M		
GOLDMAN	Awraham			Jaslo	Jaslo				M		
GOLDMAN		Rubel		Jaslo	Jaslo				F	Awraham	
GOLDNER	Adolph				Jaslo	merchant			M		
GOLDSCHMIDT	Moshe Nat			Jaslo	Jaslo	choir			M		
GOLDSCHMIDT	Tzwi Hersh			Jaslo	Jaslo	brooms			M		
GOLDSCHMIDT	Israel			Jaslo	Budapest		Tzwi Hersh		M		killed
GOLDSCHMIDT	Moshe			Jaslo	Jaslo		Tzwi Hersh		M		Palestine
GOLDSCHMIDT	Esther			Jaslo	Jaslo		Tzwi Hersh		F		USA
GOLDSHLAG	Wolf			Jaslo	Jaslo	refinery			M		
GOLDSHLAG	Maurice			Jaslo	Jaslo	salesman			M		
GOLDSTEIN	Elimelech			Dembice	Jaslo	real estate			M		
GOLDSTEIN	Benyamin			Jaslo	Jaslo	saw mill	Elimelech		M		
GOLDSTEIN	Yossef				Jaslo		Elimelech		M		
GORGAL	Mendel			Jaslo	Jaslo		adopted by		M	Ditenfast	died
GORGAL		Maltz		Jaslo	Jaslo		Nute		F	Mendel	
GORGAL	Yerucham			Jaslo	Jaslo				M		
GORGAL	Shamai			Jaslo	Jaslo				M		
GORGEL	Mendel			Jaslo	Jaslo	soap			M		died
GORGEL	Yerucham			Jaslo	Jaslo		Mendel		M		
GORGEL	Shamai			Jaslo	Jaslo	dentist	Mendel		M		USA
GORLITZER	Yudil			Gorlice	Jaslo	teacher			M		
GOTTLIEB	S.				Jaslo	lawyer			M		
GOTTLIEB	Zalmen								M		
GOTTLIEB	Rosentzweig	Eintziger				widow	Wolf		F	Zalmen	
GRABSHRIFT	Yaakow				Jaslo	timber			M		
GRABSHRIFT	Herman			Jaslo	Jaslo		dentist		M		

Last name	First name	Maiden name	Birth date	Birth place	Residence	Trade or remarks	Father	Mother	Gen.	Groom	Disposition
GRIN	Dawid			Gorlice	Jaslo				M		
GRINFELD	Yossef			Dukla	Jaslo	tailor			M		
GRINFELD	Yehoshua			Jaslo	Jaslo				M		
GRINFELD		Kalb		Jaslo	Jaslo		Yekil		M	Yehoshua	
GRINSHPAN	Tzwi Hersh			Jaslo	Jaslo				M		
GROSS	Mendel				Jaslo	kitchenware			M		
GROSS	Leib	Leon			Jaslo				M		
GROSS		Grabshrift		Jaslo	Jaslo		Yaakow		F	Leib	
GROSSMAN	I			Jaslo	Jaslo				M		survived
GROSSMAN		Freund		Jaslo	Jaslo		Elimelech		F	I	survived
GRUBTUCH	Yaakow			Tarnow	Jaslo	engineer			M		
GRUBTUCH		Kinstler		Jaslo	Jaslo		Mendel		F	Yaakow	
GUTMAN	Yeshua			Jaslo	Jaslo				M		
GUTMAN		Wagshall		Jaslo	Jaslo		Zeew		F	Yeshua	
GUTTERFREUND									M		
GUTTERFREUND	Yehoshua				Jaslo	salesman			M		
GUTTERFREUND	Chaim				Jaslo				M		
GUTTERFREUND		Citronenbaum			Jaslo		Liba		F		
GUTWIN	Dawid			Jaslo	Krakow	accountant			M		survived
GUTWIN	Yehoshua			Jaslo	Jaslo				M		
GUTWIN		Berger		Jaslo	Jaslo		Shlomo		F	Yehoshua	
GUTWIN	Elimelech			Omiszic	Jaslo	innkeeper			M		
GUTWIN	Towa			Omiszic	Jaslo				F	Elimelech	USA
GUTWIN	Awraham			Jaslo			Elimelech	Towa	M		
GUTWIN	Shmuel Leib			Jaslo	Zmigroddayan		Elimelech	Towa	M		Palestine
GUTWIN	Eliezer			Jaslo	Jaslo		Elimelech	Towa	M		
GUTWIN	Nathan			Jaslo	Jaslo	workshop	Elimelech	Towa	M		
GUTWIN	Tzirel			Jaslo	Krakow		Elimelech	Towa	F		
GUTWIN	Nechi			Jaslo	Jaslo		Elimelech	Towa	F		
GUTWIN	Gad Asher			Korczyna	Jaslo				M		
GUTWIN	Sarah	Rozner			Jaslo		Nathan		F	Gad Asher	shoa
GUTWIN	Moshe Nath			Korczyna	Jaslo		Gad Ash		M		shoa
GUTWIN	Gitche				Jaslo				F	Moshe Nath	
GUTWIN	Dudel			Jaslo	Jaslo		Moshe Nath	Gitche	M		
GUTWIN	Tzirel			Jaslo	Jaslo		Moshe Nath	Gitche	F		
GUTWIRT	Ben Tzion				Jaslo	talmudist			M		
GUTWIRT	Frida Lea	Bikower					Elimelech		F	Ben Tzion	
HABER	Moshe	Moshali		Jaslo	Jaslo	tailor			M		
HABER	Israel				Jaslo	builder			M		survived
HABER	Itzhak			Jaslo	Jaslo		Israel		M		survived
HAGEL	Hersh Chaim			Jaslo	Jaslo				M		
HAGEL	Dow			Jaslo	Jaslo		Hersh Chaim		M		

List of Jews of Jaslo Prior and During World War II

Last name	First name	Maiden name	Birth date	Birth place	Residence	Trade or remarks	Father	Mother	Gen.	Groom	Disposition
HAGEL	Mordechai			Jaslo	Jaslo		Hersh Chaim		M		
HAGEL	Baruch			Jaslo	Jaslo		Hersh Chaim		M		
HAGEL	Sheindil			Jaslo	Jaslo		Hersh Chaim		F		
HAKATAM	Shlomole				Jaslo	books			M		
HALBERSHTAM	David			Jaslo	Dobri	rabbi			M	Rachelci	
HALBERSHTAM	Awraham Chaim			Jaslo	Dobri		David	Rachel	M		
HALBERSHTAM	Tziporah			Jaslo	Dobri		David	Rachel	F		died
HALBERSHTAM	Sinai			Zmigrod	Jaslo	Zmigroder Rabbi			M		
HASS	Leibish				Jaslo				M		
HAUER	Eliezer			Jaslo	Jaslo				M		
HAZELNUSS	Elisha			Jaslo	Jaslo	shoemaker			M		
HECHT	Rachel						Elimelech	Sheindel	F	Samuel	
HECHT	Lea		1931	Bielsko	Jaslo		Shmuel	Rachel	F		
HEFNER	Israel			Tarnowca	Jaslo				M		
HEFNER	Awraham			Jaslo	Jaslo		Israel		M		
HELLER	Mordechai			Jaslo	Jaslo	horse traders			M		died
HELLER	Yaakow			Jaslo	Jaslo	horse traders			M		died
HELLER	A					hats			M		
HELMAN	Dawid			Jaslo	Jaslo	innkeeper			M		died
HELMAN		Korzenik		Jaslo	Jaslo				F	Dawid	
HEMEL	Dawid			Jaslo	Jaslo	grocery			M		
HENDLER	Israel					innkeeper			M		
HERBST	Hannah	widow			Jaslo	fish merchant			F		
HERTZ	Manes			Jaslo	Jaslo	wines			M		
HERTZ	Israel					shoemaker			M		
HERTZIG	Yaakow			Jaslo	Jaslo	attorney			M		survived
HESS	Dawid			Jaslo	Jaslo				M		
HESS	Leibish			Jaslo	Jaslo				M		
HESS	Shlomo Zal			Jaslo	Jaslo		Leibish		M		
HESS	Eli			Jaslo	Jaslo	brother	Leibish		M		
HESS	Itzhak			Jaslo	Jaslo		Eli		M		Palestine
HILLER	Shlomo			Topolina	Jaslo	innkeeper			M		died
HILPERIN	Menachem Men			Dukla	Jaslo	Dukler Rabbi			M		
HILPERIN	Yoel			Dubshitz	Dubshitz		Menachem M		M		survived
HIRSH	Awraham				Jaslo	beadle			M		
HIRSH	Kalman			Mielec	Jaslo				M		
HIRSH	Riwka			Jaslo	Jaslo		Kalman		F		Palestine
HIRSHFELD	Yaakow			Sandz	Jaslo	beadle			M		
HIRSHFELD		Lipczer		Jaslo	Jaslo		Dawid		F		
HIRSHFELD	Chaim			Jaslo	Jaslo		Yaakow		M		

Last name	First name	Maiden name	Birth date	Birth place	Residence	Trade or remarks	Father	Mother	Gen.	Groom	Disposition
HIRSHFELD		Lipcer		Jaslo	Jaslo		Chaim		F	Chaim	
HIRSHFELD	Zelka			Jaslo	Jaslo		Yaakow		M		USA
HIRSHFELD	Yehoshua			Jaslo	Jaslo		Yaakow		M		USA
HIRSHKOWIC	Ben Tzion								M		
HIRSHKOWIC		Shemesh					Asher		F	Ben Tzion	
HOFFERT	Miriam			Jaslo	Jaslo	doctor			F		survived
HOFFERT	Naphtali				Jaslo	seltzer			M		
HOFFERT		Miller		Jaslo	Jaslo		Zelig		F	Naphtali	
HOFFERT	Miriam			Jaslo	Jaslo	doctor	Naphtali		F		survived
HOFFERT	Awraham			Jaslo	Jaslo		Naphtali		M		survived
HOFFERT	Hawa	Jeramish		Jaslo	Jaslo		Moshe Yak		F	Awraham	
HOFFERT	Haya			Jaslo	Jaslo		Naphtali		F		
HOFFERT	Shlomit			Jaslo	Jaslo		Naphtali		F		
HOFFERT	Chaim			Rozwadow	Jaslo				M		
HOFFERT		Hollander		Jaslo	Jaslo		Abba		F	Chaim	
HOFFMAN	Akiva			Buczac	Jaslo	teacher			M		died
HOFFMAN	Eliezer				Jaslo	teacher			M		
HOLLANDER	Abba			Jaslo	Jaslo	eggs			M		
HOLLANDER	Leibish			Jaslo	Jaslo		Abba		M		
HOLLANDER	Yehezkel			Jaslo	Jaslo		Abba		M		
HOLLANDER	Moshe			Jaslo	Jaslo		Abba		M		survived
HOLLANDER	Shimon			Jaslo	Jaslo		Abba		M		survived
HOLOSHITZER	Yossef			Jaslo	Jaslo	webber			M		
HOLOSHITZER	Nehema			Jaslo	Jaslo			Hadassah	F	Yossef	
HOLOSHITZER	Matil			Jaslo	Jaslo		Yossef	Nehema	F		Palestine
HOLOSHITZER	Hannah			Jaslo	Jaslo		Yossef	Nehema	F		Palestine
HOLOSHITZER	Yehzkel			Jaslo	Jaslo		Yossef	Nehema	M		survived
HOROWITZ	David				Jaslo				M		
HOROWITZ	Sara				Jaslo				F		
HOROWITZ	David	Dudil		Jaslo	Mielec				M	Pessia	
HOROWITZ	Sarah				Israel		David	Pessia	F		
HOROWITZ	Yehoshua			Jaslo	Jaslo	talmudist	Yoel		M		USA
HOROWITZ	Yoel				Jaslo				M		
HOROWITZ	Yehoshua			Jaslo	Jaslo	talmudist	Yoel		M		
HOROWITZ	Bila			Jaslo	Jaslo		Yoel		M		
IGLER	Israel				Jaslo				M		
INFELD	Bracha				Jaslo				F		
INGBER	Awrahm			Jaslo	Jaslo	teacher			M		
INGBER	Moniek			Jaslo	Jaslo		Awrahm	Bela	M		survived
INGBER	Bronka			Jaslo	Jaslo				F		survived
IRMIJASH	Moshe Ya			Jasinic	Jaslo				M		
IRMIJASH	Berl			Jaslo	Jaslo		Moshe Ya		M		
JRMIJASH	Nachman			Jaslo	Jaslo		Moshe Ya		M		survived
ITZHAKOWICZ	Mordechai			Jaslo	Jaslo				M		

List of Jews of Jaslo Prior and During World War II

Last name	First name	Maiden name	Birth date	Birth place	Reside nce	Trade or remarks	Father	Mother	Gen.	Groom	Disposition
JAKUBOWICZ	Elimelech				Jaslo	grocery			M		
JAKUBOWICZ					Jaslo				M		
JAKUBOWICZ	Shmuel	Hankowker			Jaslo	milk			M		
JAKUBOWICZ	Zalman				Jaslo				M		
JERACHMIEL	Bela				Jaslo				F		
JIMNER	Naphtali			Jaslo	Jaslo				M		survived
JOHANS	Unk			Gorlice	Jaslo				M		shoa
JOHANS	Dina			Gorlice	Jaslo				F	Unk	shoa
JOHANS	Eliyahu			Gorlice	Jaslo	rabbi	Unk	Dina	M		survived
JOHANS	Dow			Gorlice	Jaslo		Unk	Dina	M		
JURTNER	A.			Jaslo	Jaslo				F		died
JUST	Dow Berish			Zmigrod					M		
JUST	Israel			Zmigrod	Jaslo	teacher	Dow Ber		M		survived
JUST	Baruch			Jaslo	Jaslo				M		
JUST	Berish			Jaslo	Jaslo		Baruch		M		
JUST	Israel			Jaslo	Jaslo		Baruch		M		survived
JUST	Alter			Jaslo	Jaslo		Israel		M		
JUST	Dawid	Tzutzenbaum			Jaslo	shoes			M		survived
JUST		Freund		Jaslo	Jaslo		Elimelech		F		survived
JUST	Yaakow			Jaslo	Jaslo		Dawid		M		
KACZKOWSKI	Simcha			Jaslo	Jaslo	barber			M		
KACZKOWSKI	Gustaw			Jaslo	Jaslo	teacher	Simcha		M		
KACZKOWSKI	Adolph			Jaslo	Jaslo	attorney	Simcha		M		
KALB	Yaakow			Jaslo	Jaslo				M		
KALB	Leibish			Jaslo	Jaslo		Yaakow		M		
KALB	Zishe			Jaslo	Jaslo	knitting	Yaakow		M		
KALB	Zalman			Jaslo	Jaslo				M		
KALB	Yossef			Jaslo	Jaslo		Zalman		M		
KALB	Moshe			Jaslo	Jaslo				M		died
KALB		Miller		Jaslo	Jaslo		Zelig		F	Moshe	USA
KALB	Motel			Jaslo	Jaslo		Moshe		M		USA
KALB	Tanchum			Jaslo	Jaslo		Moshe		M		USA
KALTER	Israel			Jaslo	Jaslo				M		
KANARIK	Zelka			Dukla	Jaslo				M		died
KANNENGISSER	Dawid				Jaslo				M		
KANNENGISSER		Rapaport		Jaslo	Jaslo		Yossef	Pearl	F	Dawid	
KANNER	Eliezer			Jaslo	Jaslo				F		
KANNER	Moshe			Jaslo	Krakow	finances			M		
KAPELNER	Cyla				Jaslo				F		
KAPLAN	P.			Sidlowca	Jaslo	shoemaker			M		
KAPLANER	L.				Jaslo				M		
KARP	Michael			Jaslo	Jaslo				M		
KARP	Moti				Jaslo				M		
KARP		Rubel			Jaslo		Itzxhak Yeh		F	Moti	

Last name	First name	Maiden name	Birth date	Birth place	Residence	Trade or remarks	Father	Mother	Gen.	Groom	Disposition
KARP	Dawid			Jaslo	Jaslo	shipper			M		
KARP		Margolies		Jaslo	Jaslo		Moshe		F	Dawid	
KARP	Beni				Jaslo				M		
KARP	Mordechai			Ulanow	Jaslo	timber			M		died
KARP	Yossef			Jaslo		lawyer	Mordechai		M		survived
KARP	Lonek			Jaslo			Mordechai		M		Palestine
KARP	Yehiel			Jaslo			Mordechai		M		shoa
KARP	Moshe	Mundek		Jaslo		lawyer	Mordechai		M		survived
KATZ	Brothers			Jaslo					M		
KATZ	Bracha			Jaslo	Jaslo				F		survived
KATZ	Mattityahu			Jaslo					M		died
KATZ	Simcha			Jaslo	Jaslo		Mattityahu		M		USA
KATZ	Benyamin			Jaslo	Jaslo		Mattityahu		M		USA
KAUFMAN		Tzimet		Jaslo	Jaslo		Leib		F		
KELLER	Mendel		1898				Hersh	Tzila	M		
KELLER	Sava			Jaslo	Jaslo				F	Naphtali	
KEMNITZER	Kopil	Hans		Jaslo	Jaslo				M		
KEMNITZER		Berger		Jaslo	Jaslo		Shlomo		F	Kopil	
KESSLER	Israel			Jaslo	Jaslo				M		
KIEHL	Eliezer			Jaslo	Jaslo	flour			M		
KIEHL	Beril			Jaslo	Jaslo	flour	Eliezer		M		
KILLIG	Moshe			Jaslo	Jaslo				M		
KILLIG	Alter			Jaslo	Jaslo		Moshe		M		
KILLIG	Avigdor			Jaslo	Jaslo		Moshe		M		
KINSTLER	Leibish			Zmigrod	Jaslo	grains			M		
KINSTLER	Mendil			Zmigrod	Jaslo	grocery			M		
KINSTLER	Kalman			Jaslo	Jaslo		Mendil		M		survived
KINSTLER	Awraham			Jaslo	Jaslo		Mendil		M		survived
KINSTLER	Leiwick			Jaslo	Jaslo		Mendil		M		shoa
KIPPEL	Yehoshua			Jaslo	Jaslo				M		
KIPPEL	Ester			Jaslo	Jaslo				F		
KIRSH	Moshe			Kobalow	Pilzno	grains			M		
KIRSH	Feiwil			Jaslo	Jaslo		Moshe		M		survived
KIRSCHNER	Yossef						Samuel	Rachel	M		
KIZELSTEIN	Chaim Zeew			Krosno					M		survived
KIZELSTEIN	Emalia	Johans		Gorlice	Jaslo		Unk	Dina	F		survived
KLAR	Feige		1885		Jaslo				F		
KLAUSNER	Berish			Jaslo	Jaslo	furniture			M		USA
KLAUSNER	Adolph			Jaslo					M		shoa
KLAUSNER	FAMILY										USA
KLAUZNER	Gittel								F	Nathan	
KLEIN									M		
KLEIN	Yehoshua			Jaslo	Jaslo	timber			M		
KLEIN	Klara			Jaslo	Jaslo				F		

List of Jews of Jaslo Prior and During World War II

Last name	First name	Maiden name	Birth date	Birth place	Residence	Trade or remarks	Father	Mother	Gen.	Groom	Disposition
KLEINBERG	Peretz			Gorlice	Jaslo	kitchenware			M		
KLEINBERG	Baruch			Jaslo	Jaslo		Peretz		M		
KLEINBERG	Kalman			Jaslo	Jaslo		Peretz		M		
KLEINBERG	rIWKA			Jaslo	Jaslo		Peretz		F		
KLEINBERG	Pesha			Jaslo	Jaslo		Peretz		F		
KLEINMAN	Feivel			Sandz	Jaslo				M		
KLEINMAN		Thaler					Elimelech		F	Feivel	
KLEINMAN	Nathanael			Jaslo	Jaslo				M		
KLEINMAN		Wilner		Jaslo	Jaslo		Israel		F	Nathanael	
KLEINMAN	Reuven			Jaslo	Jaslo				M		
KLEINMAN		Bodner		Jaslo	Jaslo		Judel		F	Reuven	
KLEINMAN	Nathanel L.				Jaslo				M		
KNOBLOCH	Shmuel				Jaslo				M		
KNOBLOCH	Reizel		1897	Jaslo	Jaslo				F	Aaron	
KNOBLOCH	Moshe			Jaslo	Jaslo		Shmuel		M		
KNOBLOCH	Israel Itz			Jaslo	Jaslo		Shmuel		M		
KNOBLOCH	Dawid			Jaslo	Jaslo		Shmuel		M		survived
KOLBER	Tzwi			Jaslo	Jaslo				M		
KOLLER	Widow				Jaslo				F		
KORMAN	Lea		1921	Jaslo	Jaslo				F		
KORMAN	Lea		1921	Jaslo	Jaslo				F	Yekutiel Ze	
KORMAN	Gershon			Jaslo	Jaslo		Yekutiel Ze	Lea	M		survived
KORMAN	Mordechai			Jaslo	Jaslo		Yekutiel Ze	Lea	M		
KORMAN	Yakow Wolf				Jaslo		Mordechai	Beila	M		
KORMAN	Awraham				Jaslo	jeweller	Yekutiel Ze		M		survived
KORMAN		Maisel			Jaslo		Ben Tzion		F	Awraham	
KORN	Chaim			Jaslo	Jaslo	hotel			M		
KORN	Chaim			Jaslo	Jaslo	hotel	Chaim		M		
KORN	Dawid Eli			Jaslo	Jaslo		Chaim		M		
KORN	Lea		1923	Jaslo	Jaslo		Shmuel	Basia	F		
KORNBLIT	Mrs			Jaslo	Jaslo	kiosk			F		
KORNBLIT	Elisha			Jaslo	Jaslo			Mrs	M		
KORNFELD	Wolf				Jaslo	kehilla president			M		
KORNFELD	Dawid Her			Jaslo	Jaslo	finances			M		
KORNFELD	Wolf			Jaslo	Jaslo	real estate	Dawid Her		M		
KORNFELD	Salo			Jaslo	Jaslo		Wolf		M		
KORNFELD	Bernard			Jaslo	Jaslo	finances	Dawid Her		M		died
KORNHAUSER	Awraham				Jaslo	lawyer			M		shoa
KORNMEHL	E.				Jaslo	doctor			M		survived
KORNMEHL		Karp			Jaslo	doctor	Mordechai		M		survived
KORNREICH	Israel Meir			Jaslo	Jaslo	spirits			M		
KORNREICH	Moshe			Jaslo	Jaslo	spirits	Israel Meir		M		

Last name	First name	Maiden name	Birth date	Birth place	Residence	Trade or remarks	Father	Mother	Gen.	Groom	Disposition
	Hersh										
KORZENIK	Yehiel			Jaslo	Jaslo	eggs			M		
KORZENIK	Shlomo			Jaslo	Jaslo	clothing			M		
KORZENIK	Eliezer			Jaslo	Jaslo				M		
KORZENIK	Hersh			Jaslo	Jaslo	baker			M		
KORZENIK	Pessel			Jaslo	Jaslo				F	Elimelech	
KORZENIK	Zelig			Jaslo	Jaslo	baker	Elimelech	Pessel	M		
KORZENIK	Moshe		1905	Jaslo	Jaslo	clothing	Zelig		M		
KRAMER	Benyamin				Jaslo	wheat merchant			M		died
KRAMER	Henech				Jaslo		Benyamin		M		died
KRAMER	Samek				Jaslo		Benyamin		M		died
KRAMER	Naptali				Jaslo	food wholesale			M		
KRANTZ	Moshe			Jaslo	Jaslo	shoemaker			M		
KRAUT	Lea			Jaslo	Jaslo		Eliezer	Ester	F		
KREBS	Dawid			Jaslo	Jaslo	baker			M		
KREBS	Roda			Jaslo	Jaslo				F	Dawid	
KREBS	Moshe			Zmigrod	Jaslo	grains			M		
KRIGER	Lea			Jaslo	Jaslo				F		
KRISHER	Sarah		1915	Jaslo	Jaslo		Yoel	Sheindel	F		
KRISHER	Fishel				Jaslo	Rabbi			M		
KRISHER	Yehoshua			Jaslo	Jaslo				M		
KRISHER	Benyamin			Jaslo	Jaslo		Yehoshua		M		
KRISHER	Motek			Jaslo	Jaslo		Yehoshua		M		
KRISHER	Ephraim Fishel			Jaslo	Jaslo		Yehoshua		M		survived
KRISHER	Yoel			Jaslo	Jaslo	toys			M		Palestine
KRISHER	Yoel			Jaslo	Jaslo	engineer	Yoel		M		
KRISHER	Elimelech			Jaslo	Jaslo	haberdashery			M		
KRISHER	Fishel			Jaslo	Jaslo	rabbi			M		
KRISHER	Itche			Jaslo	Jaslo				M		
KRISHER		Citronenbaum					Mordechai		F		died
KRISHER	Yossel			Jaslo	Jaslo		Yaakow Pinh	Sara Lea	M		
KRISHER	Chaim				Jaslo		Yaakow Pinh	Sara Lea	M		
KRISHER	Hersh				Jaslo		Chaim		M		
KRISHER	Shlomo			Jaslo	Jaslo		Chaim		M		survived
KRISHER	Miriam	Korman		Jaslo	Jaslo				F	Shlomo	
KRISHER	Yossel			Jaslo	Jaslo		Yaakow Pinh	Sara Lea	M		
KRISHER	Benyamin			Jaslo	Jaslo		Yaakow Pinh	Sara Lea	M		
KRIZWIRTH	Dawid			Jaslo	Jaslo	timber			M		
KRIZWIRTH	Betzalel			Jaslo	Jaslo	timber	Dawid		M		
KRIZWIRTH	Beril			Jaslo	Jaslo	finances	Betzalel		M		

List of Jews of Jaslo Prior and During World War II

Last name	First name	Maiden name	Birth date	Birth place	Residence	Trade or remarks	Father	Mother	Gen.	Groom	Disposition
KRONENTAL	Emanuel			Bezon	Jaslo				M		
KRONENTAL		Berger		Jaslo	Jaslo		Shlomo		F	Emanuel	
KRUPKI	Itzhak Leib			Jaslo	Jaslo	fruits			M		
KUFLICK	Betzalel Mor			Istrik	Jaslo	grocery			M		died
KUFLICK	Awraham Ye			Jaslo	Jaslo				M		survived
KUFLICK	Dwora			Jaslo	Jaslo				F		shoa
KUFLICK	Yossef			Jaslo	Jaslo				M		
KUPERBERG	Rachel			Jaslo	Jaslo				F		
KUNST	Shulem								M		
KUNST		Eintziger					Zeev Wol		F	Shulem	
KURTZWEIL	Yossel				Jaslo	cantor			M		USA
KUTZ	P.			Jaslo	Jaslo	movie house			M		

* Notes from Estelle Guzik:

NATHAN & MECHEL GUZIK were my uncles. Henia was Mechel's wife and also his first cousin. Her maiden name was also GUZIK. Their daughter was the MASHA above. They also had a son TOBJASZ (Tovia AKA TOSHAK) who was born in 1933 and was a victim of the Holocaust together with his sister and parents. Other members of the GUZIK family in Jaslo pre- and during the war were: ELAZER YEHUDA aka LAZAR GUZIK (my grandfather) and my aunt LOLA (aka Leah). Both were taken from Jaslo and were murdered in Belzec CC. My grandmother was MASHA LANDESMAN GUZIK. She died in 1927 in an accident in Jaslo. Just for the record, Nathan & Mechel were born in Uliniza (not far from Jaslo, but not in Jaslo). Lola was born in Jaslo. And Henia was born in Strzyzow. Their children, Masha and Tobjasz were born in Jaslo.
LAZAR was in Forestry. LAZAR's parents were CHAIM GUZIK & JACHET FINKEL.
MECHEL had a cattle business.

List of Jews of Jaslo Prior and During World War II

Last name	First name	Maiden name	Birth date	Birth place	Residence	Trade or remarks	Father	Mother	Gen.	Groom	Disposition

Last name	First name	Maiden name	Birth date	Birth place	Residence	Trade or remarks	Father	Mother	Gen.	Groom	Disposition
LAMBIK	Eliezer			Jaslo	Jaslo				M		died
LAMBIK	Mrs.				Jaslo	social work			F	Eliezer	
LAMPEL	Yehoshua			Jaslo	Jaslo				M		
LAMPEL		Eintziger		Jaslo	Jaslo		Zeev Wolf		F	Yehoshua	
LANG	Baruch			Jaslo	Jaslo				M		
LANGSAM	Tzwi Hersh			Jaslo	Jaslo				M		
LANGSAM	Sheindel			Jaslo	Jaslo		Melech	Miriam	F		
LANS	Yossef				Jaslo	doctor			M		
LAUFER	P			Jaslo	Jaslo	timber			M		
LAUFER		Hess		Jaslo	Jaslo		Eli		F	P	
LEFFELHOLTZ	Gedalya			Dukla	Jaslo				M		
LEFFELHOLTZ		Gutwin		Jaslo	Jaslo		Elimelech		F		
LEHR	Shmuel			Jaslo	Jaslo	furrier			M		
LEHR	Moshe			Jaslo	Jaslo		Shmuel		M		
LEHR	Eliyahu			Jaslo	Jaslo	furrier	Shmuel		M		
LEWY	Lea			Brzezow	Jaslo		Meir		F		
LICHT	Yossef			Jaslo	Jaslo	haberdashery			M		
LIEBERMAN	Issarchar D			Toporow	Boukhara				M	Rosa	
LIEBERMAN	Yehoshua Heshil				Jaslo		Dov Issa	Rosa	M		
LIPCZER	Dawid			Jaslo	Jaslo	baker			M		
LIPCZER	Itche			Jaslo	Jaslo		Dawid		M		
LIPCZER	Moshe Hersh			Jaslo	Jaslo		Dawid		M		
LIPCZER	Betzalel			Jaslo	Jaslo	baker	Dawid		M		
LIPCZER		Felderbrand		Jaslo	Jaslo		Meir		F	Betzalel	
LIPCZER	Yehoshua			Jaslo	Jaslo	brother	Dawid	Lipiczer	M		
LIPCZER	Meir			Jaslo	Jaslo		Yehoshua		M		
MAGER	P				Jaslo				M		died
MAHLER	Naphtali				Jaslo				M		
MAISEL	Ben Tzion			Jaslo	Leiptzig				M		
MALTZ	Shlomo			Jaslo	Jaslo				M		
MALTZ	Nute				Jaslo	cattle			M		
MALTZ	daughter				Jaslo	social work	Nute		F		
MALTZ	Zelig	Tarnowica			Jaslo		Zelig		M		
MALTZ	Shlomo	Tarnowica			Jaslo				M		
MANDEL	Shmuel				Jaslo				M		
MANDEL	Dawid			Jaslo	Jaslo				M		
MANDEL	Shlomo			Jaslo	Jaslo	baker	Dawid		M		
MANDEL	Yehezkel			Jaslo	Jaslo	baker	Dawid		M		
MANDEL	Regina	Gabel		Jaslo	Jaslo				F	Yehezkel	
MANDIL	Menachem			Jaslo	Jaslo	rabbi			M		

List of Jews of Jaslo Prior and During World War II

Last name	First name	Maiden name	Birth date	Birth place	Residence	Trade or remarks	Father	Mother	Gen.	Groom	Disposition
MANDIL	Yona			Jaslo	Jaslo		Menachem	Primitel	M		
MANDIL	Chaim			Jaslo	Jaslo		Yona		M		
MANDIL	Awraham Yeho			Jaslo	Jerusalem		Yona		M		survived
MARGOLIES	Yoseph		1917	Jaslo	Jaslo				M		
MARGOLIES	Moshe			Jaslo	Jaslo				M		USA
MARGOLIES		Miller		Jaslo	Jaslo		Zelig		F	Moshe	USA
MARGOLIES	Hersh			Jaslo	Jaslo		Moshe		M		USA
MARGOLIES	Abba			Trzycic	Jaslo	innkeeper			M		
MARGOLIES	Dawid			Jaslo	Jaslo		Abba		M		killed
MARGOLIES	Baruch			Trzycic	Jaslo	timber			M		
MARGOLIES		Kornreich		Jaslo	Jaslo				F	Baruch	
MARGOLIES	Nathan			Jaslo	Jaslo		Baruch		M		
MARGOLIES		Margolies		Jaslo	Jaslo		Abcze		F	Nathan	
MARGOLIES	Yoel			Trzycic	Jaslo	paper			M		died
MARGOLIES		Klinman		Jaslo	Jaslo		Feiwil		F	Yoel	
MARGOLIES	Menashe			Jaslo	Jaslo				M		died
MARGOLIES	Adolph			Jaslo	Jaslo		Menashe		M		
MARGOLIES	Moshe				Jaslo	barber			M		died
MARGOLIES	Moshe			Jaslo	Jaslo	timber			M		USA
MARGOLIES	Hawa Rach			Jaslo	Jaslo				F	Moshe	
MARGOLIES	Hersh			Jaslo	Jaslo		Moshe	Hawa Rach	M		
MARGOLIES		Altman		Jaslo	Jaslo		Berish		F	Hersh	
MARGOLIES	Sender			Jaslo	Jaslo		Moshe	Hawa Rach	M		died
MARGOLIES	Abtcze								M		
MARGOLIES	Dawid						Abtcze		M		
MARGOLIES	Rachel			Jaslo	Jaslo	property			F		
MARGOLIES	Pinhas			Jaslo	Jaslo				M		
MARKOWICZ	Lewi			Jaslo	Jaslo				F		shoa
MATA	Shimon				Jaslo	doctor			M		
MATA	Yossef			Jaslo	Jaslo				M		
MATA		Wagshall		Jaslo	Jaslo		Zeew		F	Yossef	
MAY	Israel			Jaslo	Jaslo				M		
MAY		Korman		Jaslo	Jaslo		Yekutiel Ze		F	Israel	
MEIR	Berish			Jaslo	Jaslo	slaughterer			M		
MELAMED	Israel				Jaslo	teacher			M		
MELAMED	Nathan				Jaslo	teacher			M		
MELAMED	Baruch				Jaslo	teacher			M		
MELAMED	Yudel				Jaslo	teacher			M		
MELAMED	Shimshon				Jaslo	teacher			M		
MELLER	Yossef			Jaslo	Jaslo	cattle			M		
MELLER	Hersh			Brzerzow	Jaslo	tailor			M		
MELLER	Berish	Kimchi Dov			Jaslo				M		Israel
MELLER	Mendel			Jaslo	Jaslo	leather			M		shoa

Last name	First name	Maiden name	Birth date	Birth place	Residence	Trade or remarks	Father	Mother	Gen.	Groom	Disposition
MELLER	Awraham			Jaslo	Jaslo		Mendel		M		
MELLER	Elimelech			Jaslo	Jaslo		Awraham		M		survived
MELLON	Saba		1911		Jaslo				M		
MENASHE	Yossef			Tarnow	Jaslo	clothing			M		
MENASHE	Awraham			Jaslo	Jaslo	attorney	Yossef		M		
MENASHE	Naphtali			Jaslo	Jaslo	attorney	Yossef		M		
MENASHE		Tzucker		Jaslo	Jaslo		Alter		F		shoa
MENASHE	Zigmunt			Jaslo	Jaslo	engineer	Yossef		M		shoa
MENASHE	Michael			Jaslo	Jaslo	attorney	Yossef		M		
MENASHE	Hanka			Jaslo	Jaslo		Yossef		F		
MENASHE-KAGAN	Gizelle			Jaslo	Jaslo	pharmacist	Yossef		F		
MILLER	Chaja		1925	Jaslo	Jaslo				F		
MILLER	Mooscha		1890	Jaslo	Jaslo				M		
MILLER	Zelig				Jaslo	slaughterer			M		
MILLER							Zelig		F		
MILLER	Moshe			Jaslo	Jaslo		Zelig		M		died
MILLER	Mishket			Jaslo	Jaslo				F	Moshe	
MILLER	Shmuel			Jaslo	Jaslo		Moshe	Mishket	M		
MILLER	Gedalya			Jaslo	Jaslo		Moshe	Mishket	M		
MILLER	Yaakow			Jaslo	Tarnow		Moshe	Mishket	M		
MILLER	Eliezer			Jaslo	Jaslo		Moshe	Mishket	M		
MILLER	Yehezkel			Jaslo			Moshe	Mishket	M		
MILLER	Chaim			Jaslo	Jaslo		Zelig		M		
MILLER	Pinhas			Jaslo	Jaslo		Zelig		M		
MILLER	Yaakov				Jaslo				M		
MILLER	Moshe			Jaslo	Jaslo				M		
MILLER	Henia			Jaslo	Jaslo				F		
MILLER	Frida			Jaslo	Jaslo				F		
MINTZ	Moshe			Jaslo	Vienna				M		
MOLDAUER	Nachijm		1897	Jaslo	Jaslo				M		
MOLDAUER	Eisik			Jaslo	Jaslo	factory			M		
MOLDAUER		Winfeld		Jaslo	Jaslo		Leibish		F		
MUSHEL	Meir			Jaslo	Jaslo	habedash			M		shoa
MUSHEL	Chaya	Tzimet		Jaslo	Jaslo		Moshe	Lea	F	Meir	shoa
NAGLER	P			Jaslo	Jaslo				M		shoa
NAMER	Dow			Jaslo	Jaslo	clerk			M		died
NEBENTZAHL	Leibish			Koloczyce	Jaslo				M		
NEUMAN	Abish				Jaslo	cantor			M		
NEUMAN	Yehiel				Jaslo				M		
NIRENBERG	Elimelech			Jaslo	Jaslo				M		
NIWRET	Moshe				Jaslo	cattle			M		survived
NUSSBAUM	Yossef L.			Jaslo	Jaslo	teacher			M		
NUSSBAUM	Chaim Da			Jaslo	Jaslo		Yossef L.		M		
NUSSBAUM	Tziporah			Jaslo	Jaslo		Chaim Da		F		

List of Jews of Jaslo Prior and During World War II

Last name	First name	Maiden name	Birth date	Birth place	Residence	Trade or remarks	Father	Mother	Gen.	Groom	Disposition
NUSSBAUM	Mordechai			Jaslo	Jaslo				M		
NUTMAN	Yehoshua			Jaslo	Jaslo	glazier			M		
NUTMAN		Wagshall		Jaslo	Jaslo		Wolf		F	Yehoshua	
OBERLANDER	Ludwig			Jaslo	Jaslo	attorney			M		
OBERLANDER	Nathan			Jaslo	Krakow	attorney			M		
OBERLANDER	Berthold				Jaslo	surveyor			M		
OCHERET	Dawid					wood merchant			M		
OLINER	Awraham M			Jaslo	Krakow	wines			M		died
ORENSTEIN		Winfeld		Jaslo	Krakow		Leibish		F		shoa
ORENSTEIN	Yaakow				Jaslo	beadle			M		Palestine
ORGAL	Chaim Sh	Sambor				oil			M		
ORSZICER	Chaim Sh			Jaslo	Jaslo				M		
ORSZICER		Freund		Jaslo	Jaslo		Yaakow		F	Chaim Sh	
PALEK	Michael			Jaslo	Jaslo	court manager			M		
PEARLBERG	Yossef			Jaslo	Jaslo				M		
PEARLBERG		Tzimet		Jaslo	Jaslo		Leib		F		
PELLER	Aidel	Facher		Jaslo	Jaslo		Asher	Mindel	F	Awraham	
PELIKAN	P.			Jaslo	Jaslo				M		died
PENCER	Israel			Opczi	Jaslo				M		
PEPER	Yossef			Dembic	Jaslo				M		
PEPER	Ethil	Rapaport		Jaslo	Jaslo	2nd marriage	Yossef	Pearl	F	Yossef	
PERETZ	Menachem			Jaslo	Jaslo				M		died
PERETZ		Hiller		Jaslo	Jaslo		Shulem		F	Menachem	
PETERFREUND	Yekutiel			Gorlice	Jaslo	sausage			M		
PETERFREUND	Yossef			Jaslo	Jaslo				M		
PETERFREUND	Mordechai			Jaslo	Jaslo		Yossef		M		
PIAR	Leibish			Kolbasow	Jaslo				M		
PIAR	Maltche			Kolbasow	Jaslo	midwife			F	Leibish	
PIAR	Awraham			Jaslo	Jaslo	cantor	Leibish	Maltche	M		
PIAR	Benyamin			Jaslo	Jaslo		Leibish	Maltche	M		died
PIAR	Itzhak			Jaslo	Jaslo		Leibish	Maltche	M		killed
PIAR	Moshe			Jaslo	Jaslo		Leibish	Maltche	M		
PIAR	Yaakow			Jaslo	Jaslo		Leibish	Maltche	M		
PINTER				Jaslo	Jaslo				M		
PLATNER	Sarah		1905	Jaslo	Jaslo				F		
PLATNER	Yehezkel			Jaslo	Jaslo				M		
PLATNER	Mechel			Brzostek	Jaslo				M		
PLATNER	Pesia	Wagshall		Jaslo	Jaslo		Zeew		F	Mechel	
PLATNER	Yossef			Jaslo	Jaslo		Mechel	Pesia	M		Palestine
PLATNER	Dawid			Jaslo	Jaslo		Mechel	Pesia	M		Palestine
PLATNER	Lea		1917	Jaslo	Jaslo		Mechel	Pesia	F		
PLOTZKER	Hanoch				Jaslo	timber	Henoch		M		
PLOTZKER	Israel				Jaslo	attorney	Hanoch		M		
PLOTZKER		Zilber			Jaslo		Chaim		F	Israel	

Last name	First name	Maiden name	Birth date	Birth place	Residence	Trade or remarks	Father	Mother	Gen.	Groom	Disposition
PLOTZKER	Eliezer			Jaslo	Sanok		Henoch		M		died
PLOTZKER		Faust		Jaslo	Jaslo		Moshe		F	Eliezer	shoa
PLOTZKER	Dan			Jaslo	Jaslo		Eliezer		M		shoa
POKORILES					Jaslo	pharmacist			M		died
POLANER	Moshe				Jaslo	teacher			M		
POSTIBOLER	Michael			Postibola	Jaslo	farmer			M		
PRAELBERGER				Jaslo	Jaslo				F	Yossef	
PRAELBERGER	Israel			Jaslo	Jaslo	doctor			M		
PROPER	Henia				Jaslo				F		
RAAB	Eliezer				Jaslo	innkeeper			M		died
RAAB	Kalman				Jaslo	choir	Eliezer		M		
RAAB	Leibish			Jaslo	Jaslo		Eliezer		M		
RAAB		Geminder		Jaslo	Jaslo		Shlomo		F	Leibish	
RAAB	Yehoshua			Jaslo	Jaslo		Eliezer		M		Palestine
RAAB	Pinhas			Jaslo	Jaslo				M		
RAAB		Meller		Jaslo	Jaslo		Mendel		F	Pinhas	
RAAH	Eliezer			Jaslo	Jaslo	haberdashery			M		
RAAH	Israel			Jaslo	Jaslo		Eliezer		M		
RABI	Beril			Jaslo	Jaslo		Eliezer		M		
RACHMIL		Geminder		Jaslo	Jaslo		Shlomo		F		survived
RACKER	Arieh			Gorlice	Jaslo		Itzik	Hantche	M		
RANDAL	Itzhak			Jaslo	Jaslo	grains	Itzhak		M		
RANDAL	Yaakow			Jaslo	Pilzno	grains			M		
RAPAPORT	Chaim			Rudnik	Jaslo				M		
RAPAPORT	Yuta	Gutwin		Jaslo	Jaslo		Asher		F	Chaim	shoa
RAPAPORT	Moshe Nat			Jaslo	Jaslo	author	Chaim	Yuta	M		survived
RAPAPORT	Shmuel			Jaslo	Jaslo		Chaim	Yuta	M		survived
RAPAPORT	Itzhak			Jaslo	Jaslo		Chaim	Yuta	M		shoa
RAPAPORT	Yehuda			Jaslo	Jaslo		Chaim	Yuta	M		shoa
RAPAPORT	Issachar D			Jaslo	Jaslo		Chaim	Yuta	M		shoa
RAPAPORT	Rivka			Jaslo	Jaslo		Chaim	Yuta	F		shoa
RAPAPORT	Eliyahu			Jaslo	Jaslo				M	Rivka	shoa
RAPAPORT	Hannah			Jaslo	Jaslo		Eliyahu	Rivka	F		shoa
RAPAPORT	Sarah			Jaslo	Jaslo		Eliyahu	Rivka	F		shoa
RAPAPORT	Yehezkel			Jaslo	Jaslo				M		shoa
RAPAPORT	Yossef			Jaslo	Jaslo				M		died
RAPAPORT	Pearl			Jaslo	Jaslo				F	Yossef	
RAPAPORT	Yudel			Jaslo	Jaslo		Yossef	Pearl	M		
RAPAPORT	Etil			Jaslo	Jaslo		Yossef	Pearl	F		
RAPAPORT	A			Jaslo	Jaslo	jeweller			M		
RAPAPORT	P			Jaslo	Jaslo	jeweller			M		
RAPAPORT		Hess		Jaslo	Jaslo	jeweller	Eli		F	P	
RECHFELD	Zelde	Thaler		Jaslo	Jaslo		Naphtali		F	Yehezkel	survived
RECHFELD	Naphtali			Jaslo	Jaslo		Yehezkel	Zelde	M		shoa

List of Jews of Jaslo Prior and During World War II

Last name	First name	Maiden name	Birth date	Birth place	Residence	Trade or remarks	Father	Mother	Gen.	Groom	Disposition
RECHFELD	Naala			Jaslo	Jaslo		Yehezkel	Zelde	F		shoa
RECHFELD	Hirsh				Jaslo				M		survived
REICH	Itzhak			Jaslo	Jaslo	salt			M		
REICH	Natan			Jaslo	Jaslo		Itzhak		M		
REICH	Mendel			Jaslo	Jaslo		Itzhak		M		
REICH	Shlomo			Jaslo	Jaslo		Itzhak		M		
REICH	Yehoshua			Jaslo	Jaslo		Itzhak		M		survived
REICH	Hersh			Jaslo	Jaslo		Itzhak		M		survived
REICH	Zeew				Jaslo				M		
REICH	Moshe			Jaslo	Przemysl				M		
REICH		Frei		Jaslo	Przemysl		Yerucham		F	Moshe	
REICH	Motel			Jaslo	Przemysl		Moshe		M		
RESSLER	Awraham			Jaslo	Jaslo	Hebrew teacher			M		
RESSLER	Chaim Mendel			Jaslo	Jaslo		Awraham		M		
RESSLER	Zeew			Jaslo	Jaslo		Awraham		M		
RESSLER	Yehiel			Jaslo	Jaslo		Awraham		M		
RESSLER	P.			Jaslo	Jaslo				M		
RESSLER	Mirriam	Weber		Jaslo	Jaslo	2nd marriage			F	P.	
RESSLER	Simcha Ber				Jaslo				M		
RHINHALD	Abish			Jaslo	Jaslo				M		
RHINHALD	Itzhak			Jaslo	Jaslo		Abish		M		
RHINHALD	Simcha Ber			Jaslo	Jaslo		Abish		M		
RING	Dawid			Jaslo	Jaslo				M		
RIP	Naphtali			Jaslo	Jaslo				M		survived
RIP		Werner		Jaslo	Jaslo		Moshe A		F	Naphtali	survived
RISS	Mordechai Dawid			Jaslo	Jaslo				M		
RISS		Hiller		Jaslo	Jaslo		Elisha		F	Mordechai Dawid	
RISS	Feiwil						Mordechai Dawid		M		
RITNER	Yona			Jaslo	Jaslo	brooms			M		
ROSEN	Feiga	Bindigger				candies	Hersh	Sheindil	F	Yaakow Henoch	
ROSEN	A			Jaslo	Jaslo				M		survived
ROSENBLIT	L			Jaslo	Jaslo	clerk			M		
ROSENBUSH				Jaslo	Jaslo	attorney			M		
ROSENFELD	Chaim			Jaslo	Jaslo	furniture			M		survived
ROSENFELD	Awraham			Jaslo	Jaslo	attorney	Chaim		M		shoa
ROSENFELD		Bergman		Jaslo	Jaslo		Tzwi		F	Awraham	shoa
ROSENFELD	Itzhak			Jaslo	Jaslo		Chaim		M		shoa
ROSENFELD	Dawid			Jaslo	Jaslo		Chaim		M		
ROSENFELD	Leah			Jaslo	Jaslo		Chaim		M		
ROSENFELD	L			Jaslo	Jaslo	candies			M		died
ROSENTZWEIG		Eintziger		Jaslo	Jaslo		Zeev Wol		F	L	

List of Jews of Jaslo Prior and During World War II

Last name	First name	Maiden name	Birth date	Birth place	Residence	Trade or remarks	Father	Mother	Gen.	Groom	Disposition
ROSENTZWEIG	Yehiel			Jaslo	Jaslo				M		
ROSENZWEIG*	Nathan						L		M		survived
ROSENZWEIG		Guzik					Elazar		F	Nathan	survived
ROSNER	Meir H			Jaslo	Jaslo				M		survived
ROSNER	Mordechai			Jaslo	Jaslo				M		
ROSNER	Eliezer			Jaslo	Jaslo	money	Mordechai		M		
ROSNER	Yehiel			Jaslo	Jaslo	innkeeper	Mordechai		M		
ROSNER	Chaim			Jaslo	Jaslo	innkeeper	Yehiel		M		
ROSNER	Yehoshua			Jaslo	Jaslo	innkeeper	Yehiel		M		
ROSNER	Moshe			Jaslo	Jaslo				M		
ROSNER		Shriar		Jaslo	Jaslo				F	Moshe	
ROSNER	Fabian			Jaslo	Jaslo	attorney	Moshe		M		
ROSENWASSER	Uziel			Gorlice	Jaslo				M		
ROSENWASSER	Moshe			Jaslo	Jaslo		Uziel		M		
ROSENWASSER	Asher			Jaslo	Jaslo		Uziel		M		
ROTA	Yudel				Jaslo				M		
ROTA	Hertzel			Jaslo	Jaslo				M		
ROTTER	Tertel			Jaslo	Jaslo	flour mill			M		
ROTTER	Zishe			Jaslo	Jaslo		Tertel		M		
ROTTER	Moshe			Jaslo	Jaslo		Tertel		M		
ROTTER	Rena		1933		Jaslo				F		
ROTH	Leibish			Jaslo	Jaslo				M		
ROTH	Yudel			Jaslo	Jaslo		Leibish		M		
ROTH	Meir Hillel			Brzeszow	Jaslo				M		survived
ROTHFELD	Meir Berish				Jaslo	shochet			M		
ROTHFELD		Shnirer			Jaslo	shochet	Sh		F	Meir Berish	
ROTHFELD	Hertzel				Jaslo		Meir Berish		M		
ROTHFELD		Apfel		Jaslo	Jaslo		Nahum		F	Hertzel	
ROSS	Shmuel Mendel			Jaslo	Jaslo	heder teacher			M		USA
RUBEL	Itzhak Yehuda			Jaslo	Jaslo				M		
RUBEL	Frida	Weil					Yaakow		F	Itzhak Yehuda	
RUBEL	Nehemia			Jaslo	Jaslo		Itzhak Yehuda	Frida	M		
RUBEL	Leibish			Jaslo	Jaslo		Itzhak Yehuda	Frida	M		
RUBEL	Elhanan			Jaslo	Jaslo	banker	Itzhak Yehuda	Frida	M		
RUBEL	Reuven			Jaslo	Jaslo		Itzhak Yehuda	Frida	M		survived
RUBEL	Feiwil				Jaslo		Reuven		M		
RUBEL	Leibish	Lonek			Jaslo		Reuven		M		killed
RUBEL	Itzhak				Jaslo		Reuven		M		USA
RUBIN	Freda		1912	Jaslo	Jaslo				F		
RUBIN	Tzvi			Jaslo	Jaslo		Awraham		M		shoa

List of Jews of Jaslo Prior and During World War II

Last name	First name	Maiden name	Birth date	Birth place	Residence	Trade or remarks	Father	Mother	Gen.	Groom	Disposition
	Yossef						Yehosh				
RUBIN	Elimelech			Jaslo	Jaslo		Tzvi Yossef		M		
RUBIN	Rachel	Rahelci		Jaslo	Dobri		Elimelech		F	David	
RUBIN	Dina	Dinahci		Jaslo	Dubshitz		Elimelech		F	Yoel	
RUBIN	Aaron			Jaslo	Bardajew	rabbi	Tzvi Yossef		M		
RUBIN	Mendel	Mandil		Jaslo	Lemberg		Tzvi Yossef		M		died
RUBIN	Mirele	Mirci		Jaslo	Jaslo		Tzvi Yossef		F		
RUBIN	Hersh	Hirshle		Tarnow	Jaslo				M	Mirele	
RUBIN	Asher			Jaslo	Jaslo		Hersh	Mirele	M		
RUBIN		Ressler		Frysztak	Jaslo				M	Asher	
RUBIN	Ephraim			Jaslo	Antwerp		Hersh	Mirele	M		
RUBIN					Jaslo		Feivel		M	Ephraim	
RUBIN	Elimelech			Jaslo	Jaslo		Hersh	Mirele	M		
RUBIN	Baruch			Jaslo	Jaslo		Hersh	Mirele	M		
RUBIN		Zak			Jaslo				M	Ephraim	
RUBIN	Dinah			Jaslo	Jaslo		Tzvi Yossef		F		
RUBIN	Rizli			Jaslo	Lodz		Tzvi Yossef		F		
RUBIN	Primitel			Jaslo	Jaslo		Awraham Yehosh		F		
RUBIN	Moshe	Moshale		Jaslo	Sandz				M	Yutal	
RUBIN	Eliezer Yeruham				Jaslo		Moshe	Yutal	M		
RUBIN	Pessia			Jaslo	Mielec		Tzvi Yossef		F		
RUBIN	Dina	Dinahci		Jaslo	Israel		Awraham Yehosh		F		
RUBIN	Rosa	Rizli			Jaslo		Awraham Yehosh		F		
RUBIN	Pessia				Jaslo		Tzvi Yossef		F		died
RUBIN	Itzhak	Itzhakel		Jaslo	Tzefat	rabbi			M		survived
RUBIN	Itzhak Yeh				Jaslo				M		
RUTFELD	Simcha			Jaslo	Jaslo	choir			M		

* Notes from Estelle Guzik:

NATHAN ROSENZWEIG was my uncle. His wife was my Aunt ESTHER (aka Erna) GUZIK ROSENZWEIG. Both were born in JASLO. ESTHER's father was ELAZAR. They fled to Russia to escape from the Germans and were sent to Siberia where they survived the War. They returned to Poland and then on 30 June 1950 emigrated to Israel where their daughter MASHA lives today. NATHAN's father was Leib Rosenzwieg and his mother was Feige Einziger. NATHAN had a gas station and hardware store in JASLO.

HENIA's parents were MENACHEM MENDEL GUZIK & GISELLA RETIG. They lived in Strzyzow.

Last name	First name	Maiden name	Birth date	Birth place	Residence	Trade or remarks	Father	Mother	Gen.	Groom	Disposition
SAN	Mordechai	cohen		Frysztak	Jaslo	hotel			M		Died
SAN	Sheindil	Fabian			Jaslo		Tuvia		F	Mordechai	
SAN	Yaakow				Jaslo	timber	Mordechai	Sheindil	M		
SAN	Mendel				Jaslo		Mordechai	Sheindil	M		
SAN	Chaim				Jaslo		Mordechai	Sheindil	M		Survived
SAN	Nachman				Jaslo		Mordechai	Sheindil	M		
SAN		San			Jaslo		Mordechai	Sheindil	F	Nachman	
SAN	Tzwi				Jaslo		Nachman		M		Palestine
SAPIR		Beck			Jaslo		Dawid		F		
SAPIR					Jaslo				M		
SCHECHNER	Awraham			Jaslo	Jaslo	tailor			M		
SCHECHT	Awraham				Jaslo	music			M		
SCHECHT	Elimelech				Jaslo	choir	Awraham		M		
SCHECHT	Moshe				Jaslo	choir	Awraham		M		Palestine
SCHECHT	Shlomo				Jaslo				M		
SCHECHTER	Itzhak			Ryglice	Jaslo				M		
SCHECHTER	Chaim			Jaslo	Jaslo		Itzhak		M		
SCHECHTER	Zeew			Jaslo	Jaslo		Itzhak		M		Palestine
SCHEDLISKER	A				Jaslo	locksmith			M		
SCHMIDT	Simcha			England					M		
SEGAL		Beck			Jaslo		Dawid		F		
SEGAL	Asher				Jaslo	beadle			M		
SEGAL	Nathan			Jaslo	Jaslo				M		
SEGAL		Beck		Jaslo	Jaslo		D		F	Nathan	
SEINWEL	Dawid			Jaslo	Jaslo				M		
SEINWEL	Gitcha	Miller		Jaslo	Jaslo		Zelig		F	Dawid	
SEINWEL	Emanuel			Jaslo	Jaslo		Dawid	Gitcha	M		
SEINWEL	Shmuel			Jaslo	Jaslo		Dawid	Gitcha	M		Shoa
SEINWEL		Raab		Jaslo	Jaslo		Eliezer		F	Shmuel	
SEINWEL	Chaim				Jaslo	vice-president			M		
SHADEL	A				Jaslo				M		Died
SHADEL		Winfeld			Jaslo		Leibish		F	A	
SHAFET	Pinhas			Jaslo	Jaslo	innkeeper			M		
SHAFFEL	Tziporah	Chayios		Jaslo	Jaslo		Baruch		F		
SHAFFEL	P.			Krenica					M		Shoa
SHAMES	Moshe				Jaslo				M		
SHAMES	Ben Tzion				Jaslo				M		
SHAMES	Awraham				Jaslo				M		
SHAMIR	Matityahu			Jaslo	Jaslo	clothing			M		
SHARMER	Mendel			Warzic	Jaslo				M		
SHARMER	Shmuel			Koloszyc	Jaslo				M		
SHEFFEL	A			Jaslo	Jaslo				M		
SHEFFEL		Chayos		Jaslo	Jaslo		Brochil		F	A	

List of Jews of Jaslo Prior and During World War II

Last name	First name	Maiden name	Birth date	Birth place	Residence	Trade or remarks	Father	Mother	Gen.	Groom	Disposition
SHEFFETZ	Israel			Jaslo	Jaslo				M		
SHEFFETZ		eTeller		Jaslo	Jaslo		Elimelech		F	Israel	
SHEFFETZ	Awraham			Jaslo	Jaslo		Israel		M		
SHEHNBERG	Yaakow								M		survived
SHEHNBERG		Faust					Moshe		F	Yaakow	
SHEINBORN		Steinhaus		Jaslo	Jaslo	doctor	Chaim		F		
SHENBERG	Yaakow Me			Jaslo	Jaslo				M		
SHENDEL	Mendel				Jaslo				M		
SHENDORF	Leah	Gutwin		Jaslo	Jaslo		Moshe N. Gitche		F		shoa
SHENDORF	Zelig			Jaslo	Jaslo				M	P.	
SHENDORF		Gutwin		Jaslo	Jaslo		Moshe N. Gitche		F		
SHENKOPF	P			Jaslo	Jaslo	engineer			M	Zelig	
SHENKOPF		Werner		Jaslo	Jaslo		Lipcze		F		
SHERTZ	Shmeril					shoes			M	P	
SHERTZ		Kklinman				shoes	Feiwil		F		
SHIFS	Mechel			Jaslo	Jaslo	shoemaker			M	Shmeril	
SHIKLER	Shalom			Jaslo	Jaslo				M		
SHIKLER		Unger		Jaslo	Jaslo		Benyamin		F		
SHILAT	Menashe			Dembice	Jaslo				M	Shalom	
SHILAT	Awraham			Jaslo	Jaslo		Menashe		M		USA
SHILAT	Reuven			Jaslo	Jaslo		Menashe		M		
SHILAT	Towa	Neiwirth		Jaslo	Jaslo		Reuven		F		
SHILAT	Meir			Jaslo	Jaslo		Reuven	Towa	M	Reuven	Palestine
SHILAT	Yehezkel			Jaslo	Jaslo		Menashe		M		
SHILAT	Yossel			Jaslo	Jaslo		Menashe		M		USA
SHILAT	Chaim			Jaslo	Jaslo		Menashe		M		
SHILAT		Franzblau		Jaslo	Jaslo		Natan		F		
SHILAT	Israel			Jaslo	Jaslo		Menashe		M	Chaim	Palestine
SHILAT	Hershele			Jaslo	Jaslo		Menashe		M		
SHILAT	Bluma			Jaslo	Jaslo		Menashe		F		shoa
SHILAT	Rachel			Jaslo	Jaslo		Menashe		F		shoa
SHILAT	Pearl			Jaslo	Jaslo		Menashe		F		shoa
SHILAT	Moshe			Jaslo	Jaslo				M		survived
SHILAT	Roda			Jaslo	Jaslo		Moshe		F		
SHILAT	Rachel			Jaslo	Jaslo		Moshe		F		
SHILAT	Alter			Jaslo	Jaslo				M		survived
SHILAT	Yochewed			Jaslo	Jaslo		Alter		F		
SHILAT	Roda			Jaslo	Jaslo		Alter		F		
SHILAT	Tziporah	Freund			Jaslo	attorney	Elimelech		F		
SHINDELHEIM	Naphtali			Jaslo	Jaslo	lottery			M		USA
SHINDLER	Mendil			Jaslo	Jaslo	choir			M		
SHINDLER	Dawid			Jaslo	Jaslo	candles			M		Palestine
SHINDLER	Yehezkel			Jaslo	Jaslo		Dawid		M		shoa

Last name	First name	Maiden name	Birth date	Birth place	Residence	Trade or remarks	Father	Mother	Gen.	Groom	Disposition
SHINDLER	Mendel			Jaslo	Jaslo		Yehezkel		M		
SHINGEL	Mechel			Siedlisk	Jaslo		Moshe Ye		M		
SHINGEL	Yerachmiel			Jaslo	Jaslo		Moshe Ye		M		Died
SHLANGER	Aaron			Jaslo	Jaslo				M		
SHLANGER		Bergman		Jaslo	Jaslo		Tzwi		F		
SHLAPF	Yehezkel D	cohen		Jaslo	Jaslo				M	Aaron	
SHLAPF	Shalom			Jaslo	Jaslo	rabbi	Yehezkel D		M		
SHLAPF	Israel Mosh			Jaslo	Jaslo		Yehezkel D		M		
SHLAPF	Naphtali Hert			Jaslo	Jaslo		Yehezkel D		M		
SHLAPF		Kalb		Jaslo	Jaslo		Yekil		F		
SHLAPF	Chaim			Jaslo	Jaslo		Yehezkel D		M	Naphtali Hert	Survived
SHLAPF		Kaufman		Jaslo	Jaslo		Reuven P		F		Died
SHLAPF	Riwka			Jaslo	Jaslo		Chaim		F	Chaim	
SHLAPF	Mordechai			Jaslo	Jaslo		Yehezkel D		M		
SHLAPF	Nahum			Jaslo	Jaslo		Yehezkel D		M		survived
SHLIFER	Fem				Jaslo				F		
SHLISSEL	Asher			Jaslo	Jaslo	paper			M		
SHMIDT	Shlomo			Jaslo	Jaslo	habedash			M		
SHMIDT	Moshe			Jaslo	Jaslo	habedash	Shlomo		M		
SHMIDT	Chaim			Jaslo	Jaslo	habedash	Shlomo		M		
SHMIDT	Yaakow			Jaslo	Jaslo	habedash	Shlomo		M		
SHMINDLING	i			Jaslo	Jaslo	underwear			M		
SHMUEL						attorney			M		
SHNEIDER	Shulem			Jaslo	Przemysl				M		
SHNEP		Oliner							F		
SHNEP	Dawid			Jaslo	Jaslo				M		survived
SHNEP		Oliner							F		
SHNEP	Naftali			Jaslo	Jaslo				M		survived
SHNEP	P.			Jaslo	Jaslo				M		
SHNITZER	Mendel			Jaslo	Jaslo				M		
SHNITZER		Freund		Jaslo	Jaslo		Yaakow		F		
SHOCHET	Moshe			Lemberg	Jaslo	engineer			M	Mendel	Died
SHOCHET				Jaslo	Jaslo	printing			F		Palestine
SHOCHET	Ludwig			Jaslo	Jaslo		Moshe		M	Moshe	
SHOCHET		Baumring		Jaslo			Tzwi		F		
SHOCHET	Leopold			Jaslo	Jaslo		Moshe		M	Ludwig	Died
SHOCHET	Naphtali			Jaslo	Jaslo		Moshe		M		
SHOCHET	Riszek			Jaslo	Jaslo		Moshe		M		
SHOCHET	Genia	Beck		Jaslo	Jaslo		Motil		F		Survived
SHOCHET	Nahum			Jaslo	Jaslo				M	Naftali	
SHOCHET	Elimelech				Jaslo				M		
SHOCHET	Menashe			Jaslo	Jaslo				M		

List of Jews of Jaslo Prior and During World War II

Last name	First name	Maiden name	Birth date	Birth place	Residence	Trade or remarks	Father	Mother	Gen.	Groom	Disposition
SHODAR	Shimon			Jaslo	Jaslo				M		
SHODAR		Shpringer		Jaslo	Jaslo	beauty salon			F		
SHOLAW	Abba			Jaslo	Jaslo				M	Shimon	Died
SHOMER				Jaslo	Jaslo	doctor			M		
SHOMER		Kinstler		Jaslo	Jaslo		Mendil		F		
SHORR	Shimon			Jaslo	Jaslo	doctor			M		
SHPELING	Leib			Jaslo	Jaslo				M		
SHPERBER	Menashe			Jaslo	Jaslo	innkeeper			M		USA
SHPERBER	P.			Jaslo	Jaslo	innkeeper			M		
SHPERLING	Shalom			Jaslo	Jaslo	merchant			M		survived
SHPILER	Mendel			Jaslo	Jaslo	butcher	Yehezkel		M		
SHPIRER	Dawid Tzwi			Jaslo	Jaslo	butcher			M		
SHPIRER	Zelig			Jaslo	Jaslo	butcher	Dawid Tzwi		M		
SHPIRER		Korzennik		Jaslo	Jaslo		Shmuel		F		
SHPIRER	Reuven			Jaslo	Jaslo	butcher	Dawid Tzwi		M	Zelig	
SHPIRER	Mani			Jaslo	Jaslo	soccer	Reuven		M		
SHPIRER	Zelig			Jaslo	Jaslo	soccer	Reuven		M		
SHPIRER		Hershefeld		Jaslo	Jaslo		Yaakow		F		
SHPIRER	Dawid Tzwi			Jaslo	Jaslo		Reuven		M	Zelig	Palestine
SHPIRER	Ephraim			Jaslo	Jaslo		Reuven		M		USA
SHPIRER	Shmuel Sh			Jaslo	Jaslo	butcher	Dawid Tzwi		M		
SHPIRER	Zelig			Jaslo	Jaslo		Dawid Tzwi		M		Survived
SHPIRER	Yossef			Jaslo	Jaslo		Dawid Tzwi		M		Survived
SHPIRER	Alfred			Jaslo	Jaslo	attorney			M		
SHPIRER	sister			Jaslo	Jaslo				F		Survived
SHPIRER	Meir			Jaslo	Jaslo				M		Survived
SHPIRER				Jaslo	Jaslo				F		
SHPIRER					Jaslo				M	Zelig	
SHPRINGER	Hersh			Jaslo	Jaslo	grocery			M		
SHPRINGER	Rachel			Jaslo	Jaslo		Hersh		M		Palestine
SHPRINGER	Chaim			Jaslo	Jaslo		Hersh		M		
SHPRINGER	Yehiel			Jaslo	Jaslo		Hersh		M		
SHPRINGER	Beril			Jaslo	Jaslo		Hersh		M		
SHPRINGER	Shmuel			Jaslo	Jaslo		Hersh		M		
SHPRINGER	Yehiel			Jaslo	Jaslo				M		
SHPRINGER	Moshe			Jaslo	Jaslo	money			M	brother	
SHPRINGER	Eliezer			Jaslo	Jaslo	post office			M		
SHRAIER	Martzel			Jaslo	Vienna				M		
SHTAMS	Baruch Le			Jaslo	Jaslo	accountant			M		died
SHTAMS				Jaslo	Jaslo				F		Palestine
SHTAMS	Anshil			Jaslo	Jaslo		Baruch Le		M	Baruch Le	Palestine
SHTAMS	Hershel			Jaslo	Jaslo		Anshil		M		Palestine
SHTAMS	Shulem			Jaslo	Jaslo		Baruch Le		M		Palestine

List of Jews of Jaslo Prior and During World War II

Last name	First name	Maiden name	Birth date	Birth place	Residence	Trade or remarks	Father	Mother	Gen.	Groom	Disposition
SHTAYER	Mordechai A			Jaslo	Jaslo				M		USA
SHTAYER		Freund		Jaslo	Jaslo		Yaakow		F		USA
SHTEIN		Weinstein		Jaslo	Jaslo		Hersh		F	Mordechai A	
SHTEINGOT	Israel				Jaslo				M	Hersh Eli	survived
SHTEINGOT	Reisel	Gutwin			Jaslo		Moshe N.	Gitche	F		shoa
SHTELER	FAM				Jaslo					Itzhak	USA
SHTERN	Shmuel			Jaslo	Jaslo				M		
SHTILMAN		Tzimet		Neumark		rabbi			M		
SHTOIER	Tzwi			Jaslo	Jaslo				M		Palestine
SHTOIER				Jaslo	Jaslo				F		Palestine
SHTOIER	Zeew			Jaslo	Jaslo		Tzwi		M	Tzwi	Palestine
SHTOIER	Yehezkel			Jaslo	Jaslo		Tzwi		M		Palestine
SHTOIER	Israel			Jaslo	Jaslo		Tzwi		M		Palestine
SHTOIER	Itzhak			Jaslo	Jaslo		Tzwi		M		Palestine
SHTOIER	Idelia	Brick			Jaslo		Michael		F		Survived
SHTOIER	Pinhas			Jaslo	Jaslo				M		Shoa
SHTROICH		Tzimet		Jaslo			Simcha B		F		
SHTROICH	Israel				Jaslo	President			M		
SHTRUM	Pinhas			Jaslo	Jaslo	silk weaving			M		Survived
SHTRUM	Bronka	Ganger		Jaslo	Jaslo		Yehoshua		F		Shoa
SHTURCH	Aaron			Jaslo	Jaslo	money			M	Pinhas	
SHTURCH	Yaakow			Gorlice	Jaslo	money			M		
SHTURCH	Esther	Gutwin		Jaslo	Jaslo		Moshe N		F		shoa
SHTORCH	Khana		1930	Jaslo	Jaslo		Yaakow		F	Yaakow	
SHUMAN											died
SHUMAN	Leib			Jaslo	Jaslo				M		
SHUMAN	Chaim			Jaslo	Jaslo	timber			M		Palestine
SHUMAN	Dawid			Jaslo	Jaslo	timber	Chaim		M		
SHUMAR				Jaslo	Jaslo				M		
SHUMAR		Kinstler		Jaslo	Jaslo		Mendel		F		died
SHWARTZMAN	Dawid			Jaslo	Jaslo				M		
SHWARTZMAN	unk	Beam		Jaslo	Jaslo		Zeelig		F	Dawid	
SHWARTZMAN	Pinhas				Jaslo				M		
SHWIMMER	Yehoshua			Dukla	Jaslo				M		
SHWIMMER	Asher Yehosh				Jaslo	innkeeper			M		
SHWIMMER		Rozner			Jaslo		Mordechai		F	Asher Yehosh	
SHWIMMER	Pinhas				Jaslo	innkeeper	Asher Yehosh		M		
SHWIMMER		Hertz			Jaslo		Manas		F	Pinhas	
SHWINGER	Mordechai Da			Jaslo	Jaslo	furs			M		
SHWINGER		Leher		Jaslo	Jaslo		Shmuel		F	Mordechai Da	
SHWINGER	Ephraim			Jaslo	Jaslo	furs	Mordechai Da		M		Survived
SHWINGER		Ziegfried		Jaslo	Jaslo		Natan		F	Ephraim	Survived
SIEGFRIED	Ester				Jaslo				F		

List of Jews of Jaslo Prior and During World War II

Last name	First name	Maiden name	Birth date	Birth place	Residence	Trade or remarks	Father	Mother	Gen.	Groom	Disposition
SILBERSTEIN	Naphtali Shmu				Jaslo				M		Israel
SMULOWICZ	Rachela			Jaslo	Jaslo				F		
SOKOLER	Hanina			Sczenica	Jaslo	farmer			M		
SOKOLOWSKI	A.			Jaslo	Jaslo	copper			M		
SOLOMON	Naphtali Shmu			Podzamci	Jaslo	farmer			M		
SOLOMON	Benyamin				Jaslo		Naphtali Shmu		M		
SOLOMON	Dawid				Jaslo		Naphtali Shmu		M		
SOLOMON	Awraham				Jaslo		Naphtali Shmu		M		
SOLOMON	Yehiel				Jaslo		Naphtali Shmu		M		
SOLOMON	P.			Jaslo	Tarnow				M		
SPIRER	Meir			Jaslo	Jaslo				M		
STAMS	Hersh Eli				Jaslo	Dr. President			M		
STEIN	Chaim			Jaslo	Jaslo	attorney			M		USA
STEIN	Tzwi Elim			Zmigrod	Jaslo	meat			M		survived
STEIN		Weinstein		Zmigrod	Jaslo		Hersh		F	Tzwi Elim	Survived
STEINBRECHER	Hersh			Jaslo	Jaslo	butcher			M		Auschwitz
STEINBRECHER	Mechel			Jaslo					M		
STEINER	Yossef			Jedlicze	Jaslo				M		
STEINER	Tzadok			Jedlicze	Jaslo		Yossef		M		USA
STEINHAUS	Chaim			Zmigrod	Jaslo				M		
STEINHAUS	Itzhak	Ignaci		Zmigrod	Jaslo	attorney	Chaim		M		
STEINHAUS	Wladislaw				Jaslo		Itzhak		M		Died
STEINHAUS	Baruch	Boguslaw		Zmigrod	Jaslo	attorney	Chaim		M		
STEINHAUS	Hugo				Jaslo	mathematician	Baruch		M		
STERN	Awner			Jaslo	Jaslo	accountant			M		
STERN	Menashe			Jaslo	Jaslo				M		Died
STERN	Shimon			Jaslo	Jaslo		Menashe		M		Died
STERN	Shimon			Jaslo	Jaslo	gravedigger			M		Died
STERN	Yossel			Jaslo	Jaslo	shipper			M		survived
STILLMAN	Beril				Jaslo				M		shoa
STILLMAN	Shmuel			Jaslo	Jaslo	flour	Beril		M		shoa
STILLMAN	Leibish			Jaslo	Rozwadow	attorney	Shmuel		M		shoa
STILLMAN	Wolf			Jaslo	Jaslo	flour	Beril		M		shoa
STILLMAN	Moshe			Jaslo	Bochnia	flour	Wolf		M		survived
STILLMAN	Leibish			Jaslo	Bochnia	flour	Wolf		M		shoa
STORK	Esther			Jaslo	Jaslo				F		
TCHOP		Hirshfeld			Jaslo		Yekil		F	Yehoshua	
TCHOP	Betzalel			Jaslo	Jaslo				M		
TEICHLER	Asher Yesh			Jaslo	Jaslo				M		
TEICHTAHLER	Eliyahu			Jaslo	Jaslo				M		
TEICHTAHLER		Korman		Jaslo	Jaslo		Yekutiel Ze		F		
TEITELBAUM	Moshe			Rymanow	Jaslo	skins			M		

List of Jews of Jaslo Prior and During World War II

Last name	First name	Maiden name	Birth date	Birth place	Residence	Trade or remarks	Father	Mother	Gen.	Groom	Disposition
TEITELBAUM	Awraham			Jaslo	Jaslo	shoes	Moshe		M		
TEITELBAUM	Benyamin			Jaslo	Jaslo		Moshe		M		Died
TEITELBAUM		Teumim		Jaslo	Jaslo		Ephraim		F	Benyamin	Died
TEITELBAUM	Tzwi			Frysztak	Frysztak				M		
TEITELBAUM		Thaler		Jaslo	Frysztak		Mordechai D		F	Tzwi	
TEITELBAUM	Elimelech				Jaslo				M		
TELLER	Yehezkel			Frysztak	Jaslo				M		
TEPPER	Yerachmiel	Ehrlich		Jaslo	Jaslo				M		
TEUMIM	Ephraim			Wilkocz	Jaslo		Naphtali Hertz		M		
TEUMIM	Elimelech			Wilkocz	Jaslo		Ephraim		M		
TEWEL		Wolf		Jaslo	Jaslo		Shmuel		F	Yerachmiel	
TEWEL	Abraham				Jaslo				M		
THALER	Leibish			Jaslo	Jaslo				M		survived
THALER	Elimelech			Zmigrod	Jaslo				M		
THALER		Tzanger					Yona		M		
THALER	Awraham			Jaslo	Holland		Elimelech		M		survived
THALER	Shmuel			Jaslo			Elimelech		M		survived
THALER	Mordechai D			Jaslo	Jaslo				M		died
THALER	Ber			Jaslo	Jaslo		Mordechai D		M		
THALER	Naphtali			Jaslo	Jaslo	wheat			M		
THALER	Miriam Sh			Jaslo	Jaslo				F	Naphtali	
THALER	Yaakow			Jaslo	Jaslo		Naphtali	Miriam Sh	F		
THALER	Betzalel		1895	Jaslo	Jaslo		Naphtali	Miriam Sh	F		
THALER	Roiza			Jaslo	Jaslo				F		
THALER	Leah			Jaslo	Jaslo		Betzalel	Roiza	F		
THALER	Rachel			Jaslo	Jaslo		Betzalel	Roiza	F		
THALER	Haya Beila			Jaslo	Jaslo		Betzalel	Roiza	F		
THALER	Hershale			Jaslo	Jaslo		Betzalel	Roiza	M		Died
THALER	Zelde			Jaslo	Jaslo		Naphtali	Miriam Sh	F		
THALER	Henia			Jaslo	Jaslo		Naphtali	Miriam Sh	F		
THALER	Brili			Jaslo	Jaslo		Naphtali	Miriam Sh	M		Died
THALER	Dawid			Jaslo	Jaslo		Naphtali	Miriam Sh	M		Died
THALER	Leibish			Jaslo	Jaslo		Naphtali	Miriam Sh	M		Palestine
THALER	Yaakow			Jaslo	Jaslo	grocery	brother of Naph		M		
THALER	Awraham			Jaslo	Jaroslaw	tabacco	Yaakow		M		
THALER	Yossil			Jaslo	Jaslo	hats	brother of Naph		M		
THALER	Tzwi			Jaslo	Jaslo		Yossil		M		Palestine
THALER	Awraham Yaa			Frysztak	Jaslo	baker			M		
THALER	Tonia			Jaslo	Jaslo				F		
TRACHMAN	Lea	Blank		Jaslo	Zmigrod				F	Peretz	
TRACHMAN				Jaslo		teacher			M		
TRATKOWER				Jaslo	Jaslo				M		

List of Jews of Jaslo Prior and During World War II

Last name	First name	Maiden name	Birth date	Birth place	Residence	Trade or remarks	Father	Mother	Gen.	Groom	Disposition
TREITEL	Yaakow			Krosno	Jaslo	tailor			M		
TRENCHER	Charna	Rossenwasser			Jaslo		Uziel		F	Yaakow	
TUDOR	Sarah		1917	Jaslo	Jaslo		Moshe	Hannah	F		
TUDOR	Dawid			Jaslo	Tarnow		Moshe	Hannah	M		Survived
TUDOR	Shimshon			Jaslo	Tarnow		Moshe	Hannah	M		Survived
TUDOR		Margulies		Jaslo	Tarnow		Yoel		F	Shimshon	
TUDOR	Reuven			Jaslo	Tarnow		Moshe	Hannah	M		Survived
TUDOR	Israel			Jaslo	Jaslo		Moshe	Hannah	M		
TUDOR	P				Jaslo	Cantor			M		
TURBOWSKY	fam			Tarnowici							
TZAFAT	Itzhak				Jaslo	manager			M		
TZAHLER	Gadel			Jaslo	Jaslo		Itzhak		M		
TZAHLER	Yona			Brzostek	Jaslo	rabbi			M		Died
TZANGER		Teller		Jaslo	Jaslo				F	Yona	
TZANGER	Tzvi			Jaslo					M		Palestine
TZICHNER		Austro					Eliezer		F	Tzvi	Palestine
TZICHNER	Simche Bun			Zmigrod	Jaslo	wheat			M		
TZIMET	Wolf				Jaslo	timber	Simche Bun		M		
TZIMET	Betzallel			Jaslo	Jaslo		Wolf		M		
TZIMET	Bunem			Jaslo	Jaslo		Betzallel		M		
TZIMET	Mandil			Jaslo	Jaslo		Betzallel		M		
TZIMET	Meir				Stryzow	jeweller	Wolf		M		
TZIMET		Geller			Stryzow	rabbi	Benyamin		F	Meir	
TZIMET	Leib				Jaslo	machinery	Simche Bun		M		
TZIMET	Bunem			Jaslo	Jaslo		Leib		M		
TZIMET	Yossef			Jaslo	Jaslo		Leib		M		
TZIMET	Goldzie	Reich		Brzesko	Jaslo		Kalman		F	Yossef	
TZIMET	Yaakow			Jaslo	Germany		Yossef	Goldzie	M		
TZIMET	Zacharia			Jaslo	Germany				M		
TZIMET	Lea								F	Moshe	
TZIMET	Hersh			Jaslo	Przemysl		Moshe	Lea	M		
TZIMET	Aaron						Hersh	Lea	M		
TZIMET	Leibish			Jaslo	Jaslo		Moshe	Lea	M		
TZIMET				Zmigrod	Jaslo				F		
TZIMET	Awraham			Zmigrod	Jaslo	wheat			M		
TZIMET	Lipa			Zmigrod	Jaslo	wheat			M		
TZIMET	Alter	Levi		Zmigrod	Jaslo				M		
TZIMET	Moshe Man			Zmigrod	Jaslo	habedash			M		
TZIMET	Yankel			Jaslo	Jaslo		Moshe Man		M		
TZUCKER	Ester				Jaslo				F		
TZUCKER	Shlomo			Jaslo	Sanok				M		
TZUCKER	Emanuel				Jaslo	Dr.			M		
TZUCKER		Menashe		Jaslo	Jaslo		Yossef		F		

Last name	First name	Maiden name	Birth date	Birth place	Residence	Trade or remarks	Father	Mother	Gen.	Groom	Disposition
TZUCKER	Mendel			Jaslo	Jaslo	distillery			M		
TZUCKER	Meir			Jaslo	Jaslo		Mendel		M		
TZUCKER	Shlomo			Jaslo	Jaslo	workshop	Mendel		M		Survived
TZUCKER	Pearl						Mendel		F		survived
TZUCKER	Mendel			Rudnik	Jaslo	slaughterer			M		survived
TZUCKERMAN	Bracha			Jaslo	Jaslo				F		survived
TZUCKERMAN	Chaya			Jaslo	Jaslo				F		survived
TZUCKERMAN	Emalia			Jaslo	Jaslo				F		survived
TZUCKERMAN	Sarah			Jaslo	Jaslo				F		survived
TZUCKERMAN	Mendel			Jaslo	Jaslo				M		survived
TZUCKERMAN	David				Jaslo				M		
TZUDERRER	Asher				Jaslo				M		USA
TZUKERMAN	Elimelech			Rudnik	Jaslo	cantor			M		survived
TZUKERMAN	Hadassah	Just	1882						F	Elimelech	
TZUKERMAN	Lea		1911	Jaslo	Jaslo		Elimelech	Hadassah	F		
TZUKERMAN	Kalmen			Jaslo	Jaslo				M		survived
TZUKERMAN	Meir			Jaslo	Jaslo	Dr.			M		survived
TZUTZKENBOIM	Dawid				Jaslo				M		
TZWEIG	Alter				Jaslo				M		
ULLMAN	Chaim Reuven			Jaslo	Jaslo	skins	Dawid		M		USA
ULLMAN	Dawid			Jaslo	USA		Chaim Reuven		M		
ULLMAN	Riwka			Jaslo	Israel		Chaim Reuven		F		Palestine
ULLMAN	Sarah			Jaslo	Israel		Chaim Reuven		F		Palestine
ULLMAN	Hannah			Jaslo	USA		Dawid		F		
ULLMAN	Kopil			Jaslo		feathers			M		
ULLMAN		Ressler		Jaslo					F	Kopil	
ULLMAN	Elisha			Jaslo	Tarnow		Kopil		M		
ULLMAN	Benyamin	Levi							M		
UNGER	Elisha				Tarnow				M		
UNGER	Itzhak			Jaslo	Krakow		Kopil		M		Survived
UNGER	Shmuel			Jaslo	Jaslo				M		
UNGER	Moshe			Jaslo	Jaslo				M		
UNGER	Reisil	Piar		Jaslo	Jaslo		Leibish		F	Moshe	
UNGER	Benyamin					cantor	Moshe	Reisil	M		survived
WACHNER		Apfel		Jaslo	Jaslo		Nahum		F	Yossef	
WACHNER	Philip			Jaslo	Jaslo	judge			M		
WACHTEL	Zeew			Worzic	Jaslo				M		
WAGSHALL	Israel		1897	Jaslo	Jaslo	transport	Zeew		M		
WAGSHALL		Schechter		Jaslo	Jaslo		Awraham		F	Israel	
WAGSHALL	Leibish			Jaslo	Jaslo		Awraham		M		
WAGSHALL	Dawid			Jaslo	Jaslo				M		died
WAGSHALL	Anna			Jaslo	Jaslo				F		
WAGSHALL	Max			Jaslo	Jaslo				M		
WALDHORN	Braindil	Teller		Jaslo	Jaslo				F	Dawid	died

List of Jews of Jaslo Prior and During World War II

Last name	First name	Maiden name	Birth date	Birth place	Reside nce	Trade or remarks	Father	Mother	Gen.	Groom	Disposition
WALDHORN	Rachel			Jaslo	Jaslo		Dawid	Braindil	F		Palestine
WALDHORN	Chaya			Jaslo	Jaslo		Dawid	Braindil	F		shoa
WALDHORN	Yuta			Jaslo	Jaslo		Dawid	Braindil	F		shoa
WALDHORN	Yossef			Jaslo	Jaslo		Dawid	Braindil	M		shoa
WALDHORN	Elezer			Jaslo	Jaslo		Dawid	Braindil	M		Shoa
WALDHORN	Israel			Jaslo	Jaslo		Dawid	Braindil	M		Shoa
WALDHORN	Fishel			Jaslo	Jaslo	attorney			M		
WALFELD	Shmuel			Jaslo	Jaslo	teacher	brother	Fishel	M		
WALFELD	Naphtali				Jaslo	president			M		
WALFELD	Elazar			Jaslo	Jaslo	grocery			M		
WALKER	Shmuel			Frysztak					M		
WALKER	Dow			Jaslo	Jaslo		Shmuel		M		
WALKER	Moshe			Jaslo	Jaslo				M		
WALKER	Eliezer			Jaslo	Jaslo				M		Palestine
WALKER		Stillman		Jaslo	Jaslo		Wolf		F	Eliezer	Palestine
WARSHER	Chaya			Jaslo	Jaslo		Moshe		F		
WARSHER	Mendel			Jaslo	Jaslo		Moshe		M		Survived
WARSHER	Pearl	Wienner		Jaslo	Jaslo				F		
WAX	Tzadok			Jaslo	Jaslo	butcher			M		died
WEBER	Libce			Jaslo	Jaslo		Tzadok		M		
WEBER	Motil			Jaslo	Jaslo		Tzadok		M		
WEBER		Schechter					Awraham		F	Motil	
WEBER	Itzik			Jaslo	Jaslo		Tzadok		M		
WEBER	Hersh			Jaslo	Jaslo		Tzadok		M		
WEBER	Yaakow			Jaslo	Jaslo	tenor	Tzadok		M		
WEBER	Brili			Jaslo	Jaslo	tailor			M		
WEBER	Hershel			Jaslo	Jaslo		Brili		M		
WEBER	Yaakow				Jaslo	skins			M		
WEIL	Leibish			Jaslo	Jaslo	wines			M		
WEINBERGER	Lea			Jaslo	Jaslo				F		
WEINBERGER	Shmuel			Jaslo	Jaslo				M		USA
WEINBERGER	Shlomo				Jaslo	timber			M		survived
WEINSTEIN	Fradel		1924	Jaslo	Jaslo				F		
WEINSTEIN	Menashe				Jaslo				M		
WEINSTEIN	Chaim			Gorlice	Jaslo				M		
WEINSTEIN	Yehezkel			Jaslo	Vienna	teacher	Chaim		M		
WEINSTEIN	Heshil			Jaslo	Jaslo		Chaim		M		
WEINSTEIN	Hersh	cohen		Zmigrod	Jaslo				M		
WEINSTEIN	Elazar			Podzamce		innkeeper			M		
WEINSTEIN	Nathan								M		
WEINSTEIN		Margolies					Moshe		F	Nathan	
WEINSTEIN	Feige		1925	Jaslo	Jaslo		Nissim	Sarah	F		
WEISS	Shmuel			Jaslo	Jaslo				M		
WEISS	Bat Shewa			Jaslo	Jaslo				F	Shmuel	shoa

Last name	First name	Maiden name	Birth date	Birth place	Residence	Trade or remarks	Father	Mother	Gen.	Groom	Disposition
WEISS	Cheva			Jaslo	Jaslo		Shmuel	Bat Shewa	F		
WEISS	Elazar			Jaslo	Jaslo		Leibish	Bat Shewa	M		Palestine
WEISS	Shulem			Jaslo	Jaslo				M	.	died
WEISSBERG	Sarah	Citronenboim		Jaslo	Jaslo		Leib	Liba	F	Shulem	
WEISSBERG	Israel			Jaslo	Jaslo		Shulem	Sarah	M		
WEISSBERG	Menashe			Tarnow	Jaslo				M		
WEISSBERG		Zinbal		Jaslo	Jaslo		Dawid		F	Menashe	
WEITZ	Bela	Zomer		Jaslo	Jaslo				F	Asher	
WEITZ	Dawid			Jaslo	Jaslo	choir			M		
WEITZ	Yaakow			Jaslo	Jaslo		Awraham		M		
WEITZ	Hershil				Krakow		Yaakow		M		
WEITZ	Yehoshua			Jaslo	Jaslo		Yaakow		M		
WEITZ	Mendel			Jaslo	Jaslo		Asher		M		Survived
WEITZ	Dawid			Jaslo	Jaslo		Awraham		M		
WEITZ	Mendel			Jaslo	Jaslo				M		Survived
WEITZ	Rozalia			Jaslo	Jaslo				F		
WEITZMAN		Apfel		Jaslo	Jaslo		Nahum		F	Eliezer	
WEITZMAN	Chaim						Eliezer		M		
WEKSEL	Yaakow		1910		Jaslo				M		
WEKSELBAUM	Yehoshua			Jaslo	Lejansk		Chaim		M		
WEKSELBAUM	Reuven			Jaslo	Belgium		Chaim		M		
WEKSELBAUM	Shlomo			Jaslo	Jaslo		Chaim		M		
WEKSELBAUM	Chaya			Jaslo	Jaslo		Chaim		F		
WEKSELBAUM	Yaakow			Jaslo	Jaslo				M		
WEKSELBAUM		Stillman		Jaslo	Jaslo		Wolf		F	Yaakow	
WEKSELBAUM	Lipcze			Jaslo	Jaslo				F		
WERNER	Awraham				Jaslo		Lipcze		M		killed
WERNER	Moshe Aaaron			Jaslo	Jaslo	innkeeper			M		
WERNER						dentist	Moshe Aaaron		M		
WERNER		Weingarten					Shlomo		F		
WISTREICH	Mila		1918	Jaslo	Jaslo	butcher			F		
WISTREICH	Set			Jaslo	Jaslo	attorney			M		survived
WISTREICH	Hanka	Manashe					Yossef		F	S.	survived
WISTREICH	Mendel			Jaslo	Jaslo	wines			M		
WISTREICH	Esther	Shtoyar		Jaslo	Jaslo				F	Mendel	
WISTREICH	widow			Hiclowa	Jaslo		widow		F		
WISTREICH	Munk					refinery			M		shoa
WISTREICH	Moshe			Jaslo	Jaslo				M		died
WILDSTEIN	Rivka			Jaslo	Jaslo				F		
WILDSTEIN	Yudel			Jaslo	Jaslo	cattle			M		
WILDSTEIN	Awigdor			Jaslo	Jaslo	cattle	brother	of Yudel	M		
WILDSTEIN	Shmuel			Jaslo	Jaslo				M		Died
WILDSTEIN	Cilka			Jaslo	Jaslo				F	Shmuel	
WILDSTEIN	Itzhak			Jaslo	Jaslo		Shmuel	Cilka	M		

List of Jews of Jaslo Prior and During World War II

Last name	First name	Maiden name	Birth date	Birth place	Residence	Trade or remarks	Father	Mother	Gen.	Groom	Disposition
WILDSTEIN	Bronia				Jaslo				F		
WILKPORT	Aaron			Jaslo	Jaslo		David		M		Died
WILKPORT	Awraham			Jaslo	Jaslo		David		M		Survived
WILKPORT	Lea			Jaslo	Jaslo		David		F		Survived
WILKPORT	Hanoch			Jaslo	Jaslo		David		M		Survived
WILKPORT	Israel			Jaslo	Jaslo	leather			M		
WILNER	Mindel			Jaslo	Jaslo		Israel		F		Survived
WILNER	Eliezer			Jaslo	Jaslo		Eliezer		M		
WINER	Michael				Jaslo	doctor			M		Palestine
WINER	Leibish			Zmigrod	Jaslo				M		
WINFELD	Yutali			Zmigrod	Jaslo				F	Leibish	
WINFELD	Pinhas			Zmigrod	Jaslo				M		
WINFELD	Naphtali				Jaslo				M		
WINFELD	Moshe				Jaslo	builder					
WINKLER	D				Jaslo				M		Palestine
WINKLER	David				Jaslo				M		
WISER	Pinhas			Jaslo	Jaslo				M		
WINTER	Hanah		1896		Berlin				F		
WOLF	Eisik			Jaslo	Jaslo				M		
WOLF		Budner		Jaslo	Jaslo		Yudel		F	Eisik	
WOLF	Mordechai			Jaslo	Jaslo				M		
WOLKER	Yossef			Jaslo	Jaslo				M		
WROBEL	Sarah			Zmigrod	Jaslo				F		
WROCENKO	Yaakow				Jaslo				M		
ZAIDNER	Lea				Jaslo				F		
ZAKAL	Arieh Leib			Jaslo			Michael		M		
ZAKAL	Yerachmiel			Jaslo			Michael		M		Survived
ZAKAL	Leon			Jaslo			Michael		M		Survived
ZAKAL	Awraham			Jaslo	Jaslo				M		Died
ZIDORC	Mrs.	Brandstadter					Wolf		F		
ZIFMAN	Nathan			Kolczyc	Jaslo	cattle			M		
ZIGFRIED	Mendel				Jaslo				M		
ZILBER	Naphtali			Jaslo	Jaslo				M		
ZILBER	Pearl	Tupoliner			Jaslo		Shulem		M	Naphtali	
ZILBER	Chana			Jaslo	Jaslo		Naphtali	Pearl	F		
ZILBER	Yehoshua			Jaslo	Zmigrod		Naphtali		M		
ZILBER		Ginzburg		Zmigrod	Zmigrod		H		F	Yehoshua	
ZILBER	Mendel			Jaslo	Sandz	teacher	Naphtali		M		
ZILBER	Tzwi Dawid			Jaslo	Warsaw	teacher	Naphtali		M		survived
ZILBER	Chaim			Sanok	Jaslo	timber			M		
ZILBER	Wolf			Jaslo	Jaslo		Chaim		M		shoa
ZILBER	Esther	Freund		Jaslo	Jaslo		Elimelech		F	Wolf	shoa
ZILBER		Berger		Jaslo	Jaslo		Shlomo		F	Chaim	

List of Jews of Jaslo Prior and During World War II

Last name	First name	Maiden name	Birth date	Birth place	Residence	Trade or remarks	Father	Mother	Gen.	Groom	Disposition
ZILBER	Leibish			Gorlice	Jaslo	timber			M		
ZILBER	Chaim			Jaslo	Jaslo		Leibish		M		
ZILBER	Moshe			Jaslo	Jaslo				M		
ZILBERSHTEIN		Eisenberg		Jaslo	Jaslo		Yaakow		F	Moshe	
ZILBERSHTEIN	Shmuel			Jaslo	Jaslo		Moshe		M		
ZILBERSHTEIN	Israel			Jaslo	Jaslo	refinery			M		
ZILBERSHTEIN	Julia	HamershlNowy Targ							F	Israel	
ZILPAN	Shmuel			Siniawa	Jaslo				M		
ZILPAN		Kinstler		Jaslo	Jaslo		Leibish		F	Shmuel	
ZIMMERMAN	Mania			Jaslo	Jaslo				F	Szmuel	
ZOMMER	Sh.			Jaslo	Jaslo				M		
ZOMMER		Margulies		Jaslo	Jaslo			Abtcze	F	Sh.	

INDEX

www.ingramcontent.com/pod-product-compliance
Lightning Source LLC
Chambersburg PA
CBHW061834260326
41914CB00005B/993